ReFocus: The Films of Andrei Tarkovsky

ReFocus

ReFocus: The International Directors Series

Series Editors: Robert Singer, Stefanie Van de Peer, and Gary D. Rhodes

Board of advisors:
Lizelle Bisschoff (University of Glasgow)
Stephanie Hemelryck Donald (University of Lincoln)
Anna Misiak (Falmouth University)
Des O'Rawe (Queen's University Belfast)

ReFocus is a series of contemporary methodological and theoretical approaches to the interdisciplinary analyses and interpretations of international film directors, from the celebrated to the ignored, in direct relationship to their respective culture—its myths, values, and historical precepts—and the broader parameters of international film history and theory. The series provides a forum for introducing a broad spectrum of directors, working in and establishing movements, trends, cycles, and genres including those historical, currently popular, or emergent, and in need of critical assessment or reassessment. It ignores no director who created a historical space—either in or outside of the studio system—beginning with the origins of cinema and up to the present. *ReFocus* brings these film directors to a new audience of scholars and general readers of Film Studies.

Titles in the series include:

edinburghuniversitypress.com/series/refocint

ReFocus:
The Films of Andrei Tarkovsky

Edited by Sergey Toymentsev

EDINBURGH
University Press

Edinburgh University Press is one of the leading university presses in the UK. We publish academic books and journals in our selected subject areas across the humanities and social sciences, combining cutting-edge scholarship with high editorial and production values to produce academic works of lasting importance. For more information visit our website: edinburghuniversitypress.com

Edinburgh University Press Ltd
The Tun—Holyrood Road
12 (2f) Jackson's Entry
Edinburgh EH8 8PJ

Typeset in 11/13 Ehrhardt MT by
IDSUK (DataConnection) Ltd

A CIP record for this book is available from the British Library

ISBN 978 1 4744 3723 3 (hardback)
ISBN 978 1 4744 3725 7 (webready PDF)
ISBN 978 1 4744 3726 4 (epub)

Contents

Figures

Notes on Contributors

Linda Belau is Professor in the Department of Literature and Cultural Studies and Director of the Film Studies Program at the University of Texas-Rio Grande Valley. She is the co-editor of *Topologies of Trauma: Essays on the Limits of Knowledge and Memory* (2001), Special Issue editor of *Postmodern Culture* (2002), Special Issue editor of *Women Writers* (2010), and the author of several articles on film studies and film theory, psychoanalysis, theories of trauma, and cultural studies.

Ed Cameron is Professor of Literary and Film Studies in the Department of Literature and Cultural Studies at the University of Texas-Rio Grande Valley. He is the author of *The Psychopathology of the Gothic Romance* (2010). He is also the author of numerous articles linking psychoanalysis, film studies, and cultural critique. He has most recently published on the films of Federico Fellini, Harmony Korine, David Lynch, Todd Haynes, and Steve McQueen.

Anton Dolin is a Russian journalist, film critic, and scholar. He is the chief editor of *Iskusstvo kino*, one of the earliest film magazines in Europe. He regularly writes film reviews for the journal *Afisha* and the site *Afisha—Vozdukh*. He has repeatedly received awards from the Russian Guild of Film Scholars and Critics for his contributions in film scholarship. Among his books are *Lars von Trier: Kontrol'nye rabolty, analiz, interv'iu* (2004), *Takesi Kitano: Detskie gody* (2006), *Ulovka XXI* (2010), *German: Interv'iu, esse, stsenarii* (2011), and *Jim Jarmusch: Stikhi i muzyka* (2019).

Robert Efird is Associate Professor of Russian at Virginia Tech. He extensively published on Tarkovsky and Russian cinema in *CLCWeb: Comparative Literature and Culture*, *Slavic and East European Journal Studies*, *Russian and Soviet Cinema*, *Journal of Narrative Theory*, *Transnational Cinemas*, and others.

Andrei Gornykh is Professor of Media Studies at the European Humanities University in Vilnius, Lithuania. He received his PhD in Philosophy from Saint Petersburg State University. He is the author of two monographs: *Formalism: From Structure to Text and Beyond* (2003) and *Media and Society* (2012). His research interests are in visual and cultural studies, critical theory, psychoanalysis, film theory, and visual anthropology. He is the author of a number of creative works, such as popular science films for TV, educational DVD, and video.

Mikhail Iampolski is Professor of Comparative Literature and Russian and Slavic Studies at New York University. He has authored many books and articles on film and visual representation, including *The Memory of Tiresias: Intertextuality and Film* (1998).

Zdenko Manduŝić is Assistant Professor in the Department of Slavic Languages and Literatures at the University of Toronto. He received his PhD in Slavic Languages and Literatures and Cinema and Media Studies from the University of Chicago. His dissertation entitled "Camerawork: Soviet Film Experience and Visual Poetics After Stalin" investigates how Soviet films of the Post-Stalinist period communicated cultural values through cinematographic techniques, how formal elements organized viewer perception of these values, and how these formal elements were conceptualized.

Anne Eakin Moss is Assistant Professor in the Department of Comparative Thought and Literature at Johns Hopkins University, and co-editor of the Comparative Literature issue of *Modern Language Notes* (JHU Press). She received her PhD from Stanford University in Slavic Languages and Literatures, and her BA from Harvard University in History and Literature. She is the author of *Only Among Women: Philosophies of Community in the Russian and Soviet Imagination, 1860–1940* (2019) and a number of articles on gender in Russian literature and the problem of spectatorship in Soviet cinema.

Yelizaveta Goldfarb Moss received her PhD in Comparative Literature and Film and Media Studies from Emory University. She is currently Assistant Professor in the Department of Communication, Media, and Journalism at the University of North Georgia.

Julia Shpinitskaya holds a PhD in Musicology from the University of Helsinki. She is currently a Postdoctoral Researcher at the University of Helsinki and an Associated Researcher at IRCAV (Institute for Research on Cinema and Audiovisual Media, Université Sorbonne, Paris 3). Having a long background of research on music and sound in the films of Andrei Tarkovsky and publishing on the topic since 2004, she collaborated with the international research group *Deceptive Arts. Machines, Magic, Media*, hosted by LABEX Arts-H2H (Laboratory of Excellence in Arts and Human Mediations) in Paris.

Donato Totaro received his PhD in Film and Television from the University of Warwick (UK) and has been a Film Studies lecturer at Concordia University (Montreal, Canada) since 1990. He has been the editor of the online film journal *Offscreen* since its inception in 1997 and member of AQCC "Association québécoise des critiques de cinéma" since 2004.

Sergey Toymentsev is Assistant Professor of Russian in the Department of Languages, Literatures, and Cultures at Saint Louis University. His articles and reviews have appeared in *CLCWeb: Comparative Literature and Culture*, *Comparative Literature Studies, Film International, Journal of Philosophy: A Cross-Disciplinary Inquiry, Scope, Studies in Russian & Soviet Cinema, Film Criticism, KinoKultura*, and others.

Evgeny Tsymbal is a documentary filmmaker, writer, and film historian. He began his career at Mosfilm Studios in Moscow in the 1970s where he worked as an assistant director to Andrei Tarkovsky, Nikita Mikhalkov, Larisa Shepitko, and Eldar Ryazanov, among others. After completing Eldar Ryazanov's filmmaking course, he embarked on his own directorial journey with a variety of short films, and achieved critical acclaim with the BAFTA-winning short *Defense Council Sedov* (46 mins). He crossed over to the sphere of documentary filmmaking with works such as *Roads of Commonwealth* (1995), *Ways of Agricultural Reform* (1995), *Homeland* (1996), *In Memory: Alexander Kaidanovsky* (1996), *1001 Stories About Cinema: Vladimir Naumov* (1998), the award-winning *Stalker's Dreams* (1998), *Ordinary Bolshevism* (1999), and *Dziga and his Brothers* (2002). In addition to directing, he has continued his work as a scriptwriter, historian, and critic, publishing articles in journals such as *Sight and Sound, New Statesman, Premier, Chaplin, Iskusstvo kino, Museum, Science Fiction Film & Television*, and *Russian Literature*.

Lisa Ryoko Wakamiya is Associate Professor of Slavic in the Department of Modern Languages and Linguistics and Courtesy Associate Professor of English at Florida State University. She is the author of *Locating Exiled Writers in Contemporary Russian Literature: Exiles at Home* (2009). Her current book project, *Collecting Objects, Materializing Ethics*, investigates the relationship between collections of material objects and narrative.

Sara Pankenier Weld is Associate Professor of Russian and Comparative Literature at the University of California, Santa Barbara, where she has taught since 2012. Her first book, *Voiceless Vanguard: The Infantilist Aesthetic of the Russian Avant-Garde* (2014), received the International Research Society for Children's Literature (IRSCL) Book Award in 2015. Her second book, *An Ecology of the Russian Avant-Garde Picturebooks* (2018), mounts a close analysis of image and text in little-known picturebooks by prominent Russian writers, artists, and intellectuals. She has also published numerous articles or

chapters on a variety of Russian writers and artists, including Sergei Eisen-
stein, Osip Mandelstam, El Lissitsky, Vladimir Nabokov, Daniil Kharms, Leo
Tolstoy, Vladimir Mayakovsky, Vladimir Lebedev, Marina Tsvetaeva, and
Maxim Gorky.

Slavoj Žižek is a world-renowned public intellectual who has published over
fifty books (translated into twenty languages) on topics ranging from philosophy and Freudian and Lacanian psychoanalysis, to theology, film, opera,
and politics. He is a professor of philosophy at The European Graduate
School, a senior researcher at the Institute for Sociology and Philosophy at
the University of Ljubljana, Global Distinguished Professor of German at
New York University, International Director of the Birkbeck Institute for
the Humanities, and Founder and President of the Society for Theoretical
Psychoanalysis, Ljubljana.

Introduction: Refocus on Tarkovsky

Sergey Toymentsev

Throughout his career the renowned Russian auteur Andrei Tarkovsky (1932–86) created only seven feature-length films, or seven and a half, to use Maya Turovskya's expression,[1] if we include his 1961 diploma short *The Steamroller and the Violin*. All of his features won prestigious awards at international film festivals and have gained cult status among cineastes, often being mentioned in various kinds of ranking polls and charts dedicated to the "best films ever made." The British Film Institute, for example, honored three of Tarkovsky's films in its "50 Greatest Films of All Time" poll conducted for the film magazine *Sight & Sound* in 2012: *Andrei Rublev* (1966) is ranked at No. 26, *Mirror* (1974) at No. 19, and *Stalker* (1979) at No. 29. In fact, rumor has it that the Russian director supposedly knew that he was going to make only seven features. In his essay-film *One Day in the Life of Andrei Arsenevitch* (1999), Chris Marker makes a reference to a spiritualist séance at which the soul of Boris Pasternak allegedly informed the filmmaker he would make only seven films—"but good ones." Improbable and supernatural as this legend may seem, Pasternak's prophecy is well documented in Tarkovsky's diary, where he repeatedly recalls it at moments of self-doubt and loss of confidence.[2]

Despite being a relatively small body of work, Tarkovsky's films—famous for languid pacing, excessively long takes, dreamlike imagery, spiritual depth, and philosophical allegories— have had a profound influence on world cinema. On the one hand, by having revolutionized the aesthetic possibilities of the cinematic medium, he is widely considered one of the progenitors of slow cinema, alongside other auteurs such as Béla Tarr, Theo Angelopoulos, and Tsai Ming-liang, among others; while numerous critically acclaimed directors— Lars von Trier, Alejandro G. Iñárritu, Nuri Bilge Ceylan, and many more— openly admit his substantial influence on their work. On the other hand, the "cultlike veneration and imitation"[3] of Tarkovskian stylistic features and artistic ideals have produced a phenomenon called "the Tarkovsky syndrome," or *Tarkovshchina*, which stands for unnecessary intellectualization, messianic self-aggrandizement, and elitism in film, mostly evident in the Russian cinema of the late 1980s and early 1990s.[4] Having become an integral part of global cultural heritage, his films are now regularly screened in repertory cinemas all over the world, just as his treatise *Sculpting in Time: Reflections on the Cinema* (1986) has been translated into multiple languages. The cult of Tarkovsky peaked especially in post-Soviet Russia, where the director has been exalted into a national hero whom countless hagiographic memoirs, semi-fictional biographies, and laudatory documentaries almost unanimously herald him as prophet, visionary, and martyr. Furthermore, in 2017 Russian philanthropists set up a monument to the director in Suzdal (Figure I.1), where his *Andrei Rublev* was shot in 1965, in addition to the 2009 monument at the entrance to the All-Union State Institute of Cinematography (VGIK) in Moscow, where Tarkovsky stands in the company of his no less legendary schoolmates, Vasily Shukshin and Gennady Shpalikov (Figure I.2).

Figure I.1 Monument to Andrei Tarkovsky and *Andrei Rublev*'s characters in Suzdal.

Figure I.2 Monument to Andrei Tarkovsky, Gennady Shpalikov, and Vasily Shukshin at the entrance to the All-Union State Institute of Cinematography, Moscow.

The aim of this volume is to move beyond this kind of fascination with the Russian master and take a more level-headed approach to his career by balancing cinephilic enthusiasm with academic expertise. Tarkovsky's cinema has always attracted film scholars because of the philosophical depth and aesthetic appeal of his films. As Birgit Beumers rightly points out, there is an "over-emphasis in scholarship" on Tarkovsky at the expense of other Russian filmmakers who are no less worthy of attention.[5] At the same time, despite the impressive scope of Tarkovsky criticism written in, or translated into, English—sixteen monographs and two collections of essays—most monographic studies, with the exception of Nariman Skakov's *The Cinema of Tarkovsky: Labyrinths of Space and Time* (2012), which actively engages with cultural theory, are methodologically limited to film history and formalist analysis.[6] Although all of them have done an excellent job at placing Tarkovsky's films into their biographical, historical, and cultural contexts by extensively commenting on their production history as well as overall narrative and symbolic structure, such studies nevertheless fail to capture the rich complexity of his work, while being heavily descriptive and undertheorized.

Scholars' considerable aversion or indifference to theory and their concomitant immersion in the analysis of narrative motifs and cinematic techniques became a rather consistent feature of the field that could be traced from the earliest to more recent literature on the subject. Maya Turovskaya, for example, admits from the start in her pioneering book-length study *Tarkovsky: Cinema as Poetry* (1989) that her "book was written . . . straight from the heart," that is, from her first-hand knowledge of Soviet film industry as well as personal conversations with the director.[7] Her perspective of a "knowledgeable insider," however, masks a lack of theoretical sophistication in her perceptive readings of the films. Vida Johnson and Graham Petrie's *The Films of Andrei Tarkovsky: A Visual Fugue* (1994) is acclaimed as the highest standard in the field due to its encyclopedic scope and rigorous research, yet it almost never refers to any film theory (with the exception of "post-theoretical" David Bordwell and Noël Carrol), just as it downgrades Tarkovsky's own aesthetic views as anachronistic. Johnson and Petrie's skepticism regarding theoretical abstractions is especially evident in their critical assessment of previous studies of the filmmaker by European critics (e.g. Guy Gauthier, András Bálint Kovács, and Antoine de Baecque), whose contributions they condemn as "high-blown philosophical analyses . . . [written] in that cloudy, pompous, pseudo-poetic style that has now infiltrated from its natural home in France into what was once plain English prose."[8] Contrary to the philosophical (or poststructuralist) approach to film, which is, according to Johnson and Petrie, often based on "flimsy evidence," "downright inaccuracies," "factual mistakes," and "grandiose philosophical constructs,"[9] they emphasize instead the importance of paying attention to the narrative and aesthetic details of Tarkovsky's films as well as their cultural and historical contextualization.

Robert Bird's *Andrei Tarkovsky: Elements of Cinema* (2008) continues to abstain from theoretical interventions in his detailed hermeneutical analysis of the director's visual aesthetics which he laboriously maintains at the level of neutral phenomenological description. As he states, the main focus of his book is "Tarkovsky's sense of cinematic pitch, rather than any discursive 'meaning' of his films;"[10] hence, much attention is given to the representational devices of the cinematic medium from the viewer's perspective as well as the director's statements about cinema as art, the aspects which were left out in Johnson and Petrie's study. While considering Tarkovsky as a "great practitioner" rather than a "great thinker" or a "philosophical filmmaker" (following Alexei German's observation),[11] Bird admirably succeeds in justifying the aesthetic autonomy of his films from his mystical and religious inclinations. Still, he appears far too cautious to avoid "sealing Tarkovsky's films with the glue of theory"[12] by briefly mentioning a number of theorists (e.g. Bergson, Deleuze, Lacan) without fully engaging with their ideas.

The anti-theoretical (or post-theoretical) stance in Tarkovsky studies reached its full momentum in Thomas Redwood's *Andrei Tarkovsky's Poetics of Cinema* (2010), methodologically informed by the analytical discourse of such post-theorists as David Bordwell and Kristin Thompson, namely their notion of "parametric narration" in art cinema driven by its commitment to style rather than plot development. In his neo-formalist study, Redwood out-rightly dismisses the worth of any "overarching" film theory for his project ("be it ontological, phenomenological, psychological, theological, 'cultural' or whatever") and concentrates exclusively on the interplay of subtle stylistic strategies and devices that constitute "the internal narrational dynamics of Tarkovsky's films."[13] Even though Redwood's analytical rigor does feel like a breath of fresh air in Tarkovsky criticism preoccupied with religious and spiritualist problematics, it is hard not to notice that the focus of his study is indeed "strictly and conscientiously limited," just as his perspective on the subject is "somewhat old fashioned."[14] He never allows his references to other fields—such as art criticism, musicology, psychoanalysis, or philosophy—to evolve into a mutually productive interdisciplinary engagement which Tarkovsky's work actively suggests.

The growing corpus of Tarkovsky scholarship also includes two collections of essays that follow the same tendency described above. Gunnlaugur A. Jónsson and Thorkell Á. Óttarsson's *Through the Mirror* (2006) is largely dedicated to mystical and theological themes, and includes only two out of thirteen contributions that approach the filmmaker from theoretical perspectives (e.g. Bazin and Deleuze); whereas twenty essays in Nathan Dunne's *Tarkovsky* (2008) discuss mostly aesthetic, thematic, and historical aspects of his oeuvre. As one reviewer described Dunne's volume, "the book is definitely 'post-theory': although some authors invoke a few philosophers, from Heidegger and Benjamin to Deleuze and Derrida, these references . . . do not evolve into a sustained theoretically informed analysis."[15] At the same time, Tarkovsky scholarship is being continuously enriched by journal articles and various collections' chapters from film scholars specializing in feminism, psychoanalysis, poststructuralism, diaspora studies, urban studies, and film-philosophy, thus leaving their interpretative trace on the reception of his work.[16] The purpose of this volume is therefore to reinforce the latter tendency by placing Tarkovsky in a more interdisciplinary and methodologically diverse context without, however, underestimating the value of previous achievements in the field.

Another trend in Tarkovsky scholarship, which this volume aims to counter, is the incurable idolatry of the director in Russian-language film studies. A considerable number of Tarkovsky scholars in Russia have largely contributed to the field since the early 2000s, yet most of their contributions, despite their scholarly input, are permeated by hagiographic pathos and intensely preoccupied with religious themes and symbols. Igor Evlampiev, for example, approaches the filmmaker as a religious philosopher striving for the Absolute along with other Russian thinkers grounded in the Orthodox Christian tradition, such as Fyodor Dostoevsky, Nikolai Berdyaev, and Lev Shestov.[17] In a similar vein, Nikolai Boldyrev offers several biographical studies of Tarkovsky's mysticism in connection to Zen Buddhism, German Romanticism, Carlos Castaneda, and

Rudolf Steiner.[18] Both authors, however, passionately idolize the director as a spiritual teacher, just as his films are uncritically viewed as incarnations of divine truth. Tarkovsky's reverent treatment still persists even when scholars focus on more aesthetic subjects of research. Dmitry Salynskii, for example, discusses the filmmaker's career in terms of St Augustine's hermeneutical model, in which meaning is hierarchically distributed on literal, allegorical, moral, and eschatological levels, and explains it as a "meta-film" consistently ascending towards the transcendental realm and culminating in his final film *The Sacrifice* where the eschatological dimension manifests itself to the fullest. However rich and ambitious Salynskii's 570-page opus is, it locks Tarkovsky's work in the confines of scholastic hermeneutics, while heavily discriminating the material layer in his films.[19] Mikhail Perepelkin examines the filmmaker's engagement with literature and poetry, but his allegorical perspective often results in decoding cinematic images as the signs of hidden epiphany.[20] Natalia Kononenko's monograph undertakes a rigorous audiovisual analysis of the soundtrack evolving throughout Tarkovsky's entire career, yet she ostensibly downplays the role of sound-designers in his films, Eduard Artemiev and Owe Svensson, while crediting the director with "demiurgic" powers in creating his "sounding world."[21] Such a scholarly reverence for Tarkovsky in his native country may certainly put off a Western reader accustomed to a more impartial film criticism and could be studied in its own right as a symptom of anti-modern sentiments in the present-day Russian humanities excessively concerned with the issues of spirituality (*dukhovnost'*) and patriotism, and their ideological investment in national cultural politics.

It is against the backdrop of these tendencies in Tarkovsky scholarship—namely the methodological narrowness of Anglophone auteur studies on the one hand and Russophone hagiographic zeal on the other—that this volume hopes to offer new directions and insights for the study of the filmmaker by opening up the field to various interdisciplinary approaches. While refocusing on Tarkovsky through a more theoretical lens (e.g. Green, Lacan, Bergson, Deleuze, Aristotle, Lyotard, Žižek, Merleau-Ponty, Hadot, Kristeva, Bloom, and Sloterdijk, among others), the present work by no means intends to rekindle the theory vs. post-theory debate and advocate the legitimacy of "grand theory" for its own sake.[22] The volume's emphasis on the theoretical recontextualization of Tarkovsky's legacy should rather be viewed as yet another endeavor to understand his films in their multifaceted complexity: whereas earlier studies were more grounded in empirical research of the director's career, the following chapters invite the reader to ponder over these and other findings at a more abstract and conceptual level.

The volume consists of four parts covering biographical, aesthetic, and philosophical aspects of Tarkovsky's work, as well as tracing his influence on other filmmakers. Part one, entitled "Backgrounds" (chapters one to three), discusses extra-cinematic factors that influenced Tarkovsky's cinema, such as his biography and theoretical statements. Evgeny Tsymbal's chapter focuses on the traumatic events in the director's childhood that continued to haunt him throughout his life and found their reflection in his films. Unlike scholars who emphasize the importance of Tarkovsky's trauma of paternal abandonment for interpreting his films, for Tsymbal it is the director's strained relationship with his mother that defines much of his artistic impulse. Andrei Gornykh's chapter continues the discussion of Tarkovsky's life, albeit in later periods, by offering a verbal code of his psychobiography through a close reading of his diary. Unlike earlier biographers whose work is heavily steeped in hagiography, both authors in this section present their arguments in psychoanalytic terms: Tsymbal methodologically relies on André Green's notion of the dead mother complex, whereas Gornykh's approach is informed by Lacan's theory of the Signifier. The section is concluded by Sergey Toymentsev's analysis of the filmmaker's writings on film in light of Bergson's philosophy.

Part two, entitled "Film Method" (chapters four to eight), examines Tarkovsky's cinematic techniques, including his treatment of film genre, documentary style, temporality, landscape, and sound. Sara Pankenier Weld's chapter explores how *Ivan's Childhood* (1962) transcends the genre of the Soviet war movie by foregrounding the child's eye view in multiple cinematic dimensions and thus forces the audience into a subservient and vulnerable position. Zdenko Manduŝić's chapter discusses the director's engagement with the notion of the objective and documentary representation of reality in the context of post-Stalinist aesthetic debates and its practical implementation in *Andrei Rublev*. Donato Totaro's chapter provides a detailed textual analysis of Tarkovsky's long-take technique in *Stalker* and its key role in creating the atmosphere of spatial and temporal ambiguity in the film. Yelizaveta Goldfarb Moss focuses on the innovative representation of the Russian landscape in *Nostalghia* (1983), which underscores its unmasterable infinite spatiality via framing and one-point perspectives. This section concludes with Julia Shpinitskaya's analysis of the complex nature of Tarkovsky's sound design that, despite its overall commitment to realist aesthetics, tends towards irrealism in his later films.

Part three, "Theoretical Approaches" (chapters nine to thirteen), discusses Tarkovsky's work in the contexts of psychoanalytical, philosophical, and other theoretical perspectives. The section opens with Slavoj Žižek's "The Thing from Inner Space", which argues for a materialist reading of Tarkovsky's films that present an encounter with the radical otherness of some impossible and traumatic Thing, an encounter which is devoid of religious and mystical connotations that often accompany commentators' discussions. Žižek's chapter was originally published in *Angelaki: Journal of the Theoretical Humanities*, but is presented here in its unabridged version. Another psychoanalytic reading of

Tarkovsky's films is offered in Linda Belau and Ed Cameron's chapter, which explains the auteur's spiritual longings as the religious sublimation of his melancholic attachment to the lost object. Tarkovsky's cinematic materialism, first elaborated by Slavoj Žižek, is further explored in Robert Efird's chapter, which focuses on *Solaris*'s chiasmic representation of intersubjective space and time in light of Maurice Merleau-Ponty's philosophy. Anne Eakin Moss argues for the affinity between Pierre Hadot's philosophy of spiritual practice and Tarkovsky's films, all of which are characterized by the quixotic seekers of a transcendent aim and cinematic techniques invoking the miraculous. This section concludes with Mikhail Iampolski's chapter, which focuses on the director's consistent preoccupation with memory, and delineates his cinematic representation of the past from his attempts to historically reconstruct a period setting in *Andrei Rublev*, to private and subjective memories and dreams in *Solaris* and *Mirror*, and to the impersonal and metaphysical trace in *Stalker* and *Nostalghia*.

The fourth and final part of this volume, "Legacy" (chapters fourteen and fifteen), is dedicated to Tarkovsky's long-standing influence on such prominent auteurs as Andrei Zvyagintsev and Lars von Trier, who are often hailed as the heirs of the Russian master, yet have not received sufficient critical attention in this regard. Lisa Ryoko Wakamiya examines the presence of Tarkovskian thematic and stylistic motifs in a series of Zvyagintsev's films as well as the latter's struggle for authorial autonomy from the depersonalizing influence of the inherited tradition. Sergey Toymentsev and Anton Dolin focus on von Trier's lifelong engagement with the Russian director, which begins in his student short films and continues in more recent features.

While certainly not intending to be exhaustive, this volume provides a wide coverage of topics related to the director's oeuvre, ranging from the analysis of key biographical events that influenced the genesis of his personality as an artist, to the discussion of his formative influence on other filmmakers. Furthermore, although all chapters are firmly grounded in critical theory, the present work pays equal (or balanced) attention to both empirical (aesthetic and technical) and purely theoretical aspects of his work. Overall, this volume hopes to emphasize the urgency of a more sober appreciation of Tarkovsky's films as well as inspire further critical inquiry and debate.

NOTES

1. Maya Turovskaya, *7 ½, ili fil'my Andreia Tarkovskogo* (Moskva: "Iskusstvo," 1991).
2. To be exact, at this spiritualist séance, which allegedly took place before Tarkovsky started working on *Solaris* (1972), Pasternak foretold that the director would make "another four films," which amounts to six, not seven of his features in total. As we read in his diary's entry of 27 January 1973, "Boris Leonidovich [Pasternak] was obviously right when he said

that I would make another four pictures. I've made the first—*Solaris*. That leaves another three." In an entry of 22 November 1979 he prepares a list of questions to consult with a local psychic, one of which is: "Should I believe what Boris Pasternak told me about making four films?" Finally, in an entry of 21 December 1985 Tarkovsky, already stricken with cancer, worries whether he would manage to complete his last film: "I am getting worse by the day. Boris Leonidovich Pasternak was right when he said I would make another four films. I am thinking back to those spiritualist séances at Roerich's" (Andrei Tarkovsky, *Time within Time: The Diaries, 1970–1986*, trans. by Kitty Hunter-Blair [London: Faber & Faber, 1994], 66, 210, 349).

3. Peter Rollberg, *Historical Dictionary of Russian and Soviet Cinema* (Rowman & Littlefield, 2016), 689.
4. George Faraday, *Revolt of the Filmmakers: The Struggle for Artistic Autonomy and the Fall of the Soviet Film Industry* (University Park, PA: Penn State Press, 2000), 165.
5. Birgit Beumers (ed.), *A Companion to Russian Cinema* (Hoboken, NJ: John Wiley & Sons, 2016), 4.
6. Mark Le Fanu, *The Cinema of Andrei Tarkovsky* (London: BFI, 1987); Maya Turovskaya, *Tarkovsky: Cinema As Poetry* (London: Faber & Faber, 1989); Peter Green, *Andrei Tarkovsky: The Winding Quest* (London: Palgrave Macmillan, 1993); Vida T. Johnson and Graham Petrie, *The Films of Andrei Tarkovsky: A Visual Fugue* (Bloomington: Indiana University Press, 1994); Natasha Synessios, *Mirror: The Film Companion* (London: I. B.Tauris, 2001); Robert Bird, *Andrei Rublev* (London: BFI Film Classics, 2004); Gunnlaugur A. Jónsson and Thorkell Á. Óttarsson (eds), *Through the Mirror: Reflections on the Films of Andrei Tarkovsky* (Cambridge: Cambridge Scholars Press, 2006); Robert Bird, *Andrei Tarkovsky: Elements of Cinema* (London: Reaktion Books, 2008); Nathan Dunne (ed.), *Tarkovsky* (London: Black Dog Publishing, 2008); Jeremy Mark Robinson, *The Sacred Cinema of Andrei Tarkovsky* (Maidstone: Crescent Moon Publishing, 2008); Thomas Redwood, *Andrei Tarkovsky's Poetics of Cinema* (Cambridge: Cambridge Scholars Publishing, 2010); Sean Martin, *Andrei Tarkovsky* (Harpenden: Oldcastle Books, 2011); Nariman Skakov, *The Cinema of Tarkovsky: Labyrinths of Space and Time* (London: I. B.Tauris, 2012); Layla Alexander-Garrett, *Andrei Tarkovsky: The Collector of Dreams* (Glagoslav Publications Ltd, 2012); Geoff Dyer, *Zona: A Book About a Film About a Journey to a Room* (London: Vintage, 2012); Mark Bould, *Solaris* (London: Palgrave Macmillan, 2014); Terence McSweeney, *Beyond the Frame: The Films and Film Theory of Andrei Tarkovsky* (Aporetic Press, 2015); Tobias Pontara, *Andrei Tarkovsky's Sounding Cinema: Music and Meaning from* Solaris *to* The Sacrifice (Abingdon: Routledge, 2019).
7. Turovskaya, *Tarkovsky*, xxviii.
8. Vida T. Johnson and Graham Petrie, "Andrei Tarkovskii's films," *Journal of European Studies* 20.3 (1990): 265–77, 267.
9. Ibid., 269, 273, 276.
10. Bird, *Elements*, 9.
11. Ibid., 13.
12. Robert Bird, "Gazing into Time: Tarkovsky and Post-Modern Cinema Aesthetics," *Nostalghia.com*: http://www.nostalghia.com/TheTopics/Gazing.html
13. Redwood, 12.
14. Ibid., 12, 2.
15. Andrey Shcherbenok, "Review of *Tarkovsky*, Ed. Nathan Dunne. London: Black Dog Publishing, 2008," *Studies in Russian and Soviet Cinema* 2.3 (2008): 373–6, 375.
16. See, for example, Thomas W. Sheehan, "The Production of a Woman in Andrei Tarkovsky's *The Sacrifice*," *Women & Performance: A Journal of Feminist Theory* 9.2 (1997): 199–210; Claire C. Thomson, "It's all about snow: Limning the post-human

body in *Copuc/Solaris* (Tarkovsky, 1972) and *It's All about Love* (Vinterberg, 2003)," *New Cinemas: Journal of Contemporary Film* 5.1 (2007): 3–21; Hamid Naficy, *An Accented Cinema: Exilic and Diasporic Filmmaking* (Princeton: Princeton University Press, 2001); Thorsten Botz-Bornstein, *Films and Dreams: Tarkovsky, Bergman, Sokurov, Kubrick, and Wong Kar-Wai* (Lanham, MD: Lexington Books, 2007); Stanka Radovic, "On the Threshold: Terrain Vague as Living Space in Andrei Tarkovsky's *Stalker*," in Patrick Barron and Manuela Mariani (eds), *Terrain Vague: Interstices at the Edge of the Pale* (Abingdon: Routledge, 2014): 114–29; Dominic Michael Rainsford, "Tarkovsky and Levinas: Cuts, Mirrors, Triangulations," *Film-philosophy* 11.2 (2007): 122–43.

17. Igor Evlampiev, *Khudozhestvennaya filosofia Andreia Tarkovskogo* (Sankt Peterburg: Aleteia, 2001).

18. Nikolai Boldyrev, *Stalker, ili Trudy i dni Andreia* Tarkovskogo (Chelyabinsk: Ural LTD, 2002); *Zhertvoprinoshenie Andreia Tarkovskogo* (Moskva: Vagrius, 2004).

19. Dmitrii Salynskii, *Kinogermenevtika Tarkovskogo* (Moskva: Kvadriga, 2009).

20. Mikhail Perepelkin, *Slovo v mire Andreia Tarkovskogo: Poètika inoskazaniia* (Samara: Samarskiĭ universitet, 2010).

21. Natal'ia Kononenko, *Andrei Tarkovskii: zvuchashchii mir fil'ma* (Moskva: Progress-Traditsiia, 2011).

22. David Bordwell and Noël Carroll (eds), *Post-theory: Reconstructing Film Studies* (Madison, WI: University of Wisconsin Press, 1996).

Backgrounds

Introduction to Part I

This first section of the volume is dedicated to extra-cinematic factors that influenced Tarkovsky's cinema, such as his biography and his aesthetic views. The section opens with Evgeny Tsymbal's chapter on the traumatic events in the director's childhood that continued to haunt him throughout his life. Tarkovsky scholars often point out the autobiographical nature of his cinema and, more specifically, how the divorce of his parents influenced his cinematic representation of marital relationships. According to Helena Goscilo (2010), for example, Tarkovsky's personal trauma of paternal abandonment provides a clue to the narrative structure of his films. For Tsymbal, however, it is the director's strained relationship with his mother, viewed in the context of André Green's theory of the dead mother complex, that defines much of his artistic impulse. This chapter also discusses what hardships Tarkovsky experienced during the wartime and how his father's influence inadvertently helped him choose his future profession.

Andrei Gornykh's chapter offers a close reading of Tarkovsky's diary from a Lacanian perspective by focusing on the director's recurrent use of those keywords which symbolically epitomize and organize the major the matic layers of his biography and cinema as well: namely, grass (or *trava* in Russian), persecution from the state authorities (*travlia*), and expense (*trata*). Phonetically consonant and etymologically derived from the same root *tra-* (or proto-Slavic *ter-*), these words make up a coherent cluster of signifiers (*trava-trata-travlia*) which are centered around the director's primal fantasy of the house. As the author argues, the signifying constellation "*trava-trata-travlia*" in Tarkovsky's diary could be viewed as a psychobiographical code to the internal dynamics of his visual imagery.

This part concludes with Sergey Toymentsev's chapter, which attempts to answer the question whether Tarkovsky's insights in cinema, documented in interviews and in *Sculpting in Time* (1986), could amount to a coherent film theory. Although many scholars observe that one should abandon analytical reasoning while comprehending his films, they nevertheless follow a certain logic that seems to align with many of Henry Bergson's philosophical arguments. The same could be said about Tarkovsky's theoretical propositions: namely, his preference for intuition over intellectual cognition, psychological duration over chronological time, the past over the present, as well as his foregrounding the dual nature of the film image in which subjective consciousness (spirit) and objective reality (matter) are coalesced into a single unit. Viewing Tarkovsky as being subconsciously Bergsonian, the author argues, could help us salvage his theoretical musings from being dismissed as unembarrassedly Romantic or outdated.

CHAPTER I

Tarkovsky's Childhood: Between Trauma and Myth

Evgeniy Tsymbal

Tarkovsky's early films, such as *The Steamroller and the Violin* (1961) and *Ivan's Childhood* (1962), as well as his later *Mirror* (1974) are usually viewed as his most autobiographical films in which he realistically reproduces the happiest moments of his childhood, experienced either in Moscow or in the village of Ignatievo. By narrativizing his childhood as a pastoral paradise, Tarkovsky places himself into Russian literary heritage exemplified by such prominent works as Leo Tolstoy's *Childhood, Boyhood, Youth* (1852–7), Sergei Aksakov's *Childhood Years* (1856), Alexander Herzen's *My Past and Thoughts* (1852–68), Ivan Bunin's *The Life of Arseniev* (1927–39), and Vladimir Nabokov's *Speak, Memory* (1947), to name but a few. All of these writers not only recollected their childhood to the minutest detail, they reinvented it as a blissful and enchanted realm by mixing memory with myth. Yet it would be a mistake to think of Tarkovsky's fictionalized account of his childhood exclusively in mythical terms, since its idyllic appearance is indispensable from its deeply traumatic underside. In this chapter I explore the early years of Tarkovsky's biography, presented mostly by his sister Marina Tarkovskaya, in order to trace how the traumatic events of the director's childhood found their uncanny expression in his films. I primarily focus on how young Andrei was affected by his parents' divorce as well as his mother's consequent alienation in later years. To get a better glimpse of Andrei's estranged relationship with his mother, I discuss it in the context of André Green's theory of the dead mother complex. I also examine how the collective trauma of the war in the 1940s, associated with famine and destroyed families, was experienced by Andrei personally. To conclude, I discuss how the influence and authority of his father, Arseny Tarkovsky, helped his son become an artist as well as overcome his romantic illusions in teenage years.

EARLY CHILDHOOD

The first years in the life of Andrei Tarkovsky and his sister Marina, before their father left the family, were quite fortunate, even though they lived in extreme poverty. They had this in common with the majority of the Soviet intelligentsia in the early 1930s. Arseny Tarkovsky and Maria Vishnyakova met each other at what is now known as the Maxim Gorky Literature Institute, where both of them were attending the advanced creative writing classes. After dating for a year and a half, they married.

Both Andrei (born in 1932) and Marina (born in 1934) were adored by their young parents and surrounded by caring and benevolent people. During the summer the children were taken out to Pavel Gorchakov's country house near the village of Ignatievo where they were exposed to the beauty and charm of Russian nature. They were at times visited by relatives and friends of their parents, among whom there were many writers and poets who became famous later on. Thus, from the very beginning, they were placed in an artistic environment in which they were exposed to classical music, poetic verse, and intellectual debates. One of their frequent visitors, for example, was the poet and photographer Lev Gornung, the children's godfather, whose family photographs of the Tarkovskys and their house later became the major inspiration for the creation of *Mirror*. As Marina Tarkovskaya recalls, her parents at first doted on each other and her mother, according to the poet Maria Petrovykh, used to have a "face as if it was lit up by the sun."[1] Nevertheless, she also adds, "father was rarely at the dacha,"[2] as he had to go on long business trips.

Yet the happiness of Andrei and Marina's early childhood was already overshadowed by a number of traumatic circumstances that affected their lives later on. In Stalin's Russia descendants of noble families who refused to immigrate after the Bolshevik revolution were still viewed with a sneering attitude among common people. This was also the case for representatives of the old Russian intelligentsia who were never respected as a professional middle class, but rather contemptuously disregarded as an intermediate layer between the working class and the peasantry. The rumors about serial arrests, and relatives and acquaintances either disappearing forever or ending up in remote and desolate regions of the country, also served as the disturbing background for their growing up. Furthermore, constant relocations from one apartment to another, and from Moscow to the countryside and back again, undoubtedly had a traumatizing impact on the children and their parents. The main cause was the state-controlled famine spreading through Russia and Ukraine in the early 1930s. As Andrei's grandmother wrote to his mother at that time, "Marusya, save up flour and send us some grains and flour too because all this is gone here already."[3]

ABSENT FATHER

The most powerful trauma of the young Andrei's life was the dissolution of his family and his father leaving his mother for another woman, Antonina Bokhonova. As most psychologists agree, "The most common and difficult form of emotional trauma is the sudden loss of a loved one."[4] As Tarkovsky himself comments on his early childhood, "I lived with mother, grandmother, and sister. Family without a man. This had a considerable impact on my character . . . That was a difficult time. I have always missed my father. When father left us, I was three years old. Life was incredibly difficult in any possible way."[5] Arseny Tarkovsky abandoned his children and their mother in 1936–7.[6] In fact, the proud Maria Vishnyakova willingly helped him to move out by packing his clothes in a suitcase, since she was no longer able to tolerate his sudden disappearances, coming home late at night, offering poor excuses after he started pursuing Antonina Bokhonova, who herself was married at the time. Even though he did help his ex-wife financially from time to time and always tried to maintain a decent relationship with her and the children, for them his departure was, as Nikolai Boldyrev puts it, a "cosmogonic catastrophe."[7] For both Andrei and Marina, their father—despite his occasional visits— forever remained an absent and distant figure whose desertion for another family was simply incomprehensible. As Marina Tarkovskaya writes, in 1937 they and their father's new family (his new wife also had a daughter from the first marriage) became neighbors and, because of this, they continued to see each other quite often after separation: "I was very surprised back then why my father lived on Party Street and not on Arsenyevsky Street nearby, even though his name was Arseny and he was not a party member . . . Just as why he was not living with me and Andryusha, but with some other girl Lyalya [Bokhonova's daughter], although he was our father, not hers."[8]

As Marina Tarkovskaya later observes, "Andrei dearly loved his father whose departure from the family was deeply traumatic for him." This is why, she continues, in his diploma film *The Steamroller and the Violin* (1961) "we see no father of the boy and learn nothing about him." What we see instead is "the striving of the young protagonist to find a surrogate father in his grown-up friend."[9] Helena Goscilo goes as far as to argue that most of Tarkovsky's films came out of his continuous struggles to work through his personal "trauma of paternal abandonment"[10] and reclaim his father in multiple forms. *The Steamroller and the Violin*, she argues, blatantly brings out "Tarkovsky's denigration of women and his yearning for a loving father"[11] whose role is adopted by a benevolent steamroller driver. *Ivan's Childhood* offers a number of "eager surrogate paternal caretakers" for the young protagonist who, nevertheless, prefers to perish as a fatherless martyr in "a defiant indifference to paternal absence."[12] *Solaris* (1972), on the contrary, strives "to incorporate the Lost Father into the formative paradigm of

Family" by "Tarkovsky's unexpected wish-fulfillment introduction of a wise and caring paternal figure."[13] *Mirror* delves into the unresolved issues of the director's Oedipal drama and stages "the adolescent transfer of cathexis to the father as the norm of male identity formation."[14] *The Sacrifice* (1986) promises "rebirth and independence for the son, but at the cost of the father's self-inflicted withdrawal from the son's life."[15]

It is hard to disagree with Goscilo's assertion that "the absence of [Tarkovsky's] own father created the single weightiest and psychologically most incapacitating trauma in his life."[16] The impact of this trauma is especially evident in his autobiographical *Mirror*, which is particularly rich with poignant scenes reproducing the father's absence from the family. The opening sequence, for example, depicts the mother ritually sitting on the fence and waiting for him to come back, while Arseny Tarkovsky himself is reciting his love poems dedicated to another woman; later on in the film we see his children happily rushing towards him when he returns from the front. However, I want to suggest that Tarkovsky's "chronic longing"[17] for his absent father is not the only clue in his biography that can shed light on the narrative dynamics of his films. The relationship with his mother was no less important. After their divorce, Tarkovsky's father remarried twice, while his mother remained single for the rest of her life, devoting herself to her work and children.

TARKOVSKY'S MOTHER

According to many testimonies, Tarkovsky's mother was quite a character, so to speak: she was strict, honest, straightforward, modest, and overly responsible. She was a woman of principle with a clear and unshakable sense of right and wrong, which made her difficult to deal with at times. Her parents also got divorced when she was little. When her mother, Vera Vishnyakova, left her family for another man whom she eventually married, her father, Ivan Vishnyakov, refused to let go of their daughter and thus kept her around for a few years. The mother's long absence had a traumatic impact on the young Maria, just as her mother, according to Viktor Filimonov (one of Tarkovsky's biographers), always felt guilty for their long separation. As he writes, "When Vera Nikolaevna [Andrei's grandmother] learned that Arseny Tarkovsky left the family, she decided to help Maria raise the children, as if she wanted to right the wrongs before her daughter who still couldn't forgive her the years of loneliness in her childhood."[18] As Marina Tarkovskaya recalls,

> She never told me how much she suffered while being separated from her mother. Because she had to live with her tough father, while having only secret meetings with her mother in the years of her character formation,

she became shy, reserved, and withdrawn. With time her mother became a stranger to her. Here's what her grandmother wrote to Lev Vladimirovich Gornung during the war: "Marusya never let me into her life! Since her childhood she has been terribly withdrawn. Should you come any closer to her, she would hide into her shell right away like a snail. As a teenager she couldn't stand any advice or guidance of worldly wisdom. But now you cannot even talk to her."[19]

Even though the reason for the father's sudden desertion was never discussed in the Tarkovsky family, it is possible to suggest that it had something to do with his perception of Maria Vishnyakova's personality. She never cared about her clothes or appearance, since she wore only those dresses that were sent by her mother. Her "monastery asceticism,"[20] according to Filimonov, was the exact opposite of Arseny Tarkovsky's subsequent wives, Antonina Bokhonova and Tatiana Ozerskaya, who were both glamorous ladies of literary society. Tarkovsky's mother, however, was indifferent to judgment from the outside world. As Marina Tarkovskaya testifies,

> In everyday life our mother was a nihilist: she needed nothing, even window curtains. She was beyond the household concerns. She represented the type of women popular in the 1920s who prioritized spiritual life over everything else, dismissing the rest as petty bourgeois values.[21]

> There's a proverb: everyone is the blacksmith of his own fortune. And mother was a bad smith. She couldn't really settle in life and seemed to purposefully choose the hardest paths for herself. She never married again, she went to work in a printing house with its low wages and excessive man-hours, and she declined the evacuation opportunity provided by the Literary Fund during the war. This was all because she always had to be honest even with herself. She never cared about clothing. She thought she had no right to spend money on herself, so she dressed in random clothes. She seemed to need nothing in life, except a cup of tea with a piece of bread and cigarettes.[22]

After the divorce, Maria Vishnyakova seemed to remain faithful to Arseny by keeping in her memory the image of an ideal husband—a talented poet and the father of their children—she had formed by the time of their marriage. She might have served this image throughout her later life, by idolizing his spiritual essence yet completely overlooking his erotic nature. Arseny, however, was not only a poet, he was also a handsome and down-to-earth man prone to passionate love affairs, for whom the idealistic love of his wife might have seemed rather burdensome. As Marina Tarkovskaya describes him, "Father was a man completely immersed in passion. He was madly and deeply in love with mother. But later, when the feeling for her burnt out, he fell in love with another woman with the same passion. His poet's nature was completely devoid of rationality."[23]

THE DEAD MOTHER COMPLEX: A HYPOTHETICAL RECONSTRUCTION

In the years following the divorce, the young Andrei and Marina became unwilling witnesses to their mother's mournful and sacrificial fidelity to a past love, through which she continued to maintain an integrity and moral rigor that can be compared to the passionate devotion of the Decembrist wives. As Marina Tarkovskaya recalls,

> When I asked her once why she never married again, she said no one could replace our father to us. We never saw a man around her. The problem of a lifetime companion was solved for her once and for all. Mother was so chaste and timid that everything feminine about her, such as desire to look pretty and be admired, seemed to be uncon- sciously suppressed.[24]

Maria Vishnyakova's steadfast loyalty to her absent husband could also be explained as the result of her deep emotional scarring that prevented her from finding another love interest afterwards. In contemporary psychoanalysis, the mother's experience of loss and grief is viewed as a catastrophe for the mother-child relationship predicated on the mother's undivided emotional availability. As André Green demonstrated in his essay "The Dead Mother" (1983), "the mother's bereavement modifies her fundamental attitude with regard to the child, whom she feels incapable of loving, but whom she continues to love just as she continues to take care of him."[25] The emotional withdrawal of the mother, caused by "the loss of a person dear to her . . . a change of fortune in the nuclear family or the family of origin, a liaison of the father who neglects the mother, humiliation, etc."[26] has a profoundly traumatic impact on the growth of the child who up until then had been the center of the mother's attention. Green calls this condition the "dead mother complex," which refers to "a mother who remains alive but who is, so to speak, psychically dead in the eyes of the young child in her care."[27] The child's psychical murder of the mother, "accomplished without hatred"[28] and standing for the decathexis of the maternal image, is, of course, an action of last resort taken out of des- peration. It occurs, according to Green, after "the child has attempted in vain to repair the mother who is absorbed by her bereavement, which has made him feel the measure of his impotence, after having experienced the loss of his mother's love and the threat of the loss of the mother herself."[29] Such murder results in "the constitution of a hole in the texture of object-relations with the mother,"[30] a psychical hole which redirects the trajectory of the child's psychosexual and intellectual development. Because the mother's "love has been lost at one blow" and "the baby disposes of no explication to account for what has happened," "this position . . . obliges him to find someone responsible for the mother's black mood."[31] From now on the child is destined to forever search for the meaning of the mother's bereavement and this "loss of meaning" will launch the early development of his or her imagination and cognition. As Green elaborates,

> the quest for lost meaning structures the early development of the fantasmatic and the intellectual capacities of the ego . . . The compromised unity of the ego which has a hole in it from now on, realizes itself either on the level of fantasy, which gives open expression to artistic creation, or on the level of knowledge, which is at the origin of highly productive intellectualization. It is evident that one is witnessing an attempt to master the traumatic situation.[32]

The child's premature development of imagination and cognitive abilities, manifested in his or her "compulsion to imagine" and "compulsion to think," is thus subjected to the inexplicable mystery of the mother's withdrawal and directed towards the mastery of its traumatic impact through fantasy and thought. As Green puts it metaphorically, "to surmount the dismay over the loss of the breast," the child creates "a patched breast, a piece of cognitive fabric which is destined to mask the hole left by the decathexis."[33] Another consequence of such loss is the child's "early and particularly intense attachment to the father" who is "felt to be the saviour from the conflict" but who, nevertheless, remains unhelpful and inaccessible in reality "because he leaves the mother-child couple to cope with this situation alone."[34]

Green's discovery of the dead mother complex was largely influenced by his clinical practice with patients who happened to be professionally engaged in literature and the arts. Despite their relative success in their abstract creativity, most of them were experiencing dissatisfaction in work and "profound disturbances in love, sexuality and affective communication,"[35] which Green diagnosed as the projective actualization of their early childhood struggles with the loss of the mother's love—or their compulsive reenactment of the experience of the loss—as well as their unconscious identification with the mother's depressive disposition and incapacity to love. In most cases the image of the dead or unloving mother continues to hold sway over the patients in adulthood by making them unable to commit "to a deeper personal involvement which implies concern for the other."[36] Their treatment, according to Green's clinical method, "reveals a deep-seated longing for the ideal loving mother, the good mother that preceded the depressed one"[37] whom they refuse to mourn. It is the reactivation of the positive maternal imago buried deep down in the unconscious, he argues, that can promise a cure for such patients after many stages of the analysis: namely, "the rediscovery of the early happiness that existed prior to the appearance of the dead mother complex" and the ability "to reach a transferential repetition of a happy relationship with a mother who is alive at last and desirous of the father."[38]

Even though we have little evidence to confirm "profound disturbances" in Andrei Tarkovsky's love life, the complicated relationship with his parents and the autobiographical motifs in his films may well be interpreted in terms of Green's psychoanalytic insights. It would be reasonable to assume that Maria Vishnyakova did fall into depression after her husband left the family, given her subsequent ascetic commitment to chastity and self-denying devotion to the children's upbringing. As her daughter testifies, "The sunlight coming from her face quickly went out."[39] Furthermore, given that there is "something transgenerational in the dead mother concept [because] most of the conflicts which make the mother 'dead' (while still alive) might be related to her conflicts with the previous generation: her mother, father, etc.,"[40] Maria Vishnyakova might have been more susceptible to emotional withdrawal due to the prior traumatic experience of her own mother's absence in early childhood. And yet, her affective distance as the mother could only be hypothetically reconstructed, since neither Andrei nor Marina ever complained about this in interviews or diary. As Tarkovsky says in a 1984 interview:

My mother had a greater influence on me than my father . . . When the war started, not only did she save our lives . . . Being completely inept in everyday life, she did everything so that we could get an education. I went to music school, majoring in piano, and painting school, and I have no idea how she could make this happen, because there were no proper conditions for this at that time . . . If it was not for my mother, I would never be able to become a filmmaker.[41]

The mother's bereavement, according to Green, does not prevent her from enacting her nutritious role as a caretaker. Despite Maria Vishnyakova's sacrificial investment in her children's lives, she was nevertheless "too tough" on them and, because of this, could appear emotionally distant to them. As Marina Tarkovskaya writes,

Her entire life was devoted to the benefit of Andrei and me. But she didn't spoil us, not at all. She was, on the contrary, too tough on us.

As for Andrei's upbringing, she must have made a mistake by trying to subdue him, make him follow her orders. And this was impossible, this only estranged him from her.[42]

The estrangement of the young Andrei, who "was on his own from early childhood,"[43] could certainly be explained by his personality traits. Johnson and Petrie, for example, describe him as a restrained loner, touchy and stubborn as well as recalcitrant and hyperactive.[44] According to a family friend's account, "He caused his mother a lot of worry—he was hot-tempered and uncommunicative."[45] And yet, Andrei's emphatic autonomy from his mother's supervision could also have been the result of her previous divorce trauma which might have had an alienating effect on the formation of his character. According to Green, the child's psychological loss of the mother's love is often temporary, just as its impact varies from case to case, without necessarily developing into clinical depression. But even if the mother comes back to the child after her emotional withdrawal, the latter would never treat her in the same way. As Green argues, "The return of the presence of the object is not enough to heal the disastrous effects of its too long absence. Non-existence has taken possession of the mind, erasing the representations of the object that preceded its absence."[46] It is possible, therefore, to infer that Andrei's relationship with his mother became strained after Arseny Tarkovsky left them. Both children and their mother were affected by the trauma of paternal abandonment, but it is through the mother's "bereavement" and her emotional withdrawal that they might have been traumatized most of all.

Tarkovsky's films, however, provide us with more reliable evidence to support our hypothesis about Maria Vishnyakova's dead mother complex that might have occurred after her husband's desertion. It is there that we find the most vivid manifestation ("accompanied by a richness of representation and a gift of auto-interpretation"[47]) of the compulsive reenactment of the experience of the loss that is so characteristic of Green's patients. Both *Solaris* and *Mirror* are structured by the autobiographical protagonist's narcissistic "quest for lost meaning"[48] about the hidden cause of the family dissolution, just as they strive to restore the Oedipal family by reuniting both parents in a pre-traumatic setting and thus rediscover the happy ideal mother before her grieving. Furthermore, Tarkovsky's later features *Stalker* and *Nostalghia* testify how the director's previous phantasmatic attempts to resurrect the dead mother by making her happy again miserably failed, and how her deadness continues to hold sway over the protagonist by "[drawing his] ego towards a deathly, deserted universe."[49] As Green writes, "The mother's blank mourning induces blank mourning in the infant, burying a part of his ego in the maternal necropolis." Isn't the Stalker's Zone, in the waters of which he falls asleep in fetal position, indeed a "maternal necropolis"? *Nostalghia*, dedicated to Tarkovsky's mother, is focused exclusively on the protagonist's "feeling of narcissistic depletion, expressed phenomenologically by the sentiment of emptiness,"[50] which has all the symptoms of Green's dead mother syndrome. It is therefore safe to argue that the father's absence in Tarkovsky's early childhood is not "the single weightiest and psychologically most incapacitating trauma in his life,"[51] it is rather the mother's grieving and emotional withdrawal that became most traumatizing for him and, as a result, stimulated his "intense attachment to the father"[52] as well as his quest for lost meaning in art.

BOYHOOD TRAUMAS

During World War II, Tarkovsky's family evacuated to Yurievets, about 500 km east from Moscow, to live there with Maria Vishnyakova's mother until 1943. The evacuation time became a new period of hardships for the young Andrei: whereas in Moscow he used to spend most of his time indoors, in Yurievets he was left on his own and fully exposed to street life, mingling with the tough boys of the town. As his sister writes,

> Andrei didn't want to stand out and was friends with the savvy local boys whose influence on him was not always positive. Thus, for example, while recklessly sliding down from the famous Yurievets hills, he would scream a stream of profanities across the area, which was often brought to our mother's attention. What was most striking in Andrei's behaviour was his incredible fearlessness. This trait—call it courage or bravery—later helped him to fight Soviet officials of all kinds. It is truly impressive how bravely he defended each of his films![53]

Thanks to his innate bravery, the young Andrei was able to save his mother from drowning in the river, which was one of his most traumatic experiences during their stay in Yurievets. Besides their constant shortage of food and harsh living conditions, to keep their house warm enough they were always in need of firewood, most of which could be obtained in the river. As Marina Tarkovskaya recalls,

> This was our most terrible memory. The early spring of 1942. Ice started to break on the Volga River . . . All the townsfolk came to the riverbank to catch floating pieces of timber which we all needed for heating. We were standing on the bank, collecting the wood our mother would catch in the river, jumping from one ice float to another. All of a sudden, in front of our eyes, she fell through the ice and disappeared for a moment among drifting ice floats.[54]

Risking drowning themselves, Andrei and Marina got their mother out of the dark and cold water and thus experienced the shock of almost losing her. Confronting death and tragedies of the war became somewhat common for the teenage Andrei at that time: most of his schoolmates lost their fathers in the war, just as his female teachers lost their husbands. This is probably why his *Mirror* dedicates an entire episode to the orphan Asafiev whose parents died in the siege of Leningrad. Andrei's father himself was severely wounded, while serving as a war correspondent on the front lines, and his leg was amputated as a result. Even after the war was over, the reality of death was still quite palpable: at the age of fourteen he was diagnosed with pulmonary tuberculosis, which was poorly treated at that time. Missing classes in school, he spent about two years under treatment in various hospitals and sanatoriums, where only half the patients survived. Even though he was cured, weak lungs—inherited from his father—remained a troublesome issue for him for the rest of his life.

When Andrei turned eighteen, he decided to get married. Furthermore, because of his passionate engagement with an amateur theatre at school, he was convinced that the stage was his true and only vocation to which he should dedicate his life. He kept both decisions a secret from his mother, knowing she would not approve of them, and wrote his father a letter in which he asked for his opinion. Touched by his son's request, Arseny Tarkovsky responded with caring fatherly guidance, which may have determined most of Andrei's decisions later in life:

> I do not think your childhood was too easy, but I think that you, unfortunately, almost never had a need to be active. You didn't choose a path for yourself, it was chosen for you by circumstances, and you submitted to them . . . All your problems were solved for you by your mother, not by yourself. Hence, your childhood and adolescence may have been sorrowful, but not difficult. At your age I was more experienced because I was growing up in a more difficult time. But I still remember and understand very well what an airhead I used to be. Nevertheless, it was my untamed passion for poetry that saved and served me as my guiding light back then. I was like you in everything, except poetry. I was also light-minded and ready to follow the circumstances whatever they are, but in poetry my discipline was impeccable . . . Your mother remembers with how much diligence, perseverance, and endurance I worked on my poetry. This is the only thing which was my school of life and which stops me from being ashamed of myself . . . And now I really, really regret that my education (mainly self-education) was directed only toward the path of poetry . . . I really regret that I never studied at some school where I'd needed to work much harder . . . What keeps eating at me is that I didn't go to study physics, math or natural sciences at

university when I was seventeen-eighteen. I could have turned to poetry later! How much I would have gained! Here's my advice: it's necessary you graduate from high school. Then learn any profession at university (preferably, in natural or physical sciences) and work at least a year in it. If you still have this need for art afterwards, then yes, you may do whatever you want, even get enrolled in acting school. I really wish I could pass you the understanding of my own mistakes so you could use it not to repeat them. Now about your falling in love . . . We share so much in common. We have this propensity to jump off into any abyss if it attracts us somehow and we both forget about everything else . . . And this is bad, this could be harmful. For the love of God, don't get married . . . What if your marriage turns out to be premature? Life for both of you will turn into hell for which divorce is the only way out: this would be agony for you, your wife, and your children if you have them. I am telling you this because I know it from my experience. Talk to your mother, she will tell you the same.[55]

According to Tarkovsky's sister, this letter was not the reason for Andrei's breaking up with his would-be fiancée, given his passionate and light-hearted nature always ready to move on towards a new romance. Yet what is interesting about these didactic instructions is how they set up a program or a code of rules for Tarkovsky's career path in the future. As is known, he did try to follow his father's advice to get a useful profession at university which would require serious work: in the early 1950s he studied Arabic at the prestigious Oriental Institute in Moscow for a little bit more than a year. Neither his mother nor sister could understand why Andrei decided to choose such a major, but Arabic could be viewed as his best approximation of what his father meant by natural sciences. He even worked in a profession related to natural sciences for a year, as his father requested, by participating as a prospector in a research expedition to the taiga prior to his enrolment in the All-Union State Institute of Cinematography (VGIK) in Moscow. Furthermore, as a filmmaker he fully adopted his father's poetic perfectionism, which he later idolized as if it were some sort of religious service requiring suffering and sacrifice.

CONCLUSION

Despite the poetic authority of his father, to whom he always looked up with the greatest admiration, it is nevertheless to his mother that Tarkovsky owed much of his personality formation, both as a person and an artist. As Maya Turovskaya observes, his "spiritual baggage was acquired during his none-too-happy childhood, and was little affected by subsequent external influences."[56] To this we may add that his childhood influenced his later life mainly in terms of stressing the development of such seemingly contradictory character traits as recalcitrance and victim mentality, both of which stemmed from his strained relationship with his mother and which, in turn, became constituent in the individualization of his semi-autobiographical protagonists. As shown above, in light of Green's psychoanalytic findings, it would not be a far-fetched assumption to suggest that after his father's desertion, Tarkovsky's relationship with his mother may have suffered an irreparable rift because of her subsequent emotional withdrawal, which the young Andrei attempted to overcome by alienating himself from her, while fostering his own autonomy within the realm of imagination and thought. Andrei's early estrangement from his mother resulted in his systematic disobedience to her will, which later solidified in his constant desire for transgression that manifested itself in virtually all aspects of his social behavior: hanging out with street delinquents, skipping classes in school, getting married before graduation, getting lost in the taiga, dressing up as *stilyaga* (i.e. as a member of the Soviet youth counter-culture in the 1950s), being rejected by the Komsomol (i.e. the youth division of the Communist Party), and rebelling against the Soviet status quo, fiercely defending his films from any censorship cuts, and, eventually, leaving the Soviet Union. Tarkovsky's persistent recalcitrance against social norms and traditions, developed from his adolescent defiance of the mother's authority, was always accompanied by his parallel devotion to a higher, almost divine, law of art, which he associated with his father's rigorous commitment to poetry. And so, stuck between an emotionally withdrawn mother and a physically inaccessible father, Tarkovsky still longed for the intimacy of parental love, while perceiving himself as the victim of his unresolved family drama, which he painstakingly attempted to repair in his cinematic fantasies. As his father told him through tears after the premiere of *Mirror*: "Andryusha, was it really like this? I didn't think you took to heart so much."[57] Tarkovsky's acute sense of victimhood was not attached exclusively to the familial context. In his later features it acquired a theological dimension that added a messianic component to his characters. By honing them into self-styled martyrs, rejected by society yet driven by transcendental aspirations, and foregrounding the Christian motif of sacrifice, he thus sublimated his personal traumas into the romantic myth of an artist-savior.

Translated by Sergey Toymentsev

NOTES

1. Marina Tarkovskaya, *Oskolki zerkala* (Moskva: Vagrius, 2006), 120.
2. Ibid., 64.
3. Marina Tarkovskaya, "Vospominaniya," in *Arkhetip detstva-2: deti i skazki v kulture, literature, kinematografii i pedagogike*, ed. A. V. Tarasov (Ivanovo, 2004), 109–15, 113.

4. Mikhail Reshetnikov, *Psikhicheskaya travma* (Sankt Peterburg: Vostochno-Evropeiskiy Institut Psikhoanaliza, 2006), 85.
5. Andrei Tarkovsky, "Dlya tselei lichnosti vysokikh: Andrei Tarkovsky o sebe," *Forum: obshchestvenno-politicheskiy zhurnal*, 18 (1988): 97–103, 97.
6. Tarkovsky's biographers often diverge in giving the exact year of his father's leaving the family. Tarkovsky himself refers to 1935 but it would be more accurate to agree on the time around 1936–7, since Arseny Tarkovsky started an affair with Antonina Bokhonova right after he met her in 1936.
7. Nikolai Boldyrev, *Zhertvoprinoshenie Andreia Tarkovskogo* (Moskva: Vagrius, 2004), 22.
8. Tarkovskaya, *Oskolki*, 11.
9. Marina Tarkovskaya, "Biograficheskie motivy v filmakh Andreya Tarkovskogo," in *Andrej Tarkovskij: Klassiker–Классик–Classic–Classico: Beiträge zum internationalen Tarkovskij-Symposium an der Universität Potsdam*, vol. 1 (Universitätsverlag Potsdam, 2016), 41–8, 42.
10. Helena Goscilo, "Fraught Filiation: Andrei Tarkovsky's Transformations of Personal Trauma," in Helena Goscilo and Yana Hashamova (eds), *Cinepaternity: fathers and sons in Soviet and post-Soviet film* (Bloomington: Indiana University Press, 2010), 247–81, 277.
11. Ibid., 252.
12. Ibid., 257.
13. Ibid., 262, 257.
14. Ibid., 263.
15. Ibid., 267.
16. Ibid., 252.
17. Ibid., 268.
18. Viktor Filimonov, *Andrei Tarkovsky* (Moskva: Molodaya Gvardiya, 2012), 26.
19. Tarkovskaya, *Oskolki*, 111.
20. Filimonov, 26.
21. Marina Tarkovskaya, "Interview zhurnalu 'Bul'var Gordona,' Media-arkhiv 'Andrei Tarkovsky,'" 2007: http://www.tarkovskiy.su/texty/vospominania/MTarkovskaya04.html
22. Tarkovskaya, *Oskolki*, 120.
23. Tarkovskaya, "Interview zhurnalu 'Bul'var Gordona.'"
24. Tarkovskaya, *Oskolki*, 70.
25. André Green, *On Private Madness* (Abingdon: Routledge, 2018), 151.
26. Ibid., 148.
27. Ibid., 142.
28. Ibid., 151.
29. Ibid., 150.
30. Ibid., 151.
31. Ibid., 150.
32. Ibid., 152 (italics in the original).
33. Ibid.
34. Ibid., 150.
35. Ibid., 157.
36. Ibid., 153.
37. André Lussier, "The Dead Mother: Variations on a Theme," in Gregorio Kohon (ed.), *The Dead Mother: The Work of André Green* (Hove: Psychology Press, 1999), 151–64, 151.
38. Green, 161.
39. Tarkovskaya, *Oskolki*, 120.
40. Gregorio Kohon, "The Greening of Psychoanalysis: André Green in dialogues with Gregorio Kohon," in Kohon (ed.), *The Dead Mother: The Work of André Green* (Hove: Psychology Press, 1999), 9–58, 55.

41. Andrei Tarkovsky, "Ya nikogda ne stremilsya byt' aktual'nym", *Forum: obshchestvenno-politicheskiy zhurnal* 10 (1985): 227–36, 232.

42. Tarkovskaya, *Oskolki*, 120.

43. Tarkovskaya, "Vospominaniya," 112.

44. Vida Johnson and Graham Petrie, *The Films of Andrei Tarkovsky: A Visual Fugue* (Bloomington: Indiana University Press, 1994), 18.

45. Natalia Baranskaya, "Summer Evenings," in Marina Tarkovskaya (ed.), *About Andrei Tarkovsky* (Moscow: Progress Publishers, 1990), 24–6, 25.

46. André Green, "The Intuition of the Negative in *Playing and Reality*," in Gregorio Kohon (ed.), *The Dead Mother: The Work of André Green* (Hove: Psychology Press, 1999), 207–24, 220.

47. Green, *On Private Madness*, 161.

48. Ibid., 152.

49. Ibid., 167.

50. Ibid.

51. Goscilo, 252.

52. Green, *On Private Madness*, 150.

53. Tarkovskaya, "Vospominaniya," 114.

54. Quoted from Nikolai Boldyrev, *Stalker, ili trudy i dni Andreia Tarkovskogo* (Ural Limited, 2002), 76.

55. Tarkovskaya, *Oskolki*, 85–7.

56. Maya Turovskaya, *Tarkovsky: Cinema as Poetry* (London: Faber & Faber, 1989), 17.

57. Marina Pork, "Andrei Tarkovsky. Strat' s raschetom: Pisatel' Ol'ga Surkova o godakh, provedennykh ryadom s Andreem Tarkovskim . . ." *7days.ru*, 26 June 2016: https://7days.ru/caravan-collection/2016/6/olga-surkova-strast-s-raschetom.htm#

CHAPTER 2

Trava-Travlya-Trata: Tarkovsky's Psychobiography *à la Lettre*

Andrei Gornykh

In this chapter I offer a close reading of Tarkovsky's diary from a Lacanian psychoanalytic perspective by focusing on the director's recurrent use of those keywords that symbolically epitomize and organize the major thematic layers of his biography and cinema: grass (or *trava* in Russian), persecution or harassment from the party authorities of Goskino (*travlya*), and spending (*trata*). Phonetically consonant and etymologically derived from the same Russian root *tra-* (or proto-Slavic *ter-*), these words make up a coherent cluster of signifiers (*trava-travlya-trata*) that are centered (and circling) around Tarkovsky's primal fantasy of the house, a cinematic motif in his work which metaphorically stands for the maternal womb (e.g. the Zone and "the room of desire" soaked with water in *Stalker* (1979)). In real life this cinematic motif of the house is paralleled by his lifelong obsession with living in a country house surrounded by grass (*trava*), which he viewed as a refuge to hide from the Goskino officials' persecution (*travlya*). At the same time, he was also preoccupied with all kinds of expenses (*trata*) which would prevent him from getting settled there. I will demonstrate that Lacan's model of signifying chains, which establishes symbolic trajectories of representations— that maintain their distance from the Real (*das Ding*) and thus predetermine their modes of associations and displacements of affects—allows us to grasp the symbolic mechanisms underlying Tarkovsky's artistic imaginary. As I will argue, in Tarkovsky's diary the signifying constellation *trava-travlya-trata* presents itself as a psychobiographical code to the internal dynamics of his visual imagery.

THE HOUSE THAT ANDREI BUILT

The house occupies a central place in Tarkovsky's biography by serving as the pivotal point around which his domestic and professional activities always revolved. In his memories it is represented by various locations: first, as the place of birth in 1932 in the village of Zavrazhye in the Yurievets district and later as a hideout from the war during evacuation to the town of Yurievets in the Ivanovo Region in 1941–3. Between them lies Pavel Gorchakov's farmstead near the village of Ignatievo where Andrei and his sister Marina spent their happy summers in 1935–6. As he recalls about this period, "Happiness is tied to my childhood. The time when my mother and I lived in a steading near Moscow I remember as that of enormous happiness. It was a very happy time for me because I was still a child, connected with nature, and we lived in the woods. I felt completely happy. I did not feel anything like that later on."[1] The persistent repetition of the word "happy" in this passage points to the fact that at the moment of this recollection Tarkovsky as an adult was, on the contrary, quite unhappy and could remember his childhood only in terms of the lost happiness, whose toponymical particles were nostalgically projected into the names of his cinematic characters, such as Ignat from *Mirror* (1975) or Gorchakov from *Nostalghia* (1983).

In his grown-up life, however, the house for Tarkovsky was associated with nothing but problems. In fact, it is with the purchase of a house in the village of Myasnoye in 1970 that he started his famous diary titled "martyrology," which he decided to keep to record his hardships in everyday and professional life. Almost immediately the house purchase turned out to be a black hole in Tarkovsky's family budget. As he writes in an entry of 20 October 1970, "Our house in Myasnoye burned down. The entire middle part is gone . . . Everything should be rebuilt in the Spring, as we wanted earlier. It will cost three thousand rubles. Will see. In any case, reconstruction should be complete by the Summer."[2] Tarkovsky's preoccupations with home renovations became, therefore, the recurrent subject of his diary entries. The house was literally swallowing up his income, time, and even his wife: he personally had to do a lot of housework, just as Larisa Tarkovskaya worked there for weeks when Tarkovsky stayed in the city. And yet, despite getting mired in debts, he stubbornly clung to the idea of building his own house which, he thought, could bring "some sense" to his life. Along with his plans to rebuild the house, the diary is full of lists of items necessary for reconstruction as well as corresponding costs for them. Instead of serving him as a refuge from the stress at work, the house required increasing investments without the relief of ever getting any closer to its completion. Even after immigration Tarkovsky continued to pursue his obsession with houses. In Italy he bought an old two-story cottage in the town of San Gregorio, which also required major repairs and thus threatened to become yet another black hole for his income. Until his final days he kept designing layouts for this house and never abandoned his plans to reconstruct it.

In his films—from *Solaris* (1972) to *The Sacrifice* (1986)—Tarkovsky steadily reincarnates various models of his childhood house. For *Mirror*, for example, in 1973 he built a replica of Gorchakov's log cabin (which was dismantled long ago)

Figure 2.1 Replica of Tarkovsky's childhood house in *Mirror*.

in the village of Ignatyevo by following the exact same dimensions of its exterior and interior. Even his mother, during her visit to *Mirror*'s set, was struck by the uncanny resurrection of the original (Figure 2.1). These mimetic replicas, however, serve only as the façade appearances of Tarkovsky's imagination of the house, behind which the unsettling drama of a dysfunctional family takes place: from Stalker's utter neglect of home maintenance resulting in the alienation of domestic space, to the invasion of ghosts into the grief-stricken house in *Solaris*. Tarkovsky's houses are always flooded with water: in *Solaris* rain comes in through the roof; in *Mirror*, likewise, water bursts through the ceiling with pieces of plaster crumbling and falling in slow motion; in *Stalker* water leaks through the walls, shimmers through the large floor cracks, and keeps trickling in from above. As Evgeniy Tsymbal recalls, Tarkovsky was trying to achieve the "mucus-like appearance of the slimy walls in Stalker's bedroom by covering them with varnish, while the kitchen and the hall were coated with glistening greasy graphite."[3] The watery nature of Tarkovsky's cinematic house manifests itself to the fullest as an abandoned half-ruined dwelling with the room fulfilling unconscious desires, placed inside the deserted and derelict landscape of the Zone. The walls here could be interpreted as representing the maternal membranes enclosing the womb flooded with amniotic waters, which resonates with *Mirror*'s dream sequence, where streams of water from the ceiling merge with the mother's long hair being washed in the basin.

DAS DING AND THE INSTANCE OF THE LETTER

Tarkovsky's house as the locus of the impersonal maternal Thing at its core may serve as the perfect illustration of what Freud calls the uncanny, or *unheimlich*, which refers to "that class of the terrifying that leads back to something long known to us, once very familiar."[4] The German term *unheimlich* is, for Freud, the opposite of cozy and comfortable, and is at the same time hidden and secret, best left unseen. As Freud explains, the meaning of the word *heimlich* "develops in the direction of ambivalence, until it finally coincides with its opposite, *unheimlich*."[5] That is, the *unheimlich* experience, in which the terrifying affect is produced by what seems to be most attractive, is characterized by radical ambivalence, best exemplified by the figure of the mother. Whereas initially she serves as the primary object of the child's desire, after the resolution of the Oedipus complex and the child's internalization of the Law-of-the-Father, she becomes fundamentally unattainable and any attempt to get back to the maternal space inevitably turns that space into something unbearable and hostile.

Compulsive repetition constitutes the essence of one's relation to the maternal. To further develop the Freudian approach to the nature of desire, Lacan introduced the notion of *das Ding* (the Thing), referring to the Kantian thing-in-itself, understood as ultimately inaccessible and unknowable yet exciting and affecting the soul: "Right at the beginning of the organization of the world in the psyche, both logically and chronologically, *das Ding* is something that presents and isolates itself as the strange feature around which the whole movement of the *Vorstellung* turns."[6] According to Freud, *Vorstellung* stands for representations or mental images in which sensations, recollections, and expectations interweave. In Lacan's reading, our representations do not unfold in linear time but revolve around *das Ding* as some invisible gravity center. Their meaning is constituted not so much by their content as by their movement of re-presenting (*Vor-stellung*), while always keeping *das Ding* at a distance as the eternally absent sought-after object. As Lacan writes,

> The transference of the quantity [of psychic energy] from *Vorstellung* to *Vorstellung* always maintains the search at a certain distance from that which it gravitates around. The object to be found confers on the search its invisible law; but it is not that . . . which controls its movements. The element that fixes these movements, that models the return—and this return itself is maintained at a distance—is the pleasure principle.[7]

Finally, in one's compulsive repetition to approach *das Ding*, what one finds is not *das Ding* but representations that function not so much as image but rather as "associative," "combinatorial" elements or "constellations of representations."

As Lacan argues, "these *Vorstellungen* gravitate, operate exchanges and are modulated according to . . . the fundamental laws of the signifying chain."[8]

The basic laws of the signifying chain were already discovered by Freud as that of displacement and condensation. In *Interpretation of Dreams* (1899), the material for such operations is provided not only by dream images and hidden thoughts but by words as well. As he writes,

> The condensing activity of the dream becomes most tangible when it has selected words and names as its object. In general, words are often treated as things by the dream, and thus undergo the same combinations, displacements, and substitutions, and therefore also condensations, as ideas of things. The results of such dreams are comical and bizarre word formations.[9]

For example, Freud continues, one of his patients had a dream about a non-existent verbal compound "Maistollmutz" which, after analysis, turned out to be a condensed constellation of various words referring to different affectively charged representations: *Mais, Meissen, miss, toll, mannstol, Olmutz*. For Lacan, this is the essence of Freud's discovery: it is precisely the words, or the "instance of the letter," that should count as the formal elements, or "signifiers," which, through their combinations, lay out the channels for psychic energy and determine associative series of representations as well as their trajectories around *das Ding*. As he argues, "The space of the signifier, the space of the unconscious, is effectively a typographical space, which we must try to define as being constituted along lines and little squares, and as corresponding to topological laws."[10] That is to say, it is the correlations of words in which letters, not only meanings, blend with each other, that regulate the dynamics of the transition of one representation into another, as well as the intensity of their affective charge.

TRAVA: GRASS AS PHANTASMATIC DEFENSE

Let us now turn to our analysis of one of the verbal complexes in Tarkovsky's diary, that of *trava-travlya-trata*, or grass-persecution-spending, that organizes the network of representations in his psychobiographical narrative. The first component of this cluster is the word *trava* or "grass" that functions in Tarkovsky's imagery as a phantasmatic enclosure around the Thing.

In Tarkovsky's memories, his mother, Maria Ivanovna Vishnyakova, always remained a guardian and caretaker: she kept him and his sister Marina in a rural house in Zavrazhye near Yuryevets away from the traumatic events of the 1930s and 1940s, such as the stress of living in a Moscow communal apartment, the war, and the famine. While hiding her children in a quiet abode in the countryside, she exposed them to the beauty and serenity of nature by taking them for long walks in the woods and meadows where they could pick straw-berries and even stay overnight in a self-made shelter. When his mother passed away in 1979, Tarkovsky experienced her death as an ontological catastrophe, throwing him into a deep emotional crisis. As he writes in his diary, "Mama's funeral. It was in Vostryakovsky Cemetery. Now I feel quite defenseless; and no one in the world is ever going to love me as she did . . . God! how utterly wretched I feel! To the point of nausea, to the point of hanging myself. I am so lonely . . . I am afraid to be alone. I do not want to live. I am frightened. My life has become intolerable."[11] Even years after her death he continued to remember her as his beloved guardian. As he writes in an entry of 10 July 1981,

> I went to the cemetery today, to Mama's grave . . . I prayed to God, wept, complained to Mama, and asked her to pray for me, to intercede . . . As I was leaving Mama, I picked a wild strawberry leaf from her grave. It drooped on the way home, so I put it into warm water and the leaf revived. And I felt calmer and purer in my soul. And suddenly there was a phone-call from Rome. It was Norman, to say that the Italians are coming here on the 20th. Of course, it was Mama. I don't doubt it for a second. My dear, good Mama . . . my darling . . . thank you.[12]

In this passage Tarkovsky's mother is metaphorically represented as a strawberry leaf resurrected from the earth, an image which stems from a series of other recollections of his childhood: the house safely enfolded by trees and grass saturated with moisture; a strawberry as the sweet gift of the earth com-ing out of its humid depths; a strawberry-like drop of blood which appeared after his mother hit the little Andrei with a can for romping around during his bathing; the feelings of frustration and humiliation for her as she was forced to sell wildflowers at the marketplace during the famine; a photograph from his childhood with Andrei standing in the middle of a meadow covered with flowers. The mother's chthonic affinity with the earth and its vegetation is most pronounced in one of Tarkovsky's dreams recorded in his diary: "Last night I dreamt that I had woken up in some place I did not know, lying on the ground, where I was sleeping next to Mama. A country landscape, half familiar. I walked over to a stream, and washed my face. I could not understand at all how it was that I came to be there . . . *Could it mean I am going to die?*"[13] In an entry of 9 July 1979, Tarkovsky describes the following dream:

> Oh, God, what a beautiful dream I had! It was one of the two dreams which have recurred all through my life but which I had not had for a very long time. It was summer, not far from the house (which I don't remember). It was sunny, with a little breeze. I was out walking, and walking somehow rather fast, as if heading somewhere specific. But I was following a path I had never been along before. And immediately

I came to a most beautiful, wonderful place, a paradise. Overgrown with all sorts of different, untended flowers. In the distance I could hear screams, as if someone was struggling in the grass . . . It was not at all a long walk. I glanced to the right, and stopped—at my feet was a precipice. Down below was a broad, clean, beautiful river, its surface covered in ripples, and on the far bank grass, and a leafy, cosy wood. It was peaceful and silent! How was it that I had never been to this place before! I lay down in the grass at the very edge of the precipice. In front of my eyes—along the path—was fresh grass, a little meadow covered in blue flowers, perhaps hemp; and beyond that the picture rounded off in a darkish area—partly of pine?—while at the far end of the meadow grew two enormous flowers (in the background, but looking as if they were right in front of my eyes, and resembling the violets that grow on my windowsill) . . . A little to the right, through the trees, I glimpsed the convex brick wall of some ancient building, not very obvious, either a tower or a rounded wall. Silence. Sunshine; flowers; breeze; cool; peace! I lay there, looking in front of me at that amazing scene, my whole being filled with a sense of happiness attained . . . [14]

The word "grass" is mentioned four times in this passage. But what is interesting here is that this diary entry is almost the only one that mentions "grass" at all, despite the fact that Tarkovsky claims that this dream had haunted him throughout his life. The ostensible redundancy of this word symptomatically testifies to the condensation of speech signifying the place of "happiness regained" or "paradise" which is "overgrown with all sorts of different, untended flowers." This place is located "not far from the house" or, rather, between the two houses: one "which [he doesn't] remember" at the beginning of the dream and, towards its end, "some ancient building" which is also "not very obvious." This bifurcated house, whose contours are obscure, marks the boundaries of the phantasmatic zone of the grass.

The emphatic contiguity of the grass meadow with the house constitutes the topology of the front garden, which is yet another frequent motif in Tarkovsky's diary. Its location could be understood as the metonymical extension of the house—"not far from the house" or "close to the house"—that could allow one to come closer to *das Ding*. He even wanted to make a film about the front garden. As he wrote in a diary entry of 31 December 1978, "Tonino and I have had the idea that I should make a 16mm film about the [village]. It is to be a confession, based on Myasnoye . . . The story of how the front garden was improved to the point where it became an eyesore."[15] A month later he developed this idea into a short story draft:

Some people arrive in a new place and start to live in houses built close to one another. Suddenly one of them dies. There are no graveyards.

You can't just bury a person in the middle of a field! And you can't have a graveyard with just one grave! The corpse can't just be dumped all by himself, with no other dead around him, but all alone. So they bury the dead person close to the house, in the front garden, under the windows.[16]

Cinematically, Tarkovsky's fixation on the front garden was fully realized in *Stalker*'s Zone that surrounds the house with the "room of desire" at its center. On the one hand, this place is strictly transitional, it wards off any inhabitation and one cannot dwell here for too long since it can turn into an "eyesore." On the other hand, it is viewed as a "paradise" in which death is absorbed and domesticated by the derelict landscape and the deceased buried under the earth and sprouting through the grass. The Zone's ambivalent symbolism of the grass, which joins the sunlit surface with the dark underground as well as the maternal with the dead, resonates with the image of the Mother Moist Earth in Russian folklore, which appears both as the "maternal life force" and "destroyer who holds men in her grasp and lures them to their deaths."[17] In Tarkovsky's cinematic imagery, the grass manifests itself as the ambivalent metonymy of the house and death. In *Solaris*, the house is metonymically represented by the image of riverweeds in the water stream, toll-grass vegetation in the field, and even a flower planted in a pot in the space station. In *Stalker*, Stalker dives into the grass with the words "we are home" on arriving at the Zone, while the Writer hides in the grass from the bullets of the Zone's guards. As death, it is also associated with the irreparable loss in *Mirror*—when the abandoned mother awaits her husband in vain or when the wind ruffles the foliage in the narrator's nostalgic dream about the childhood house—or with danger and obstruction in *Stalker*.

It is not by accident that Tarkovsky almost never uses the word *trava* in his diary, except in his description of the oneiric grass given above. Such avoidance can only be explained as his highly controlled repression that forces the word *trava* out of his everyday language and pushes it towards *das Ding* which, in turn, holds it back within its own gravitational reach. As a return of the repressed, the grass nevertheless reappears in his films in the form of uncanny dream-like images. Thus, the unbearable affective tension caused by the haunting memory of his childhood house is being compulsively discharged or sublimated into numerous visual representations of the grass serving as a phantasmatic defense against the proximity of *das Ding*.

TRAVLYA: PERSECUTION BY GOSKINO

We now turn to the next component of Tarkovsky's psychobiographical keyword cluster, which is that of *travlya* or persecution. Tarkovsky strongly believed that his professional career in the Soviet Union was determined not so much by his success among viewers or awards at international film festivals as it was by the party bureaucrats of Goskino, whose administrative actions towards himself he perceived as persecution, bullying, and harassment. He was certainly spared the kind of persecution allotted to some of his fellow film-makers, such as Sergei Paradzhanov, imprisoned for several years on charges of bribery, rape, and homosexuality, or Alexander Askoldov, forbidden to make any more films because of his anti-Soviet film *Commissar* (1967). Nevertheless, with the exception of *Ivan's Childhood* (1962), all of his Soviet films were sub-jected to interference from the state censors during the filmmaking process, especially at the stage of post-production. That is to say, to shoot a film was only half the work for Tarkovsky, he also had to fight for it in order to save it from numerous censorship cuts and revisions to which he was painfully sensi-tive. As he recalled in a 1984 interview with Radio Liberty,

> It was very difficult to work in the sense that I made just a few movies, only six . . . That is too few and unsatisfactory for me. I spent a huge amount of time trying to convince the leaders, governing bodies of the importance of making the films that I was proposing. Then it took a lot of time for the finished film to be accepted. Then there were always grievances against my films: there were attempts to change some word-ing, the length, and some scenes. Time was spent trying to organise the relationship with Goskino so as to save the movie. *Rublev*, for instance, was shelved for five and a half years after its acceptance by Goskino. And during all that time I did nothing, I didn't work, because it was presumed that if I made an "ideologically unseasoned" picture, then I would have no further right to work until that conflict was settled . . . I continuously submitted proposals, ideas to the Goskino, in order to start a new film, but they were always refused . . . [18]

In his diary and letters Tarkovsky's professional hardships related to Gos-kino's revisions of his films are summarized in one word: *travlya*. For example, after *Andrei Rublev* was eventually approved by the artistic council at Mosfilm in 1966, yet severely criticized for its length and graphic violence, Tarkovsky responded with a letter to Alexei Romanov, the chairman of Goskino, defend-ing the integrity of his film and complaining about the countless requests for cuts. Characteristically enough, *travlya* or persecution becomes the keyword in his appeal to the boss. As he writes, "I consider all this campaign with its wicked and foul allegations against me as no less than a persecution. Nothing but a persecution." "I have to write to you as our supervisor and ask for your help to stop this unprecedented persecution . . . The friendly polemics on my film has long developed into—I apologize for repeating myself—an organized persecu-tion."[19] In a diary entry of 21 January 1972, he uses the same word mentioned during his meeting with Philip Yermash, the Minister of Cinematography: "I went to see Yermash. Didn't say a word about *Solaris* and the alterations. I asked him if I was an underground director and how long this persecution was going to go on [for]."[20] In another entry of 1 March 1982, right before his trip to Italy, he writes, "I am not compatible with the Soviet cinema. None of my films has been presented at any Soviet film festival! I haven't received a single award for my films in USSR. This is just a systemic and continuous persecution!"[21] Already in Rome, he continued to refer to Moscow as the site of his never-ending *travlya*: "Larissa and I telephoned Moscow. Rumours are being spread all over the place about my film being a flop at Cannes. Vindictive slander-mongering [*travlya*]."[22]

Johnson and Petrie, however, refuse to take Tarkovsky's "extreme claims of martyrdom" at face value by skeptically dismissing it as a self-imposed "myth of his own persecution."[23] As they suggest, his "insistent struggle with the authorities and his almost pathological conviction of being a martyred artist can perhaps best be understood as a reaction to a probably subconscious fear of repeating his father's fate."[24] Tarkovsky's father, Arseny Tarkovsky, indeed couldn't get published for a long time due to the apolitical nature of his poems. Yet the period of his poetic silence took place predominantly in Stalin's Russia, while from the early 1960s his work was widely recognized and venerated. In the 1970s, therefore, the father's literary fame was an example for the son to follow. Nevertheless, Johnson and Petrie's skepticism regarding Tarkovsky's persecution complex is understandable, since in comparison with other artists he, they write, "seems to have been relatively fortunate": all of his "original and daring films" were generously sponsored by the state and none of them were banned, many influential people supported him, and he did have a chance to travel abroad. The Goskino bureaucrats did place their obstacles in his way, but they also enabled him to make the films "which can be ranked among the best in contemporary Russian—and world—cinema."[25]

However, the purpose of our analysis is not to judge whether Tarkovsky's accusations of Goskino for persecution were adequate. What is more interesting is to look at how his persecution anxiety is intimately tied up with his fantasies of the house and the garden around it. Etymologically, *travlya* stems from the Slavic word *traviti*, which is itself a derivative of *trava* and the proto-Slavic root *ter-* (*terti* or to rub). In Slavic languages *traviti* denotes "exterminate," "devour," "poison," and "feed with grass."[26] In contemporary usage the semantic link between *travlya* and *trava* is no longer active, yet in Tarkovsky's vocabulary these words are subconsciously intertwined: the former accumulates the negative charge of the latter's ambivalence by manifesting itself through the haunting anxiety of invisible hostility. Just as the Russian word *travlya* homonymously overlaps with *trava* by sharing the same root *trav-*, Tarkovsky's anxiety of persecution is similarly expressed in his dreams about the grass, or the front garden, and the house. As we read in his entry of 7 March 1983,

> I had a dream last night. It was a warm and cloudy summer day. Some sort of a front garden with flowers, or a small lawn, where I meet Yermash. He's dressed casually, not like a Minister as usual, in some canvas jacket that is thoroughly soaked, while I am myself completely wet and freezing too. Probably it was raining, and we couldn't escape it. Yermash is in a nasty mood. We talk. He has changed a lot and I even seem to calm him down. All of a sudden, I feel like I am losing my voice. I open the faucet nearby, which is for watering flowerbeds, and then start drinking a strong and thin stream of warm water smelling of iron. After this I regain my voice. Yermash is drinking too from another pipe.[27]

In this dream Tarkovsky meets Philip Yermash, who chaired Goskino from 1978 to 1986 and fully controlled the censorship organ in the Soviet film industry. In his diary Tarkovsky frequently mentions him as the conservative party bureaucrat who kept standing in the way of his artistic creativity. He also complains how dependent he is on his employers and colleagues, and how they do not really hear him. In the dream Tarkovsky is unable to speak in the presence of Yermash, yet thanks to the faucet in the garden he clears his throat and regains his voice. Thus, the dream restages the drama of the artist in front of the authorities by bringing together the motifs familiar from Tarkovsky's films: those of grass, house, rain, excessive moisture, and regaining voice. As is known, the autobiographical theme of regaining one's own voice is metaphorically presented in *Mirror*'s prologue featuring a stuttering boy cured after a hypnosis session.

In a similar dream Tarkovsky meets Nikolay Sizov, the head of Mosfilm Studios from 1970 to 1984:

> Last night I had a really strange dream. Sizov was talking to me with love and unusual tenderness. It was cold and we were lying in some armchairs on the terrace at night. We talked to each other with fondness, as if we were brothers. I even remember his unshaved cheek when he kissed me.[28]

Just as Philip Yermash, Sizov was also actively involved in censoring Tarkovsky's films as well as authorizing them for release. In an entry of 17 March 1971, he writes, "More corrections to *Rublyov*. It's more than I can bear . . . The worst of it is that Sizov is categorically for the changes."[29] In another entry on *Solaris*, he writes, "Sizov is expecting to see me on Thursday. He obviously intends to bully me into making corrections."[30] At the same time it was Sizov who approved of most of Tarkovsky's projects and promoted them at higher bureaucratic levels. As we read in an entry of 30 December 1971, "Larissa went to see Sizov, who told her that he likes *The Bright Day*, likes it 'very much'."[31] In another entry Tarkovsky explains how *Solaris* was saved from cuts: "*Solaris* was accepted without a single alteration . . . I heard that Sizov showed the film to three officials . . . and their authority is too great for their opinion to be ignored. It's nothing short of miraculous."[32] Tarkovsky's relationship with the party authorities was therefore deeply ambivalent: he blamed them for persecution, yet he was also grateful to them for their support and protection, although subconsciously in his dreams, which placed his "persecutors" in the context of homey comfort and mutual sympathy. That is to say, for Tarkovsky *travlya*, besides being an obvious bureaucratic obstacle, also served as an indispensable condition and stimulus for his return to the maternal *trava* surrounding the house.

TRATA: SPENDING MONEY AND LIFE

Tarkovsky's next keyword *trata* is etymologically less straightforward than the other two discussed above. Most linguists suggest it stems from the proto-Slavic verb *tratiti* which denotes "spend," "waste," "lose," and "squander." Yet for other scholars *tratiti* could be the result of the contamination of proto-Slavic *traviti* (to poison/exterminate) and *ratiti* (to fight/struggle). It is also possible that *tratiti* is, on the contrary, a derivative of the noun *trata* (with the suffix -*ta*) that itself, just as *traviti*, stems from the proto-Slavic root *ter*- (*terti* or "rub") and is related to proto-Slavic *treva*, from which the modern Russian word *trava* is derived.[33] As we will see below, the etymological interrelatedness within the keyword cluster *trava-travlya-trata* is parallel to Tarkovsky's biographical psychodynamics of associations provided by these words.

The Russian noun *trata* could be translated as expense or spending. In Tarkovsky's diary it refers primarily to his financial hardships in both professional and personal matters. At times his diary resembles a ledger in which he meticulously registers and calculates his daily expenses, making lists of future costs and irritated creditors as well as expressing hopes to get some extra cash in addition to his official employment at Mosfilm Studio. As he writes in an entry of 15 August 1970, "Penniless. And appalling debts. What's going to happen? I just can't imagine."[34] In an entry of 28 June 1978, he recalls his stay in the sanatorium with the writer Arkady Strugatsky: "Arkady Strugatsky has shown himself to be petty and calculating. To hell with him. I am going to owe him 1200 roubles for our shared expenses."[35] The diary especially dwells on casual expenses during his travelling abroad. For example, while in Italy in 1980, he wrote, "Today I fell; I bought two pairs of shoes; I spent 130,000 lire. Quite mad."[36] "I have to spend money wisely. Not sure I'll get back here soon."[37] During his work on *Nostalghia* in Italy, Tarkovsky was also often worried about difficulties with financing the project: "It's difficult to work because we haven't got the money yet on film-related expenses."[38] "Sovinfilm is neither able nor willing to spend a penny on preparatory works before signing the contract."[39] Yet the biggest expenditure for Tarkovsky was, of course, his continuous investment in the country house he purchased in 1970. As he wrote right after the purchase,

> Now I don't care what happens. If they don't give me any work I'll sit in the country and breed piglets and geese, and tend my vegetable patch, and to hell with the lot of them! We shall gradually put the house and garden in order, and it will be a wonderful country house; Now I must earn as much as possible so that we can finish the house by the autumn. It has to be habitable in winter as well. Three hundred kilometres from Moscow—people won't come dragging out here for nothing.[40]

For Tarkovsky the house in the village of Myasnoye served as a paradisal retreat far from the city's adversities, such as debts to his creditors and professional misfortunes. As he put it in one of his entries, "Here I am, back in Myasnoye . . . It's paradise."[41] Furthermore, becoming a subsistence farmer, who would grow vegetables and raise piglets and poultry, seemed for him like a viable alternative to his filmmaking career often put on hold by the Mosfilm bureaucrats. As he reiterates, "Garden, vegetable patch, household, sauna, house, car—all that together would solve most of the problems arising from the physical lack of work."[42] Besides his subconscious gravitation towards the maternal *Ding*, personified by the country house, Tarkovsky's obsession with getting settled there, away from work, money, and social obligations, could also be explained by his nostalgic desire to recreate the communal environment of the 1960s in which the Moscow intelligentsia, including Vladimir Vysotsky, Robert Rozhdestvensky, Vasily Shukshin, and many others, together attempted to establish their autonomous utopian space outside the Soviet status quo. In the 1970s, however, the bohemian lifestyle within the dissident urban commune was no longer in fashion due to the pervasive professionalization and monetization of their artistic endeavors. But for Tarkovsky the inevitable extinction of communal inhabitation, devoid of bureaucratic interference and bourgeois materialism, only meant that he was increasingly determined to find a proper replacement for it, either in the lifestyle of his dedicated film crew, whose members were often ready to sacrifice anything on the altar of cinema, or in the idyllic ambience of a country house. As he wrote in 1973, "I feel restricted, my soul is restricted inside me, I need another living space."[43] Such an alternative "living space" nevertheless required proper maintenance and substantial financial support, which quickly became a burden for Tarkovsky:

"there are repairs to be done in the country—that means more money."[44] As is mentioned above, five months after the house was purchased, it burned down and had to be rebuilt. It took Tarkovsky over three years to finish it, which left him quite exhausted. As he writes in an entry of 18 December 1973, "The Myasnoye house is nearly finished . . . When shall I be able to stop worrying about house, mod. cons., and my chances of working!"[45]

But *trata* was not only related to money issues. Tarkovsky also repeatedly uses the word in relation to recklessly wasting his time, energy, emotions, and health and losing relatives, friends, home, and eventually life, which adds melancholy to the tone of his diary. His complaints about feeling tired are especially constant: "I am tired. In April I shall be forty. But I'm never left in peace, and there is never any silence."[46] "I am tired. I shall soon be forty two, and I have never had my own place."[47] "Tired as a dog, tired as a son of a bitch! Can hardly stand."[48] "I am terribly tired. I have pain in every inch of my body."[49] In one entry he even includes Tolstoy's saying on *trata*, "Goodness means service of God, accompanied by the sacrifice, the constant loss [*trata*] of one's animal life, just as light is accompanied by a constant loss [*trata*] of fuel."[50] That is to say, *trata*, understood as burning out, was eventually adopted by Tarkovsky in the context of his martyrdom rhetoric, as a spiritual vocation or self-imposed sacrifice inseparable from his devotion to cinema.

CONCLUSION

Tarkovsky's recurrent use of keywords such as *trava*, *travlya*, and *trata*, which make up a coherent verbal cluster in his psychobiography, gives shape to the utopian structure of his personality. Imagining himself as a martyr persecuted by the Goskino censors, he was hoping to find shelter in the village outside the city, which was also viewed as an attempt to reproduce the tranquil environment of his childhood. To put this drama in Tarkovsky's own terms, we could say that in order to escape from *travlya* or persecution in the city, he wanted to hide in *trava* near the country house, which required him to spend much of his energy and money, or *trata*. These three words, derived from the same root *tra-* (or proto-Slavic *ter-*), denote the principal trajectories of semantic associations in Tarkovsky's life as well as the psychoanalytic logic of his anxieties and fantasies, all of which are centered around his primal fantasy of the house. Throughout all his adult life he kept striving to return to the house of his childhood by recreating it in both cinematic and personal contexts. In light of Lacanian psychoanalysis, Tarkovsky's house, metaphorically standing for the maternal *Ding*, cannot yet must be attained and replicated by always manifesting itself as a void in the symbolic order that needs to be filled out, the black hole of the Real into which significations will pour and vanish. In his films, such significations become recurrent representations of the house, all of which are essentially flawed to various extents: illusory in *Solaris*, crumbling in *Mirror*, alienated in *Stalker*, distant in *Nostalghia*, and burned down in *The Sacrifice*. In his diary, the key signifiers, which keep circling around the house by trying to compensate for its fundamental unrepresentability, are all the derivatives of *trava* or grass, whereas grass itself serves as a phantasmatic defense against the proximity of the *Ding*. As we read in his dreams, the "sense of happiness" Tarkovsky managed to attain was not inside the house but in the grass surrounding it, as if he knew that grass in a lawn or a front garden was the closest he could get to it. Just as grass and front garden function as metonymic ruins of the repressed, *travlya* and *trata* similarly manifest themselves as unconscious signifiers referring back to the house via an etymological association with *trava*. In this regard, Tarkovsky's fixation on his own persecution should not, of course, be taken at face value, but rather be viewed as his chief impetus to finally get settled in the country house that eventually became associated with nothing but *trata*, both financial and emotional. Tightly knit together, the signifiers of *trava*, *travlya*, and *trata*, therefore, constitute a verbal code to Tarkovsky's psychobiography by forming a signifying chain around the always empty space of the house.

Translated by Sergey Toymentsev

NOTES

1. Nikolai Boldyrev, *Zhertvoprinosheniye Andreia Tarkovskogo* (Moskva: Vagrius, 2004), 78.
2. Andrei Tarkovsky, *Martirolog. Dnevniki 1970–1986* (Florentsiya: Mezhdunarodnyy institut imeni Andrey Tar-kovskogo, 2008), 48.
3. Georgiy Rerberg, Marianna Chugunova, and Yevgeny Tsymbal, "Fokus na beskonechnost': razgovor o "Stalkere,"" *Iskusstvo kino*, vol. 4, 2006: http://kinoart.ru/2006/n4-article20.html#11
4. Sigmund Freud, "The Uncanny," in David Sandner (ed.), *Fantastic Literature: A Critical Reader* (Santa Barbara, CA: Praeger, 2004), 74–101, 76.
5. Freud, 80.
6. Jacques Lacan, *The Ethics of Psychoanalysis: The Seminar of Jacques Lacan (Book VII, 1959–1960)*, edited by Jacques-Alain Miller, trans. by D. Porter (New York: W. W. Norton & Co., 1992), 57.
7. Ibid., 58.
8. Ibid., 62.
9. Sigmund Freud, *The Interpretation of Dreams*, trans. by A. A. Brill (New York: Macmillan, 1913), 277.
10. Jacques Lacan, *The Seminar of Jacques Lacan, Book V: Formations of the Unconscious (1957–58)*, edited by Jacques-Alain Miller, trans. by R. Grigg (Cambridge: Polity Press, 2017), 132.
11. Andrei Tarkovsky, *Time within Time: The Diaries, 1970–1986*, trans. by Kitty Hunter-Blair (London: Faber & Faber, 1994), 207–10.
12. Ibid., 284.

13. Ibid., 257.
14. Ibid., 187–8.
15. Ibid., 161.
16. Ibid., 172.
17. Joanna Hubbs, "The Worship of Mother Earth in Russian Culture," in James J. Preston (ed.), *Mother Worship: Theme and Variations* (Chapel Hill: University of North Carolina Press, 1982), 123–44, 123.
18. Quoted from Galina Gornostaeva, "Soviet Film-Making Under the 'Producership' of the Party State (1955–85)," in Andrew Dawson and Sean Holmes (eds), *Working in the Global Film and Television Industries: Creativity, Systems, Space, Patronage* (London: Bloomsbury Academic, 2012), 39–56, 51.
19. Tarkovsky, *Martirolog*, 163–4.
20. Tarkovsky, *Time*, 51.
21. Tarkovsky, *Martirolog*, 390.
22. Tarkovsky, *Time*, 329.
23. Vida Johnson and Graham Petrie, *The Films of Andrei Tarkovsky: A Visual Fugue* (Bloomington: Indiana University Press, 1994), 13.
24. Ibid., 260.
25. Ibid., 13.
26. Rick Derksen, *Etymological Dictionary of the Slavic Inherited Lexicon* (Leiden: Brill Academic Publishers, 2007), 496.
27. Tarkovsky, *Martirolog*, 475.
28. Ibid., 427.
29. Tarkovsky, *Time*, 38.
30. Ibid., 53.
31. Ibid., 46.
32. Ibid., 55.
33. Pavel Chernykh, *Istoriko-etimologichesky slovar' sovremennogo russkogo yazyka*, vol. 2 (Moskva: Izdatel'stvo "Russkiy yazyk," 1999), 258–9.
34. Tarkovsky, *Time*, 7.
35. Ibid., 155.
36. Ibid., 250.
37. Tarkovsky, *Martirolog*, 303.
38. Ibid., 294.
39. Ibid., 305.
40. Tarkovsky, *Time*, 3.
41. Ibid., 110.
42. Ibid., 29.
43. Ibid., 79.
44. Ibid., 19.
45. Ibid., 82.
46. Ibid., 52.
47. Ibid., 82.
48. Ibid., 207.
49. Ibid., 335.
50. Ibid., 319.

CHAPTER 3

Does Tarkovsky Have a Film Theory?

Sergey Toymentsev

TARKOVSKY'S CHALLENGE TO FILM THEORY

Tarkovsky's cinema often poses a considerable challenge to film studies by blurring the boundaries between subjective experience and objective reality. Widely acknowledged as one of the most technically accomplished representations of dream imagery, his visual language has become a constitutive part of cinematic vocabulary in general and is easily recognizable by a range of stylistic characteristics: extremely lengthy tracking shots, decelerated motion, dedramatized action, eerie atmosphere, hallucinatory ambiguity, dissolution of spatial and temporal continuity, scenes of characters' levitation, illogical combinations of objects, uncanny non-diegetic film sound, extensive use of natural elements (water, fire, air, earth) that are often combined together within a single shot. The tactile image in his films often exceeds the limits of representation by becoming the direct, non-mimetic expression of a natural and phantasmatic world where a human being is stripped from all the coordinates of everyday consciousness and rendered passively drifting through various dreamscapes. It is one of his highest achievements that in his later films all these oneiric cinematic effects are no longer coded as dreams *per se* but rather saturate the entire film with a dream-like aura. In *Stalker* (1979), for example, there is no single traditionally coded dream that could be distinctly separated from daytime reality. In a scene titled "The Stalker's Dream" in the DVD chapter selection we see the travelers preparing to rest, yet we do not enter their dreams while they are sleeping. What we see instead is the slow camera movement following the flow of water with piles of garbage underneath. In his diary, Tarkovsky refers to this four-minute sequence as a dream.[1] Yet it is not quite a dream since no cut or dissolve marks the transition from external reality to the characters' inner world, and what we see is the same Zone, only from a close-up perspective. While dwelling on the Zone's debris, we are still outside the character's consciousness. The same goes for *Nostalghia* (1983), where the protagonist's dream visions of his past in Russia are often merged with his present time in Italy via long tracking shots that establish seamless continuity between temporally and spatially distinct realities.

Given the constitutive inseparability of dream and reality in Tarkovsky's work, especially in his late period when the pre-reflective dimension of his vision becomes predominant, it is rather difficult to apply any interpretive approach to his films. As Vlada Petric observes, "Tarkovsky's films transcend the Freudian significations of dream images in that they do not so much function as latent symbols as they contribute to a subliminal experience of a dream world. Instead of reading his films from an ideological or psychoanalytical point of view, it seems more justified to examine the author's dream imagery rendered through cinematic devices."[2] Robert Bird similarly points out the pre-theoretical nature of Tarkovsky's work which makes any neat interpretation of his films virtually impossible. In his discussion of Tarkovsky's enigmatic image of the Zone, for example, he demonstratively refuses to define its meaning and concludes that it "is where one goes to see one's innermost desires. It is, in short, the cinema."[3] Thus, to avoid the intentional fallacy, most commentators prefer to approach Tarkovsky's films from a rather descriptive perspective by carefully abstaining from any systematic explanation and only registering the viewer's sensorial response as well as the distortion of everyday perception. As Natasha Synessios points out, in Tarkovsky's films "the mesmerizing camera movements, together with the unusual events taking place within the frame, confound all attempts to interpret the image. The emphasis is on directly experiencing it and allowing it to affect a deeper layer of our consciousness."[4] For Ian Christie, the hyper-realism of Tarkovsky's dreams expresses the director's desire to encourage the viewer "to attend *first* the rhythm and framing of the images, to experience the film on an aesthetic-intuitive level, *before* considering it intellectually."[5] According to Angela Dalle Vacche, Tarkovsky's images of natural elements are not intended as meaningful symbols but, on the contrary, as "primal images, so natural and therefore inexhaustible in their signifying power that they are capable of reorienting our imagination away from a rational, technocratic world view toward something infinite and unspeakable."[6]

Understandably enough, Tarkovsky's film language, because of his consistent emphasis on mysticism and the subjective rhythm of duration, posits a number of obstacles and traps for film studies. And yet, it seems rather reductive to perceive Tarkovsky's "pre-cognitive" images only intuitively and thus deny him a consciously systematic and analytical approach to art. Sergei Filipov, in this regard, goes as far as to claim that Tarkovsky's cinema exemplifies the cognitive activities of the right hemisphere of the brain because of his explicit preference of intuition over logic, observation over meaning, holistic

reasoning over linear, image over dialogue, indivisible duration over chronological discreteness, stylistic plenitude over plot development, etc.[7] Filipov's
right-hemisphere approach certainly sheds some light on the director's work
as a whole, yet it ultimately neglects the internal logic by which his film components are correlated, a logic which is unequivocally rational. As Tarkovsky
writes in his diary, "I am convinced that system is what is important . . . System
is what can organize a man, his emotions, and intellect into the condensed and
concentrated whole . . . System is a closed circle, it is a rhythm of its vibrations that come to existence only because of their fidelity to that system."[8] In
his study *Tarkovsky's Cine-Hermeneutics* (2009), Dmitrii Salynskii seems to
take Tarkovsky's valorization of the system at face value by viewing his films
from the perspective of medieval scholasticism in light of which the director
reappears as a strangely systematic artist and rigorous schematist allowing no
contingency in engineering his images.[9] Nevertheless, however rich and helpful
Salynskii's hermeneutic findings, his hyperrationalistic approach is arbitrary
and speculative, since he often considers only those motifs that are already
inscribed in his quasi-Augustinian paradigm that views the director's entire
career as a coherent spiritual path toward the Absolute and spiritual transcendence climaxed in Tarkovsky's last film *The Sacrifice* (1986). In such a projective reading, plenty of motifs associated with "lower" (profane or empirical)
hermeneutic layers are thus necessarily left out or underdeveloped.[10]

Mikhail Perepelkin's attempt to systematize Tarkovsky's aesthetics in
terms of literary studies similarly results in downgrading the raw materiality
of things expressed in his images.[11] By defining the director's method as the
"poetics of allegory," he views Tarkovsky's imagery as the cinematic elevation
of everything empirical and mundane onto metaphysical heights. While the
allegorical approach does help us to see how Tarkovsky's camera pervasively
"spiritualizes" matter, in his zeal of arbitrary decoding Perepelkin too often
overblows the director's demiurgic motifs into what Žižek terms "cheap religious obscurantism"[12] by compulsively converting each and every image under
consideration into a purveyor of some hidden epiphany with frequent references to "God," "Creator," and "divine truth."

It seems equally counter-intuitive to approach Tarkovsky's images exclusively
from the perspective of narratology that entirely subordinates the visual data to
the narrative form. David Bordwell's approach to the European art film as style-
centered "parametric" cinema, which shifts the function of narration from the
film's plot to its "decorative" stylistic subtleties, would only partially account for
Tarkovsky's imagery by persistently stumbling against the overall "incoherence"
and "incomprehensibility" of his narrational dynamics.[13] Thomas Redwood's
neo-formalist study of the narrative aspects of Tarkovsky's cinematic style
emphasizes such narrative autonomy of stylistic devices in his films (e.g. color
coding, distorted sounds, motific correlations between characters, objects, and

natural elements, framing and staging strategies, etc.), yet the researcher's spectator-oriented model based on *average* comprehension skills unavoidably reduces the director's cinematic and philosophical insights to a set of "incomprehensible" deviations from common sense.

Furthermore, Bazin's ontology of cinematic fact as well as Kracauer's genetic reduction of cinematic image to photographic image would hardly account for the psychological origin of Tarkovsky's empiricism. Bazin does celebrate the use of the long take, which brings "an added measure of realism on the screen"[14] and confirms "our sense of natural reality."[15] But for Tarkovsky, the use of the long take serves the intensity of *inner, subjective* reality. For example, in Tarkovsky's later films, the average length of shots significantly increases (from 25 to 70 seconds), while the "sense of natural reality" dramatically decreases. Yet the longer the sequence shot, the more we believe in the virtual dimension of illuminated things.

Nor would we benefit much from dogmatically aligning Tarkovsky with Eastern Orthodoxy and Dostoevsky's humanism[16] or the existentialist tradition of Russian philosophy.[17] As Tarkovsky claims in an interview, "I don't agree with all [Berdyaev's] opinions. He approaches problems as if he's above them, as if he's resolved them. I don't believe people like that, like Steiner, or Berdyaev."[18] Furthermore, in his diary he writes that he is an agnostic[19]—the knowledge of either God or the Universe is but an individualist illusion which can be psychologically explained. As is known, Tarkovsky planned to shoot a biographical film on Dostoevsky. Yet again, as we learn from his diary notes, Dostoevsky for Tarkovsky is a very troubled man who does not believe in God. He desperately tries to do so only because it is impossible to relate to the world otherwise, on a logical ground; for Dostoevsky, according to Tarkovsky, the world perceived rationally is absurd. It is for this doubt and hesitation that Tarkovsky embraces Dostoevsky, and it is for the clarity of an ethical system that he rejects Berdyaev.

It has become commonplace in Tarkovsky studies that Dostoevsky's Prince Myshkin, a crazy knight of faith, is a prototype for his late protagonists (e.g. Stalker, Domenico). That is, unable to adapt *The Idiot*, he molded his heroes under the influence of Myshkin's personality. Tarkovsky did not shoot *The Idiot*, yet he directed a production of *Hamlet* on stage, where the main hero is emphatically hesitant and inactive because he does not know how to relate to the world since "time is out of joint." For Tarkovsky, Hamlet perishes as the victim of disconnected time, as "self-sacrifice"[20] to "set it right." It is therefore much safer to argue that Tarkovsky's heroes owe as much to Shakespeare as to Dostoevsky, since all of them are stricken by the clash of multiple temporalities and are in search of a synthesis of disjointed time.

How would Tarkovsky's own "theoretical" writings on cinema help us understand his representation of dream and reality? Would they appear to us as "aesthetic-intuitive" as his images? Many commentators remain skeptical about Tarkovsky's contribution to film theory because of its seemingly anachronistic nature. As Johnson and Petrie critically observe: "Tarkovsky's free and unembarrassed use of such terms as 'genius', 'transcendence', 'spiritual vision', 'beauty', etc. may seem to place him as an inheritor of a Romantic tradition that is widely regarded in the West as being outmoded and discredited."[21] Nevertheless, a closer look at his writings and interviews could help us discern an internal philosophical logic which underlies his cinematic method.

TARKOVSKY'S ANTI-INTELLECTUALISM

At first sight, most of Tarkovsky's statements do support commentators' emphasis on the pre-reflective dimension of his films. As he writes,

> Understanding in a scientific sense means agreement on a cerebral, logical level; it is an intellectual act akin to the process of proving a theorem . . . Understanding an artistic image means an aesthetic acceptance of the beautiful, on an emotional or even supra-emotional level . . . For the empirical process of intellectual cognition cannot explain how an artistic image comes into being—unique, indivisible, created and existing on some plane other than that of the intellect.[22]

> Art does not think logically, or formulate a logic of behaviour; it expresses its own postulate of faith.[23]

> The artist cannot, and has no right to, lower himself to some abstract, standardised level for the sake of a misconstrued notion of greater accessibility and understanding.[24]

> The artist cannot make a specific aim of being understandable—it would be quite as absurd as its opposite: trying to be incomprehensible.[25]

> I had the greatest difficulty in explaining to people that there is no hidden, coded meaning in the film, nothing beyond the desire to tell the truth. Often my assurances provoked incredulity and even disappointment. Some people evidently wanted more: they needed arcane symbols, secret meanings. They were not accustomed to the poetics of the cinema image.[26]

As is evident, Tarkovsky's committed resistance to and depreciation of intellectual or logical thinking could hardly help the audience understand the meaning of his works since intellectual cognition as such is not what he expects from them. For Tarkovsky, rational understanding is fundamentally a profane relation to art. The power of art, he argues, necessarily exceeds the viewer's cognitive capacities to grasp its transcendent and spiritual meaning. As he refers to the Russian symbolist Vyacheslav Ivanov, artistic images "cannot be stated or explained, and, confronted by their secret meaning in its totality, we are powerless." Their meaning is "inexhaustible and unlimited" because they are "formed by organic process, like a crystal."[27] It might appear that Tarkovsky's rejection of the primary role of intellect in both creation and reception of the film image points to a supposedly higher, irrational, and mystical communion with it, a path which was taken in much Russian-language studies on Tarkovsky, characterized by heavily impressionistic and hagiographic readings of his work. Nikolai Boldyrev's writings are exemplary in this regard: instead of the expected analytical commentary of Tarkovsky's films, the critic purposefully takes an emphatically mystical, almost apophatic stance on the issue by offering an ecstatic prayer-meditation inspired by his film images.[28] A more modern and critically oriented viewer would be turned off by such an unabashed affirmation of anti-intellectualism. And yet, a closer reading of Tarkovsky's ostensibly old-fashioned rebuttals against intellect would suggest that what the director vehemently resists is not a thought or meaning *per se* but a thinking governed by preconceptions and stereotypes, that is, by such cerebral processes of consciousness which Deleuze characterizes as "the stereotypes, clichés, ready-made visions and formulas"[29] of the movement-image supervised by the model of recognition and pre-given categories of thought. As Ian Christie observes, "No doubt it was . . . his experience working in Soviet cinema that fueled Tarkovsky's intense hostility to any interpretation of his films, at least in the sense of revealing a hidden meaning. Officially sponsored critiques of works of art have an altogether more sinister significance in the Soviet context than our journalistic tradition comprehends."[30] Tarkovsky does invoke the power of the artistic genius to transcend the imposed constraints of the everyday consciousness, but this should be read as his own "romantic," albeit anachronistic, way to deterritorialize the dogmatic image of thought. As he writes,

> The birth and development of thought are subject to laws of their own, and sometimes demand forms of expression which are quite different from the patterns of logical speculation.[31]

> A vast number of clichés and commonplaces . . . found a resting-place in the cinema.[32]

> A mass of preconceptions exists in and around the profession . . . those hackneyed ways of thinking, clichés that grow up around traditions and gradually take them over. And you can achieve nothing in art unless you are free from received ideas.[33]

A convention dictated by necessity has turned into a preconception, a cliché.[34]

There are too many temptations on every side: stereotypes, preconceptions, commonplaces, artistic ideas other than one's own.[35]

It is because of his rejection of the pre-established forms of perception and rationalization imposed on the film image that Tarkovsky sweepingly rejects Eisenstein's intellectual montage for its exclusive focus on the viewer's analytical competence. As he writes,

The idea of 'montage cinema'—that editing brings together two concepts and thus engenders a new, third one— . . . seems to me to be incompatible with the nature of cinema. Art can never have the interplay of concepts as its ultimate goal.[36]

I reject the principles of 'montage cinema' because they do not allow the film to continue beyond the edges of the screen: they do not allow the audience to bring personal experience to bear on what is in front of them on film. 'Montage cinema' presents the audience with puzzles and riddles, makes them decipher symbols, wonder at allegories, appealing all the time to their intellectual experience.[37]

In his critique of Eisenstein, who "makes thought into a despot" by using "the frame to codify intellectual formulae,"[38] Tarkovsky goes as far as to claim that *Ivan the Terrible* (1944) "almost ceases . . . to be a cinematic work" because it is "so close to the theatre" and "consists of a series of hieroglyphics. There is not a single detail that is not permeated with the author's intent."[39] It is for the same reason that Tarkovsky is starkly opposed to Pasolini's "poetic cinema." "'Poetic cinema', as a rule," he writes, "gives birth to symbols, allegories and other such figures—that is, to things that have nothing to do with the imagery natural to cinema."[40] In it, "everything is deliberately made incomprehensible and the director has to think up explanations for what he has done."[41]

Tarkovsky's critique of the intellectual and allegorical composition of film images, i.e. a composition that directly reflects the director's authorial intention, may still seem somewhat puzzling to his viewers since most images in his films are indeed saturated by plenty of "hieroglyphic" details and innovative compositional strategies that provoke our hermeneutic zeal to decipher them. As mentioned above, Dmitrii Salynsky's *Tarkovsky's Cine-hermeneutics* focuses precisely on this aspect of the director's oeuvre, i.e. the hidden layers of meaning (e.g. psychological, cultural, mythological, religious) inscribed in the architectonics of his films. In fact, many scholars have noticed Tarkovsky's "customary self-contradiction"[42] or the discrepancy between his theoretical statements and film practice.[43] I would argue that the director's notorious "self-contradiction" appears to be caused by the insufficiency of his theoretical vocabulary, derived mainly from the Soviet film aesthetics still dominated by the socialist realism doctrine, rather than from his intention to confuse the viewer. By insisting on the "uniqueness"[44] and "singularity"[45] of the film image, free from "vulgar symbolism"[46] and "inexhaustible and unlimited in its meaning,"[47] Tarkovsky strives to disengage his cinematic vision from any prior ideological or intellectual investment and dedicate it to the expression of the raw facticity of "life itself . . . in its simplest manifestations."[48] It is in his commitment to realism and, sometimes, naturalism as the aesthetic basis of the film image that his methodological views prove to be most consistent. Although Tarkovsky's use of the term "realism" is rare and obscure (e.g. "Realism is a striving for the truth, and truth is always beautiful;"[49] "Bach's D-minor choral prelude is realistic, because it expresses a vision of the truth"[50]), judging by his formulations of the film image, in which the realist representation of an object is to be refracted through the psychological processes of the character's individual consciousness (e.g. memories, dreams, and hallucinations), we may safely suggest that his cinematic method could be categorized as "oneiric realism."

TARKOVSKY ON THE FILM IMAGE

The cornerstone of Tarkovsky's writings on film can be considered his notion of the film image, which in turn determines his understanding of other aspects of film: cinematic time, *mise-en-scène*, editing, script, acting, and soundtrack. Here are a number of his formulations of the film image:

> The image is independent and elusive, dependent upon our consciousness and on the real world it seeks to embody.[51]

> In cinema it is all the more the case that observation is the first principle of the image . . . But by no means every film shot can aspire to being an image of the world   Naturalistically recorded facts are in themselves utterly inadequate to the creation of cinematic image. The image in cinema is based on the ability to present as an observation one's own perception of an object.[52]

> To be faithful to life, intrinsically truthful, a work has for me to be at once an exact factual account and a true communication of feelings.[53]

As we can see, for Tarkovsky the film image must meet two conditions: it must be adequate to both real life and psychological state. That is, the film image is born when these two conditions become one: when the objectivity of the camera blends with the subjectivity of the filmmaker (or character). In a sense, Tarkovsky's film image stands between the world and the subject, and equally reflects the two; it serves as the medium of both inner and outer worlds. In this regard, Tarkovsky does not believe in the pure objectivity of documentary cinema, which strives for the unbiased depiction of reality. Such a demonstrative naturalism for him is an artificial stylization of life. As he writes,

> Every artist is . . . limited in his perception, in his understanding of the inner connections of the world about him. It's therefore meaningless to talk about naturalism in cinema as if phenomena could be recorded wholesale by the camera, irrespective of any artistic principles, so to speak in their 'natural state'. This sort of naturalism cannot exist.[54]

Neither does he accept an experimental visionary film with its emphasis on the unrestrained spontaneity of the inner world, which ultimately neglects the physical laws of empirical reality. Tarkovsky's hysterical reaction against Stan Brakhage's objectless abstract work at the 1983 Telluride Film Festival is quite exemplary here. As Brakhage paraphrases, Tarkovsky's furious assessment had no single word of appreciation for his experimental shorts: "this is too scientific to be Art," "this-is-too-rapid-it-hurts-the-eyes," "this is sheer self-indulgence," "the color is shit," "what is this paint? Why do you do this?"[55] For the same reason he disagrees with German Romanticists who, according to Tarkovsky, almost ideologically oppose subjectivity to reality. As he comments in an interview,

> Romantics are people who have always tried to imagine life different than it was. The most terrible thing for them is routine, the daily habit, the relationship to life as something fixed. Romantics are not fighters. When they perish, it's the result of chimeras they themselves created. For me romanticism as a way of looking at the world is very dangerous, where personal talent is regarded as something of capital importance.[56]

In his screenplay *Hoffmanniana* (1975), Tarkovsky attempted to demonstrate the danger of the romanticists' "chimeras." Written right after he completed *Mirror* (1974), *Hoffmanniana* elaborates on the theme of the indiscernibility of imagination and reality by using the motifs of mirror, doppelgänger, and dream. Yet, unlike in *Mirror*, this indiscernibility acquires a more sinister and pathological character. For Tarkovsky, the primacy of the subjective world over the external one is "sickness."[57] His project is, on the contrary, to harmoniously unite them, that is, to overcome the dualism between the subject and the object, which is more utopian.

Tarkovsky's pursuit of the "complete and unconditional factual truth"[58] is therefore inseparable from his treatment of it as a reflection of "the interior world of the individual imagination." Given that "the [film] image can only be realised in factual, natural forms of visible and audible life," memories, fantasies, dreams, and hallucinations should necessarily be "made up of exactly these same observed, natural forms of life."[59] The ideal synthesis of outer and inner worlds (i.e. perception and imagination) is exemplified for Tarkovsky by Japanese haiku poetry, in which images "mean nothing beyond themselves."[60] Whereas for Eisenstein the tripartite structure of haiku, which juxtaposes and unifies different elements within a single poetic form and "creates something different in kind from any of them,"[61] illustrates the central aspect of his theory of montage (in which shots should be combined according to the dialectical logic of conflict and synthesis), for Tarkovsky haiku underscores the facts of "pure observation" that "make us feel [the author's] mood."[62] That is to say, Eisenstein sees in haiku the linear narrative logic of sequential juxtapositions, whereas Tarkovsky sees the union between mind and nature via "a precise observation of life." As he demonstrates this union in the process of reading haiku, "the reader of haikku [sic] has to be absorbed into it as into nature, to plunge in, lose himself in its depth, as in the cosmos where there is no bottom and no top."[63] The same effect of the viewer's absorption into the reality of the film image the director seeks in his representation of dreams and memories by ultimately rejecting conventional "old-fashioned filmic tricks,"[64] such as shooting "at high speed," "through a misty veil," "mysterious blurring," bringing in "musical effects,"[65] etc. For Tarkovsky, "the actual, material facts of the dream . . . which were refracted in that layer of the consciousness which kept vigil through the night" constitute the only possible basis for his oneiric phenomenology. The hyperrealism of dreams in our actual lives should therefore be replicated on screen in its pristine originality without any unnecessary distortion involved. As he claims, "the most interesting or frightening dreams are the ones where you remember everything down to the minutest detail."[66]

TARKOVSKY ON TIME

For Tarkovsky, cinematic time, "*captured in its factual forms and manifestations,*"[67] is what glues together the objective and subjective dimensions of the film image. It preserves the "concrete life and emotional content of the object filmed."[68] It is important to emphasize that it is from time rather than space that Tarkovsky derives the factual material for his films: time for him is the original source of the living facts to be observed. That is, to observe life cinematically is to follow its flow in time:

For the cinema image is essentially the observation of a phenomenon passing through time.[69]

> The cinema image . . . is basically observation of life's facts within time, organised according to the pattern of life itself, and observing its time laws . . . The image becomes authentically cinematic when (amongst other things) not only does it live within time, but time also lives within it, even within each separate frame.[70]

Given that time is the primary substance from which the film image is molded, the filmmaker becomes the sculptor of time, who, "from a 'lump of time' made up of an enormous, solid cluster of living facts, cuts off and discards whatever he does not need, leaving only what is to be an element of the finished film, what will prove to be integral to the cinematic image."[71] In Tarkovsky's aesthetics, editing serves as the main function of such sculpting in time: that is, by cutting time in pieces, assembling them into various temporal sequences and discarding those which do not fit the image, the director "brings together shots which are already filled with time, and organises the unified, living structure inherent in the film; and the time that pulsates through the blood vessels of the film, making it alive, is of varying rhythmic pressure."[72] As a result of editing, the chain of shots filled with various "time-pressures" constitutes the film's overall temporal rhythm. Rhythm, in this regard, is not a quantitative category; it is rather defined by a certain psychological intensity invested in a given shot. As he writes, "The distinctive time running through the shots makes the rhythm . . . Rhythm is not determined by the length of the edited pieces, but by the pressure of the time that runs them."[73] That is, each and every shot is supposed to be charged with a distinctly unique time-pressure which materializes the psychological singularity of a moment. This time-pressure or time-thrust inhaled into a shot becomes the basic unit of a film. The entire film succeeds only when these rhythmically divergent temporal units constitute an organic whole that channels the flow of time. Tarkovsky doesn't explain how to measure a particular time-pressure within a shot. Since the purpose of the time-thrust is to create the intensity of a moment and not its meaning, the calculating methods of editing aimed at the creation of concepts are of no use here. For Tarkovsky, the sense of time which regulates the temporal rhythm of an entire film is purely intuitive; it is a gift similar to the absolute pitch of a musician or the poet's sense of a right word in a poem. As he writes, "Feeling the rhythmicality of a shot is rather like feeling a truthful word in literature. An inexact word in writing, like an inexact rhythm in film, destroys the veracity of the work." For Tarkovsky, each director has his or her own unique sense of temporal rhythm: no director feels time in a similar way; the time-pressure inflated in a shot is rather a prime factor for their difference. "It is above all," he argues, "through sense of time, through rhythm, that the director reveals his individuality."[74] In this regard, it is quite erroneous to align Tarkovsky's long take with that of Theo Angelopoulos; the former, in his diary, ultimately dismisses the latter for his unreasonably long sequence shots which feel like a "pointless stretching of a rubber band."[75]

TARKOVSKY AND BERGSON

Tarkovsky's theoretical statements on intuitive comprehension, image, memory, and time, however romantic and anachronistic they may seem, are strangely resonant with Henry Bergson's insights on the same subjects.[76] More specifically, Tarkovsky's dual commitment to pure observation and subjective imagination or "feeling" as the fundamental constituents of the film image is strikingly parallel to Bergson's notion of consciousness coextensive with matter and time via perception- and memory-images. Just as Tarkovsky refuses to attach any meaning to the image of wind, fire, or water,[77] that is, to represent the *idea* of the object filmed, so Bergson removes any intellectual or psychological mediation between consciousness and the object by claiming that, according to Deleuze, "all consciousness *is* something."[78] For Bergson, image is identical to matter which consciousness can perceive without threatening its objectivity. Bergsonian consciousness completely immersed in the material universe is "pure" or inhuman perception, i.e. the lowest form of consciousness merging with matter ("where subject and object coincide"),[79] which is only theoretically posited as the consciousness' limit of objectivity yet can never be achieved in reality since our perception is always intermeshed with memories. For Bergson, human perception is necessarily limited. As he writes, "'Pure', that is to say, instantaneous, perception is, in fact, only an ideal, an extreme. Every perception . . . prolongs the past into the present, and thereby partakes of memory."[80] Tarkovsky similarly considers documentary cinema's striving for pure objectivity (or "pure perception" devoid of subjectivity) as an impossible ideal, since "things that exist 'in themselves' only come to have existence 'for us' in the course of our own experience."[81] Furthermore, just as for Tarkovsky memories and dreams can only be represented in tangible forms of present perception—because of which he thoroughly discredits the abstract experimental cinema that aims to represent consciousness in its objectless purity—so for Bergson virtual "memory can only become actual by means of the perception which attracts it. Powerless, it borrows life and strength from the present sensation in which it is materialized."[82] For both Bergson and Tarkovsky, "it would be a chimerical enterprise to try to free ourselves from the fundamental conditions of external perception." Without perception, "the memory-image itself, if it remained pure memory, would be ineffectual."[83] That is, the latter would agree with the former that "we shall never reach the past unless we frankly place ourselves within it. Essentially virtual, it cannot be known as something past unless we follow and adopt the movement by which it expands into a present image."[84]

Furthermore, Tarkovsky's protagonists often manifest their Bergsonian nature as well: they are suspended between their memories of the past and present reality, unable to completely join either side. Nether fully in the past nor fully in the present, but rather half here/half there, they keep dwelling in a strange kind of temporality that fuses recollection-images with the perception of current reality. We may even say that their temporal as well as spatial suspension is dictated by the dual structure of Tarkovsky's film image itself consisting of the objective observation of empirical reality refracted through the characters' individual consciousness. That is, his characters perceive the world only through their memories, yet what they compulsively remember can no longer be attainable in the present. We may say that all Tarkovsky's characters are Bergsonian dreamers and time travelers withdrawn from the present and traversing from one memory layer onto another to the point of losing themselves in the infinity of time.

Tarkovsky's writings on cinematic time, however, do not share the Bergsonian ontology of the virtual or pure memory, according to which the impersonal past is preserved in itself beyond the limits of our consciousness and actualizes itself in it via (personal) memory-images. He may seem to favor the psychological notion of time when he argues that "[t]ime is a state: the flame in which there lives the salamander of the human soul;"[85] "it is a subjective, spiritual category. The time we have lived settles in our soul as an experience placed within time."[86] As Nariman Skakov pointed out, Tarkovsky's "temporal 'sculptures' are overwhelmingly anthropocentric."[87] His heavily subjective (and anthropocentric) approach to memory is best illustrated by his most autobiographical film *Mirror*, where the protagonist's mother is played by the director's actual mother, the voice of the actor playing his father is dubbed by the voice of his actual father, his second wife plays a doctor's wife, his stepdaughter one of the characters of his memories. The country house of his childhood is an exact replica of the original rebuilt for the set on the foundation of the old house, the childhood landscape (the buckwheat field) is resurrected directly from his memories, many film shots directly follow Tarkovsky's family photographs, *Mirror*'s dream sequences are his own dreams recorded in his diary. Furthermore, in the end the protagonist lying on the deathbed is played by Tarkovsky himself, and he is also seen in the mirror reflection in the earring sale episode. In each and every film, Tarkovsky recounts one and the same story of his nostalgia for the lost harmony of his childhood. Yet this should not imply that time, according to Tarkovsky, is confined within our consciousness and ceases to exist beyond its limits. In fact, time may leave consciousness if one dedicates oneself to a purely materialistic existence, just as it "can vanish without trace in our material world." As he writes, "falling out of time, [a person] is unable to seize his own link with the outside world—in other words he is doomed to madness." "The human conscience is dependent upon time for its existence."[88] That is, Tarkovsky's personal feeling and valorization of time and memory, which "merge into each other" as if they were "the two sides of a medal,"[89] should be understood as the result of his radical openness to time in general, which is most evident in his films demonstrating the eventual dissolution of the characters' subjectivity within time. He does perceive the world in terms of multiple durations by observing phenomena "passing through time"[90] and "printing on celluloid"[91] their diverse rhythmicality, yet his highly personal and subjective sense of duration opens up to a larger, impersonal, or ontological dimension of time, of which we can judge by his images conflating multiple temporalities beyond individual consciousness.

In a similar vein, Tarkovsky's praise of cinema for its ability to capture the actuality of time "in its factual forms" as well as to preserve it "in metal boxes for a long period of time"[92] may seem like a gesture toward a spatialization and domestication of time rather than its direct presentation, of which Deleuze speaks in *Cinema II*. But for Tarkovsky, "the fact that the [film] image can only be realised in factual, natural forms of visible and audible life" is "[o]ne of the most important limitations of cinema."[93] The totality of time can certainly not be captured in the finite film image, but what we see in the frame, he writes, "is not limited to its visual depiction, but is a pointer to something stretching out beyond the frame and to infinity."[94] Given that for Tarkovsky "the image stretches out into infinity, and leads to the absolute,"[95] so should time factually "imprinted in the frame."[96]

Tarkovsky's commitment to realism, therefore, should not be seen as an obstacle to a direct presentation of time precisely because his vision of the raw materiality of things is thoroughly temporalized by being refracted through memory. It is in this respect that Tarkovsky shares much affinity with Bergson. For both of them, memory signifies the final and ultimate spiritual activity. Just as Tarkovsky claims that "[m]emory is a spiritual concept,"[97] Bergson similarly argues that "pure memory is a spiritual manifestation"[98] and "it is really into spirit that we penetrate by means of memory."[99]

CONCLUSION

Tarkovsky's implicit "Bergsonism" could certainly be further elaborated through Deleuze's *Cinema II*, in which the director is credited to "set out the greatest crystal-images in the history of the cinema."[100] For Deleuze, the notion of the crystal-image stands for the Bergsonian "coalescence" between memory and perception, where "perception and recollection, the real and the imaginary, the physical and the mental, or rather their images, continually [follow] each other, running behind each other and referring back to each other around a point of indiscernibility."[101] The process of the continual and indiscernible exchange between the actual present and the virtual past is evident in almost all Tarkovsky's images, easily rendering themselves to the Deleuzian framework of film analysis, quite often implemented in recent literature on the director.[102] However tempting it is to extend this line of analysis here, our purpose was rather to demonstrate that Tarkovsky becomes one of Deleuze's favorite directors because the former holds essentially Bergsonian views on cinema: namely, in his preference of intuition over intellectual cognition, psychological duration over chronological time, the past over the present, as well as in his foregrounding of the dual nature of the film image, in which subjective consciousness (spirit) and objective reality (matter) are coalesced into a single unit. Viewing Tarkovsky as being subconsciously Bergsonian could certainly help us salvage his theoretical musings from being dismissed as unembarrassedly Romantic or outdated.

NOTES

1. Andrey Tarkovsky, *Time within Time: the Diaries 1970–1986* (Kolkata: Seagull Books, 2004), 168.
2. Vlada Petric, "Tarkovsky's Dream Imagery," *Film Quarterly* 43.2 (1989–90): 28–34, 30.
3. Robert Bird, *Andrei Tarkovsky: Elements of Cinema* (London: Reaktion Books, 2008), 69.
4. Natasha Synessios, *Mirror: The Film Companion* (London: I. B.Tauris, 2001), 50–1.
5. Ian Christie, "Introduction: Tarkovsky and His Time," in Maya Turovskaya, *Tarkovsky: Cinema as Poetry* (London: Faber & Faber, 1989), ix–xxvi, xviii.
6. a Dalle Vacche, *Cinema and Painting: How Art Is Used in Film* (Austin: University of Texas Press, 1996), 137.
7. Sergei Filippov, "Teoriya i praktika Andreia Tarkovskogo," *Kinovedcheskie zapiski*, vol. 56 (2002), 41–74.
8. Andrei Tarkovsky, *Martirolog: dnevniki 1970–1986* (Istituto internazionale Andrej Tarkovskij, 2008), 369.
9. Dmitrii Salynskii, *Kinogermenevtika Tarkovskogo* (Moskva: Kvadriga, 2009).
10. Salynskii's hermeneutic hyperrationalism is best exemplified in his analysis of the film composition according to the golden ratio and narrative symmetry. By interpreting Tarkovsky's films in terms of what happens at the proportionally accentuated points—the film's center, the center of its first and second halves, and the point of the golden ratio— he attributes a number of arbitrary codes and rules, called "the canon of Tarkovsky," to the overall composition of his cinematic narration, even though the director never consciously divided his films into such points.
11. Mikhail Perepelkin, *Slovo v mire Andreia Tarkovskogo: Poètika inoskazaniia* (Samara: Samarskiĭ universitet, 2010).
12. Slavoj Žižek, "The Thing from Inner Space," *Angelaki: journal of the theoretical humanities* 4.3 (1999): 221–31, 228.
13. Thomas Redwood, *Andrei Tarkovsky's Poetics of Cinema* (Cambridge: Cambridge Scholars Publishing, 2010), 201, 203.
14. André Bazin, *What is Cinema?*, Vol. 2 (Berkeley: University of California Press, 2005), 27.
15. Ibid., 110.
16. Salvestroni Simonetta, "The Science-Fiction Films of Andrei Tarkovsky," *Science-Fiction Studies* 14 (1987): 294–306.
17. Igor Evlampiev, *Khudozhestvennaia filosofiia Andreia Tarkovskogo* (Aleteia, 2001).
18. Gianvito, *Andrei Tarkovsky: Interviews*, 186.
19. Tarkovsky, *Martirolog*, 366.
20. Tarkovsky, *Time within Time*, 378.

21. Vida T. Johnson and Graham Petrie, *The Films of Andrei Tarkovsky: A Visual Fugue* (Bloomington: Indiana University Press, 1994), 31–2.

22. Andrey Tarkovsky, *Sculpting in Time: Reflections on the Cinema* (Austin: University of Texas Press, 1987), 40.

23. Ibid., 41.

24. Ibid., 166.

25. Ibid., 167.

26. Ibid., 133.

27. Ibid., 47.

28. See Nikolai Boldyrev, *Stalker, ili trudy i dni Andreia Tarkooskogo* (Cheliabinsk, Russia: Izd-vo Ural Ltd), 2002; Nikolai Boldyrev, *Zhertvoprinoshenie Andreia Tarkovskogo* (Moskva: Vagrius, 2004).

29. Gilles Deleuze, *Cinema II: The Time-Image* (Minneapolis: University of Minnesota Press, 1989), 182.

30. Christie, "Introduction: Tarkovsky and His Time," xvii.

31. Tarkovsky, *Sculpting in Time*, 20.

32. Ibid., 26.

33. Ibid., 59.

34. Ibid., 70.

35. Ibid., 80.

36. Ibid., 114.

37. Ibid., 118.

38. Ibid., 136.

39. Ibid., 67.

40. Ibid., 66.

41. Ibid., 223.

42. Helena Goscilo, "Fraught Filiation: Andrei Tarkovsky's Transformations of Personal Trauma," in Helena Goscilo and Yana Hashamova (eds), *Cinepaternity: Fathers and Sons in Soviet and Post-Soviet Film* (Bloomington: Indiana University Press, 2010), 247–82, 274.

43. See, for example, Sergei Filippov, "Teoriya i praktika Andreia Tarkovskogo," *Kinovedcheskie zapiski* 56 (2002): 41–74; Robert Bird, *Andrei Tarkovsky: Elements of Cinema*; Shusei Nishi, *Tarkovsky and His Time: Hidden Truth of Life* (Alt-arts LLC, 2012); Maia Turovskaya, *Tarkovsky: Cinema as Poetry* (London: Faber & Faber, 1989).

44. Tarkovsky, *Sculpting in Time*, 111.

45. Ibid., 141.

46. Ibid., 216.

47. Ibid., 47.

48. Ibid., 106.

49. Ibid., 113.

50. Ibid., 154.

51. Ibid., 106.

52. Ibid., 107.

53. Ibid., 23.

54. Ibid., 185.

55. Stan Brakhage and Jennifer Dorn, "Brakhage Meets Tarkovsky," *Chicago Review* 47.4 (2001): 42–7, 43.

56. John Gianvito, *Andrei Tarkovsky: Interviews* (Jackson: University Press of Mississippi, 2006), 184–5.

57. Ibid., 176.

58. Ibid., 78.

59. Ibid., 71.
60. Ibid., 106.
61. Ibid., 66.
62. Ibid., 112.
63. Ibid., 106.
64. Ibid., 30.
65. Ibid., 71.
66. Ibid., 72.
67. Ibid., 63 (emphasis in original).
68. Ibid., 69–70.
69. Ibid., 67.
70. Ibid., 68.
71. Ibid., 63–4.
72. Ibid., 114.
73. Ibid., 117.
74. Ibid., 120.
75. Andrei Tarkovsky, *Martirolog*, 439.
76. There have been scholars, of course, who compellingly argued for the affinity between the two. Nariman Skakov, for example, explored the phenomena of space and temporality in Tarkovsky's cinema by extensively applying Bergson's and Deleuze's philosophies of time (see Nariman Skakov, *The Cinema of Tarkovsky: Labyrinths of Space and Time* (London: I. B.Tauris, 2012)). More importantly, Donato Totaro, twenty years earlier, demonstrated how Bergson's concept of indivisible duration could be illustrated by Tarkovsky's film aesthetic, namely his long takes, editing, and camera movements (see Donato Totaro, "Time and the Film Aesthetics of Andrei Tarkovsky," *Canadian Journal of Film Studies* 2.1 (1992): 21–30). In his review of the English translation of Tarkovsky's *Sculpting in Time*, Totaro also mentions in passing that both are "like-minded souls who happened to share a common worldview," such as emphases on intuition, inner world of consciousness, non-chronological time, and memory (see Donato Totaro, "Art For All 'Time'," *Film-Philosophy* 4.1 (2000)). My close reading of Tarkovsky's theoretical statements along Bergsonian lines is partly inspired by these findings.
77. Ibid., 212.
78. Gilles Deleuze, *Cinema I: The Movement-Image* (Minneapolis: University of Minnesota Press, 1986), 56 (emphasis in original).
79. Henri Bergson, *Matter and Memory* (Zone Books, 1990), 221.
80. Ibid., 244.
81. Ibid., 185.
82. Ibid., 127.
83. Ibid., 187.
84. Ibid., 135.
85. Ibid., 57.
86. Ibid., 58.
87. Skakov, *The Cinema of Tarkovsky*, 5.
88. Ibid., 57–8.
89. Ibid., 57.
90. Ibid., 67.
91. Ibid., 63.
92. Ibid., 62.
93. Ibid., 71.
94. Ibid., 117.

95. Ibid., 104.
96. Ibid., 117.
97. Ibid., 57.
98. Ibid., 240.
99. Ibid., 180.
100. Gilles Deleuze, *Cinema II: The Time-Image* (Minneapolis: University of Minnesota Press, 1989), 73.
101. Ibid., 69.
102. See, for example, Anna Powell, *Deleuze, Altered States and Film* (Edinburgh University Press, 2007); Alexander Kozin, "The Appearing Memory: Gilles Deleuze and Andrey Tarkovsky on Crystal-Image," *Memory Studies* 2.1 (2009): 103–17; Robert Efird, "Deleuze on Tarkovsky: The Crystal-Image of Time in 'Steamroller and Violin,'" *The Slavic and East European Journal* 58.2 (2014): 237–54.

Film Method

Introduction to Part II

This section discusses Tarkovsky's cinematic techniques, including his treatment of film genre, documentary style, temporality, landscape, and sound. It opens with Sara Pankenier Weld's chapter, which explores how *Ivan's Childhood* (1962) critically transcends the genre of the Soviet war movie by employing the child's perspective on the war. Through his poetically and autobiographically enriched cinematic version of Vladimir Bogomolov's original story "Ivan" (1957) that foregrounds the patriotic celebration of a child hero, Tarkovsky juxtaposes wartime violence with childhood as such and the protagonist's private subjectivity, by letting the viewer enter his memories and dreams and thus assume a subservient and vulnerable position.

Zdenko Mandušić's chapter discusses Tarkovsky's appreciation of newsreel-documentary films in the context of the Soviet film discourse over new documentary style in the 1960s. As Mandušić demonstrates, the sixties' cult of authenticity achieved through the documentary representation of reality was one of many ways for the Thaw cinema to counter late-Stalinist movies notorious for their excessive mythologization. Against the backdrop of these debates, Tarkovsky devised his theory of documentary realism in his essay "Imprinted Time" (1967), which he practically implemented in *Andrei Rublev* (1966). Aimed to recreate the authentic experience of time and space rather than accurately reconstruct the historical environment of medieval Russia, *Andrei Rublev* applied visual strategies—extended duration, stable or static frames, composition in depth—that constitute his method of direct observation.

Donato Totaro's chapter concentrates on Tarkovsky's 1979 film *Stalker* and in particular how his expression of temporality through his long-take aesthetic impacts on narrative meaning. In his close reading, Totaro breaks down the film into three sections that comprise the narrative and character journey—

pre-zone reality, the fantastical zone, and the post-zone reality—and examines how time is represented in the long take across these sections. As *Stalker*'s narrative progresses, he argues, time in the long take becomes an expression of creation and invention, moving from the so- called "drab-time" of the initial pre-zone city scenes, to a "creation-time" in the middle-zone section, to a more ambiguous expression of time in the post-zone city scenes.

Yelizaveta Goldfarb Moss' chapter discusses how Tarkovsky's *Nostalghia* (1983) organizes its *mise-en-scène* to frame a relationship with mental and spatial infinity that speaks to timelessness, fluid immobility, and spiraled untraversability. By employing Aristotle's terminology, the author demonstrates how Tarkovsky represents space as becoming through *tableaux vivants* and superimpositions of architectures. In support of this argument, she turns to optical geometry, theories of painting, and architectural framings. She also discusses an excess of vision in the film that parallels its treatment of time and space. In opposition to traditional notions of cinema as Cartesian monocular vision, she argues, Tarkovsky values curved, non-mechanical perspectives that align with Lyotard's theories of painting and theater architecture.

This section concludes with Julia Shpinitskaya's analysis of Tarkovsky's sound design that underwent several transformations throughout his career. Whereas in his early features the director employed a regular music track composed by Viacheslav Ovchinnikov, in his later films made in the 1970s he worked with composer Eduard Artemiev, who created original and highly experimental soundtracks. As Shpinitskaya demonstrates, Tarkovsky primarily strived for the realistic sound aesthetic, requesting a variety of noises and natural sounds, in conjunction with electronic arrangement. At the same time his sonic realism progressively tends toward irrealism in his later films, when selected natural sounds manifest their otherworldly dimension. His preference for natural sounds sounding unnaturally is especially evident in his last film *The Sacrifice* (1986), when Tarkovsky decided to work with the sound mixer only, Owe Svensson, without a composer.

CHAPTER 4

The Child's Eye View of War in
Ivan's Childhood

Sara Pankenier Weld

In his first full-length feature film, *Ivan's Childhood* (*Ivanovo Detstvo*, 1962), Andrei Tarkovsky employs the child's eye view in multiple cinematic dimensions to create an unparalleled depiction of a child at war.[1] The film transcends the genre of the Soviet war movie in part because of the dramatic confrontation of childhood and war it depicts through its evocative poetic form. Far from a patriotic tale of a child hero specific to one national context, Tarkovsky's film offers a fervent critique of war. Indeed, Tarkovsky himself remarked, "I wanted to convey all my hatred of war. I chose childhood because it is what contrasts most with war."[2] This chapter examines how Tarkovsky's film *Ivan's Childhood* assumes a child's eye view in order to offer a personal critique of war by juxtaposing wartime violence with childhood.

Overall, in the transformations he makes to Vladimir Bogomolov's original story "Ivan" (1957), Tarkovsky emphasizes the child's perspective.[3] Having taken over film production after a failed earlier attempt to adapt Bogomolov's story to the screen, Tarkovsky took a radically different approach to that of his predecessor. His emphasis on the child within the film is underscored by the fact that he changed the title of the film by adding the word 'childhood' to the title of Bogomolov's story,[4] thereby emphasizing the young age of Ivan, who thus becomes not just an everyman but an every child.[5] In so doing, Tarkovsky also makes the title of *Ivan's Childhood* significantly more ironic and less reflective of the true subject matter of the film—war—which the film dramatically opposes to the childhood Ivan has lost, or any idyllic childhood nostalgically or Romantically construed.

Unlike the failed first adaptation, Tarkovsky's film further emphasizes the contrast between idyllic childhood and the morbid implications of war by returning to the story's original tragic ending, wherein the narrator learns of

Ivan's death at the hands of the Germans.[6] Its title notwithstanding, it is the death of Ivan that is the true subject of the film, including the spiritual death that precedes a physical one. This deathliness is underscored by the film's setting, since Ivan emerges from and disappears into the liminal space of the river, which, like the River Styx, denotes his closeness to the underworld. Ivan only ever escapes from this nightmarish setting through memories, dreams, and nightmares. In his adaptation, Tarkovsky preserves the structure of Bogomolov's story, but goes significantly further in taking the perspective of Ivan, since the story's narrative perspective necessarily remains at a certain remove, due to its being narrated by lieutenant Galtsev. By contrast, the more widely ranging cinematic eye in Tarkovsky's film even enters into Ivan's private subjectivity, memories, and dreams, which remained inaccessible to Bogomolov's narrator.

In assuming a child's eye view, however, Tarkovsky also in some senses stays true to the spirit of Bogomolov's story, since it too focuses on the enigmatic figure of Ivan, who passes through the life of the narrator. For example, Bogomolov's initial, and final, descriptions of the boy focus particularly on his eyes. The first description of Ivan's first appearance concludes with an evocative description of his large, wide-set eyes: "He approached, examining me with the guarded and focused gaze of his large, unusually widely-spaced eyes. [. . .] In his gaze [. . .] an internal struggle was detectable and, as it seemed to me, mistrust and enmity."[7] The description of these wary, focused eyes, which look guardedly at the narrator before they are themselves seen, transforms into a description of his gaze and his expression that hints at the depths of his experience, including his mistrust and enmity. After the lieutenant's own mistrust gives way to respect and even, perhaps, awe, the boy's overall aspect changes to that of a fair-haired and pale-skinned child, while his eyes remain remarkable. "Notable in his high-cheekboned face were his eyes, which were large, greenish and surprisingly widely spaced; it is most likely that I had never before seen eyes so widely spaced."[8] Ivan's large, green eyes now strike the narrator even more, as he wonders about the secrets of this boy and what he has seen. Tarkovsky's film takes us deeper into those eyes and reveals the secrets of his interior experience at the outset, even before depicting the scene where the story's narrator Galtsev first encounters the boy. For before this opening scenario, the film adds an evocative childhood sequence where we enter into Ivan's interior experience. From the first scene in the film, the viewer watches Ivan seeing. The fragmented view of the boy through a spider's web[9] and the fragmented view of the world it implies, foreshadows the shattering of the childhood nature idyll depicted in the first dream scene as the dark film begins, plunging the orphan into a time and space defined by war.

Through his poetically enriched cinematic version of the story, which assumes a child's eye view, Tarkovsky takes the viewer into the striking and enigmatic eyes Bogomolov describes. For both writer and filmmaker, then, Ivan's eyes stand as a poetic synecdoche for the tragic figure of the child as a whole. Similarly, the child's experience stands for that of many others and, as Lury observes, "the child's narrative function is effectively to act as a metonym for wider suffering."[10] Ultimately the boy is reduced to those eyes, as a witness to horror who becomes an almost inhuman, vengeful, and astonishingly adult military scout, who sees, spies, and reconnoiters, but must not himself be seen. In Tarkovsky's film, these eyes find a striking portrayal in many scenes where the boy's eyes, as depicted skillfully by Nikolai Burlyaev, form the centerpiece of the composition; however, the child's eye view finds many other expressions as well.

The film assumes the child's perspective by showing Ivan's experiences more from the child's own point of view, rather than from the limited perspective of the original narrator in Bogomolov's story. Notably, it adds representation of the interior experience of the child through the inclusion of childhood memory and dream sequences, which punctuate the film at key moments, thereby framing a nightmarish reality of war with a dream-like and nostalgic childhood idyll that is irrevocably lost and, even in memory or dream, shadowed by the darkness of the future, present, and past. Tarkovsky's emphasis on the child's eye view thus goes far beyond the focus on the thematics of the child's aspect, vision, and eyes evident in Bogomolov's story. It even replicates for audiences the child's eye view itself through formal methods that emphasize the perspective of the child, or that of the adult on the child. I would argue that in Tarkovsky's film the child's eye view becomes the artistic dominant, as it were, for the unique thematic and formal aspects of this striking film, as well as being key to its message. Although other formal aspects contribute to the cinematic eye in this film, this chapter will focus on the child's eye view primarily through visual elements of the film.

THE CHILD'S EYE VIEW

Attention to the child's perspective has roots in film theory. Consider, for example, Béla Balázs' claim in *Visible Man* that *"Children see the world in close-up."*[11] In her discussion of "The close-up as child's eye view,'" Melinda Szaloky observes that "Artistic sensibility at its best is akin to that of children for Balázs."[13] More recently, Gilles Deleuze speaks in *Cinema 2* of the child as a figure, whose "motor helplessness [. . .] makes him all the more capable of seeing and hearing."[14] Recent work by scholars of cinema and childhood, such as Vicky Lebeau and Karen Lury, has focused particularly on the child in film, while some recent scholarship examines the uses of the child's perspective in film. In *Childhood and Cinema*, Vicky Lebeau discusses how cinema can offer access to both the child as spectacle and child as subject as it delivers "the points of view that help to put the adult audience back *in the place of the child*" and "take the position of that child to show us what he or she sees . . . to deliver a child's point of view."[15] When she lists a number of World War II films that make "use of the child—as point of view, as image—to drive home the destruction of war,"[16] and includes *Ivan's Childhood* in this list, Lebeau moves in the direction of this chapter. Other recent scholarship explores formal specifics surrounding the child's point of view in the analysis of contemporary films. For example, Emma Wilson speaks of contemporary films that attempt "to offer new representations of a child's subjectivity" and mold "the medium to child perceptions" using certain tropes and devices "associated with child subjectivity."[17] Wilson cites recent films that seek "to show the subjective perceptions" of their child subjects, such as how Veysset uses a close-up that allows the viewer to enter the child's "subjective reality"[18] or uses camera angles to this effect.[19] If Emma Wilson identifies the use of such devices to enter the child's subjectivity in contemporary films, this chapter locates such cinematic devices in Tarkovsky's earlier film *Ivan's Childhood*.

Like children's literature research conceptualizing the dual audience of children and adults addressed within children's literature[20] and theories of autobiography distinguishing between the layering of adult and child selves,[21] contemporary film scholars have begun to attend to the double-voicedness of films about children. In *The Child in Film*, Karen Lury observes, "In each case the child figure is double-voiced; the child's limited and often unconventional view of the world and war is framed by the adult's knowingness and retrospective understanding."[22] Indeed, a film for adults about children necessarily contains both of these perspectives at once. In an article on recent French films on children, Phil Powrie employs Foucault to consider the heterotopic space in such films. He observes: "The child's view defamiliarizes the world . . . [T]he heterotopic space is both 'here' and 'there', combining the recognizable, and the recognizable displaced into a heterotopic elsewhere so that it becomes unrecognizable."[23] Powrie also expands the notion of heterotopic space to consider space-time in films about children: "What makes these films so interesting is that the child's view allows spectators to inhabit both space-times. As spectators, we are, like the children themselves, on a threshold, looking back to our past and looking forwards to the present of our viewing from the place to which we are looking back."[24] Powrie defines this duality as heterospection: "Put more simply, heterospection is being-adult while also being-child, inhabiting two different but complementary space-times."[25] Double-voicedness and heterospection apply to the play of adult and child perspectives, and glimpses of present and past, that coexist in a poetic form in Tarkovsky's *Ivan's Childhood*.

TARKOVSKY'S USES OF THE CHILD'S EYE VIEW

In assuming the child's perspective in his adaptation of Bogomolov's story for the screen, Tarkovsky achieves the defamiliarizing heterospection of which

Powrie speaks by adopting the child's eye view as his own. In so doing, he offers to the film his own personal experiences of childhood and of war. In a 1962 interview, Tarkovsky admits to having made this a film by looking "through the eyes of a person" of his own age, thereby underscoring how he deliberately takes us into the perspective of his own childhood's coeval:

> The search for a new formal structure is always determined by thoughts that demand a new means of expression. For example, it is impossible today to see the war through the eyes of those who consciously experienced it. In my film, I try to see it through the eyes of a person of my age. I am judging the past from a contemporary point of view. I am illustrating what I could have experienced if I had taken part. I have witnessed how war can mentally cripple someone.[26]

The defamiliarizing perspective of childhood assumes a central function in Tarkovsky's critique of war, just as Tarkovsky's own childhood experiences of war and its impact on his father and family colored his own view of the war.[27] As noted earlier, he openly confessed, "I wanted to convey all my hatred of war. I chose childhood because it is what contrasts most with war. The film isn't built upon plot, but rests on the opposition between war and the feelings of the child."[28]

War and childhood thus emerge in direct opposition in Tarkovsky's account. As Maya Turovskaya observes, "what attracted [Tarkovsky] in the subject matter of *Ivan*, was not so much the achievements of the young hero as the terrible significance of what they masked: the destruction of the bright and natural world of childhood, and Ivan's violent and tragic coming of age."[29] Coming of age, however, seems the wrong term in this case, since this is no *Bildungsroman*; rather, Ivan has already been shaped into a monstrously adult child conscripted to war by a desire to avenge what is irretrievably lost. There is no further development possible for the (in Tarkovsky's own phrase) "mentally crippled" Ivan, only death. As Tarkovsky observes in *Sculpting in Time*,

> A third thing moved me to the bottom of my heart: the personality of the young boy. He immediately struck me as a character that had been destroyed, shifted off its axis by the war. Something incalculable, indeed, all the attributes of childhood, had gone irretrievably out of his life. And the thing he had acquired, like an evil gift from the war, in place of what had been his own, was concentrated and heightened within him.[30]

In other words, war has brutally stripped Ivan of his childhood and all he has gained in return is a gift of preternatural sight that proves to be a curse.

At the same time, Tarkovsky counters, or at least contrasts, this wartime reality with idyllic interior experiences of the child. In a radical modification of Bogomolov's original, Tarkovsky adds Ivan's childhood memory or dream sequences to his film adaptation, as well as imaginary episodes and traumatic flashbacks from which Ivan suffers as a result of his experiences and nerves. From the very first scene of the film, which dwells in the natural idyll of Ivan's childhood and predates his direct experience with war and the death of his mother, these augmentations of the story assume the perspective of the child and enter into his interior subjectivity. Unlike the figure of Ivan in Bogomolov's story who remains enigmatic, these additions grant the viewer entry into the hardened Ivan's private personal world of memory and dreams that contrasts maximally with his present reality. Tarkovsky's innovation enhances the story and advances his own rhetorical cause by bringing childhood and war into maximal contrast. They also offer Tarkovsky's own deeply personal interpretation of the enigmatic character of Ivan and achieve a deeper heterospection and doubling of voice and space-time. This dividedness replicates how Ivan's own consciousness is torturously and involuntarily split between the childhood he had lost, traumatic involuntary memories of his past, and the adulthood he strives to embody in his conscious wartime existence.

In *Sculpting in Time*, Tarkovsky remarked, "The most beautiful memories are those of childhood"[31] and confessed that Ivan's dreams derive from his own childhood memories. He notes, "All four dreams, too, are based on quite specific associations. The first, for instance, from start to finish, right up to the words, 'Mum, there's a cuckoo!' is one of my earliest childhood recollections. It was at the time when I was beginning to know the world. I was four."[32] This fact perhaps explains the evocative power of these images and shows how personal Tarkovsky made his film adaptation of Bogomolov's story. Consider here the words of Gaston Bachelard: "By certain of its traits, *childhood lasts all through life* . . . First, childhood never leaves its nocturnal retreats. Within us, a child sometimes comes to watch over us in sleep . . . One needs, and sometimes it is very good, to live with the child which he has been . . . Poets will help us find this living childhood within us, this permanent, durable immobile world."[33] In this sense, adulthood can be characterized by its heterospection insofar as "the durable character of childhood" of which Bachelard speaks offers the retention of childhood through dreams, as in Ivan's traumatized existence.[34] Bachelard's description of childhood memories also resonates with Tarkovsky's remarks that, if there is any realm where the distinction between imagination and memory "is especially difficult, it is the realm of childhood memories, the realm of *beloved images* harbored in memory since childhood."[35] Reflecting on creative work, he adds, "the memory dreams, and reverie remembers. When this reverie of remembering becomes the germ of a poetic work, the complex of memory and imagination becomes more tightly meshed."[36] In this view, Tarkovsky fuses memory and imagination in the childhood consciousness he (re)creates for Ivan in his film. Ivan's dreams prove redolent with poetic symbolism originating in childhood impressions, but they are also colored and enhanced by contrast with the rest of the film. For example, Tarkovsky observes, "We wanted to capture in that scene the child's foreboding of imminent tragedy."[37] Thus even the poetic beauty of the child's interior subjectivity portends tragedy and betrays the reality that surrounds him, like the spider's web fragmenting his face and vision or shadows falling over his brow.

As illustrated in many of the most striking scenes in the film, Tarkovsky's framing often emphasizes the child's aspect, vision, and eyes. The camera often focuses on the child's eyes, thereby enhancing and visually underscoring the film's attempt to enter into the child's perspective. Many scenes dwell upon the expressions of his countenance and, particularly, his expressive large eyes. In one case, Ivan is crying, not out of suffering or pain, nor from fear, since he seemingly knows none; but from the threat to send him away to a safer place, and thereby deprive him of the military service and vengeance he craves. In such scenes, the film displays Ivan's interior experience and affect, as communicated to the film's audience, by his exterior, and particularly his eyes. Often shadows fall over his eyes from the outside, his eyes seem entirely dark, or are darkened around or underneath. The darkness and shadow signify what has taken over his life in a time of war. Even in the idyllic moments or memories that return in his dreams, from their "nocturnal retreats," such shadows fall over his face, brow, and eyes. These signify his doom, like a mark of death, as does the cuckoo as a harbinger of death in the opening scene with his mother.

In the film Tarkovsky also assumes a child's eye view through camera angles that replicate the perspective of a younger person. These defamiliarizing angles compel the viewer to take the disempowered position or naïve perspective of a child in witnessing events. For example, in one image from the film, where Ivan stands behind Kholin and Galtsev, looking up at them, the low camera angle replicates and even exaggerates the angle of the child's vision by looking up at the adults from the other side. It is the perspective of the child that is taken in this low angle, as shown in another scene between these three characters (Figure 4.1). Other scenes also employ an oddly low or upward camera angle, often slightly below the boy, in order to focus on his face or to frame his form with ominous surroundings, symbolically penning him in and pointedly threatening his existence. Particularly noteworthy in this respect is a striking scene of Ivan surrounded and framed by the radiantly angled points of the timbers that remain in the old man's burned-down home. It achieves its effect by being shot from a low angle that emphasizes this oppressive and threatening superstructure, as demonstrated at the end of this sequence (Figure 4.2). Such images disempower the spectator too and force the audience into a subservient and vulnerable position, as if small and cowering as well. The camera often privileges this naïve viewpoint, looking up at Ivan or other characters through the use of an at times disconcerting and unusual angle that replicates a child's eye view.[38]

Figure 4.1 Ivan with Kholin and Galtsev in *Ivan's Childhood*.

Figure 4.2 Ivan in burned ruins in *Ivan's Childhood*.

It is from the same low angle that the viewer may observe the religious fresco on the wall of the church ruin behind Kholin, when he smokes before Ivan's final trip over the river near the end of the film. It is a naïve perspective that looks upward, as if reverently, at the beloved parental surrogate of sorts, as a piece of timber and cigarette burn instead of a candle before an icon or in church. Meanwhile, the iconic depiction of mother and child—Mary and Jesus with their bright halos—that remains on the church wall behind him visibly exposes the fact that the men's military quarters are the ruins of a church, thus illustrating the complete dissolution of civilization. This holy sanctuary clearly has been violated by the enemy before, having become a place of torment for captives awaiting execution; evidently its sanctity no longer obtains in the hell of war. Moreover, its representation of maternal love and the embrace of parent and child in the realm of God contrasts maximally with Ivan's reality.

At the same time, however, the torment, death, and martyrdom of the adult Jesus, who is depicted here in infancy, compares with that of Ivan and what he has and will suffer. Indeed, in an early scene, after Ivan has completed his mission, the sleeping boy is cradled in the arms of lieutenant Galtsev in the limp posture of a child who has completely surrendered to sleep. Yet the scene also has a deathly aspect, in the way the boy's thin limbs dangle down, as if a *pietà*— where Mary cradles Jesus's lifeless body taken from the crucifix. Indeed, as a child martyr, Ivan's unruly bright shock of hair often resembles a halo. Ivan's representation by child actor Nikolai Burlyaev in some respects also resembles Nesterov's painting *The Vision to the Youth Bartholomew*. But this comparison is ironic, since the knowledge Bartholomew, the future St Sergius, receives is the gift of book learning, while Ivan's military knowledge and gifts as a scout prove a curse. Ivan's keen vision is not cosmological or prophetic, but simply reports the movement of the enemy. It fails to foresee his own capture and death, thus dooming him to repeat the fate of those who scrawled a final plea for vengeance on the wall of the church.

CHILD AS SUBJECT OR SPECTACLE?

After Ivan again goes over the river and disappears from view, we witness a final episode in Ivan's life, after the fact, through the documentary evidence of a still photograph (Figure 4.3). In the screenplay, Galtsev's "heart freezes. Ivan is looking out at him from a photograph glued to a form. He is looking up from under his eyebrows, frowning, full of hatred. There is a dark bruise on his left cheek."[39] The theme of Ivan's gaze recurs once more: "Ivan's face looks out from the photograph. The eyes are those of an adult, filled with wild hatred."[40] Through the visual medium of film, the spectator sees this Gestapo photograph recording a final moment in the life of Ivan, as he glares back at the camera.

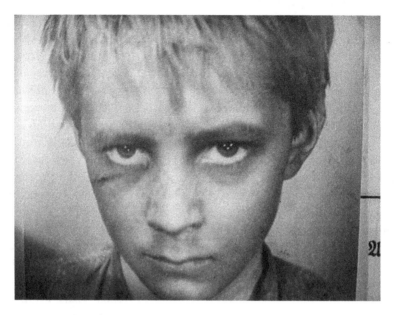

Figure 4.3 Final photograph of Ivan after capture in *Ivan's Childhood*.

Like famous documentary images, this image provokes the conscience. In *Childhood and Cinema*, Lebeau compares the photograph and memory, and cites Susan Sontag on memory as a "freeze frame," noting that "such images may well have a unique capacity to haunt us [. . .] as evidence of the destruction of children and childhoods, cultures and communities."[41] The final image of Ivan's stunted and truncated life and his intense gaze back at the camera indeed sums up the battered child's perspective on the world, both broken and defiant, as he faces imminent death. This image emphasizes the dark, shadowed eyes and his inscrutable brow. Even in this, Tarkovsky stays true to the spirit of Bogomolov's story, which offers its final vision of Ivan and his eyes: "I knew him immediately by his high-cheekboned face and large, wide-spaced eyes—I never had seen such widely spaced eyes. He looked warily from under his brow, like a bull, as he had then at our meeting in the dugout on the bank of the Dneiper. A bruise darkened his left cheek, under his cheekbone."[42] In the context of this chapter's examination of the child's eye view, it proves noteworthy that the angle of this photograph depicts Ivan from a definitively adult eye view. The high camera angle points downward at the child, as indicated by his upward gaze and the liquidly dark pupils accentuated by the whites of his eyes below. Suddenly this angle, his defiant glower, and downturned chin make the child appear younger than his years, a small child again. At the same time, his ferocious and unforgiving look levels an accusation at his captors, and all who witness it, including the spectator.

The photograph at the end of *Ivan's Childhood* visually gives voice to the unspeakable final moments of Ivan's life and mutely speaks volumes to the adult spectator. In *The Child in Film*, Karen Lury observes that the child figure as witness or participant in events provides a form of "prosopopoeia: that is, a conversation between the living (the adult survivor) and the dead (the child self, who may or may not be alive at the end of the film)."[43] Yet "what is being projected on to the 'dead' (here the child) may not be true. This is because just as the dead cannot really speak to the living, the child cannot speak 'properly' to the adult they have since become. Whereas the dead are beyond or without speech, the child cannot speak because as a child they are (or were) yet to become fully articulate (sensible)."[44] In this mute ekphrastic moment, the film offers its concluding critique of war from a child's eye view and on behalf of every child who suffers as a result of war, as Andrei Tarkovsky also did personally, if not so directly.

Yet both story and film prove complicit in constructing Ivan as a martyr and thereby making Ivan's death inevitable. As Tarkovsky declares: "First there was the fate of the hero, which we follow right up to his death. Of course many plots have been constructed in this way, but it is by no means the case, as it is with *Ivan*, that the *denouement* is inherent in the conception and comes about through its own inner necessity. Here the hero's death has a particular significance."[45] A martyr's end is indeed inevitable, especially in the retrospective account of a martyr's life, which necessarily ends with death. In the story of Ivan, however, the significance of that death proves very different. Tarkovsky elaborates, "At the point where, with other authors, there would have been a comforting follow-up, this story ends. Nothing follows."[46] It is precisely in this absence that meaning lies for Tarkovsky: "In Bogomolov's story, this stage, cut off by death, becomes the final and only one. Within it is concentrated the entire content of Ivan's life, its tragic motive power. There is no room for anything else: that was the startling fact that made one unexpectedly and acutely aware of the monstrousness of war."[47] The film thus concludes with a focus on Ivan's deprivation, torment, and death for the sake of its rhetorical message.

Indeed, the cinematic eye revels in Ivan's sufferings throughout the film for dramatic or rhetorical effect. The impact of the visual delivery of such content, in contrast to the verbal description in Bogomolov's story, proves more horrifying. As Vicky Lebeau observes in *Childhood and Cinema*, "As an institution that pleasures the eye, cinema has a complex, often fraught, relation to images of suffering—images to which, from its very origins, it is deeply indebted. How do you film the death of a child? What wishes are at work in the visual archive of a child in pain?"[48] The numerous close-ups in the film that fixate on the suffering child's experience, face, and eyes indeed archive Ivan's pain. Considering also the fraught relations of adult and child,[49] we might also ask, "what is the child *for* cinema? What does cinema *want* of the child?"[50] If, in

Tarkovsky's film, the suffering child functions to offer a critique of war itself, then Tarkovsky himself conscripts the child to this cause, even if the child's death here serves to deliver an ideological message against war.

This conscription of Ivan also proves problematic, since one cannot disentangle the "collusion between horror and pleasure, politics and pain, in the various uses of a child's suffering on screen."[51] Does Tarkovsky's *Ivan's Childhood* offer audiences "child as subject" through its uses of a child's eye view, or does Ivan emerge as "child as spectacle"?[52] Does the visual display of mute childhood suffering give voice to the child as subject so displayed? Or does it objectify the child and exploit his voicelessness and usurp his voice? As Lebeau observes in *Childhood and Cinema*, the cinematic child investigates the limits of language and death:

> [T]he spectacle of the child on screen has been one site of such negotiation, integral to the modern investigation of children and childhoods, its attempts to capture—to tell, to give image to—the child. No surprise, then, that infancy and death have been described as the two limits of an aesthetic grounded in knowing and showing the mind of another, or that the child should so often bring us up against the limits of language, of knowledge, of sexuality, of death. Such limits are inseparable from the concept of the *infans*, from modern constructions of the difference of the child, as at once known and not known.[53]

For Tarkovsky, the child serves to navigate the unspeakable horrors of war and the significance of death. Through earlier attempts to take the child's eye view, as well as this final visual display, Tarkovsky lets the life and death of Ivan speak for itself, while inviting the spectator to see through the child's accusatory child's eye view to critique the world as it is.

The ritual or psychoanalytical significance of the death of a child, as seen at the end of *Ivan's Childhood*, is highlighted by psychoanalyst Serge Leclaire, when he writes, "A child's death is unbearable,"[54] and observes that in a child's death, which simply cannot be, "We rediscover the sacred horror."[55] This same response is detectable in the thoughts a journalist who once penned, "You don't bomb babies. You don't shoot children. You don't single them out for hatred," but then corrected himself, "this is a sentimental delusion. Babies are bombed. Children are shot," and concluded, "Children are waged war upon and wage war themselves."[56] From this perspective, Bogomolov's fiction and Tarkovsky's film, however fictionalized or artificial, speak the truth about the world, where children do suffer, fight, and die in the wars waged by adults. Lury makes a similar point, when she states, "children caught up in war are not simply witnesses but agents" and "neither just the mute and traumatised witnesses to this war, nor merely its innocent victims. They also lived in the war [. . .] the war invaded their imaginations and the war raged inside them."[57] This distinction highlights the issue of agency in Tarkovsky's film, where Ivan achieves preternatural agency as a military scout in a time of war, but remains powerless to escape his inevitable death. Yet his death proves significant, since, as Lebeau notes, "the death of a child, the threat to a child, can breach the fictional frame of the image, reaching out towards the spectator" with a threat that provokes fear for the lives of other children.[58] From this perspective, the still photograph, with its "unreadable face of the child,"[59] ekphrastically opens up toward the audience by radically confronting the spectator with the still image, which demands to be read although it signifies only mutely.

In the final photograph, Ivan functions like a child witness to an adult world, who attests to and protests the atrocity of war and terror, while wordlessly forcing such reflections upon the audience. Recall how for Deleuze, as Sutton paraphrases, the child witness is one who "in the adult world [. . .] is affected by a certain motor helplessness, but one which makes him all the more capable of seeing and hearing."[60] For cinema, the child also functions to make the audience more capable of seeing and hearing as well, by enhancing affect and allowing different modes of vision. As Szaloky observes of Balázs, "A child's experience is assumed to be less distancing and ocular-centric and more immediate and immersive than that of adults. It is 'the heart not the eye,' feelings and intuitions, rather than views, which guide the child's-eye-view as manifest in the close-up."[61] In this sense, the final close-up image of Ivan speaks to the heart and not to the eye, as it takes a child's eye view upon the child himself. Sutton further reflects on how, "Thus for Deleuze, the child remains ultimately passive, despite the active spectatorial affects that his or her optical witness might provoke."[62] Perhaps this passivity and privileged optical witness even enhances the effect upon (and affect of) the audience. If so, perhaps it is this that cinema wants of the child.

The true tragedy of the film, then, becomes Ivan's fundamental passivity and objectification as a child in the arena of adults and war, despite his fierce desire to achieve adult agency in the world. Rather than achieving agency or voice, he is captured and forever silenced, reduced to one deathly still photograph. Although Tarkovsky immortalizes in the film his own deeply personal childhood memories and impressions of war, and seeks to grant entry into the child's eye view in multiple dimensions in *Ivan's Childhood*, he concludes the film with a mute visual representation of Ivan's sufferings that also exposes the film's visual exploitation of the child. Lury cites André Bazin's implication that we perceive the otherness of children "as entirely open to interpretation rather than 'other'"[63] and that "in many films about war adults use children as a blank screen on to which they can project adult emotions and fears."[64] Ivan's childhood, Ivan, his face, and his eyes function precisely as such a screen for the cinematic projections of adult ideology. He is no actual child, since as is so often the case with the child in film, "children are often ciphers for adult anxieties, fantasies and fears."[65]

Tarkovsky thus uses the juxtaposition of childhood and war and a critical child's eye view in *Ivan's Childhood* in order to underscore the brutality, pointlessness, and suffering of war. The final images of Ivan in the film, including in the final photograph that preserves the unforgiving gaze of the child's eyes before his certain death, make this point abundantly clear. Yet it also levels a universal accusation at everyone and anyone who exploits or victimizes children, whatever the cause to which childhood is conscripted or the rhetorical or aesthetic aim of that exploitation. From a child's eye view, this image condemns all who see children without seeing them or project their own adult aims upon the child, including the filmmaker or spectators making meaning out of what they see.[66]

NOTES

1. Andrei Tarkovsky, *Ivanovo detstvo/Ivan's Childhood*, Criterion Collection (Moscow: Mosfilm Studios, 1962).
2. John Gianvito (ed.), *Andrei Tarkovsky Interviews* (Jackson: University of Mississippi Press, 2006), 4.
3. Vladimir Bogomolov, "Ivan," *Roman, povesti, rasskazy* (Moscow: Russkaia kniga, 1994), 409–66.
4. Maya Turovskaya, *Tarkovsky: Cinema as Poetry*, trans. by Natasha Ward (Boston: Faber & Faber, 1989), 31.
5. Denise Youngblood remarks, "*Ivan's Childhood* is more than a film about one child's childhood; it is a film about the fate of all children during the Second World War. (Tarkovskii's use of the generic Russian name 'Ivan', the name given protagonists in most folktales, is one important clue.)" Denise Youngblood, "Post-Stalinist Cinema and the Myth of World War II: Tarkovskii's *Ivan's Childhood* (1962) and Klimov's *Come and See* (1985)," *Historical Journal of Film, Radio and Television* 14.4 (1994): 416. Quoted in Karen Lury, *The Child in Film: Tears, Fears and Fairy Tales* (New York: I. B.Tauris, 2010), 107.
6. Bogomolov, "Ivan," 465–6.
7. Ibid., 409–10.
8. Ibid., 417.
9. Cf. Lury, *The Child in Film*, 114.
10. Ibid., 107.
11. Béla Bálazs, *Early Film Theory, Visible Man and The Spirit of Film*, edited by Erica Carter, trans. by Rodney Livingstone (New York: Berghahn Books, 2010), 62 (italics in the original).
12. Melinda Szaloky, "Close-up," *The Routledge Encyclopedia of Film Theory*, eds. Edward Branigan and Warren Buckland (New York: Routledge, 2014), 95.
13. Ibid.
14. Gilles Deleuze, *Cinema 2: The Time-Image*, trans. by Hugh Tomlinson and Roberta Galeta (Minneapolis: University of Minnesota Press, 1989), 3. For more on Deleuze and children, see Anna Catherine Hickey-Moody, "Deleuze's Children," *Educational Philosophy and Theory* 45.3 (2013): 272–86.

15. Vicky Lebeau, *Childhood and Cinema* (London: Reaktion Books, 2008), 41.
16. Ibid., 141.
17. Emma Wilson, "Children, emotion and viewing in contemporary European film," *Screen* 46.3 (Autumn 2005): 332.
18. Ibid., 339.
19. Ibid.
20. Barbara Wall, *The Narrator's Voice: The Dilemma of Children's Fiction* (London: Macmillan, 1991).
21. Philippe Lejeune, *On Autobiography* (Minneapolis: University of Minnesota Press, 1989).
22. Lury, *The Child in Film*, 109.
23. Phil Powrie, "Unfamiliar places: 'heterospection' and recent French films on children," *Screen* 46.3 (Autumn 2005): 350–1.
24. Ibid., 352.
25. Ibid.
26. Gianvito, *Andrei Tarkovsky Interviews*, 8.
27. Lyudmila Boyadzhieva, *Andrei Tarkovsky: A Life on the Cross* (London: Glagoslav Publications, 2014), 38.
28. Gianvito, *Andrei Tarkovsky Interviews*, 4.
29. Turovskaya, *Tarkovsky: Cinema as Poetry*, 31.
30. Tarkovsky, *Sculpting in Time*, 17.
31. Ibid., 29.
32. Ibid.
33. Gaston Bachelard, *The Poetics of Reverie: Childhood, Language, and the Cosmos*, trans. by Daniel Russell (Boston: Beacon Press, 1971), 20.
34. Ibid., 20.
35. Tarkovsky, *Sculpting in Time*, 20.
36. Bachelard, *The Poetics of Reverie*, 20.
37. Ibid., 31.
38. Even in the absence of Ivan, such as in the famous scene where Kholin embraces Masha over a ditch, the camera angle comes from below, so the naïve perspective and child's eye view goes beyond obvious motivations.
39. Andrei Tarkovsky, *Collected Screenplays*, trans. by William Powell and Natasha Synessios (London: Faber & Faber, 1999), 124.
40. Ibid., 124.
41. Lebeau, *Childhood and Cinema*, 138–9.
42. Bogomolov, "Ivan," 465.
43. Lury, *The Child in Film*, 111.
44. Ibid.
45. Tarkovsky, *Sculpting in Time*, 16.
46. Ibid., 16–17.
47. Ibid., 17.
48. Lebeau, *Childhood and Cinema*, 19.
49. Cf. Rose, *The Case of Peter Pan or The Impossibility of Children's Fiction*, 1984.
50. Lebeau, *Childhood and Cinema*, 12.
51. Ibid., 19.
52. Ibid.
53. Ibid., 84–5.
54. Serge Leclaire, *A Child is Being Killed: On Primary Narcissism and the Death Drive*, trans. by Marie-Claude Hays (Stanford: Stanford University Press, 1998), 2. Cf. Lebeau, *Childhood and Cinema*, 137.

55. Ibid., 2.

56. Quoted in Lebeau, *Childhood and Cinema*, 137.

57. Lury, *The Child in Film*, 144.

58. Lebeau, *Childhood and Cinema*, 157.

59. Lury, *The Child in Film*, 109.

60. Cf. Deleuze, *Cinema 2*, 3. Quoted in Paul Sutton, "The *bambino negato* or missing child of contemporary Italian cinema," *Screen* 46.3 (Autumn 2005): 357.

61. Szaloky, "Close-up," 95. Cf. Bálazs, *Early Film Theory*, 56.

62. Sutton, "The *bambino negato* or missing child of contemporary Italian cinema," 357.

63. Lury, *The Child in Film*, 106.

64. Ibid.

65. Ibid.

66. I am grateful to Peter Bloom, Michael Brodski, Oksana Bulgakowa, and Sergey Toymentsev for their suggestions and references.

CHAPTER 5

The Truth of Direct Observation: *Andrei Rublev* and the Documentary Style of Soviet Cinema in the 1960s

Zdenko Mandušić

As the officially unfinished *Andrei Rublev* was being denounced in 1967 for excessive violence, nudity, and animal cruelty, as well as its sheer length, Andrei Tarkovsky wrote the essay "Imprinted Time," defining his theory of film and the aesthetics of his troubled production. Unlike his previous texts, "Imprinted Time" was a scholarly, critical essay, which presented Tarkovsky's conception of cinema's ability to capture an impression of time, this unique capacity defining the medium's specificity. Tarkovsky's claims in "Imprinted Time" are notably grounded in terms associated with the production of newsreels or cine-chronicles and early non-fiction filmmaking. Tarkovsky asserted: "I see chronicle as the ultimate cinema; for me it's not a way of filming but a way of reconstructing and recreating life."[1] Associating the production of *Andrei Rublev* to cine-chronicles, Tarkovksy wrote of wanting to reconstruct for a modern audience the real world of the fifteenth century, with the goal of achieving "the truth of direct observation, what one might almost term physiological truth."[2] The appeal to physiology brings to mind nineteenth-century physiological sketches, which were supposed to provide accurate, almost scientific observations of reality and portrayals of everyday life.[3] Along with this claim to documentary observation, Tarkovsky's veneration of the cine-chronicle raises questions about the confluence of historical recreation and the documentary modes of production. Furthermore, such statements connect Tarkovsky's cinema aesthetics and his theory of film to discourses over cinema's relationship to reality within post-Stalinist Soviet cinema and beyond to developments in international film style.

Over the course of the 1960s Soviet feature-length fiction films were increasingly discussed in terms of their perceived documentary qualities. Along with Tarkovsky, other filmmakers considered the cine-chronicle as a model for modern filmmaking. Andrei Mikhalkov-Kochalovsky, Tarkovsky's friend and co-writer of *The Steamroller and the Violin* (*Katok i skripka,* 1961), *Ivan's Childhood* (*Ivanovo detstvo,* 1962), and *Andrei Rublev,* claimed that ideally he would like to have filmed his second film, which came to be called *The Story of Asia Kliachina, Who Loved but Did Not Marry* (*Istoriia Asi Kliachinoi, kotoraia liubila, da ne vyshla zamuzh*), as a cine-chronicle (*khronikal'nyi fil'm*).[4] What was described as the collision of fictional and factual interests was usually addressed with the abstract noun *dokumental'nost'* ("documentary-ness"), and sometimes *dokumentalizm.* In his text Tarkovsky describes the new stylistic trend in Soviet cinema using the term *khronikal'nost'* ("chronicle-ness"), in reference to newsreel films as well as the historical registers of events and the years of their occurrence. As he locates in the cine-chronicle the origin of cinema's ability to depict time, Tarkovsky also seems to be playing on the origin of *khronika* and *khronikal'nost'* from the Greek word *khronikos* "of time" and *khronos* "time." Although no uniform definition was adopted, the appeal to veracity and authenticity through these terms expressed a renewed engagement with the problem of referentiality and how cinema could be used to provide accurate knowledge of the world.

Beyond his textual and semantic references, Tarkovsky's engagement with the discourse on *dokumenta'nost'* is also made apparent by the fact that "Imprinted Time" was first published in the 1967 annual edition of *Problems of Film Art* (*Voprosy kinoiskusstva*), alongside several other essays, which discussed documentary filmmaking and the new documentary style of Soviet cinema. These articles included Iakov Varshavskii's "Documentary and Fictional Cinema" ("Dokumental'noe i igrovoe") and N. Abramov's "Man in Documentary Cinema" ("Chelovek v dokumental'nom fil'me"). Along with the Soviet discursive and stylistic context, statements regarding cine-chronicles and the observational-documentary mode of production in "Imprinted Time" relate *Andrei Rublev* and Tarkovsky's cinema aesthetics to developments in international cinema, specifically the *cinéma vérité* and direct cinema movements in France, Canada, and the United States.

Russian film scholar Evgenii Margolit characterizes the documentary realism of Soviet cinema in the 1960s as an aesthetic of trust in the reality of film image.[5] His work provides a global overview of the visual and narrative style of Soviet films in this period, associating *dokumental'nost'* with post-Stalinist developments in Soviet culture. Josephine Woll relates the documentary style of the 1960s, especially Tarkovsky's stylistic choices for *Andrei Rublev,* to the desire of directors to "generate their own singular vision and version of [reality]."[6] Maya Turovskaya doubts that Tarkovsky really wanted to produce a historical account of medieval Russia in the manner that cine-chronicles/newsreels reconstruct life. He only wanted, claims Turovskaya, for his vision of Rublev's Russia to look like a documentary. "In fact, it was only in the most philosophical sense that Tarkovsky's ideal form of cinema was newsreel footage. In practice, even the precisely dated episodes of *Andrei Rublev* were variations on a theme: his personal perception of the subject, successfully made to look like a documentary observation."[7] Expanding on such previous work, this essay will locate Tarkovsky's film poetics within the Soviet film discourse regarding *dokumental'nost'*, examining his writing and filmmaking as direct participation and responses to debates over *dokumental'nost'*, cinema's relationship to reality, and the veracity of the film image.

Although Tarkovsky later revised and incorporated "Imprinted Time" as a chapter into his book *Sculpting in Time* (1986), this essay will focus on the original 1967 version of the text, approaching it as a historical document. Combining the investigation of discursive frameworks with Tarkovsky's film poetics and theoretical claims, I argue that what he wrote in "Imprinted Time" and staged in *Andrei Rublev* constitute responses to contemporary claims about the reality of fiction films, which competed to define the new documentary style in Soviet cinema. Delineating his film poetics, Tarkovsky associated the documentary veracity of the film image with the viewer's temporal experience of cinema, revising, in the process, what it meant for films to document and represent reality. Moreover, while most Soviet films referenced in this discourse had contemporary plots, *Andrei Rublev* and Tarkovsky's theory of film connect *dokumental'nost'* to questions of historical representation.

THE DISCOURSE ON *DOCUMENTAL'NOST'*

Growing distrust in cinema's representation of reality motivated the new documentary style of Soviet cinema. Nikita Khrushchev provoked this crisis at the Twentieth Party Congress in February 1956 when he repeatedly cited

Figure 5.1 Watching the Jester's performance in *Andrei Rublev*.

the complicity of Soviet cinema in the veneration of the Stalin cult of personality. Even though Khrushchev cited other offending forms of cultural production, including novels and historical studies, he specifically indicted films of the late-Stalinist period, such as Mikhail Chiuareli's *The Fall of Berlin* (*Padenie Berlina*, 1949), for creating a false image of Soviet history and society, and for promoting an idealized image of the leader.[8] Late-Stalinist films about the Great Patriotic War were especially problematic because they depicted Stalin as infallible and omniscient, controlling the outcome of distant battles from the Kremlin. These films were defined as fictionalized documentaries (*khudozhestvenno-dokumental'nyie fil'my*), which were supposed to objectively represent the war and some of which integrated documentary footage.[9] Before Khrushchev, Andre Bazin criticized the mythical representation of Stalin in these films and their corruption of historical representation in his essay "The Stalin Myth in Soviet Cinema," written in 1950.[10] Bazin specifically called into question the purported historical realism of films such as *The Battle of Stalingrad* (*Stalingradskaia bitva*, Vladimir Petrov 1949–50), which portray Stalin ultimately in control of historical events. Six years later, Khrushchev's speech compromised the documentary claims of these films and brought into question the use of film to depict historical reality.

The Twentieth Party Congress prompted film critics and filmmakers to question how cinema could be used to provide knowledge of the world.[11] New films subsequently presented previously forbidden themes and stylistic innovations that altered the relationship between the viewer and the screen. Critics responded by delineating stylistic differences between late-Stalinist cinema and the cinema of the Thaw, characterizing films of the late 1940s and early 1950s as pompous and decorative (*pompezno-dekorativnyi*), while discussing the work of young filmmakers during the Thaw in terms of their simplicity and authenticity.[12] Developing from this differentiation, the discourse regarding *dokumental'nost'* featured attempts to discern the formal, visual, and narrative strategies of the new style. One of the central concerns of these efforts was what separates documentary from fictional films. Filmmakers and critics addressed multiple methods of incorporating elements of documentary filmmaking into fiction films, including the use of equipment developed for documentary productions, the incorporation of documentary sequences within fiction films, and the imitation of documentary visual strategies to film staged or rehearsed events. According to Evgenii Margolit, select filmmakers in the 1960s "were discovering for themselves in documentary films a source of innovative artistic strategies, which would completely revive the language of cinematography in general."[13]

Thaw-era film critics discussed the new style of documentary realism as the combination of two approaches to representing reality. Documentary filmmaking suggested objectivity, evidence, dispassion, and fact, while fiction films implied subjectivity, emotion, and individual voices.[14] According to this dichotomy, documentary filmmaking "attends to the analytical observation of reality," offering direct access and a scientific instrumentality, whereas fiction film "readily deals with openly subjective representations."[15] In this regard, documentary techniques were the panacea for Soviet cinema's representational crisis, by providing alternatives to aesthetics associated with late-Stalinist cinema. Particular formal elements were identified as denoting documentary realism, including "capricious and even illogical editing, very mobile and at first a seemingly senselessly wandering camera, careless pans and camera movement in general, and especially careless composition of the shot, far removed from any conventions of painting."[16] Mikhail Romm emphasized the ultimate benefit of these new methods, writing that the purpose behind the use of these elements was "an attempt to return to film its original *dokumental'nost'*, to restore the viewer's belief that a shot is before all else a material fact recorded on film, an authentic event, not an imagined patch of a tailored whole."[17] The goal of restoring belief in film images fixated on the Soviet viewer and their relationship to the screen. In this regard, the reproduction of documentary aesthetics in fiction films was an appeal to the viewer's perception of films and the evaluation of what they viewed and heard as being either realistic or misleading.

The discourse over Soviet cinema's new documentary style looked past the Stalinist fictionalized documentaries, drawing on earlier polemics regarding film's essential purpose and its relation to reality. The central concepts of the discourse as well as how documentary and the artistic-played film related to each other originated in the virulent debates of the 1920s, which revolved around non-fiction films, "cine-facts," documents, and archives. The quarrel between Sergei Eisenstein and Dziga Vertov provides a model for understanding the use of documentary elements as not simply an aesthetic mannerism, consisting of grafting methods of documentary filmmaking onto fiction cinema. This was the charge Vertov leveled against Eisenstein, claiming that *Strike* (*Stachka*, 1925) was "cut and filmed in imitation of *Kino-Pravda* and *Kino-Eye*."[18] Responding to this attack, Eisenstein positioned himself as moving beyond cine-chronicles in terms of organizing filmed materials to affect viewers as opposed to just attracting their attention. After characterizing Vertov's method as "montage of fragments of real life," Eisenstein defined his own approach as "snatching fragments from our surroundings according to a conscious and predetermined plan calculated to launch them at the audience in the only correct combination that would subjugate this audience, infect it with the appropriate associations with an eye to motivating it ideologically."[19] In his drafts for the opening volume of *The History of Soviet Cinema*, Eisenstein would go on to define the chronicle as the initial stage of the artistic film.[20] Choosing to reenact history instead of using factual elements, Eisenstein, in the words of François Albera, "made the chronicle explode, seizing hold of it and giving it a new expressive quality in *Strike* and *Potemkin*."[21] Eisenstein himself stated "*Potemkin* looks like a chronicle (or newsreel) but functions as a drama."[22]

In the post-Stalinist period, critics referred to *Strike* and *Potemkin* as examples of film poetics being "enriched" and "revitalized" through use of documentary methods in artistic cinema, while documentary films *Turkskib* (Victor Turin, 1929) and *Salt for Svanetiia* (*Sol' Svanetii*, Mikhail Kalatozov, 1930) were held up as examples which combined subjective poetics and documentary objectivity.[23] Echoing the Thaw-era veneration of the 1920s Avant-Garde, Eisenstein's early films were promoted as legitimizing precedents for the post-Stalinist *dokuemntal'nost'*, which was, in turn, traced through the various absorptions of documentary methods and equipment in the production of fiction films. Frequently cited was Sergei Urusevskii's use of the Konvas-Avtomat handheld camera, initially designed for documentary filmmaking, as well as Iurii Ekel'chik's use of the wide-angle 18mm and 22mm lenses on the production of *The First Echelon* (*Pervyi eshelon*, Mikhail Kalatozov, 1955).[24] According to Roman Il'in, Urusevskii's and Ekel'chik's borrowings produced shots which "resembled in their substance, materiality, and texture those [views] we know well from life, with a greater amount of specificity and detail."[25] More than just adopting equipment, Urusevskii was especially credited with replicating the visual aesthetics of documentary films. Regarding *The Cranes Are Flying* (*Letiat zhuravli*, Mikhail Kalatozov, 1957), Iakov Varshavskii wrote that the cinematographer "takes up the 'Konvas-avtomat' camera, the trade instrument of a newsreel-cinematographer, and shoots a feature film as if he's reporting from the street, moving in the crowd, observing his characters from the heart of action."[26] In this manner, documentary aspects were associated with creating the impression of immediacy.

Marlen Khutsiev's *I am Twenty* (*Mne dvadtsat' let*, 1964) was credited with introducing a distinct form of poetic documentary-ness through its depiction of Moscow.[27] The film features multiple sequences shot on location of characters traversing the streets of Moscow. One particular sequence, in which the film's protagonist follows his romantic interest through the city, was shot with a hidden camera amid real crowds of people, some of whom puzzlingly look straight at the film apparatus they have spotted. As Natal'ia Baladina claims, Khutsiev and his cinematographer Margarita Pilikhina here utilize Dizga Vertov's "Life-Caught-Unawares" shooting strategy to map their fictional narrative onto the material reality of Moscow.[28] Mikhail Romm's *Ordinary Fascism* (*Obyknovennyi fashizm*, 1965), which was assembled from a vast trove of Nazi documentary footage as well as contemporary footage of

Moscow children and students, was described as "destroying the wall between feature and documentary film, and enriching the latter with artistic passion, brave new ideas, and emotional color."[29]

Film historians have associated developments in Soviet cinema of the 1960s with both a regional, East European documentary style and the wider documentary trend in France's *cinéma vérité*, Britain's free film movement and the New York School.[30] In contemporaneous discussions, Soviet *dokumental'nost'* was positioned as a response to *cinéma vérité* experiments in France and the United States. At the 1962 conference of the Union of Filmmakers, film critic Aleksandr Karaganov defined this opposition in terms reminiscent of Eisenstein's criticism of Vertov. Western filmmakers were said to desire naturalism in their films, "the camera capturing life as it is, the artist not interfering in the action, the film reproducing parts of life, snatched from (life's) flow, taken in all their raw naturalness."[31] Soviet filmmakers, on the other hand, were said to depict and interpret reality. In "Imprinted Time," Tarkovsky vaguely criticizes Jean Rouch and Edgar Morin's *Chronicle of a Summer* (*Chronique d'un été*, 1961), Shirley Clark's *The Connection* (1961), and John Cassavetes' *Shadows* (1959) for an "inadequate adherence to principle" and not consistently pursuing "complete and unconditional factual truth." Soviet critics, on the other hand, attacked *cinéma vérité*'s claim to objective representation of reality, arguing that reality filmed directly does not fully represent reality's truth. In order to reveal the "meaningful content of unrehearsed reality," filmmakers had to decipher this reality and direct the viewer's perception.[32] Dziga Vertov's writings were mobilized as the theoretical grounds for this critique as a way to posit the preeminence of Soviet cinema and to largely dispel the claim that *cinéma vérité* filmmakers such as Rouch and Morin were continuing the Vertovian approach. However, some *vérité* films were celebrated. Rostislav Iurenev praised Chris Marker and Pierre Lhomme's *The Lovely Month of May* (*Le Joli Mai*, 1962) for its Vertovian methods associated with the film's large collection of ordinary Parisians, Marker's active interventions in the reality being filmed, and the use of montage to produce semantic juxtapositions.[33]

While Soviet critics disparaged *cinéma vérité* for not interpreting reality, many Soviet films associated with the documentary style also faced criticism in studio discussion, from film industry bureaucrats, and in newspapers as well. Along with *Andrei Rublev*, a host of other films were accused of "naturalism," the catch-all charge, which implied an uncritical presentation of reality, including Khutsiev's *I am Twenty*, which had to be considerably altered, and Konchalovskii's *The Story of Asia Kliachina* and Kira Muratova's *Brief Encounters* (*Korotkie vstrechi*, 1967), both of which were shelved. Censorship halted the stylistic development of documentary realism in Soviet fiction films and hindered critical reflections.

Figure 5.2 Watching the persecution of pagan peasants in *Andrei Rublev*.

THE DOCUMENTARY DILEMMA OF *ANDREI RUBLEV*

Tarkovsky is reported to have ideally wanted to film *Andrei Rublev* as if a hidden camera was placed on the streets of a medieval town.[34] This statement speaks to his desire to avoid the look of stylized historical illusions in favor of achieving the appearance of direct observation. The visual strategy of *Andrei Rublev* combines overt aesthetic choices, deceptive filmmaking techniques, and Tarkovsky's signature long takes to produce a sense of time and space of medieval Russia. Tarkovsky's pursuit of the look of authenticity collided with anxiety over historical accuracy. Although he and Konchalovsky claimed to have diligently studied historical documentation and scholarship on the period, Tarkovsky did not want *Andrei Rublev* to be scrutinized from the perspectives of science, historiography, or art history.[35] The film, however, provoked a fervent debate about historical inaccuracies and Tarkovsky's deviation from the historical biographical film genre. Responding to this line of criticism, Tarkovsky shifted the terms of discussion away from historical accuracy toward the use of historical material as an occasion to express personal ideas and create contemporary characters.

The goal was to construct a believable medieval reality, through the experience of time and perception of space, which would be free of any jarring markers of historical stylization. The film's costume, dialogue, depictions of the medieval way of life, and even architecture were not supposed "to give any sense of being relic or of antiquarian rarity."[36] The language spoken in the film was a neutral-contemporary Russian dialogue, with the exception of the Church-Slavonic words Kiril utilized as part of his self-stylization.[37] Instead of museum artifacts, Rublev's Russia is further constituted by means of simple and tangible materials, such as bread, milk, canvas, sheepskin and fur, log walls, white stone, plaster, apples, and cabbage.[38] These objects constitute a generalizable sensory texture, and even though the title cards locate them in history by giving the year and location of the film's episodes, their lack of specificity produces "a timeless setting somewhere in the past."[39]

Film color in *Andrei Rublev* further indicates Tarkovsky's attitude toward depicting Rublev's historical reality. He explained the transition from black and white to color at the end of the film in terms of black-and-white cinema being more realistic, due to the fact that film color had not yet attained the stage of realism, remaining an exotic effect.[40] Despite Josephine Woll's claim that Tarkovsky's decision to depict medieval Russia in black and white represented a desire to generate his own singular vision and version of reality, his visual strategy accorded with the documentary impulse of the 1960s. Tarkovsky asserted that black-and-white film stock was more suitable for representing Rublev's "everyday, realistic, rational life," while color was used to express "the convention of the artistic expression of this life."[41] Like other filmmakers of the post-Stalinist Thaw, Tarkovsky perceived black-and-white film stock as "a signifier of reliability and truthfulness."[42] As an aesthetic statement, filmmakers who chose monochromatic aesthetics mobilized the expressive graphic qualities of black-and-white photography while also consciously mobilizing the film stock's associations with documentary filmmaking and the Soviet avant-garde film tradition.

The desire to make the world of *Andrei Rublev* appear authentic prompted Tarkovsky to develop a visual strategy anchored in material reality. The film was shot on authentic locations referenced in the narrative and Tarkovsky utilized long takes to delineate the spaces of scenes and establish the atmosphere of the narrative. Nariman Skakov defines the long take as "an uninterrupted—and in Tarkovsky's case usually slow-paced—cinematic shot which lasts longer than the conventional editing pace of the film."[43] The continuity of time these shots register combines with the continuity of space unfolding within the frame, producing what Lev Anninskii defined as *dokumental'nost'*—"the cinematographic immutability of the filmed material."[44] Yet the film also includes film tricks and visual uncertainty, which mark the constructed-ness of the film's realism. Close viewing of the film reveals geographic discrepancies within scenes depicting specific settings, some of which include shots from multiple locations.[45] Shots of fortifications from Pskov and the Cathedral in Vladimir were sutured together during the sacking of the latter city in episode five of *Andrei Rublev*, recreating Lev Kuleshov's "creative geography", to suggest the attack occurred in a continuous place at a continuous time. In a similar fashion, some long takes in *Andrei Rublev* contain internal discontinuities, which means, as Robert Bird points out, that they "both assert and undermine the realistic temporal continuity of the scene, inspiring both the confidence that the viewer is seeing everything and the fear of the things unseen."[46] This combination of claims to realism and the manipulation of reality does not indicate a compromise of

Tarkovsky's desire for authenticity, but, instead, the handling of historical references to depict fifteenth-century Russia. "Our aim was not to minutely expose all the events that took place at the time. Our purpose was to trace the road Roublev followed during the terrible years, wherein he lived, and to show how he overcame his epoch."[47] Authenticity thus lies in the depiction of Rublev's experience and the viewer's perception of this as motivation for his artwork.

Tarkovsky's disinterest in accurate historical details and rejection of complete reenactment indicates that his definition of the newsreel/cine-chronicle as the ultimate cinema is predicated on the chronicle's claim to historical time and reality. In "Imprinted Time" he delineates cinema's relation to reality, its function as a form of art, and his preferred visual strategies utilizing concepts related to the cine-chronicle and *khronikal'nost'*. The essay's central argument about cinema's relationship to time is couched in the language of documentary objectivity as evident when Tarkovsky states that "time appears in cinema in the form of fact" or that a film image can be a fact itself ("Eto obraz, kotoryi est' fakt"). Events, human movement, and any real object, even unmoving and unchanging ones, can appear as a fact ("vystupat' v kachestve fakta"), as long as they are located in the flow of time. In this manner, Tarkovsky ascribes factuality to the medium and reformulates the Soviet and international shift toward documentary realism as a question of medium specificity instead of a stylistic shift. Central to his intervention is the relation between the chronicle and the chronicled event. The chronicle, as Tarkovsky understood it, is an account of the real, which functions as a document and records the past physically and temporally on the medium of film. He mobilized this sense of observed and recorded actuality in his representation of medieval Russia through visual and narrative strategies.

TARKOVSKY'S POLEMICAL INTERVENTIONS

"Imprinted Time" allowed Tarkovsky to differentiate the principles of his approach to filmmaking in contrast to popular trends in cinematography. At the same time, he accounted for the aesthetic of *Andrei Rublev* in terms of medium-specific qualities as opposed to questions about the accuracy of his depiction of medieval Russia. On the level of film style, Tarkovsky's discussion of documentary tendencies in "Imprinted Time" reveals how his strategies diverged from other pretenders to documentary realism, especially in the way camera techniques position viewers in relation to the events unfolding on the screen. Pivotal for the understanding of cinema delineated in "Imprinted Time" is the view of cinematography as direct observation. "The cinema image, then, is basically observation of life's facts within time, organized according to the pattern of life itself, and observing its time laws."[48] In the essay, Tarkovsky argues for specific principles of visual composition required for this kind of observation. Although he doesn't refer to long-take shots by name, the principles he defines—extended duration, stable or static frames, composition in depth—are distinctive features achievable by this type of shot. Given his conception of cinema's capacity to depict time, Tarkovsky's reliance on the long take might appear determined by his theory of film, but his film poetics are not without a cultural context.

The long take in *Andrei Rublev* emerges in contrast to other cinematographic trends associated with *dokumental'nost'*. Tarkovsky distinguishes between his film poetics and competing visual strategies in terms of how their formal qualities relate to cinema's factual basis. In this regard, "Imprinted Time" opposes the ornamental usage of cinematography and documentary stylization to strategies utilized "to convey the specific, unique form of the developing fact." Addressing stylistic developments toward the chronicle in Soviet cinema, Tarkovsky criticizes the prevalent use of trembling, unfocused handheld camera movement to achieve the impression of spontaneity and direct observation. "It's not the point of contemporary factuality and chronicle-ness to shoot by hand, with a wobbling camera, even making blurred shots—as if the camera-man hadn't quite managed to focus—or by any other gimmicks of that kind."[49] Despite their suggestion of casualness, Tarkovsky claimed such shots often appear as contrived and pretensions as carefully constructed frames filled with symbolism.

In the post-Stalinist period this technique came to prominence through the camerawork of the previously mentioned Sergei Urusevskii. Beginning with *The Cranes Are Flying*, Urusevskii utilized the handheld Konvas-Avtomat camera to communicate physiological sensations and emotional states, as well as to replicate the experience of motion and spontaneous movements of the body, producing the sensation that viewers were immersed in the action on the screen. Tarkovsky did not wholly reject handheld camera shots as a cinematographic technique, nor the work of Urusevskii, with whom he wanted to work before teaming up with Vadim Iusov.[50] In "Imprinted Time" Tarkovsky addresses the roundly criticized visual style of the second film Urusevskii made together with director Mikhail Kalatozov, *The Unsent Letter* (*Neotpravlennoe pis'mo*, 1959). Presenting the story of a group of geologists who become trapped in the Siberian taiga, *The Unsent Letter* is predominantly composed of handheld shots filmed with the Konvas-Avtomat camera. As opposed to the praise they received for *The Cranes Are Flying*, critics attacked Kalatozov and Urusevskii for excessively focusing on expressive handheld camerawork in *The Unsent Letter* while failing sufficiently to define the psychologies of the film's characters. Contrary to the prevailing negative reception, Tarkovsky wanted Kalatozov and Urusevskii to completely forsake the narrative subplots and focus on the experience of the stranded explorers; he wanted Urusevskii's camera to relentlessly track the fate of the trapped geologists.

Although Tarkovsky ultimately claims, "It's not *how* you shoot that is going to convey the specific, unique form of the developing fact," his discussion of handheld camerawork casts in relief the observational mode of vision privileged in his long takes.[51] The kind of handheld shots popularized by Urusevskii's camerawork were associated with the "presence effect" (*effekt prisutstviia*), the illusion of participatory involvement of viewers in the action unfolding on the screen. Urusevskii conceptualized his work with the handheld camera and other cinematographic elements as performing together with the actor. For him it was not enough to simply move or run with the actor when filming with the handheld camera. "It's not just a matter of running with [actors]. Camera movement is very active. I express my attitude toward what is happening through the camera and it becomes a co-participant. The viewer also."[52] Thus the operator brings his camera and the viewer into a participatory position through the perspective of the apparatus, its rhythm and speed of movement. This kind of involvement runs counter to the uninterrupted continuity of Tarkovsky's long takes as well as the studied pace of his camera movements.

As opposed to the kind of sensory contiguity between the moving handheld camera, the space it traverses on the screen, and the viewers stimulated to experience a sense of participation, Tarkovsky's camera takes on the guise of detached observation surveying the physical world of the film. This function is on display in the first episode of *Andrei Rublev*, where long pans meticulously survey the inside of a barn where Rublev, Kirill, and Daniil take shelter from the rain. These shots establish the presence of everyone in the hut, tracing across the faces and bodies of peasants young and old, while also delineating the space where the action of the episode will take place. Maya Turovskaya writes: "The camera pans unhurriedly, giving us time to take in the rough hewn logs with which the hut [where the monks stop] is built, the tiny apertures of the windows, the crude benches, the peasants in their hempen shirts, the ragged children on the floor."[53] Rublev himself remains an observer for much of the film, which diverged from his actions in Konchalovsky and Tarkovsky's script, where the monk intervened in fighting between peasants, battles a Tartar, and attempts to prevent the Duke's men from leaving to attack the stonemasons.[54]

Tarkovsky's concern with observation reaches toward the hyperbolic when he describes his ideal piece of filmmaking as the ability to accumulate millions of meters of films, which recorded "systematically, second by second, day by day and year by year, a man's life, for instance, from birth to death."[55] This fantasy has implications for the narrative structure of *Andrei Rublev* since the discussion of filming someone's entire life can be interpreted as an indirect reference to the production of a film about Rublev and the fact that this film by its title and genre is biographical in nature. The episodic structure of the film rigidly marked by episode titles and dates spans quarter of a century, providing *Andrei Rublev* with the structure of a chronicle.

The fantasy of documenting someone's life prompts a discussion of assembling all of that material into a film and leads to a critical statement about film editing, which reveals how Tarkovsky expanded the idea of the newsreel/cine-chronicle beyond linear accounts of history. Regarding editing, Tarkovsky states:

> And even though it would not be possible to have those millions of meters, the 'ideal' conditions of work are not as unreal as all that, and they should be what we aspire to. In what sense? The point is to pick out and join together the bits of sequential fact, knowing, seeing and hearing precisely what lies between them and what kind of chain holds them together. That is cinema.[56]

The process of "picking out and joining together" echoes Tarkovsky's radical revision of *Andrei Rublev*. When he cut the film from the original 205-minute version to 185 minutes, Tarkovsky combined and altered several episodes and left out characters, places, and events that related events in the film, creating an elliptical narrative and purposefully obscuring narrative connections between episodes. He would go on to say: "editing must be infinitely spontaneous, like nature itself."[57] In "Imprinted Time" cinema's potential for spontaneity is explored through an anecdote immediately preceding the fantasy of documenting someone's life. Here Tarkovsky discusses a casual dialogue he once taped and then later marveled at for its spontaneity, which made attempts to represent reality seem stylized and pretentious. In this manner, Tarkovsky utilizes the long take to leave open the possibility of interactions and spontaneous moments.[58] Only by resisting linear narratives and refraining from constantly following the main character in *Andrei Rublev* does Tarkovsky generate the film's authentic sense of history and achieve the desired truth of direct observation.

CONCLUSION

Beyond what it reveals about the relation between direct observation, long takes, and his editing strategies, Tarkovsky's criticism of handheld camera shots raises questions about the degeneration of cinema's factuality toward aesthetic mannerism. After the critical and popular success of *The Cranes Are Flying* handheld camera shots were frequently emulated in Soviet films and by the early 1960s critics began to call attention to the growing tendency for handheld sequences.[59] Whereas initially these shots were celebrated for their newsreel/documentary qualities, this cinematographic technique became a cliché as directors began inserting handheld shots to imitate the effects Urusevskii had achieved. In the

April 1962 issue of *Iskusstvo kino*, V. Shumskii wrote: "Instead of original compositions of the frame, a number of cinematographers have produced imitative eccentricities, instead of utilizing film technology to produce their own organic composition, they aimlessly subordinate their production [to technology]."[60] As mannerism erodes the claim to actuality, Tarkovsky identified the solution for this degeneration in newsreel/chronicle aesthetics.

Like Eisenstein, Tarkovsky seized the chronicle and repurposed its visual style and its claim to actuality. His reconstruction of fifteenth-century Russia was anchored visually and narratively in the documentary mode. Along with the episodic narrative of *Andrei Rublev*, the film's color strategy, and its carefully chosen props, the long take allowed Tarkovsky to depict medieval Russia in the mode of documentary observation. These elements of style combine to ascribe to *Andrei Rublev* features of a historical document, which some have even cited in the course of historical studies.[61] The film addresses viewers with medieval brutality and existential hardships so that they can perceive the monk's lived experience as the motivation for his moral ideas. In this manner, *Andrei Rublev* animates perception and projects consciousness onto the world presented on the screen. The Soviet film discourse on *dokumental'nost'* and the post-Stalinist developments in Soviet film style provide the historical context for these aesthetic and theoretical decisions. *Andrei Rublev* and "Imprinted Time" were the result of Tarkovsky working within the particular system of Soviet state-controlled filmmaking. But his engagement with this system extends beyond the problems with *Andrei Rublev*. His theory of film and distinctive aesthetics show Tarkovsky in dialogue with a wider film culture at home and abroad. His words and images were actively engaged in stylistic developments in Soviet cinema and contributed to efforts aiming to revise how cinema engaged viewers and represented reality.

NOTES

1. "Ideal'nym kinematografom mne predstavliaetsia khronika: v nei ia vizhu ne sposob s"emki, a sposob vosstanovleniia, vossozdaniia zhizni." Andrei Tarkovsky, "Zapechatlennoe vremia," in *Voprosy kinoiskusstva*, *Voprosy kino iskusstva*, Vol. 10 (Moscow: Iskusstvo, 1967), 84. Throughout this essay I quote the translation of "Imprinted Time" included in Andrei Tarkovsky, *Sculpting in Time: Reflections on the Cinema*, trans. by Kitty Hunter-Blair (Austin: University of Texas Press, 1989). Tarkovsky's statement on the chronicle as ultimate cinema is on p. 65 of *Sculpting in Time*.
2. ". . . dobit'sia pravdy priamogo nabliudeniia, pravdy, esli mozhno tak skazat' 'fiziologicheskoi' . . .", "Zapechatlennoe vremia", 99; *Sculpting in Time*, 78.
3. For the history of Russian physiological sketches and their connection to similar French texts, see the Introduction of *The Physiology of Petersburg*, trans. by Thomas Gaiton Marullo (Evanston, IL: Northwestern University Press, 2009).
4. Andrei Mikhalkov-Konchalovskii, "Nekotorye soobrazheniia po postanovke 'Pervogo uchitelia'," *Iskusstvo kino* (January 1967): 44.

5. Evgenii Margolit, "Kinematograf 'ottepeli': K portrety fenomena," *Kinovedcheskie zapiski* 61 (2002): 214.

6. Josephine Woll, *Reel Images: Soviet Cinema and the Thaw* (New York: I. B.Tauris, 2000), 195.

7. Maya Turovskaya, *Tarkovsky: Cinema as Poetry* (London: Faber & Faber, 1989), 86.

8. Quoted in Jay Leyda's *Kino: A History of the Russian and Soviet Film*, 3rd edn (Princeton: Princeton University Press, 1983), 399.

9. Elena V. Barban, "The Battle of Stalingrad in Soviet Films," in Elena V. Baraban, Stephan Jaeger, and Adam Muller (eds), *Fighting Words and Images* (Toronto: University of Toronto Press, 2012), 237–58; Judith Devlin, "The End of the War in Stalinist Film and Legend," in Alexander Lyon Macfie (ed.), *The Fiction of History* (London: Routledge, 2014), 106–17.

10. Bazin, Andre, "The Stalin Myth in Soviet Cinema," in Bill Nichols (ed.), *Movies and Methods*, Vol. II (Los Angeles: University of California Press, 1985), 29–40.

11. *Iskusstvo kino* published excerpts from the Twentieth Party Congress in the March 1956 issue, using the term "cult of personality" as well as reporting that Khrushchev had called for all artists, including film workers, to "lead a tireless fight 'against untruthful representation of Soviet reality, against attempts to varnish it or, on the contrary, to decry and defame, that which has been conquered by the Soviet people'." ("S"yezd prizval rabotnikov iskusstv vesti neustannuiu bor'bu 'protiv nepravdivogo izobrazheniia sovetskoi deystvitel'nosti, protiv popytok lakirovat' ee ili, naoborot, okhaivat' i porochit' to, chto zavoyevano sovetskim narodom'.") Anon, "Istochnik vdokhnoveniia", *Iskusstvo kino* 3 (March 1956): 3–6.

12. For an example of this, see Iakov Varshavskii, "Estetika chestnosti," in N. R. Mervol'f (ed.), *Molodye rezhissery Sovetskogo kino* (Moscow: Iskusstvo, 1962), 40–66.

13. Evegenii Margolit, "Kinematograf ottepeli: epokha vizual'nogo kino," in *Zhivye i mertvoe: zametki k istorii sovetskogo kino 1920–1960-kh godov* (Sankt-Peterburg: Masterskaia "Seans", 2012), 445.

14. Woll, *Real Images: Soviet Cinema and the Thaw*, 192.

15. Iakov Varshavskii, "Dokumental'noe i igrovoe", *Voprosy kino iskusstva*, Vol. 10 (Moscow: Iskusstvo, 1967), 157.

16. This abbreviated list comes from Mikhail Romm's article, "Dokumentalizm khudozhestvennogo fil'ma", *Sovetskii fil'm* (20 May 1965): 1. Similar enumerations are also found in Sergei Iutkevich, "O dokumental'nosti kino televideniia," in *Kinematograf segodnia* (Moscow: Iskusstvo, 1970), 59–78, and in Aleksandr Macheret, *Real'nost' mira na ekrane* (Moscow: Iskusstvo 1968), 5–82.

17. Mikhail Romm, "Dokumenalizm khudozhestvennogo fil'ma", *Sovetkii fil'm* (20 May 1965): 1–2.

18. Dziga Vertov, "Kino–Eye on Strike", in Yuri Tsivian (ed.), *Lines of Resistance: Dziga Vertov and the Twenties*, trans. by Julian Graffy (Gemona, Udine: Le Giornate del cinema muto, 2004), 125.

19. Sergei Eisenstein, "The Problem of the Materialist Approach to Form", in *Lines of Resistance: Dziga Vertov and the Twenties*, 128.

20. Sergei Eisenstein, "In Praise of the Cine-Chronicle," in Naum Kleiman and Antonio Somani (eds), *Notes for a General History of Cinema* (Amsterdam: Amsterdam University Press, 2016), 225.

21. François Albera, "'The Heritage We Renounce': Eisenstein in Historiography," in Sergei Eisenstein, *Notes for a General History of Cinema* (Amsterdam: Amsterdam University Press, 2016), 284.

22. Sergei Eisenstein, "The Structure of the Film," in Jay Leyda (trans. and ed.), *Film Form: Essays in Film Theory* (New York: Harcourt, Inc., 1977), 162.

23. Varshavski, "Igrovoe i dokumental'noe kino", 158–60.
24. Urusevskii replaced Ekel'chik on the production of *The First Echelon* after the latter became ill.
25. Roman Il'in, "Nekotorye problem izobrazitel'nogo resheniia sovremennogo fil'ma," in *O kinoiskusstve: spetsifika, obraznost', masterstvo* (Moscow: Iskusstvo, 1965), 235.
26. Varshavskii, "Dokumental'noe i igrovoe", 153.
27. Macheret, *Real'nost' mira na ekrane*, 72.
28. Natal'ia Baladina, "Obrazy goroda i doma v kinoiskusstve: na materiale otechestvennogo i frantsuzskogo kino kontsa 50-kh - 60-kh godov" (Doctoral thesis, Gerasimov Institute of Cinematography, 2008).
29. V. Baskakov, "Khoroshaia rabota," in *Ekran 1967–1968* (Moscow: Iskusstvo, 1968), 74.
30. For the East European discussion, see Peter Wuss, "The Documentary Style of Fiction Film in Eastern Europe Narration and Visual Style," in Lennard Hojbjerg and Peter Schepelern (eds), *Film Style and Story: A Tribute to Torben Grodal* (Copenhagen: Museum Tusculanum Press, 2003), 215–38; Josephine Woll discusses the international context in *Reel Images: Soviet Cinema and the* Thaw, 192.
31. RGALI Fond 2936, op. 1, delo 484, 28–9.
32. V. Furtichev, "Kinoproavda i kinolozh'," *Iskusstvo kino* 10 (1968): 83.
33. R. Iurenev, "V poiskah pravdy", *Sovetskaia kul'tura* (25 June 1964): 4.
34. Evegenii Margolit discusses this statement in "Kinometograf 'ottepeli'. K portretu fenomena", *Kinovedcheskie zapiski* 61 (2002): 218.
35. Quoted in M. Dolinskii and S. Chertok, "Vek piatnadtsatyi—vek dvadtsatyi," *Sovetskii ekran* 3 (1966): 11.
36. Tarkovsky, "Zapechatlennoe vremia," 99–100; *Sculpting in Time*, 78.
37. Robert Bird, *Andrei Rublev* (London: British Film Institute, 2004), 26.
38. Maya Turovskaya, *Tarkovsky: Cinema as Poetry*, 88.
39. Pascal Vandelanoitte, "An Icon of Change: *Andrei Rublev* (1966) as Historical Film about the Birth of Russia," in Leen Engelen and Roel Vande Winkel (eds), *Perspectives on European film and history* (Ghent: Academia Press, 2007), 35.
40. Michel Ciment with Luda Schnitzer and Jean Schnitzer, "The Artist in Ancient Russian and in the New USSR," trans. Susana Rossberg, in John Gianvito (ed.), *Andrei Tarkovsky: Interviews*,(Jackson: University Press of Mississippi, 2006), 24.
41. Ibid.
42. Irina Shilova, "Cherno-beloe kino," *Kinovedcheskie zapiski* 32 (1996–7): 25–9.
43. Nariman Shakov, *The Cinema of Tarkovsky: Labyrinths of Space and Time* (New York: I. B. Tauris, 2012), 2.
44. Lev Anninskii. *Shestidesiatniki i my* (Moscow: Soiuz kinematografistov SSSR, 1991), 194.
45. Bird, *Andrei Rublev*, 27.
46. Robert Bird, *Andrei Tarkovsky: Elements of Cinema* (London: Reaktion Books, 2008), 196.
47. Ciment et al., "The Artist in Ancient Russian and in the New USSR," 18.
48. Tarkovsky, "Zapechatlennoe vremia," 87; *Sculpting in Time*, 68.
49. Tarkovsky, "Zapechatlennoe vremia," 88; *Sculpting in Time*, 69.
50. Bird, *Andrei Tarkovsky: Elements of Cinema*, 57.
51. "Sut' ne v tom, kak postavlena ili ne postavlena kamera, sut' v tom, chtoby to, chto vy snimaete, peredavalo konkretnuiu i nepovtorimuiu formu razvyvaiushchegosia fakta" Tarkovsky, "Zapechatlennoe vremia", 88; *Sculpting in Time*, 69.
52. ". . . delo ne tol'ko v tom, chto bezhish' s nimi. Dvizhenie kamery ochen' aktivno. Cherez kameru ia vyrazhaiu svoe otnoshenie k sobytiiu, I ona stanovitsia souchastnikom. Zritel'— tozhe." Maiia Merkel', *Dialogi s Urusevskimi* (Moscow: Iskusstvo, 1980), 58.
53. Turovskaya, *Tarkovsky: Cinema as Poetry*, 39.

54. Vida T. Johnson and Graham Petrie, *The Films of Andrei Tarkovsky: A Visual Fugue* (Bloomington: Indiana University Press, 1994), 95.

55. Tarkovsky, "Zapechatlennoe vremia," 84.

56. "I khotia v deistvitel'nosti imet' eti million metrov nevozmozhno, 'ideal'noe' uslovie raboty ne tak uzh nereal'no, k nemu mozhno i sleduet stremit'sia. V kakom smysle? Delo zakliuchaetsia v tom, chtoby otbirat' i soediniat' kuski posledovatel'nykh faktov, tochno znaia, vidia i slysha, chto mezdu nimi nakhoditsia, chto za nepreryvnost' ikh sviazyvaet. Eto i est' kinematograf." Tarkovsky, "Zapechatlennoe vremia," 84; *Sculpting in Time*, 65.

57. Ciment et al., "The Artist in Ancient Russian and in the New USSR," 20.

58. For further discussion of this, see Bird, *Andrei Tarkovsky: Elements of Cinema*, 205.

59. See Maiia Merkel', "Dolzhno li operator videt'?", *Iskusstvo kino* 10 (October 1961): 51–7; Shumskii's, V. "Lozhnye uvlecheniia", *Iskusstvo kino* 4 (April 1962): 98.

60. V. Shumskii, "Lozhnye uvlecheniia", *Iskusstvo kino* 4 (April 1962): 98.

61. Discussing the banning of Pagan practices in the church law of Kievan Rus', historian Richard Hellie, a scholar of medieval and early modern Russian history, wrote: "Andrei Tarkovskii's film *Andrei Rublev* reveals that the Church was still having difficulty enforcing those interdicts in the beginning of the fifteenth century." See Richard Hellie, "Foreword," in Daniel H. Kaiser (trans. and ed.), *The Laws of Rus' —Tenth to Fifteenth Centuries* (Salt Lake City, UT: Charles Schlacks, Jr., Publisher, 1992), xxi.

CHAPTER 6

Temporality and the Long Take in *Stalker*

Donato Totaro

W ith the advent of digital camera technology, the craft of the long take is less a feat of cinematic athleticism than in years past. In the digital age films are no longer limited to the ten-minute length of a 35mm film magazine, and even the once-complex interaction of stage-trickery *mise-en-scène* and hidden edits to surpass that limit is made easier by the digital camera and computer-generated visual effects. The aesthetic potential of the long take to manipulate narrative time and challenge viewer perception of both narrative and subjective time continues as a potent formal choice for filmmakers. Yet there is still a mystique surrounding the original masters of the long-take aesthetic—directors such as Carl Dreyer, Orson Welles, Kenji Mizoguchi, William Wyler, Jean Renoir, Theo Angelopoulos, Max Ophuls, Miklos Jançso, Alexandr Sokurov, Hou Hsiao-hsien —which goes beyond pure technical virtuosity. Standing at the top of this list is Andrei Tarkovsky, whose fans and acolytes speak of his command and control of the long take in hushed tones of reverence and awe.

As evidenced by his gradually increasing average shot lengths (ASL), Tarkovsky carved a career of dedication to the long take: *Ivan's Childhood* (ASL 17.9*), *Andrei Rublev* (ASL 26*), *Solaris* (ASL 27*), *Mirror* (ASL 24.2*, 25), *Stalker* (ASL 66, 64*), *Nostalghia* (ASL 62, 56*), *The Sacrifice* (ASL 72, 72*).[1] Tarkovsky's use of the long take is never just a formal feat but remains at the service of a film's narrative and thematic underpinning and, of equal importance, is at the heart of Tarkovsky's nuanced understanding of how to magnify *both* a viewer's subjective perception of time, and time as a material, philosophical, and spiritual property.

This union of the long take, narrative, and philosophical/thematic import reached its peak, I would argue, in Tarkovsky's second foray in science fiction,

Stalker (1979). The central thematic/philosophical meaning which I will explicate through close textual analysis of *Stalker* is that time in the long take is
introduced as an expression of "drab" realism in the opening city scenes, but
then is transformed in the Zone and becomes an expression of creation and
invention.[2]

ESTABLISHING 'DRAB TIME'

Stalker begins with a static long take of approximately 3m05s that immediately
establishes the drab, depressive mood that permeates the "real world" of the
fictional city. The camera is placed inside a dark, dank, dingy bar. We see a
small table in the middle ground and a door in the background. A bartender,
dressed in a white lab coat, enters through the door and walks off-screen right.
A second man, the Scientist (or Professor), enters from the left foreground,
walks to the bar, and then settles at the table. The bartender leaves through the
back door. This is all the "action" that takes place.

The sense of "drab," linear time is carried over into the third shot/scene,[3] a
long take of 01m15s where the camera dollies in ever so slowly toward a set of ajar
double doors in the Stalker's bunker-like living quarters, stopping at the threshold of the door and then passing through into the bedroom. The scene cuts to
an overhead shot of a small, round night table. Vibrations from an approaching
train cause the table and objects on it to move. From this overhead angle, the
camera slowly tracks laterally left over the figures lying in the bed—the Stalker's
wife, his daughter Monkey, and the Stalker—then retraces its movement back to
where it started (with the vibrations now subsided).

A few minutes later the film returns to the bar and the meeting between the
three men, with the camera assuming the same position inside the gloomy bar
as shot one, only now tracking forward agonizingly slowly for the duration of
its 4m42s, shifting from a full view of the three men to a medium close-up of
the Stalker. The scene does nothing to explicate the film from the drab tonality
of the overall aesthetics of the opening city scenes, sinking us further into the
arrested emotional and spiritual state of the three main characters, the Writer,
the Scientist, and the Stalker.

Two things relative to the long take and time can be said about these opening scenes that reflect general points of the film and will eventually factor into
the progression from drab time to creation time: agonizingly slow camera
movements into space, and direct overhead camera angles that move perpendicular to the ground/floor/objects. These two interrelated qualities (since
some of the overhead shots are also slow-moving) affect the quality of time and
the spectator's subjective experience of the shot's time. This quality of "slow"
time is also achieved with static long takes, but for the moment, I will discuss
long takes that feature extremely slow inward movement.

Figure 6.1 Minimalism in the long take: opening camera position in *Stalker*.

Figure 6.2 Minimalism in the long take: closing camera position in *Stalker*.

DURATIONAL COMPLEXITY

Vlada Petric points to two types of camera movements in *Stalker* (and *Mirror* (1974)): lateral movements with telephoto lenses that obscure all but one plane of the image, and overhead perpendicular tracking movements over objects and spaces (often nature).[+] The latter camera movement is used emphatically in *Stalker*. Petric notes that this movement (along with other aspects of the *mise-en-scène*) "estranges" the objects recorded by placing us in a physical position we rarely assume in life. Tarkovsky often uses this camera movement, in conjunction with other formal elements such as sound, as a unique signifier for dream-time and subjective states. In some instances, as in the Stalker's lakeside dream, the movement can be said to be approximating an out-of-body experience. In these and other cases, the effect is a form of estrangement from natural and everyday objects.

In a similar sense, the agonizingly slow camera movements inward are a form of "temporal estrangement," largely because we have no physical correlative in our real-life experience of moving at such a retarded pace. Relative to our perceptual schemata, the faster the camera moves, the more it compresses the intervening space and shortens the time; the slower the movement and the longer time feels. And most camera movements, unless dictated by a specific context, like being mounted in front of a moving car or in a helicopter, fall within our normal sense of moving through space. All things being equal, cinema conventions dictate that unless we are told otherwise by strict codes, such as slow/fast motion, freeze-frames, the use of extreme long/short lenses, etc., the passing of time and movement exist in a state comparable to how we would perceive them in the real world. But the deliberate and extremely slow camera movements in *Stalker* function to retard our normal perception of time; they alter the convention of normal or physical time (our perceptual schemata) by reducing movement to a speed alien to human locomotion (and most film-viewing experiences). In fact, to find movement at such a retarded pace in our normal everyday experience would entail unusual situations or very particular forms of attention (daydreaming, extreme concentration, fixation, decreased arousal states such as being inebriated or drugged, etc.). This temporal estrangement is strongly implicated in their durational complexity: slow, foregrounded time that may be experienced as "time standing still," or as feeling longer or shorter than the sheer external time (length of the take).

DURATIONAL COMPLEXITY THROUGH MINIMALISM

I will expand on this notion of temporal estrangement by bringing in a form of music whose history is contemporaneous with Tarkovsky's career: minimalism. Though writers have referred to Tarkovsky's later films (*Stalker*, *Nostalghia*

(1983), *The Sacrifice* (1986)) as bearing a 'minimalist' style, no one has articulated or developed the implication the term minimalism may have to the sense of time in Tarkovsky's long takes. As I will demonstrate, the parallel to minimalist musical form may have an important relevance to an understanding of the temporal dimension of *Stalker*'s noted slow-moving long takes.

Minimalism is a term in currency since the early 1970s used to define various compositional practices, "the features of which—static harmony, patterned rhythms and repetition—aim radically to reduce the range of compositional materials."[5] Relevant to my cinematic context is that when listening to a typical minimalist composition what is most striking to the listener, or what we are most conscious of, is this sense of a restricted musical palette, through repetition and/or stasis. Yet if you compare the opening passage of most minimalist musical pieces to the ending, there will be a noticeable difference in instrumentation, notation, rhythm, pitch, or tempo. This gradual change is an important aesthetic feature of minimalist music. Steve Reich, a leading minimalist composer, called one of his live musical performances (*Drumming* 1971) "music as a gradual process."[6] The reason for our not being very aware of these differences through the course of listening to the composition is that the change(s) has been brought about incrementally. The change is only, or mostly, noticeable when you compare the opening of the musical piece to its closing.[7]

A similar effect is achieved in some of the agonizingly slow long takes in *Stalker*, meaning that if you compare the first frame to the last frame there will be an appreciable difference in either scale, lighting, framing, etc. For example, the second long take in the bar, which starts at 16m30s and lasts 04m42s, begins on an extreme long establishing shot of the bar, with Scientist, Stalker, and bartender standing around, but ends on a medium close-up of the Stalker seated at the round table. In the long take in the sand room (1h45m50s, running 04m35s),[8] the camera travels from a long shot of the Writer lying on the ground to a medium close-up of the Writer seated on the well. In each of these examples, change does exist from the beginning to the end but at a remarkably measured pace.

As in a minimalist musical piece, we are not aware of this change at every instance because it occurs so gradually. To bring out a second related point, change is often acknowledged as a key element of time. As William James put it, "Awareness of change is . . . the condition on which our perception of time's flow depends."[9] If this is true, then "time's flow" is relative to the conscious awareness of change, so if the flow of time is dependent on the rate at which change is perceived, as Williams James observed, then we can hypothesize that the rate at which time is perceived in Tarkovsky's agonizingly slow camera movements is affected relative to our awareness of change in them (granting these basic formal similarities to minimalist music). As our awareness of change is slowed down, then so too is our awareness of time passing. I realize this is speculative, but I offer this hypothesis as one possible explanation for why the slow, contemplative temporal tonality in *Stalker* does not produce the sensation of eternity or boredom (at least in this viewer).[10]

THE TROLLEY JOURNEY AND THE NEW TEMPORAL EXPERIENCE

Up until the famous trolley (or rail car) scene, the temporal tonality of the long takes have been marked by what I am calling "drab time," a combination of dreary *mise-en-scène* slow pacing, static camera, low contrast/monochromatic black and white, and mostly diegetic natural sounds, which has been placed in support of a linear narrative progression from scenes 1 to 6 inclusive: 1) we see a man, the Scientist, waiting at a bar; 2) an intertitle explains the origins of the Zone; 3) the Stalker wakes up, argues with his wife, and leaves for the bar; 4) he meets a second man outside the bar, the Writer, talking to a lady; the Stalker tells the lady to "get lost" and together he and the Writer join the Scientist in the bar; 5) the three men leave the bar and use a jeep to evade a government barricade; 6) they find and board a train trolley and begin their journey to the Zone. My point here is that the trolley ride scene, which starts at 35m09s, is a vital transitional moment in the film's triad structure (pre-Zone city, Zone, and post-Zone city), forming a literal and figurative bridge between the drab time of the City and the unpredictable creation time of the Zone. A close analysis of the trolley scene will pinpoint the visual and aural elements that make the sequence's temporality feel elongated, compressed, distorted, and subjective in ways not seen thus far.

Tarkovsky has always downplayed the importance of montage in his films, but the cut that takes us from the three men boarding the trolley still in the city perimeter to the journey on course to the Zone is a powerhouse edit, a sledgehammer coming down to sever the viewer from the drab reality of the city scenes and—perhaps—change forever our experience of the city after contact with the magical Zone. Firstly, the cut is abrupt because it covers a drastic change in shot scale from extreme long shot to close-up. Secondly, there is a stark change in sound from the loud, distant whirring of the trolley engine to the nearer clanking sound of the wheels on the tracks. In the second shot a non-diegetic sound is subtly introduced to the diegetic sounds of the wheels on the train track, an unnatural electronic sound akin to the sound of bending sheet metal.

Cut to the third shot, a close-up of the Writer, in profile with his head tilted downward, and then to a shot of the Stalker in close-up, standing upright looking steadfastly ahead (screen left). By this point the diegetic trolley track sound is overwhelmed by the non-diegetic electronic sound. Moreover, the diegetic sound of the trolley wheels begins to take on the properties of the electronic sound. This aural merging of diegetic and non-diegetic sound plays a great formal role in elongating the perception of time. The bending sound pitch creates an aural equivalent of stretched time.

The fifth shot and final long take (1m02s) colors the whole scene's temporal tonality by emphasizing stillness and inactivity. The Writer is framed in profile and positioned with his head bowed down. Throughout this shot the camera, while it moves ever so slightly, never veers from the Writer. He turns his head once and brings his hand up to his face, but that is the extent of the action. Of the five, this shot has the least amount of information for the viewer to digest, which underscores that there is little happening dramatically in the scene. And yet, as this shot begins the Writer appears to be asleep, or at least in a state of semi-consciousness (when he raises his head the sluggish movement of his eyelids implies this), which suggests that the trolley journey has been considerably longer than the elapsed screen-time. The shot ends with a cut to a color image of a lush, wooded landscape. The unnatural, non-diegetic sound abruptly stops and is replaced by a return to the diegetic sound of the wheels and tracks.

Although the trolley ride consumes only 3m42s of screen-time, there are hints of temporal compression. In the second shot after the journey ends, the Stalker rises and stretches his arms over his head, as if limbering up after a long trip (corroborating the Writer's sleep-state in the last shot on the trolley, and that *he has* been asleep for some time). All these abrupt changes, in shot scale, sound, and black and white to color, subtly affect the temporal whole of the scene by giving the impression of a larger span of duration. In the end we can surmise, given how slow the trolley is moving, that it would take considerably longer than 3m42s to travel from the city to the Zone, which we know to be in the countryside. Philosophically, this temporal vagueness symbolizes the spiritual journey that the three travelers are about to embark upon, as well as foreshadowing the unreal or irreal time-space properties of the Zone.[11]

ENTERING THE ZONE: CREATION TIME

Time is invention, or it is nothing at all.[12]

Once in the Zone, temporality becomes unpredictable and divorced from rational teleology. In contrast to the first part of the film, the city scenes, time in the long take now assumes an element of spontaneity, invention, novelty, and creation, which provides an interpretive strategy whereby, in certain key long takes, time functions to let things happen in front of the spectator's eyes, to surprise us in the same way that the three characters are surprised by the physical surrounding of the Zone. This sense of mystery and magic is transmitted in time, through the long take.

The first of such long takes occurs about ten minutes into the Zone at 50m15s, and is especially important because it embodies a physical passage through a threshold into the precarious spatial-temporal nature of the Zone. The shot, which lasts 2m31s, begins with a medium long shot of the rusted frame of an abandoned car nestled within deep foliage. The camera begins to track toward the car's open hollow frame and continues into and through its empty hull, until we see only the three travelers standing together on the other side of the empty frame. Only when the Scientist and Writer step down the steep side and leave the frame line does the camera zoom in to reveal a deep gully littered with derelict army vehicles and armaments. Slowly and minimally, the camera movement has taken us beyond the car into a wholly new space, one we could never have envisioned from the beginning of the long take and which makes it another example of the earlier noted affinity with minimalism—*gradual* change.

As such, this revelation in time establishes the mercurial, shifting spatial-temporal nature of the Zone, which forms a major part of the film's dramatic tension and narrative drive. The camera tracks forward passing through a

Figure 6.3 Creation time in the long take: opening camera position in *Stalker*.

Figure 6.4 Creation time in the long take: closing camera position in *Stalker*.

threshold (into the past? into the future? into a sphere of timelessness?), yet still produces twists and turns because, as the Stalker says, "In the Zone the direct way is not the shortest." When the three men pass through this threshold—in the symbolical sense, since it is the camera that moves through it— the Stalker looks straight ahead and tells his two voyagers, "The room is over there." But then proceeds to throw the weighted cloth in a different direction! The experience of time is likewise non-linear and prey to the whims of the Zone's supra-natural environment, expressive of a sentiment from Tarkovsky's diaries: "I am convinced that Time is reversible. At any rate it does not go in a straight line."[13]

One of the Stalker's first acts once in the Zone is to lie down face first in the deep foliage, breathing a sigh of comforting relief. A striking formal manifestation of this strange affinity between the Stalker and the Zone is the scene sometimes referred to as the Stalker's "Apocalyptic Dream," which marries the Zone's non-rational spatial-temporal properties with the Stalker's subjectivity, using an enigmatic and perplexing spatial teleology to manifest *creation time*. The 3m26s long take begins close-up on a dark object, indistinguishable until it tilts up to reveal the Stalker's sleeping face. The camera pans away from the Stalker's face to a stream of clear, shallow water and begins to slowly track perpendicularly over a series of varied objects submerged under the clear water, and then finally to an upturned hand resting in the water. The camera pulls back slightly, tilting up to reveal a sweater sleeve and dark leather coat. Is this the Stalker's hand? Spatial logic dictates that it cannot be, since the camera travelled in a straight line. However, if observant we will remember (or soon notice) that only the Stalker is wearing such clothing, confirming that it is/ was his hand, and recalling the Stalker's words about there being "no straight lines" in the Zone. One can also see the shot as the sleeping Stalker's dream image, which would make this one of the most literal visualizations ever of stream of consciousness.

As a viewer, we are seduced by the sensuous beauty of the image and the odd collage of objects, but this long take offers no predictable sense of teleology. We may be surprised when the camera returns us to where we began, but we cannot have prefigured this or envisioned when/where the movement would end. Hence one's perception of time is not conditioned by a knowing or anticipatory sense of expectation. *Stalker* contains other examples of long takes with spatial and geographical ambiguity where an unpredictable teleology leads to a revelation. Tellingly, these long takes only occur *after* the opening city scenes and lead to the important thematic, formal, and philosophical integration of time and the long take in *Stalker*: creation time.

Tarkovsky employs the Zone's temporal-spatial unpredictability and creation time in a mesmerizing long take during the "Dry Tunnel" scene. The scene begins with the Writer and the Scientist resting in front of a tiled wall. The sound of unseen water drops is faintly heard off-screen. The scene cuts on the sound of a splash to an overhead shot of a vat of silver liquid, into which a stone has fallen. The long take in question begins at 70m48s on a close-up of the Writer. The camera begins to slowly track right, past the tiled wall, and past a series of hanging lamp fixtures. The sound of running water has swelled, but is oddly contrasted by a dry creaking sound (the swinging lamps?). Ambient electronic music appears, as if to underscore the mysterious sound of rushing water. The camera movement continues screen right and reveals the source of the loud running water: a huge waterfall visible through periodic arched openings in the stone wall. The camera continues to track laterally to a close-up of the perplexed-looking Writer, who, like us, is wondering: where did this waterfall come from? Two shots later they find themselves back at the tiled room as it was at the beginning of the scene, with the Scientist sitting quietly next to his knapsack having a sandwich and drink.

This temporal/spatial circularity is not unlike the straight forward camera movement over the objects in the stream that defies spatial logic by returning to the point of origin. Like the shot through the shell of the car, we slowly experience an unexpected physical and geographical change, from barely audible dripping water to a deafening, surging waterfall, from a relatively dry, tiled room area to the same space transformed into a tropical-like jungle. Through the continuous time of the long take (2m42s), we share the sense of wonder and surprise with the characters.

Another such moment of creation-time long take (4m40s) occurs at a crucial juncture in the film: when the three men finally arrive at the wish-fulfilling room, but are unable to make the moral commitment to enter (2h19m11s to 2h24m01s). After arguing among themselves, the three exhausted men sit on the wet ground outside the room's threshold. The camera, positioned inside the room, slowly dollies back to a long shot of the three seated men. Several inches of water cover the tiled floor inside the room. We see a reflection of the three men in the water—ironically, their shadows have entered the room, but their bodies remain outside. A shaft of bright light comes down directly from above, casting a reflecting shine on the water, then darkens to a brownish hue. The sound of dripping water gives way to a spontaneous rain shower, which produces a rippling rainbow effect on the water. As in the dry tunnel, water is connected to sudden and surprising events and accorded a mysterious presence. The rain tapers off as quietly and unexpectedly as it started. The three men observe the moment in quiet contemplation. The lighting in the room changes once more. The faint sound of an oncoming train is heard, as it was in the Stalker's home at the beginning of the film. Perhaps in less dramatic fashion, but this is another long take where something spontaneous and unpredictable occurs in the extended time of a very long take. And, as in most of these "creation time" long takes, the spontaneous event is connected to nature.

The qualities discussed above coalesce in perhaps the richest and most complex long take in the film. The shot of 4m37s begins at 1h45m54s with the Writer in long shot lying in a puddle in front of a well-like vat sticking out of the sand dunes. He wakes up, picks up a stone and drops it into the well. Several seconds later we hear the thud of the stone hitting the bottom. He sits on the edge of the well and then several seconds later we hear a *second* sound, this time a splash. The two sounds clearly present a non-rational series of events. The Writer's reaction suggests as much. He stares into the well and says, "Another experiment. Experiments, facts, truth at the last boundary. There is no such thing as facts, especially here." The mystery of that earlier overhead shot of a stone splashing into a well is now placed in a retroactive context, with the cause coming forty-minutes *after* the effect.

This shot's complexity is centered in the way it encapsulates the film's formal and thematic integration of time. The incrementally slow inward dolly movement from the initial long shot to the camera's final medium close-up position expresses durational complexity through minimalism, while the unpredictable nature of time, underscored through key dialogue, echoes the central thematic and philosophical concern of the film. If we recall an early exchange before he enters the Zone, the Writer is seen talking to a woman about the existence of the Bermuda Triangle. He tells her, "Don't count on it.

There's no telepathy, no ghosts, no flying saucers. They can't exist. The world is governed by cast-iron laws . . ." Later, in the Zone, the Writer counters the Scientist's objective certainty: "Forget your crawling empiricism. Miracles lay beyond empiricism." And then in this scene, about forty minutes later, we hear the Writer's patently non-rationalist refrain in response to the sound of the stone falling twice ("Once, the future was only a continuation of the present. Its change loomed beyond the horizon. But now the future's a part of the present"). The Writer has gradually changed his belief system. Once a cynic and non-believer, the Writer now courts a philosophical position held dearly by the Stalker: the necessity to believe in values beyond the strictly rational, scientific, and material.

In summary, this long take of 4m36s is exemplary of how time and the long take fuse form, theme, and philosophy in *Stalker*. The durational complexity of the shot, achieved by the minimalist advancement of change from long shot to medium close-up, helps to formally underscore the (potentially) creative nature of time. Unpredictable, non-linear time is represented by the double sound of the stone falling, by the temporal loop the shot forms with the earlier shot. Hence in this long take the narrative advances while thematic and philosophical meaning is imparted through the unique temporal tonality of the shot.

CREATION TIME BEYOND THE ZONE

When the three men appear back at the bar, little seems to have changed. In fact, if it were not for the black dog from the Zone, one would be inclined to think they never left the bar! (And how they return is left to our imagination.) But two long takes at the end of the film, both featuring the Stalker's daughter Monkey, represent the final stage in the film's philosophical and thematic progression from drab time to creation time. Close textual analysis reveals that up until the scene where the three men reach but do not enter the room, the only long takes to exhibit the notion of creation time have been within the Zone. The scenes leading up to the entrance into the Zone, from the start to approximately thirty-five minutes (scenes 1 to 6), were marked by "drab time." That is, none of the long takes before the Zone exhibited the spontaneity, surprise, or sense of discovery associated with creation time. Additionally, none of the non-Zone long takes were marked by the sort of unpredictable teleology defined earlier (only temporally estranged in one instance, the second bar shot, by a minimalist long take). But once the wife and daughter arrive to collect the Stalker, things do seem to have changed.

The first of the two long takes that introduce the shift to a Zone-affected (or should it be infected?) city occurs at the end of the first scene back in the city, when the wife and daughter come to meet the Stalker at the bar to accompany

Figure 6.5 Color and surprise "infects" the city in *Stalker*.

him home. With Monkey waiting outside on a bench, the Stalker and his wife exit the bar. The long take in question begins after this shot, in a profile close-up of Monkey, who appears to be walking screen right. This surprises the viewer, since in the Zone we learn that the Stalker's daughter, perhaps contaminated genetically because of her father's contact with the Zone, was born without legs. So how can she be walking? As the camera tracks right to follow her, Monkey begins to veer off left, away from the camera's straight lateral line of movement. The magical illusion of her walking lasts about one minute, until the moment she walks far enough away from the camera to reveal that she is being carried on her father's shoulders. Our expectation is thwarted and we are witness to a revelation of a slightly different order (something apparently magical is explained by natural law). However, for the first time outside the Zone we have a long take that contains an element of surprise or wonderment that was absent from the city prior to the trip to the Zone. Adding to the mystery is that, for the first time in the film, color, seen in Monkey's gold headscarf, appears in the non-Zone city. In fact, as if to cement this link between Monkey and the magical Zone, the shift from the city's black and white to color here symbolically mirrors the earlier edit that shifted from black and white to color when the men first arrive in the Zone.

This long take has introduced the possibility of surprise and unpredictability in the real world outside the Zone. The previously depicted pre-Zone "drab time" has now attained a magical quality of surprise that it did not previously possess. The thematic implication is that magic and wonderment is potentially not only in the guarded Zone but all around. And that the possibility for selfless love and spiritual rejuvenation is in every person. This point is driven further in the powerful final long take, where once again the possibility for magic is brought to bear.

The concluding long take of 04m20s (beginning at approximately 2h37m38s), full of mystery and ambiguity, offers the interpretive possibility that things have changed in the real world outside the Zone. To begin, this is the first full-color shot in the city. The shot begins in a right profile close-up of Monkey seated at the kitchen table intently reading a book of poetry. We hear the off-screen sound of a distant train. The camera dollies back slowly and reveals three glasses lined up diagonally on the table: a short glass half-filled with a dark liquid; a thick jar filled with broken eggshells and other objects; and a tall milk-smeared glass. Monkey puts the book down on the table and looks off-screen. We then hear a female voice-over reading a love poem by nineteenth-century Russian poet Fyodor Tyuchev, "The Dull Flame of Desire." By the time the voice-over stops, the camera has dollied back a considerable distance across the table. Monkey bends her head down angled toward the tabletop and stares at the glass closest to her. The glass begins to move of its own volition. The black dog that the Stalker brought back from the Zone whimpers off-screen, as if sensing an alien or unusual presence. The glass moves ahead past the tall milk-smeared glass to the left edge of the table. Her eyes are riveted on the glass. It stops a few inches short of the edge of the table. She then shifts her eyes to the second glass, the jar, and it moves ahead a few inches; then the third tall milk glass moves forward. At 2h40m15s, nearly three minutes into the shot, she places her face directly on the table; a moment later the milk glass falls below frame line to the floor, crashes, rolls, but does not shatter. Seconds later the window, table, and the glasses begin to vibrate, like in the opening scene, as the rhythmic clanking sound of an oncoming train swells. The sound of the train gets louder, shaking the tabletop. Beethoven's "Ode to Joy" begins to play, and builds to a cacophony with the sounds of a human choir and the oncoming train. The camera dollies forward toward Monkey. The shot slowly fades as the train sound and vibrations diminish and the music fades out.

Was this an act of miracle? Did the Stalker bring back "powers" from the Zone that he transmitted to his mutant daughter and which caused her to move the glasses telekinetically? The film ends on this exclamative long take which carries over the sense of mystery and the unknown quantity that previously resided only in the Zone. But it is important that Tarkovsky does not provide a simple, definitive explanation but leaves open the possibility of a natural expla-nation: the movement of the glasses across the table could have been caused by the vibrations of the oncoming train. Retaining this hesitation between a natural and supra-natural explanation serves the very point of the film: that one must resort to faith to believe in a supra-natural explanation when empirical and rational laws are insufficient or inconclusive. Monkey's seemingly miraculous act in the film's final long take leaves open the possibility that creation time (a non-linear, non-teleological, inventive, subjective understanding of time) has seeped into a world previously governed by "cast-iron laws." The sense of surprise, ambiguity, and going beyond the empirical that was exclusively present in the Zone (scenes 8–18, or from 39m00s to 2h24m38s) is now seemingly present outside the Zone, all centered on Monkey: first through the striking appearance of the color gold in her headscarf, introducing color into the dull, drab post-Zone reality; then the playful deception of her miraculous ability to walk; and then the unresolved ability to move matter with her mind. The first line of dialogue from the Writer that signaled his skepticism toward the unexplainable took place before the Writer came in contact with the peculiar and life-altering force of the Zone. Being mute, the mutant daughter is unable to express herself through the Writer's medium: words. Instead her mental/physical act completes the evolution of the Writer's change in belief system by extending creation time outside the Zone.

CONCLUSION

As a starting point for my analysis of *Stalker*, I organized my case study around a thematically designed progression of the long take. Close textual analysis revealed a shift in temporal tonality from the "drab time" in the initial city scenes (1–6), to the dramatic appearance of non-teleological time during the famous Trolley scene/Journey to the Zone (scene 7), to creation time in the Zone scenes (8–18), to the transmigration of creation time into the city in the concluding scenes (19–22). The thematic implication is that the experience of the Zone has changed the once- cynical Writer and materialist Professor/Scientist into potential believers of the paranormal and non-natural. I offer this progressive reading of time (from drab time to creation time) partly because, in *Stalker*, the pseudo-trappings of science fiction are secondary to the journey of self-discovery. And time, a subject dear to Tarkovsky, becomes a medium through which this self-discovery occurs. As Tarkovsky writes, "Time is a condition for the existence of our 'I' . . . Time is necessary to man, so that, made flesh, he may be able to realize himself as a personality . . ."[4] Once in the Zone, the Writer's and Scientist's preconceived notions of time and space are shattered, and replaced by a new sense of time and space brought on by the surprise and wonder of the Zone, a new reality which profoundly alters their sense of self. Most importantly, the change of belief system introduces into the once-drab city the non-materialist, non-rationalist qualities and values that are held dearly by the Stalker (and exemplified in its pure state by his wife): love, self-sacrifice, faith, and hope.[15]

NOTES

1. The statistics with asterisks are taken from the Cinemetrics website. When there was more than one entry per title in the database, I took the average of them. Totals without an asterisk were from my own calculations.

2. My use of the words "creation" and "invention" intentionally invokes Henri Bergson's phrase from *Creative Evolution*, "time is invention or it is nothing at all" (Henri Bergson, *Creative Evolution*, trans. by Arthur Mitchell (London: Macmillan & Co. Ltd, 1911), 361.

3. Third if you count the intertitle as a scene. In my calculation, there are twenty-two scenes in the film. For the curious, they are: Scene 1: The Bar; Scene 2 (intertitles): What is the Zone?; Scene 3: The Stalker Awakes; Scene 4: Meeting the Writer and the Scientist; Scene 5: Trespassing the Protected Barrier; Scene 6: Preparing the Trolley; Scene 7: The Trolley Journey; Scene 8: Arrival into the Zone; Scene 9: Entering the Zone Proper; Scene 10: The Warning; Scene 11: The "Dry" Tunnel; Scene 12: Resting near the Tiled Room; Scene 13: The Stalker's Apocalyptic Dream; Scene 14: The Meatgrinder; Scene 15: At the Well; Scene 16: The Telephone Room; Scene 17: Struggling at the Room's Threshold; Scene 18: Looking into the Room; Scene 19: Back at the Bar; Scene 20: Consoling the Stalker; Scene 21: The Wife's Monologue; Scene 22: Monkey's Miracle?

4. Vlada Petric, "Tarkovsky's Dream Imagery," *Film Quarterly* 43.2 (Winter 1989–90): 29.

5. Stanley Sadie (ed.), *The Grove Concise Dictionary of Music*, assist. ed. Alison Latham (London: Macmillan Publishers Ltd, 1988 [1994]), 525.

6. Ibid.

7. Other important minimalist musicians/bands include Tangerine Dream, Klaus Schulze, Manuel Göttsching (formerly Ash Ra Tempel), Philip Glass, Michael Nyman, Brian Eno, Morton Feldman, John Cage, Bill Nelson, and Harold Budd. It is interesting to note that contemporaneous with this musical movement there were filmmakers also experimenting cinematically with minimalism through protracted long takes, static framing, electronic music, looping, re-photography, and other formal qualities (Andy Warhol, Chantal Akerman, Jean-Marie Straub & Danièle Huillet, and Michael Snow).

8. All time calculations were taken from the Criterion Blu-ray of *Stalker* available on Blu-ray and DVD via the Criterion Collection.

9. Quoted in Peter Hartocollis, *Time and Timelessness* (New York: International Universities Press, Inc., 1983), 3.

10. When I teach *Stalker* I often have my class listen to a minimalist piece of music before the film and then ask them to estimate how long they think the piece was. In all cases the students guess a length *shorter* than the actual length. I take this to be *some* empirical evidence that supports the speculative connection I am making between Tarkovsky's "minimalist"-like long takes and the perception of time.

11. See Julia Shpinitskaya's chapter in this volume on the irreal audio effect of Tarkovsky's sound design.

12. Henri Bergson, *Creative Evolution*, trans. by Arthur Mitchell, 1911 (London: Macmillan & Co. Ltd, 1964), 361.

13. Andrei Tarkovsky, *Time Within Time: The Diaries*, trans. by Kitty Hunter-Blair (Kolkata: Seagull Books, 1991), 122.

14. *Sculpting in Time: Reflections on the Cinema*, trans. by Kitty Hunter-Blair (London: The Bodley Head, 1986), 57.

15. As Tarkovsky writes in *Sculpting in Time*, "Her [the Stalker's wife] love and her devotion are that final miracle which can be set against the unbelief, cynicism, moral vacuum poisoning the modern world, of which both the Writer and the Scientist are victims" (198).

CHAPTER 7

Framing Infinity in Tarkovsky's *Nostalghia*

Yelizaveta Goldfarb Moss

If the western European landscape is a plentitude of form in the narrowest space, the Russian landscape is antipathy to form running out to infinity.[1]

Perhaps the most striking and famous scene of *Nostalghia* (1983) is its ending shot which supcrimposes a Russian dacha and landscape within the ruins of an Italian cathedral (Figure 7.1). The shot makes it seem as though Russian land is so nebulous and expansive that it infects other lands, other architectures. For Russian philosophy, this is the shape of Russian infinity, expressed in its landscape: it is oppressive in its unboundedness and impossibility of escape. Andrei Tarkovsky wrote on the potential for cinema to uniquely address infinity through finite *mise-en-scène*. For him, man accesses a sense of infinity in dreams, memory, and spirituality. And it is precisely the "on top" quality of a film aesthetic that allows for such a sense of infinity to be manifested. But rather than an overtonal sense of aesthetic sublation, as in Eisenstein, Tarkovsky's work layers disjunctive images on top of one another in the same frame. So Tarkovsky's dream, memory, and spiritual shots jam together two differently functioning images into one space.

The distorted quality of this opposition creates a new sense of the world and of thought, a "catharsis" with a depth of artistic images, ultimately "accumulat[ing] to form an all-embracing sphere that grows out into infinity."[2] Tarkovsky argues that even though we cannot avoid using the finite in order to evoke the infinite, by substitution "it is possible to create the illusion of the infinite: the image."[3] In Tarkovsky, images iterate, and they unfold slowly over time so that enjambments of disparate spaces and *tableaux vivants* do justice to infinity's spiraling form.

Figure 7.1 The final static shot in *Nostalghia*.

The marriage of contradictory spaces necessitates a new set of aesthetic rules and a radically new sense of genre. In Tarkovsky, we find this radicality in his treatment of time. As encouraged by the title of his aesthetic treatise *Sculpting in Time*, readings of Tarkovsky's work have lauded his molding of time in a genre that by nature is spatial. But in the focus on temporality, these readings have dismissed what should be seen as a radical formation of space, a disjunctive layering which exceeds the bounds set by any one aesthetic genre, yet is made possible only through an unusual, cinematic molding of time. In Tarkovsky's work, we see a unique *tableau* created through cinema, not as the filming of painting, but as the emergence of nature's infinity through a markedly slow reflection on *mise-en-scène* and a relationship to infinity through the distorting framing of architecture.

In *Nostalghia*, Tarkovsky organizes his *mise-en-scène* to frame a relationship with mental and spatial infinity that speaks to timelessness, fluid immobility, and untraversability. Like Aristotle, who resisted the ossification of infinity into a stable, metaphysical entity, Tarkovsky represents boundlessness through concepts of becoming and unending motion. Tarkovsky's methods of unfolding space in time through *tableaux vivants* and superimpositions of architectures allow for a representation of infinity that is counter-metaphysical. Rather than perceiving infinity as a closed loop or motionless totality, these representations uncover an Aristotelian "potential" infinity and treat space as an unfolded becoming, a spiraled untraversability. *Nostalghia*, while representing the haunting of an "infinite" Russian landscape, also recreates the form of infinity as described by Aristotle, Fedor Stepun, and Jean-François Lyotard.

Nostalghia uses several strategies to make infinity visible within art. It manipulates the Russian landscape, long considered to be a topographical manifestation of infinity, to force it within windows and between walls of an Italian cathedral. With every attempt to frame, Tarkovsky shows off the impossibility of controlling space with theatrical constructions. The film also forces its audience's gaze to wander without locking on any one subject, without resting in linearly rendered, mappable space. In fact, *Nostalghia*'s one-point perspectives through door frames and columns are set up as foils before turning actors to odd angles or panning the camera to disrupt any clear rectilinearity. Attempts to move linearly and attempts to translate clearly are consistently proven to be faulty maneuvers. Characters either become engulfed by the weight of this endless space (Gorchakov, Domenico) or are left to wander the world as aimless nomads (Eugenia).

For Tarkovsky, infinity is an all-embracing substance that can be built out of finite material, accumulated into a sense of limitlessness. Though the film style of *Nostalghia* has often been interpreted as a spiritual statement on memory and loss, Tarkovsky's own view of infinity opens up a spatial interpretation of the film. The false continuities—eyeline matches, cross-cutting, point-of-view shots, slow pans, and *tableaux vivants*—stitch together a filmic limitedness that works in tandem with Aristotle's counter-metaphysical, "potential" infinity.

TABLEAUX VIVANTS

When Gorchakov and Eugenia step out of the car in the second scene of the film, she looks out onto the fog and exclaims "it's a marvelous painting," as though the landscape before her is a painting itself. The line is intentionally ambiguous, and it harkens back to the first shot of the film: a long take of a monochrome Russian landscape in which the characters of Gorchakov's life scatter across the hill. The *tableau vivant* feels simultaneously random in its distribution of human figures and carefully composed as they evenly fill the frame, like in a landscape painting which catches its momentary subject over many hours of work. Its staging is confirmed when the scene almost imperceptibly turns into a freeze-frame, a snapshot of a painting within the movement of cinema, a *mise-en-abîme* of framings. Confirming this connection between "marvelous painting" and landscape, Eugenia's tears ("I cried the first time I saw it") are reserved for Gorchakov's wife, not the Madonna del Parto painting, as one might assume.

Infinity, as recognized in the Russian landscape, is framed, but not aesthetically reproduced as a sublime view. Instead, in *Nostalghia*, a sense of infinity is imposed by the matrix of framings and by the intersection of temporal planes. The film constructs a representation of infinity, but maintains Aristotelian qualities of spatial untraversability and unmasterability through its unique treatment of time, a slowing to a standstill according to traditions of *tableaux vivants* and a merging of time as a way of expanding on spatial routes. This aesthetic route grapples with the particular difficulties of drawing the unbounded. It struggles to present a coherent vision of abstract space in infinity while maintaining the uniquely incoherent qualities of an Aristotelian untraversability.

Tarkovsky provides a resistance to metaphysical infinity, instead allowing for a view of spatial infinitude that unfolds in time, that does not assume a unity of any dimension. Most often, philosophical notions of spatial infinity presuppose a metaphysical temporality—a wholeness of time against which space can expose its limits, as in European Romanticism's natural sublime. Yet Aristotle's "potential infinity" concerns itself with a fluid spatiality that is constructed in time, in a never-ending state of "becoming." Thus, for Aristotle, infinite space is always in flux, and this consistent movement makes it untraversable.[4] For Tarkovsky, creating untraversability, as in Gorchakov's impossible journey from one side of a pool to the other, mimics the form of counter-metaphysical, "Russian" infinity.

To separate the various notions of the infinite, Aristotle writes of two infinities: actual and potential. Actual infinity, which many of Aristotle's predecessors (and successors) uphold, would exist wholly at a particular *point in time*. In this actual infinity, metaphysics and Romanticism can experience infinity as sublime, as though overlooking the great abyss of infinity in one terrifying look. As we will see, Tarkovsky disagrees with this representation, arguing for a temporally unfolding sense of infinite iteration. Potential infinity, for which Aristotle argues, exists *over time*: "Nothing is complete which has no end and the end is a limit."[5] Aristotle's infinity is always, by necessity, "potential" since its spatial traversal can only be conceived *over time*. Tarkovsky plays with this notion of "over time"—he intentionally works in cinema, an art of movement, yet he consistently denies his films the quick movements associated with commercial films. His pacing is slow, he lingers for entire scenes on *mise-en-scène*, and his actors double back and repeat movements, like broken records. Over time, *Nostalghia* generates a sense of space: not with establishing shots which mean to orient, but with false eyeline matches and long pans that alternately miss and catch up to their subjects. In fact, even when the film gives us an extreme long shot, it is filled with so much fog that it fails to do the work of an establishing shot. Instead, the film takes up techniques of disorientation and untraversability as its central art of movement.

Though Tarkovsky was skeptical of incorporating formal traditions of painting and theater into cinema, his films are filled with painting-like shots and re-presentations of paintings. He found that the clichés established by these other art forms were clouding the potential for cinema to function as a profound experience of time. But even in his resistance to other forms of art, Tarkovsky could not help but focus attention on paintings and labor over the *mise-en-scène* of his films. He was fond of *tableaux vivants*, and his shots, with their reflective stillness, are often described as paintings themselves.[6]

Tarkovsky's *Stalker* (1979), for example, was intended to feel like a single shot, "time and its passing . . . revealed":[7] no montage, no "dislocation of time" by cutting. Tarkovsky has an Aristotelian respect for the unknowable whole of time. We can only understand infinity as a spiraling, unfolding in time, and Tarkovsky could not envision such an unfolding, a state of "becoming," as a quickening aesthetic. So his films, especially his later *oeuvre*, slow down to a near standstill with almost imperceptible zooms.[8] This sort of "extreme immobilization" is lauded in Lyotard's discussion of cinema:

> We should read the term *emotion* as a *motion* moving toward its own exhaustion, an immobilizing motion, an immobilized mobilization. The representational arts offer two symmetrical examples of these intensities, one where immobility appears: the tableau vivant; another where agitation appears: lyric abstraction.[9]

At the pole of *tableau vivant*, Lyotard's "acinema" absorbs all fantasy, movement, disjunction into a core of absolute entropy. It exposes all potential combinations, contradictions, and representations. And in placing these potential interactions together, we see both the visible "real" and invisible "potential." In the moments when actors hold their poses, "all motion on the stage ceases, a temporally circumscribed and 'out-of-time' moment" that harkens to Diderot's tableaus and *apothéose* of staged melodrama.[10] Tarkovsky's filmed "paintings" continue to move imperceptibly, touching the order of infinity, accessing the non-recurrent and unrepresentable.[11] These *tableaux vivants* allow for Tarkovsky to instill a "most intense agitation through [the work's] fascinating paralysis"[12] in both their radical stillness and their unorthodox construction of impossible spaces. His filmed places and times fold in on each other—not in a Vertovian jumping from place to place, but into a single, reflective shot (Figure 7.1).

Tarkovsky's work is propagated by still lifes: carefully staged *mise-en-scènes* which are presented as living photographs. Often tabletops filled with objects or scattered relics lying just below the surface of water, these *mise-en-scènes* appear to almost breathe, as though they are enacting an imperceptible animation. Just as with Aristotle's potential infinity, Tarkovsky's temporality is stuck in a state of becoming, a living standstill. He writes on his still lifes and landscapes: "I am . . . puzzled when I am told that people cannot simply enjoy watching nature, when it is lovingly reproduced on the screen, but have to look for some hidden meaning they feel it must contain."[13] Rather than contain the image of nature, Tarkovsky's frames guide our gaze and force us to grapple with infinity's and cinema's excess of vision.

PROSCENIUMS

The architecture ruins featured in Tarkovsky's *Nostalghia* take on framing functions in their photogenic lacework. Characters wander through the ruins, even dwell in them, but the building carcasses have lost their original utility. They have no doors; they are overgrown; they leak. This architecture is left only with aesthetic value, and the framing of dream, memory, and infinity through their walls takes on a theatrical substance: "Italy . . . stretches out above [Gorchakov] in magnificent ruins which seem to rise up out of nothing. These fragments of civilisation at once universal and alien, are like an epitaph to the futility of human endeavour, a sign that mankind has taken a path that can only lead to destruction."[14] Though *Nostalghia* is filled with the architectural remnants of human endeavors, these carcasses serve to frame a relationship with infinity rather than mark the metaphysical boundary between immortality and finitude. The architecture pushes our gaze into the strange, untraversable space which resists our attempts to navigate it. Looking into Tarkovsky's film frame is to struggle with an Aristotelian infinity constantly in flux, denying a wholeness to time. The "magnificent ruins which seem to rise up out of nothing" are resurrected for the purpose of focusing our attention, for without them, Tarkovsky's characters and audience would become lost under the Chekhovian weight of "too much space."

Stepun, in his *The Russian Soul and Revolution*, argues that the Russian landscape relates the form of a European topographical "plentitude" and extends it to an infinity.[15] The Russian horizon is a particularized cultural figure that forces the Russian "eye" to roam endlessly:

> In this repeated flight of the gaze to the horizon, in the way these horizons, holding nothing in their arms, waver, cross, disappear, and yet remain ever the same, the eye exiled in the Russian landscape experiences its lone, invisible beauty; a beauty without scenic effects, a distance without far views, more melody than picture.[16]

The unfettered Russian horizon is an unmasterable figure of self-sameness that seems always to be in motion. The eye travels across such a landscape endlessly without seeing anything new, yet it continues to attempt to see the

Russian infinitude, this "lone, invisible beauty" of Russian land. The eye travels as though looking at a landscape painting, but in the empty plenitude of infinity it cannot hold on to any particularity—of object, of moment—and so it must continue to look without seeing, experiencing the landscape in a necessary state of "exile." This monotony of form comes to feel like a *mise-en-abîme*—endless replications of near self-same material, an infinite set of superfluous, null elements.

Russian infinity escapes visual concretization by its unending, iterative movement, which throws the gaze into a "flight," an "exile," as it consistently fails to master the landscape. Attempts to capture Russian infinitude in aesthetic representation will necessarily fail by virtue of this iterative movement. When Tarkovsky freeze-frames his Russian landscape or frames it in an Italian window, he points to these common attempts to control Russian infinity through proscenium framings. But Tarkovsky also links Russia with Italy in their monochrome color schemes, infecting foreign lands with the self-sameness of Russian landscape; he overflows and explodes the Italian window with Russian landscape, as though it cannot be framed and controlled at a distance.

As a figure of Aristotelian infinity, and thus also of an iterative self-similarity, the Russian horizon holds a power that extends beyond mere aesthetic contemplation of nature. The dual force of Russia's landscape, Stepun argues, is mimicked in the Russian soul, which holds a tension "between holiness and barbarism,"[17] endlessly wavering and crossing between one and the other. This tension, manifested in *Nostalghia* as iterative spatial movement between two

Figure 7. 2 Outside landscape spilling into Domenico's house through the window frame in *Nostalghia*.

lands and two architectures, expresses itself as fatal nostalgia in Gorchakov and as fatal guilt in Domenico.

Nostalghia's natural Russian landscape, framed as though it were a perspective painting in its rendering of deep space, stands as both its authentic self and its representation, a semiotic *mise-en-abîme* which simultaneously represents the present moment, memory, and the impossible future. The invisible movement of the Russian landscape, with its infinite, iterative horizon revealed between columns, is maintained by Tarkovsky's refusal to represent it. He frames infinity without trying to master it, thus forcing his audience's gaze into wandering "exile" as they search the "scenic views" for some reliable ground of a fixed image. But the landscape behind the proscenium of doorway or window, even as it is framed, does not function as a painting at all. It is constantly moving, a living artwork of sorts; yet it remains the same in its centrifugal motion which disperses any reliable particularity or temporal marker. Unlike metaphysics and Romanticism's accounts of infinity, which argue for a static sense of space in any singular point in time, Tarkovsky welcomes temporal shifts as they help to show the progression of infinity from dreamy fullness to stark nothingness.

This anchored point of view might sound like Romanticism's treatment of infinity in that the proscenium frame seems to be a stable lens that directs our view onto the terrifying grandiose scope of the horizon, given to us all at once. But Tarkovsky's proscenium frame does not inhibit the movement of infinity on the other side. Rather, this preserved iterative movement is the very quality of infinity that makes it unpredictable and unstable. As we saw earlier, Aristotle makes a point to distinguish the shape of a "potential" infinite series. It is not linear, growing progressively larger in an additive measure of magnitudes. Rather, infinity functions iteratively, in a circular fashion, yet not in a circle shape which would cover the same moment *ad infinitum*.[18] Each moment must be unique and distinct from its set, even as the whole of infinity rotates back on itself.

Though Domenico's banner "1+1=1" may seem to be an iterative, accumulating series of self-sameness, he also warns "It's wrong to keep thinking the same thing." Rather than an iterative series, 1+1 gets us nowhere new while still progressing forward ("one drop and one drop make a bigger drop, not two drops"). The film continually shows us that lingering does not mean standing still. Even Eugenia, who is a contemplative character of grand monologues, is twitchy, fidgety, constantly tripping over herself. Even the camera, given still lifes and immobile ruins, cannot sit still. It lingers with slow pans and zooms. And it refuses to break into shot/reverse-shots in dialogues, instead letting characters speak to one another off-screen and never quite catching up with the speakers. In this way, the camera denies 1+1=2, maintaining our focus, denying a traditional journey, yet never quite standing still.

Nostalghia does not give us a true accumulation of plot and shots; but it does divide the Russian and Italian world into minutia which we would have otherwise passed over. In other words, the "1+1=1" mantra may not be about additive movement at all, but about metonymy: the parts of a whole circulating back to the whole itself. Dividing a concept into smaller and smaller portions, an infinity of division takes on something extra into its set, even as we cannot predetermine what these extra somethings will be (they are not patterned, like an arithmetic progression): "The infinite turns out to be the contrary of what it is said to be. It is not what has nothing outside it that is infinite, but what always has something outside it."[19] Such a progression perhaps looks more like a spiral, like Dante's hell, a circle that continually reveals new sights.[20] The spiral is in a constant state of becoming, and it cannot be determined from outside as a wholeness or unity.[21] Rather, this creative motion implies a self-same perpetuation. And this is precisely the sort of iterative infinity—incrementally in motion yet maintaining an impression of self-sameness—which interests Stepun in Russia's infinitude. For Tarkovsky, the accidental, fixed point of view is *meant* to be repeated and iterated in a plurality of *mise-en-scène*, all with their own particularities. It is in such an unmathematical set of iterations that an appropriate infinity can be revealed and that the impossible shape of nostalgia can be drawn.

The Russian landscape is infinite, yet "always the same," filled with "silent fields, unadorned woods, dusty country roads, swamps, slow streams, shaky hump-backed bridges, thatched-roofed wooden houses—all homely, all quickly built and erected casually from materials accidentally at hand. Nothing attracts the eye, nothing satisfies it, nothing dazzles it."[22] The sense of infinity implicit in such vastness is enhanced by inconsequential human life. There is no impetus to construct one's own fate, such as in monumental European architecture or as in St Petersburg's superman complex. It is no surprise that Russia's infinitude has long served as a weapon in human trifles: this "land-ocean" has defeated Napoleon and has swallowed Moscow's political exiles. Chekhov attributes the particularity of Russian suicide to this same unlivable expanse of space:

> Russian life oppresses the Russian man, to such a degree that he disappears without trace, it bears down on him like a ten-ton rock. People in the West perish because their life is too cramped and suffocating; here, they perish from too much space. There is so much space that a little human being hasn't the strength to get his bearings in it. That's what I think about Russian suicides . . . [23]

In the unnavigable, untraversable Russian terrain, a landscape scattered only with "accidental" constructions which may just as well not exist, the human cannot help but to become lost.

In Gorchakov we see this loss immediately. He wanders aimlessly, gives up on trajectories and goals easily, and allows for the pressure of Russia to take over his mind at every new Italian sight. He feels a kinship with Domenico, who perishes, as people in the West do, from suffocation. It is hard to take Domenico's story of caging his family over many years seriously, but as an organizing narrative for his being, claustrophobia has certainly driven him to madness. Though the film dovetails Gorchakov and Domenico—creating guilt in Gorchakov for Domenico's crimes, mirroring their faces, conjoining their fates—Gorchakov's family is always portrayed outside of the house, wandering in the open Russia landscape. Gorchakov cannot get his "bearings," as though Russia is haunting him and impressing its spatial oppression on him at a distance. If he left Russia to escape this weight, he fails to understand that nomadism is historically ingrained in Russian life and that exile will not free him from oppression.[4]

ONE-POINT PERSPECTIVE

A spontaneous play, of sorts, takes place in St Catherine's Pool, a steaming bath which fills a recess in a ruined building. Some remaining walls and arches surround the pool, and Tarkovsky's camera watches the baths from behind the columns, from behind the wings, in a "third limit" of the stage, so that it has a clear view of both inside the pool and of its skirting stage area. Bathers sit in St Catherine's Pool like an audience, so the narrative action happens at the corner, on two sides of them—they are at the center, looking out, commenting on the action on the raised "stage." When they approve of Domenico's recitation of God's words to St Catherine, they clap and yell: "*Bravo*, Domenico!" Startled by the outburst of this audience, the three actors look around sheepishly until the camera zooms closer to them, eclipsing our view of the bathing audience with the actors' heads. In the intimacy of this framing, no longer reliant on the architectural staging of ruins, we are back in the mode of cinematic identification. The architectural *mise-en-scène* gives us a theatrical staging, reversed. We see the audience's gaze pointed back toward us, as it watches the actors who mediate the space between the two audiences, between the chorus and the camera.

Nostalghia constantly gives off the eerie remnants of a stage. Tarkovsky alternates the placement of the camera: it will sometimes take the place of the audience, and it will sometimes take the place of the actors off-stage in the wings. At times the placement is ambiguous, and Tarkovsky enhances our disorientation by denying us the classic filmic representations of dramatic dialogue and staging. When characters speak to one another, they are often not filmed in shot/reverse shots; instead, they speak to one another off-screen, in the wings.

When Tarkovsky does cut between characters in dialog, he gives us an establishing shot only after the conversation, so that our seeming orientation, built out of cuts between speakers, is proven false by the subsequent long view.[25] Spatial mismatches seem to be a privilege of cinema, which has classically worked hard to create a formal system of coherent space in order to imitate the spatial clarity of the stage. Tarkovsky realizes this, and his play between dramaturgical aura and filmic disorientation creates an odd quality of unease and tension.

Though the notion of visual perspective changes with the advent of film—we see the depth of three dimensions projected equally on a flat surface—the architecture of the theater remains largely the same. Beginning with early Greek theater, around 425 BC, the proscenium stage frame has marked the boundary between mimesis and its audience, much like the earlier-noted painting frame that marks the difference between the wall and the representation while also interrogating these distinctions of inside/outside. The proscenium frame also established direction of vision, perspectival lines that would come to determine art's technical representation of the world. Lost for many centuries to a circular-stage custom, the proscenium reemerged in the Renaissance by the influence of perspectival painting[26] and Neoclassicism. Forced perspective from the Greek tradition is adopted and improved upon in several capacities: audience seating is arranged in a semicircle and raised for improved sight lines; the stage floor is sloped and stage wings are angled to encourage a sense of depth; actors are grouped symmetrically around a central axis and in recessive diagonals.[27]

In the transition from theater to cinema, many of these same forced perspective traditions—depth of field, lines of acting, invisible fourth walls—were maintained. But, as Erwin Panofsky argues, even though theater architecture has not changed, the perspective of the spectator has mobilized with cinema projections:

> In theater, space is static, that is, the space represented on the stage, as well as the spatial relation of the beholder to the spectacle, is unalterably fixed. The spectator cannot leave his seat, and the setting of the stage cannot change, during one act . . . With the movies the situation is reversed. Here, too, the spectator occupies a fixed seat, but only physically, not as the subject of an aesthetic experience. Aesthetically, he is in permanent motion as his eye identifies itself with the lens of the camera, which permanently shifts in distance and direction.[28]

In his static, fixed position, the spectator witnesses a radical treatment of space: not just bodies moving in space as on the stage, but space itself in motion, "approaching, receding, turning, dissolving and recrystallizing" through the camera, editing, and special effects.[29]

The relationship of the camera to the screen is similar to that of Brunelleschi's box to painting—the designed perspective gives a mechanical impression of space, a constructed representation of reality.[30] Tarkovsky, who greatly disliked the trend of "filmed theater," found fault with this mechanized reproduction of space. His work enacts a different representation that is not married to a purely perspectival notion of reality, as in classical painting or theater. In fact, *Nostalghia* pokes fun at film's adoption of theatrical orthogonals by constantly setting up one-point perspectives, only to step out of them. Columns of a cathedral will be lined up around a classic central axis with recessive diagonals, but then the camera will start panning, turning the columns into an unnavigable forest. Doorways in hotel lobbies will be organized symmetrically in receding geometrical patterns; but doorways will also be left raw, as in Domenico's house, filmed laterally so that we can see that door frames are mere props.

This shift in perspective from geometrically directed to disorientingly askew is essential to *Nostalghia*'s point about space and its visibility. To direct one's vision into a particular direction, Lyotard writes, is to "always [be] surrounded by a curved area where visibility is held in reserve yet isn't absent."[31] The potential of perception is ever-present in the blurred curve skirting a linear focus. But as soon as the line of vision is shifted to sharpen and domesticate this blurred space, the skirting swings just out of reach. One cannot hold all points in focus simultaneously put them into the kind of imaginary perspective of landscape painting or organized theater. This problem of vision is analogous to the difficulty of viewing infinity, which is why Tarkovsky uses film form, not a landscape-painting backdrop, to represent Russian land.

Vision is non-Euclidean, and so cannot be fully represented by a linear perspective of orthogonals. Recognition of curved space and our physical experience of space runs counter to a Cartesian mechanics, to which the camera eye is so often bound. Rather than a segmented Cartesian grid which isolates monocular experience, from a peephole structure, Tarkovsky's space revels in its excess of vision, in its unpresentable places. Subjective perception cannot hold all possibility within itself, and so alternates irreducibly between vision and the invisible, presentation and the unrepresentable, finite and the infinite.

Both painting frame and theater footlights demarcate a space that separates us from the work of art, and this demarcation allows for the work to have a contemplative, inward orientation. The stage is set up as a labyrinth: its wings, décor, curtains, and backdrop establish a space inaccessible and unnavigable by the audience. The footlights center attention on the actors onstage, but the centripetal focus is an illusion that disperses in the back space, receding from the audience's view.

Lyotard argues that both theatrical backstage and representative painting have three spatial limits that perform distinct functions. The theater or museum firstly sets up the space that allows for representation. Within it, the frame— the proscenium, stage edge, painting frame—is a second limit, a window onto a particular representation. The third limit is invisible; it functions by setting up the possibility of representation, while hiding itself from view as representation. In his theatrical setups, Tarkovsky points to the "third limit" by simultaneously representing the space of the audience, stage, and off-stage (off-screen actors and sound). In painting, this "third limit" is identified as the distance point, often traced out of frame, invisible in the painting itself, yet fundamentally constructing that which has been made visible.[32] In creating distance points through one-point perspectives and open Russian landscapes only to ruin them or contain them, Tarkovsky jabs at the limits of these aesthetic constructions also.

Gorchakov opens an Italian door onto a Russian landscape which seems to be spilling into the room from the window frame (Figure 7. 2). Some of the landscape lies in miniature before the open window, across which the camera travels as though it were in flight over a motionless, muddy river. The camera frame lifts into the window, and the landscape framed within it merges seamlessly with the microcosm which lies in the foreground before it. In *Nostalghia*, the Russian infinitude cannot be held at a distance, framed tentatively by the *mise-en-scène*. It rushes back through the stage frame, leaking into the side of human finitude. The Apeiron (the Greek word for "infinity") appropriately resists its imposed bounds and refuses to be framed passively as an aesthetic object, a rendered painting. Or it is as though the Lyotardian invisible backstage, the third limit, has seeped out from behind the wings, and both visible and invisible are rendered on the same plane.

In acknowledging non-Euclidean vision and the "third limit" of staging, *Nostalghia* registers the boundlessness of memory and "profound alienation" of spatial infinity. Tarkovsky writes that his *Nostalghia* expresses the "hopelessness of trying to grasp what is boundless."[33] In his films, the characters' static struggle to navigate infinity's invisible movement often renders them part of this horizon. Like the immobile statues of Sosnovsky's dream, they become arbitrary anthropomorphic structures under the weight of Russian space. Tarkovsky's emphasis on memory and alienation over the characters themselves perhaps is indicative of a Russian literary tradition of the superfluous man. It is arguably the very pressure of Russia's infinitude that rushes man to his superfluity—if not in Chekhovian suicide, then in his integration with the horizon.

NOTES

1. Fedor Stepun, *The Russian Soul and Revolution*, trans. by Erminie Huntress (New York: Scribner's Sons, 1935), 20.
2. Andrei Tarkovsky, *Sculpting in Time: Reflections on Cinema* (Austin: University of Texas Press, 1994), 39.
3. Ibid., 38.

4. Aristotle considers three possible untraversabilities—incompletion (as in traveling a circle), physical difficulty (as in crossing a roaring river), unlimitedness (as in moving through unending space)—and he ascribes only the last to "potential" infinity. Aristotle, *Physics*, trans. by Jonathan Barnes (Princeton: Princeton University Press, 1991), 204a3–204a6.

5. Ibid., 207a14.

6. Though Tarkovsky resisted direct adaptation between aesthetic genres, his films make extensive reference to paintings, and his background as a painter inflects his cinema. Tarkovsky's writings make reference to Carpaccio, Cézanne, Dali, Magritte, de La Tour, van Gogh, Goya, El Greco, Picasso, Dürer, Raphael, Leonardo da Vinci, Giotto, among many others. And setting aside *Andrei Rublev* for its direct thematization of painting, Tarkovsky's films make extensive visual reference to particular paintings: *Mirror* lingers over Leonardo's *A Young Woman with a Juniper Twig* and his instructional writings on battlefield painting; *Nostalghia*'s narrative is motivated by Piero della Francesca's *Madonna del Parto*, a fresco featured in the film, and the heroine is a dead ringer for one of Piero's painted women; van Eyck's *The Adoration of the Lamb* is featured in the abandoned ruins of *Stalker*'s Zone; *Mirror* enacts Pieter Bruegel's *January (Hunters in the Snow)*; and *Nostalghia* enacts Caspar David Friedrich's *Ruins of Abbey at Eldena* as *tableaux vivants*; Solaris replicates the earthly scene of *Hunters in the Snow*, which also hangs in the spaceship. But also, Tarkovsky's compositions have been widely recognized as painterly. His symmetrical framing is reminiscent of Renaissance perspective paintings. Often his *mise-en-scène* are ordered as frontal perspectives with one vanishing point, flattening the image. For more on Tarkovsky's painting influence, see James Macgillivray, "Andrei Tarkovsky's Madonna Del Parto," in *Tarkovsky*, trans. by Nathan Dunne (London: Black Dog Publishing, 2008); Juhani Pallasmaa, "Space and Image in Andrei Tarkovsky's 'Nostalgia': Notes on a Phenomenology of Architecture in Cinema," in *Chora 1: Intervals in the Philosophy of Architecture* (Quebec: McGill-Queen's University Press, 1994), 143–66.

7. Tarkovsky, *Sculpting in Time*, 194.

8. Jennifer M. Barker recognizes a similarly near-imperceptible zoom in Tarkovsky's *Mirror*: "the forward-tracking camera performs a barely perceptible reverse zoom. Both movements, forward and reverse, continue for a brief few seconds . . . The slowness of the forward tracking motion and the slightness of the reverse zoom yield an effect that, though subtle, is dizzying." Jennifer M. Barker, *The Tactile Eye: Touch and the Cinematic Experience* (Berkeley: University of California Press, 2009), 13.

9. Jean-François Lyotard, "Acinema," in Phillip Rosen (ed.), *Narrative, Apparatus, Ideology: A Film Theory Reader*, trans. by Paisley N. Livingston (New York: Columbia University Press, 1986), 356.

10. Brigitte Peucker, *The Material Image: Art and Real in Film* (Stanford: Stanford University Press, 2007), 30.

11. Lyotard argues that the classic problem of representational arts is their "exclusion and foreclosure of all that is judged unrepresentable because nonrecurrent" (Lyotard, "Acinema," 355).

12. Lyotard, 357.

13. Tarkovsky, *Sculpting in Time*, 212.

14. Ibid., 205.

15. Stepun, *The Russian Soul and Revolution*, 20.

16. Ibid., 20.

17. Ibid., 23.

18. Though it may seem that a circular path would constitute an infinite untraversability—in that the traversal would be unending—the circle does not satisfy Aristotle's notion of infinity: "it is necessary also that the same part should never be taken twice. In the circle, the latter condition is not satisfied: it is true only that the next part is always different." Aristotle, *Physics*, 206b34–207a6.

19. Ibid., 206b34–207a6.

20. Virgil to Dante: "You know that the place is circular; and though you have come far, always to the left in descending to the bottom, you have not yet turned through the whole circle; wherefore if aught new appears to us, it should not bring wonder to your face." Dante Alighieri, *The Divine Comedy*, trans. by Charles S. Singleton (Princeton: Princeton University Press, 1970), 149.

21. Aristotle does not name the spiral as the shape of infinite motion, but he does point to a modified circle as something of an approximation: "This is indicated by the fact that rings also that have no bezel are described as infinite, because it is always possible to take a part which is outside a given part. The description depends on a certain similarity, but it is not true in the full sense of the word. This condition alone is not sufficient: it is necessary also that the same part should never be taken twice. In the circle, the latter condition is not satisfied: it is true only that the next part is always different." Aristotle, *Physics*, 206b34–207a6.

22. Stepun, *The Russian Soul and Revolution*, 20.

23. Andrei Chekhov, *Pis'ma v dvenadtsat' tomakh* (Moskva: Izdatel'stvo "nauka," 1980), 292.

24. As Petr Chaadaev argues in his critique of city-dwelling, Russians become nomadic in times of revolution, and this nomadism allows for artistic productivity on a national, even legendary, level. According to Chaadaev, the Russian man can be susceptible, just like the European man, to losing himself by disorientation: "a man gets lost when he can find no means to bind himself with what has come before him and what will follow him. Then all consistency, all certainty escapes him. Lacking the guiding sense of continuous duration, he finds himself lost in the world." Petr Chaadaev, "Pis'mo pervoe," in *Stat'i i pis'ma* (Moskva: Sovremennik, 1989), 45.

25. For example, when Gorchakov and Eugenia speak in the lobby chairs, he turns back to speak to her through the camera when she is revealed later to have been to the right of him. She turns right to speak to him through the camera when he is revealed later to have been behind her.

26. Several scientific perspective systems were developed in the Renaissance for perspectival painting and continued to be improved upon in subsequent aesthetic traditions. Linear (or central) perspective, attributed to Alberti, traces orthogonal lines into one vanishing point. Angular (or oblique) perspective uses two vanishing points. Inclined perspective uses three vanishing points and avoids objects drawn parallel to the picture plane. Synthetic perspective, attributed to da Vinci, curves some parallel edges to more realistically mimic optics. In parallel perspective—often seen in Asian art—parallel edges remain parallel in the representation, and orthogonal lines do not converge. In inverted perspective, orthogonals converge in front of the picture plane (we will return to this in Lyotard's discussion of Brunelleschi's box). In vanishing area perspective, orthogonals converge into a general region (not a vanishing point). In axial (or vanishing axis) perspective, orthogonals converge at a vertical axis. In bifocal perspective, orthogonal lines converge at two incompatible vanishing points.

27. For more on aesthetic perspective, see Erwin Panofsky, James J. Gibson, Julian Hochberg, Margaret A. Hagen, Rudolf Arnheim, Richard L. Gregory, and E. H. Gombrich.

28. Erwin Panofsky, "Style and Medium in the Motion Pictures," in Irving Lavin (ed.), *Three Essays on Style* (Cambridge, MA: The MIT Press, 1995), 96.

29. Panofsky, 96–8.

30. Brunelleschi's box was a mechanism which revolutionized perspectival painting before even Alberti's advent of linear perspective. The box, open at the top, contained Brunelleschi's drawing of the Dome of Florence façade and a back panel of buffed metal (in effect, a mirror). At the correct angle, viewed through the peephole of the box, the drawing would merge with the mirrored image of the actual Dome, thus proving that Brunelleschi's representation matches point-by-point with the image of the Dome. The peephole view denies peripheral vision. And the reflected image, as viewed through the box, is already a flattened representation of the actual Dome. It excludes optical curvature, and in its central focal perspective, the reflected image is more adaptable to aesthetic representation than a view of the Dome itself with the naked eye. For more on denied optics in Brunelleschi's box, see Jean-François Lyotard, "Veduta on a Fragment on the 'History' of Desire," in *Discourse, Figure*, trans. by Antony Hudek and Lydon (Minneapolis: University of Minnesota Press, 2011), 157–204.

31. Jean-François Lyotard, *The Inhuman: Reflections on Time*, trans. by Geoffrey Bennington and Rachel Bowlby (Stanford: Stanford University Press, 1991), 16.

32. Jean-François Lyotard, "Painting as Libidinal Set-Up (Genre: Improvised Speech)," in Keith Crome and James Williams (eds), *The Lyotard Reader and Guide*, trans. by Keith Crome and Mark Sinclair (New York: Columbia University Press, 2006), 302–29.

33. Tarkovsky, *Sculpting in Time*, 203.

CHAPTER 8

Approaching the Irreal: Realistic Sound Design in Andrei Tarkovsky's Films

Julia Shpinitskaya

Nature exists in cinema in the naturalistic fidelity with which it is recorded; the greater the fidelity, the more we trust nature as we see it in the frame, and at the same time, the finer is the created image: in its authentically natural likeness, the inspiration of nature itself is brought into cinema.

Andrei Tarkovsky[1]

REALISTIC SOUND AND A SOUND DESIGNER

Viewers of *Solaris* (1972) may remember Berton's lengthy car drive along multi-lane urban motorways and through long tunnels after his meeting with Kris Kelvin and his father at their countryside house (Figure 8.1). The episode lasts almost five minutes, which seems like an eternity, and adds very little to the film's narrative since it suspends the action and does not feature any dialogue. What we see is Berton sitting in the car in his pensive state of mind, occasionally interrupted by his restless son in the back seat, and watching through the windscreen passing vehicles and concrete structures of Tokyo's futuristic landscape alternating between color and monochrome. Even though the entire sequence is wordless, its sound solution vividly exemplifies Tarkovsky's realistic sound design in his later period: all the visuals are accompanied by what Elizabeth Fairweather calls "a permanent drone of traffic noise" mixed with a variety of synthetic sounds, such as "an intrusive, high frequency and an ear-piercing timbre," "ascending arpeggios, descending glissandi that call to mind sci-fi laser-guns, a 'solar wind' effect, and clouds

Figure 8.1 The Tokyo sequence in *Solaris*.

Figure 8.2 The Stargate sequence in *2001: A Space Odyssey*.

of indistinguishable 'cocktail party' chatter."[2] The continuously increasing urban noise cuts abruptly into the silent landscape of the countryside, thus establishing a sharp audio contrast between the two settings.

Berton's linear journey on highways and through tunnels might have been modelled after the much longer Stargate sequence in Stanley Kubrick's *2001: A Space Odyssey* (1968), which features the astronaut's trip through the nebula corridor asymmetrically splitting apart, shot with the help of slit-scan photography (Figure 8.2).[3] Furthermore, just as the latter is accompanied by György Ligeti's highly dissonant music characterized by "the thick texture of many instruments playing at once,"[4] Tarkovsky similarly strived to achieve the same disturbing effect of cacophony in the soundtrack for his Tokyo sequence, although without recourse to a preexisting music. Eduard Artemiev's electronic score here resembles the *musique concrète* style by starting off with the real noise of a working engine and then adding disharmonic technical sounds and its multilayered transformations later on. As Tarkovsky said to Artemiev during the sound-editing of this scene, "It is necessary that electronic music sounds much stronger here so that everyone would throw up."[5]

Solaris was a turning point in Tarkovsky's career that revealed basic principles of the realistic audiovisual design in his films, especially explicit in the long-lasting reality episodes with no action or dialogue involved. Enveloped in the realism of sounds, these episodes make the viewer become an observer. Too long for an ordinary film scene, they are constructed from monotonous visual sequences filled with undifferentiated realistic noises: sounds that imitate naturalistic conditions or sounds whose origins and sources are concealed. *Mirror* (1974) also emphasizes realistic moments to a great extent, but it is in *Stalker* (1979) where Tarkovsky's sound naturalism fully unfolds: namely, in his technique of long naturalistic sequences in which audiovisual components are entirely subjected to the principle of realism. As Eduard Artemiev comments on Tarkovsky's idea of the film score: "There was a great sequence in *Stalker* known as the 'meat grinder passage' . . . I came up with a strange, gloomily tense music for it with gradual escalation, but Andrei rejected everything: 'No music at all: footsteps and echo only.'" "He had some kind of purely biological sense of form, a hunch for everything superfluous," he continues. "He used to say, 'No need for that.' And he was right, there was no need for that at all. He himself acutely felt all the sound score of a film."[6]

Before venturing into further analysis, let us clarify what is meant by sound naturalism and authentic sound design. First of all, for Tarkovsky the sound that originally belongs to all sound sources in a shot is not identical to the sound that provides a sequence with authenticity. He understood the sound design as a complex process that should include several stages: such as eliminating the original sounds of a shot, selecting sounds (or a sound) that could make a scene expressive (based on the sounds that belonged to it), stressing and expanding selected sounds in the audio space, and removing side effects that would distract attention from the basic sound. As he argues in his *Sculpting in Time*, "As soon as the sounds of the visible world, reflected by the screen, are removed from it, or that world is filled, for the sake of the image, with extraneous sounds that don't exist literally, or if the real sounds are distorted so that they no longer correspond with the image—then the film acquires a resonance."[7] Tarkovsky praised Bergman as "a master of sound"[8] and referred to his sound technique as an example to follow:

The sounds of the world reproduced naturalistically in cinema are impossible to imagine: there would be a cacophony. Everything that appeared on the screen would have to be heard on the soundtrack, and the result would amount to sound not being treated at all in the film. If there is no selection then the film is tantamount to silence, since it has no sound expression of its own . . . For instance, when Bergman uses sound apparently naturalistically—hollow footsteps in an empty corridor, the chime of a clock, the rustle of a dress, the effect is in fact to enlarge the sounds, single them out, hyperbolise them . . . He singles out one sound and excludes all the incidental circumstances of the sound world that would exist in real life.[9]

While working on the film sound, Tarkovsky primarily aimed at creating a realistic sound environment and, because of this, had little need for the traditional film music, the absence of which he often compensated with electronic music, still a new trend in the Soviet art of the 1970s, as well as natural sounds and noises that at times steadily accompany an entire episode. As he writes, "It may be that in order to make the cinematic image sound authentically, in its full diapason, music has to be abandoned . . . Properly organised in a film, the resonant world is musical in its essence—and that is the true music of cinema."[10] "Above all, I feel that the sounds of this world are so beautiful in themselves that if only we could learn to listen to them properly, cinema would have no need of music at all."[11] That is to say, natural sounds and noises replacing traditional film music were expected to be heard as music *per se*, whereas electronic music served to stand for natural sound and noise. Meanwhile, a composer was to become a sound designer and arranger.

Tarkovsky believed that natural resonant sounds heard as music could fill the audio space of a film and thus organically complement the visuals. Such sounds would provide the visual sequences with authenticity because music is so strong in meaning that it could form its own channel of signification. Given its complex and autonomous nature, instrumental music usually presents considerable technical challenges in being smoothly assimilated with the film narrative without overlapping it, whereas electronic music, because of its sound and rhythmic malleability, provided Tarkovsky with a much greater resource for experimentation. As he writes, "Electronic music has exactly that capacity for being absorbed into the sound. It can be hidden behind other noises and remain indistinct: like the voice of nature, of vague imitations . . . It can be like somebody breathing."[12] The origins of electronic music, however, must be carefully concealed and it must closely approximate the authenticity of natural sounds or be mixed with them. According to Tarkovsky, "The moment we hear what it is, and realize that it's being constructed, electronic music dies . . . Electronic music must be purged of its 'chemical' origins, so that as we listen we may catch in it the primary notes of the world."[13]

Tarkovsky's emphasis on real-life experience and sound naturalism required sound-work with attention to a number of details: the sound origin, the synthesis and treatment of sound, the emergence of sound within the film's resonant space, and experiments with ways to introduce sounds into narration. My observations on Tarkovsky's sound space are based on his own comments on film music made in his *Sculpting in Time* as well as the interviews with the electronic composer Eduard Artemiev and the Swedish sound mixer Owe Svensson, who shared their experience of designing the sound for his films. Tarkovsky worked together with Artemiev on three films in succession, *Solaris*, *Mirror*, and *Stalker*,[14] whereas in his last two films he decided to work without a composer, while still managing to employ music and sounds along with his aesthetic statements.[15] According to Artemiev, instead of music, Tarkovsky primarily asked for the organization of sounds and noises; what he needed was not a composer making music but rather a sound-mixer with the composer's ear, an expert in rustles, rumbles, and echoes.[16] The director fully gained such experience only in his last film, *The Sacrifice* (1986).

UNDERSTANDING SOUND-WORK

In his endeavor to create cinema without music, Tarkovsky focused on the experimental conjunctions of sound and image that would produce new expressive senses. After *Solaris* he decided to dispense with a regular music track altogether by making sound enter his films by other means.[17] Speaking about Tarkovsky's sound-work and sound-making strategies, it is important to keep in mind that his cinematic spaces are highly heterogeneous and comprise different sound realities or soundscapes. In the final sound form, however, all these realities interweave and interact synergistically, resulting in a coherent whole. There are several sound sources regularly used in the sound design of his films (including sounds that are selected, synthesized, and composed):

- natural sounds produced by animals, weather phenomena, and inanimate objects;
- industrial and urban noises produced by human activities, such as the noise of cars or equipment;
- electronic music composed especially for the films in accordance with his audio ideas;
- musical quotations from historical sources or, more generally, a preexisting recorded sounding.[18]

In Tarkovsky's sonic universe, sounds serve as essential elements that interplay with image; they are, therefore, introduced as autonomous audio units without interruption, independently of the characters' speech and dialogue. At times, however, sounds intermingle with music, blurring the boundary between the two. Furthermore, Tarkovsky's soundtracks do not accompany the visual order continuously but build up a discrete line within the film body by presenting an elaborate gradation of audio levels between sound proper and its opposite, silence or non-sound. Dialogues are often placed into a completely silent soundscape devoid of music as well as natural ambient sounds. And whenever sounds intrude into such silent sequences, they are treated as if they were truly extraordinary audio events.

Based on our analysis of the sound material in Tarkovsky's features (especially in his late period) and the valuable testimonies of the sound designers he used to work with, the director's approach to sound could be best understood in terms of metamorphosis. Most sound-work procedures implemented in the sound design of his films are directed primarily at the transformation of an initial target sound, such as

- sound differentiation that consists in the application of a variety of sounds and their variations to a single episode;
- mixing procedures that involve combining and blending sounds in order to make the film's soundscapes cross over or interlace with each other;
- masking procedures that include disguised electronic music or covert quotations, also aimed at the interplay of the film's sound realities.

Tarkovsky's treatment of sound differentiation could be well illustrated by his collaboration with Owe Svensson on *The Sacrifice*. As Svensson recalls, after the director requested 253 different examples of sound effects to work with, such a great number appeared far too unrealistic to him as it would threaten to overburden the film: "And straightaway I realized this wasn't going to be possible. There was no space left; the film was going to be crammed with a load of diverging sounds. To begin with, I cut out half, and then I started to work."[19] Apart from reducing the abundance of sound effects requested for *The Sacrifice*, he proposed more advanced sound-work strategies for the film and thus considerably enriched Tarkovsky's ideas on the film sound. For Svensson, the same kind of sounds must differ and have a dynamic curve because sound as a living phenomenon is never constant. In terms of its treatment of environmental and everyday sounds, *Nostalghia* appeared to him "very poorly done" because of their monotony. "The sound of someone walking," he says, "always sounds like click-clack, click-clack, click-clack . . . No two footsteps would sound alike and they'd have a life of their own." Given this, for *The Sacrifice* he suggested "an entirely different approach" by providing each sound occurring inside Alexander's house with its own distinct character. As he says,

This wooden house, where many things happen, has floorboards which sound different depending on where one stands in the room. I decided I should produce these sounds at my own country cottage. It is an old, turn-of-the-century house that has resounding walls and floors. So all the footsteps were produced by me; that is, I physically walked in different pairs of shoes, even ladies' shoes size 45. The voices must be given their own character, so that you can experience them in their own personal environment . . . The voice must develop, it must change. So if you're speaking up or down, sideways or back, the character of the voice changes constantly. Even if you have 100 per cent location recording and it sounds even, you would still have to work with spatial dimensions and reverberation in the mix. If people are at different points in the space, every voice must have its own distinct character, its own reverberation. And that's really to create the sense of credibility and the right emotion. There are many ways of achieving that.[20]

Sound individuation, therefore, became one of the main principles in *The Sacrifice*'s sound production. Svensson similarly contributed to the naturalism of mixing and masking procedures in the film's sound-editing. Both techniques are implemented to distort certain aspects of the sound formation: whereas mixing is used for the actual alteration of the sound origin, masking aims at covering up a given sound with other natural or artificial sounds by making its source less evident and intrusive. In Tarkovsky's films made in the USSR, sound mixing and masking are applied to noises, instruments, electronic music, and quotations. More specifically, in *Solaris*, *Mirror*, and *Stalker* musical quotations are variously mixed with electronic, instrumental, and natural sounds as well as their technical transformations. In *Solaris*, for example, Bach's Chorale Prelude in F Minor "Ich ruf zu dir, Herr Jesu Christ" is played four times as a refrain and each time it is progressively mixed with different natural and electronic sounds: in its second playing it is mixed with footsteps in the snow and bird chirping, while in its final occurrence it becomes saturated with the electronic sound of Solaris. In *Stalker* the electronic sound is meticulously masked as noise-like effects, whereas historical music quotations are mixed with sounds of other origins, the most famous example of which is the brief appearance of the "Ode to Joy" from Beethoven's Ninth Symphony through the metallic clamor of the passing train at the end.[21]

During *The Sacrifice*'s sound production Tarkovsky's main requirement for Svensson was that of authenticity. In search of something utterly original, Tarkovsky opted for the traditional Swedish herding calls or *kulning* that are very rare and difficult to find in recordings. Finally, after long searches, they came across a distorted singing which was genuine yet improperly recorded. It was integrated into the film's soundscape and disguised among other sounds. As Svensson recalls, while they were looking for the recording it was important to find one with the most realistic sound, regardless of the quality:

We thought of looking for these calls in the Swedish Radio archives but didn't find many that were recorded realistically. There were some that had been arranged musically, but he rejected those. He wanted it to be real. And then we came across a rather old recording that had been made via a telephone cable from Rättvik in the Swedish countryside to Swedish Radio in Stockholm. It was mastered on one of those wax cylinders. It was of very poor quality—there was crackling and static—but he still thought it was marvelous. In the soundtrack, it was mixed into the outdoor environment with a certain amount of reverberation, so the quality didn't matter.[22]

This process is evidence of Tarkovsky's particular accuracy in selecting a sound sample or preexisting recording according to its authenticity. For the viewer's perception, the authenticity of a selected sound is further enhanced in the context of the film's soundscape when its origin and imperfect source are hidden by being blended with other ambient sounds that potentially belong to the scene.

FRAMING THE IRREAL

Naturalistic sound effects reconceived as musical events are usually employed by Tarkovsky in the sound-making of extended sequences in which odd natural and electronic sounds are integrated into the film's score. In such seemingly uneventful scenes as the car passage through Tokyo in *Solaris*, the journey on the railway trolley into the Zone in *Stalker*, long-lasting rain in Gorchakov's dream and his nine-minute messianic walk with a candle across the spa-pool in *Nostalghia*, time is dilated to the extent of its emancipation from the confines of everyday temporality, just as sound serves as a key device to both enhance the authenticity of real-life experience as well as transcend its empirical coordinates. Such "slow" sequences, which constitute the signature of Tarkovsky's "transcendental style,"[23] are inspired by his methodological conviction that "observation is the first principle of the image, which always has been inseparable from photographic record," and that cinematographic image must "present as an observation one's own perception of an object."[24] That is to say, the auteur's subjective vision of an object overlaps with its objective or photographic observation and thus adds a mode of spiritual contemplation to the authenticity of the real-life experience represented in a film.

Despite Tarkovsky's outspoken commitment to realism, his filmmaking (and sound-making) practices could be best described in terms of irrealist aesthetics. First promoted by the American philosopher Nelson Goodman, irrealism as a philosophical concept refers to the assertion of the plurality of worlds and the relativity of representation directed against the universality of truth claims. Rather than being the opposite of realism, irrealism denotes neither the negation of reality (anti-realism) nor its illusory nature and immateriality (idealism); it emphasizes instead the presence of parallel versions of reality that all have an equal right to exist simultaneously.[25] In the context of literature, irreal narratives are characterized by the events complying with fundamentally unknown laws of physics that cannot be explained away either by hidden circumstances of a story or genre conventions (e.g. fairy tale, sci-fi, fantasy, surrealism). Kafka's narratives, in this regard, serve as the most exemplary illustration of literary irrealism, since their "events, characters, and physics . . . cannot be satisfactorily reduced to one such interpretation"[26] and the only logic that is applicable to his fiction is that of the absurd. In Tarkovsky's films, the irreal amply manifests itself in oneiric and levitation scenes, magic places (e.g. Solaris, Zone, and spa-pool), and mysterious characters. Furthermore, his films have often been interpreted in terms that are quite compatible with irrealism: the Freudian uncanny,[27] Todorov's notion of the fantastic,[28] and the Formalist estrangement or *otstranenie*.[29] As for the sound, many scholars have noticed that "Tarkovsky uses sound in order to define place . . . as some kind of parallel reality."[30] Michel Chion, for example, argues that his sounds "seem to come from the other side, as if they're heard by an immaterial ear, liberated from the hurly-burly of our human world . . . [calling] to another dimension . . . disengaged from the present."[31] In a similar vein, according to Andrea Truppin, "Tarkovsky's use of sound permits his films to travel smoothly through multiple and equally weighted layers of experience. These layers flow simultaneously through one another without the rigid hierarchy that separates most filmic worlds into 'reality' and 'fantasy.'"[32]

In his collaboration with Tarkovsky, Artemiev achieved the effect of the irreal mainly by blending together a variety of environmental, electronic, and musical sounds, which could be best illustrated by *Solaris*' library sequence where both musical and visual quotations resonate: Bach's choral prelude and Pieter Bruegel the Elder's *The Hunters in the Snow* (1565). The sequence starts off with the medium close-up of Hari contemplating Bruegel's painting and then continues as the detailed examination of its winter landscape from her point of view. The animated landscape is represented panoramically by being fragmented into multiple parts as if a moving camera were filming a real vista from a distant point. The camera's slow sliding across the painting is accompanied by various sounds that would voice each of its static images: chatting men, barking dogs, chirping birds, ringing church bells, and even blasting hunter's horn. The metamorphosis applied to the painting transposes the viewer into the realm of the irreal where the distinction between the painterly image and reality is blurred. The ekphrasis of the painting switches to the levitation scene non-diegetically accompanied by the Bach prelude with new electronic sounds laid over the organ, which further enhances the meditative mood.

The creation of a certain contemplative state was the first and foremost prerequisite Tarkovsky presented to the sound designer. As Artemiev says,

> I have always composed music to make it "fit the screen." Tried to work with exact timing, coordinate everything in seconds. It has always been like this in cinema . . . But not with Tarkovsky! To him it was not timing that was important but a 'state'. Perhaps, his very aesthetics was different, he had very few rapid shots in general. He said, "Music should be here. Start from here . . . however, you can start even earlier."[33]

Given the predominance of musical quotations in *Mirror*'s score, Artemiev's involvement in its sound design was relatively lesser than in other Tarkovsky features. Nevertheless, his contribution to the irreal effect of few episodes was quite significant. The one known as "Crossing Sivash" is especially noteworthy among them: the documentary footage of the Soviet soldiers crossing Lake Sivash in December 1943. Artemiev proposed to accompany this sequence with a simple yet sinister sound laid over the splashes in the water:

> According to Tarkovsky's idea, it was a kind of biblical Exodus . . . How to render this musically? And then I invented a thing for which Andrei thanked me with words: "Man, you are just a genius!" It was the simplest thing ever: a variation to one chord. It was the sound of real acoustic E-flat major triad in the form of slowly revolving 'rings' that I set on a 24-channel sound board [that is, "single chords—orchestral, choral, electronic—as if they were hanging in space in endless repetition"]. As a result, what came out was a strange, extending and sufficiently 'mystical' sounding.[34]

In another scene of *Mirror*, featuring a small boy who comes to the village for the first time, Tarkovsky wanted to create the ambience of a "scary forest." When Artemiev proposed to mix the forest's background noise with the sounding of a full symphony orchestra, Tarkovsky rejected it as being too intentional and artificial. Instead, he requested to somehow incorporate the sound of a pipe which seemed to him "strange" when he was a child. Thus, the rustle of leaves in the scene irreally intertwines with an uncanny timbre of pipe.[35]

In *Stalker*'s sound design, Tarkovsky and Artemiev pushed their sonic irrealism to yet another level by demonstrating the literal mutation of the sound in the context of the narrative transition to an otherworldly dimension. The characters are transported into the Zone by a motorized rail trolley and their four-minute journey is accompanied by nothing more than the rhythmical sound of the train's wheels clattering along the tracks that is electronically transformed. In this scene the camera never captures the source of the sound and, from various angles, focuses instead on the protagonists' heads and faces pensively staring out into space. As Artemiev comments on the scene,

> Heroes depart from a more or less normal world to an abnormal one, the Zone . . . And nothing happens on the screen. Merely a trolley with the heroes is rushing forward. However, the viewer must feel that something is changing. The reality is changing in itself, something like a new reality is emerging. I had been thinking for a long time what clue I could get to it. Then it occurred to me: the rumble of wheels. What if I play with it? At first I simply added reverberation—in one place more, in another less. Then I replaced an acoustic rumble by "artificial." Then I laid this sounding over a male choir (by transposing it down by an octave). Then I added other background acoustic noises by the smallest, literally homeopathic doses. As a result, the rumble of wheels, first as the natural sound, started to sound, with an interval of ten seconds, more fantastically, strangely, "otherworldly."[36]

That is to say, the characters' transition into the magic space of the Zone is demarcated by the sound which itself becomes "otherworldly." Electronic music composed for the scene is masked as an ambience, or technical noise, which imperceptibly works as a substitute while the resounding is made. Above all, it is more about concrete music than electronic sound. The trolley's reverberation transfers the listener into the Zone, focusing perception on a monotonous static state with the interplay of color, rhythm, and tone inside the structure, which produces a hypnotizing effect and involves the listener in the meditation. This scene parallels the naturalistic sound design of *Solaris*' long sequence featuring the car passage along futuristic highways and clearly demonstrates how Artemiev's approach to sound evolved in terms of his emphasis on the irreal by blurring the distinction between the electronic and the acoustic.

As noted, in his last two films made abroad Tarkovsky had to manage without a composer since Artemiev was unable to work with him. However, his collaboration with Owe Svensson for *The Sacrifice* brought his sound design to an entirely new level. Besides stressing the differentiation of natural sounds described above, Svensson similarly contributed to the sound solution of irreal episodes in the film by gathering and mixing different sound sources, including a musical instrument, recorded music, and noises. In *The Sacrifice*, the irreal sound is most tellingly implemented in the scene of Alexander's visit to Maria: convinced by Otto that she is a witch, he hopes to persuade her to perform a love ritual in order to save the world. Seeing him kneeling beside her with the words "love me . . . save us all" and even putting a handgun to his head, Maria reluctantly complies with his bizarre supplication and the two embrace each other, levitating and rotating in the air. The levitation scene cuts to Alexander's black-and-white recurrent vision of the apocalypse, followed by the fragments from his dream in which Maria is dressed as his wife Adelaide and naked Marta is shooing away chickens in the house. Just as the electronic transformation of the trolley's sound in *Stalker* announces the characters' transition into a magic space, in this scene the sound equally serves as an audio marker of the narrative's switch to a dream reality and thus invokes the experience of meditation. Here the two musical quotations (or preexisting recordings) share the same soundscape in which they, like the characters, interlace with each other: the recording of the Japanese bamboo flute *hotchiku*, performed by the Rinzai Zen master Watazumido Shuso, and the Swedish herding calls *kulning* mentioned above. The sequence is also accompanied by an array of other natural sounds associated with the apocalypse: the roar of fighter jets flying overhead, clinking glasses and dishes, and stomping footsteps of panic-stricken people in a devastated city. Svensson comments on the sound components of this sequence:

> In the case of the dreams it was all very evident what needed to be done. The main component is naturally the overhead flights. In order to conjure up threats of war we had to create a sense of great anxiety, to make it seem as if a war was actually going on. It's a composition of many Swedish jet fighters with added bits of rumble and a few other things. Another sound component is the Japanese flute, a kind of a long tube, which we took from a vinyl recording. Strangely enough, Tarkovsky wanted us to do a mix of the Japanese flute in combination with the voice of the woman—the cow calls. And remarkably it worked; music was made out of two seemingly unrelated components. And there's another ingredient: there were ships' horns in the distance that sometimes reach the pitch of the Japanese flute. There are a number of different ship sirens as well as lighthouses that sound foghorns. So, in the end, the dream is heard as a combination of the woman's voice, the Japanese flute and various ship sounds.[37]

The sounds of the Japanese flute and Swedish herding calls start during Alexander's visit to Maria and continue until he wakes up in his own room. Both sounds, therefore, create a counterpoint, introducing a new layered and mixed sounding. The meaning of these quotations can be interpreted as references to the characters' cultural backgrounds: the flute represents Alexander's personality due to his passion for Japanese culture, whereas the herding calls stand for Maria as a local living in the countryside. Both sounds appear multiple times in the film but separately. It is only at the moment of the characters' love-making and levitation that we hear them at the same time. Furthermore, not only are the herding calls the typical sounds of the Swedish countryside, in *The Sacrifice* they obtain a real sense of otherworldly signals, since their actual purpose is to call. Given that we have no confirmation of Maria being a witch, *kulning* could be the only evidence of her mysteriousness in the film. Svensson interprets this sound in relation to Maria:

> The important thing was that there was the presence of a woman that comes into the film quite early. And then she enters the dream; and that represents a connection with human emotions, which is of course a contrast to the threat of war. Both Otto . . . and Alexander are in contact with her. Otto seems to hear her call when he suddenly collapses on the floor while walking through the house telling his strange tales. One never really discovers what is going on.[38]

In addition to Otto's collapse in response to the herding calls he might have heard, their mystical origin could be evidenced in the scene in which Otto comes to Alexander and tells him about Maria's magic powers, insisting that Alexander should visit her. In this moment a single call is heard and both of them receive the signal:

> Otto: Have you heard?
> Alexander: What?
> Otto: What is it?
> Alexander: I don't know. I thought it sounded like music.
> Otto: In any case, you must go to Maria!

Right after this conversation, Alexander flees to Maria's house in secrecy. The following levitation scene with cuts to his disaster vision and dream images is accompanied by the four-minute interaction of the flutes and calls, interspersed with the characters' incoherent verbal exchange (e.g. Maria says "there" and "poor," while Alexander stutters "No!" and "I can't"). When the oneiric sequence smoothly morphs into the next scene, when Alexander wakes up in the morning and everything seems to be back to normal, we discover that the sound of the Japanese flute is, in fact, diegetic: as a recording, it comes from his home sound system, which he turns off and the tune discontinues. The same could be said about the herding calls which are often heard in the Swedish countryside. And yet, whether these sounds are diegetic or not is still hard to tell in the context of the film's narrative, the ambivalence of their sources seeming to be parallel with the irreal plausibility of the levitation sequence itself.

CONCLUSION

As observed by Andrea Truppin, in Tarkovsky's irreal episodes different sounds serve as "sound bridges" used to "join together heterogeneous worlds," "the real with the unreal, making each more like the other," and "subverting our expectations of conventional depictions of reality that the films initially seem to follow."[39] To extend this metaphor, both Eduard Artemiev and Owe Svensson could be viewed as such sound bridgemakers who helped the auteur to establish an audible connection and interflow between this world and its otherworldly dimension by defamiliarizing sound via various techniques. Whereas Artemiev, being an avant-garde composer, contributed to Tarkovsky's sound design by merging the acoustic with the electronic via his ANS synthesizer, Svensson as a sound-mixer further refined the naturalistic aspects of the film sound by transforming diverse recorded material through elaborate procedures of sound editing and post-production. Tarkovsky's irreal sound design follows the same aesthetic principles as his long-take sequences embedded in real-life experience and observation: just as time and space transcend their empirical limitations through the excess of their materiality in such sequences, the irreal ambiguity of their sound similarly comes from pushing its firm anchorage in concrete reality to the limit.

NOTES

1. Tarkovsky, *Sculpting in Time: Reflections on the Cinema* (Austin: University of Texas Press, 1986), 212.
2. Elizabeth Fairweather, "Andrey Tarkovsky: The Refrain of the Sonic Fingerprint," in James Wierzbicki (ed.), *Music, Sound and Filmmakers* (Abingdon: Routledge, 2012), 32–44, 39.
3. As many scholars have noticed, for Tarkovsky it was a matter of principle to create something entirely opposite of Kubrick's *2001*, "a kind of 'anti-2001' sf movie," which would rather emphasize humanistic ideals instead of special effects of space travel (see James M. Purcell, "Tarkovsky's Film *Solaris* (1972): A Freudian Slip?" *Extrapolation* 19.2 (1978): 126–31, 126). Nevertheless, in his 1970 letter to the Department of Culture of the Central Committee of the Communist Party, arguing to extend the funding for *Solaris*, Tarkovsky referred to the high production level of Kubrick's *2001* as an example to follow and a reason why the Tokyo trip, being under the threat of cancellation, was indispensable for the representation of an authentic "city of the future." *Solaris* conceived as the "Soviet answer to *2001*" was, therefore, much dependent on Tarkovsky's ability to shoot the car-drive sequence in Tokyo (see Dmitry Salynsky, *Fil'm Andreia Tarkovskogo "Solaris"* (Moscow: Astrea, 2012), 369).
4. Christine Lee Gengaro, *Listening to Stanley Kubrick: The Music in His Films* (Lanham, MD: Rowman & Littlefield, 2013), 95.
5. Salynsky, *Fil'm Andreia Tarkovskogo*, 393.
6. Arkady Petrov, "Eduard Artemiev i Andrei Tarkovsky ('Muzyka v fil'me mne ne nuzhna . . .')," *Elektroshock.ru*: http://www.electroshock.ru/edward/interview/petrov3/index.html
7. Tarkovsky, *Sculpting in Time*, 162.
8. Ibid., 159.
9. Ibid., 159–62.
10. Ibid., 159.
11. Ibid., 162.

12. Ibid., 163.

13. Ibid., 162.

14. On creating the sound design for *Solaris*, *Mirror*, and *Stalker*, Artemiev worked with the ANS and Synthi 100 synthesisers. See Julia Shpinitskaya, "Deconstructing Andrei Tarkovsky's Magic Realism. Sound Design and the Category of Irreal," in Jean-Marc Larrue, Servanne Monjour, and Marcello Vitali Rosati *Sens public*, *Authentique artifice*, ed. Jean-Marc Larrue, Servanne Monjour, Marcello Vitali Rosati (eds), 20 May 2019: http://sens-public.org/article1401.html. On the use of the ANS synthesizer in the Soviet context during the 1960s and 1970s, see Peter J. Schmelz, "From Scriabin to Pink Floyd. The ANS Synthesizer and the Politics of Soviet Music between Thaw and Stagnation," in Robert Adlington (ed.), *Sound Commitment: Avant-garde Music and the Sixties* (Oxford and New York: Oxford University Press, 2009), 254–77.

15. *Nostalghia* (1983) and *The Sacrifice* (1986) were made abroad, in Italy and Sweden respectively. It is said that the Italian Musicians' Union insisted on Tarkovsky hiring an Italian composer for *Nostalghia*, yet he wanted to work with Artemiev only.

16. Petrov, "Eduard Artemiev."

17. The first two, *Ivan's Childhood* (1962) and *Andrei Rublev* (1966), do have a regular music track composed by Viacheslav Ovchinnikov. Consider, for instance, Paul Schrader's observation on Tarkovsky's sound design: "The more a director is committed to slow cinema, the less he or she uses musical scoring. Andrei Tarkovsky and Theo Angelopoulos, for example, began their careers by using composed music, and ended by using little or none" (Paul Schrader, *Transcendental Style in Film: Ozu, Bresson, Dreyer* (Berkeley: University of California Press, 2018), 14).

18. On the use of quotations in Tarkovsky's films, see Julia Shpinitskaya, "Andrei Tarkovsky's Musical Offering: The Law of Quotation," in *New Semiotics: Between Tradition and Innovation: Proceedings of the 12th World Congress of Semiotics* (NBU Publishing House and IASS Publications, 2017), 608–16.

19. Owe Svensson, "On Tarkovsky's *The Sacrifice*: Video Interview, Sunday April 18, 1998, Institut Français, London," in Larry Sider, Diane Freeman, and Jerry Sider (eds), *Soundscape. The School of Sound Lectures 1998–2001* (London and New York: Wallflower Press, 2007), 113.

20. Svensson, "On Tarkovsky's *The Sacrifice*," 114.

21. See Tobias Pontara, "Beethoven Overcome: Romantic and Existentialist Utopia in Andrei Tarkovsky's *Stalker*," *19th-Century Music* 34.3 (2011): 302–15.

22. Svensson, "On Tarkovsky's *The Sacrifice*," 113.

23. Schrader, *Transcendental Style*, 6–14.

24. Tarkovsky, *Sculpting in Time*, 107.

25. Nelson Goodman, *Ways of Worldmaking* (Cambridge, MA: Hackett Publishing, 1978).

26. G. S. Evans, "What Is Irrealism?" in G. S. Evans and Alice Whittenburg (eds), *The Irreal Reader* (Guide Dog Books, 2013), 152–8, 156.

27. Daniel McFadden, "Memory and Being: The Uncanny in the Films of Andrei Tarkovsky," *Verges: Germanic & Slavic Studies in Review* 1.1 (2012).

28. Nariman Skakov, *The Cinema of Tarkovsky: Labyrinths of Space and Time* (London: I. B. Tauris, 2012), 93.

29. Thorsten Botz-Bornstein, *Films and Dreams: Tarkovsky, Bergman, Sokurov, Kubrick, and Wong Kar-Wai* (Lanham, MD: Lexington Books, 2007).

30. Stefan Smith, "The Edge of Perception: Sound in Tarkovsky's *Stalker*," *The Soundtrack* 1.1 (2007): 41–52, 43.

31. Michel Chion, *Audio-Vision: Sound on Screen* (New York: Columbia University Press, 1994), 123–4.

32. Andrea Truppin, "And Then There Was Sound: The Films of Andrei Tarkovsky," in Rick Altman (ed.), *Sound Theory. Sound Practice* (New York and London: Routledge, 1992), 235–48, 243.
33. Petrov, "Eduard Artemiev."
34. Ibid.
35. Ibid.
36. Ibid.
37. Svensson, "On Tarkovsky's *The Sacrifice*," 115.
38. Ibid., 113.
39. Truppin, "And Then There Was Sound," 244.

Theoretical Approaches

Introduction to Part III

Andrei Tarkovsky may be more of a "great practitioner" than a "great thinker," as the prominent Russian auteur Alexei German skeptically observed. Yet the aesthetic power of his film images only intensifies their thought-provoking impact on the viewer. This section aims to demonstrate how theoretical discussions generated by his films can helpfully contribute to a deeper understanding of their meaning. The section opens with Slavoj Žižek's chapter, which offers a Lacanian reading of Tarkovsky's films in terms of an encounter with the radical otherness of the Kantian thing-in-itself, illustrated by the planet Solaris or Stalker's Zone, which is structurally quite similar to more commercial horror movies dramatizing an encounter with the unknown.

In a similar vein, Linda Belau and Ed Cameron provide a psychoanalytically inflected analysis of the complex nature of Tarkovsky's melancholia as the predominant affect in his films, functioning as a poetic critique of the reality principle, eschewing our symbolic separation from the Thing. Engaging with the theories of melancholia developed by Sigmund Freud, Jacques Lacan, and Julia Kristeva, the authors trace its various configurations in Tarkovsky's last three Soviet films: *Solaris* (1972) exhibits the melancholic clinging to the impossible past brought about by narcissistic withdrawal and interminable mourning; *Mirror* (1974) dramatizes the impossible return to a pre-symbolic childhood; the story of *Stalker* (1979) circulates around the unknown that grounds the world of the melancholic.

Robert Efird's chapter explores *Solaris'* chiasmatic interpenetration of the real and the phantasmatic in the context of Maurice Merleau-Ponty's concept of the flesh defined as the non-physical substrate of the visible world and the virtual. Thanks to its genre of science fiction, Efird argues, *Solaris* accomplishes more convincingly the physical realization of the characters' dream imagery, which vividly exemplifies Tarkovsky's cinematic materialism. Besides numerous scenes with mirrors, the dynamic chiasm of the flesh, which is both physical and spiritual, fully manifests itself in the ambiguous figure of Hari who is simultaneously the object of Kelvin's memory as well as the self-conscious subject on her own.

Anne Eakin Moss' chapter examines Tarkovsky's cinema in relation to contemporary philosopher Pierre Hadot's concept of spiritual exercises. As she demonstrates, each of his films could be seen as such spiritual exercises because of numerous parallels with Hadot's theory: all his protagonists demand of themselves extreme forms of mental concentration, focused on goals that depart from the everyday and can only be seen as metaphysical, and all of them are quixotic seekers passionately involved in spiritually transcendent quests characterized by deep attention to the world around them. Furthermore, the viewer's experience could also serve as an example of Hadot's idea of how spiritual exercises might be practiced via deepening and transforming habitual perception.

This section concludes with Mikhail Iampolski's chapter tracing the evolution of Tarkovsky's engagement with memory throughout his career. Whereas in *Andrei Rublev* (1966) he attempts to reconstruct Russia's medieval environment by applying his method of direct observation, in *Mirror* the integration of the past into the present becomes thoroughly subjectivized through his modelling of material reality after his personal memories and photographs. Furthermore, by sharing the director's individual realm of memory with viewers and making them accept it as their own, *Mirror* also aims to transcend it on the impersonal level. In his late features, Iampolski argues, Tarkovsky finally overcomes the subjective dimension of the past by shifting his attention to the objective trace of time expressed by the material indexality of things.

CHAPTER 9

Andrei Tarkovsky, Or the Thing from Inner Space

Slavoj Žižek

Jacques Lacan defines art itself with regard to the Thing: in his Seminar on the *Ethics of Psychoanalysis*, he claims that art as such is always organized around the central Void of the impossible-real Thing—a statement which, perhaps, should be read as a variation on Rilke's old thesis that Beauty is the last veil that covers the Horrible.[1] Lacan gives some hints about how this surrounding of the Void functions in the visual arts and in architecture; what we shall do here is not provide an account of how, in cinematic art also, the field of the visible, of representations, involves reference to some central and structural Void, to the impossibility attached to it—ultimately, therein resides the point of the notion of *suture* in cinema theory. What I propose to do is something much more naive and abrupt: to analyse the way the motif of the Thing appears within the diegetic space of cinematic narrative—in short, to speak about films whose narrative deals with some impossible/traumatic Thing, like the Alien Thing in science-fiction horror films.[2] What better proof of the fact that this Thing comes from Inner Space than the very first scene of *Star Wars*? At first, all we see is the void—the infinite dark sky, the ominously silent abyss of the universe, with dispersed twinkling stars which are not so much material objects as abstract points, markers of space coordinates, virtual objects; then, all of a sudden, in Dolby stereo, we hear a thundering sound coming from behind our backs, from our innermost background, later rejoined by the visual object, the source of this sound—the gigantic spaceship, a kind of space version of *Titanic*—which triumphantly enters the frame of screen-reality. The object-Thing is thus clearly rendered as a part of *ourselves* that we eject into reality . . . This intrusion of the massive Thing seems to bring a relief, cancelling the *horror vacui* of staring at the infinite void of the universe; however, what if its actual effect is the exact opposite? What if the true horror is that of

Something—the intrusion of some excessive massive Real—where we expect Nothing? This experience of "Something (the stain of the Real) instead of Nothing" is perhaps at the root of the metaphysical question "Why is there something instead of nothing?"

The exemplary case of the Thing is, of course, the mysterious undead alien object falling from the universe, an object which is inhuman, but nonetheless alive and often even possessing an evil will of its own, from *The Thing* (John Carpenter, 1982) or *Smilla's Sense of Snow* (Bille August, 1997). However, what one should not forget is that one of Lacan's examples of *das Ding* in his Seminar on the *Ethics of Psychoanalysis* is Harpo Marx, the mute Marx brother, identified as the monster apropos of whom we are never sure if he is a witty genius or a total imbecile, i.e. in whom childish innocence and goodness overlap with extreme corruption and sexual dissolution, so that one doesn't know where one stands with him: does he stand for the Edenic, prelapsarian innocence or for the utter egotism which does not know of the difference between Good and Evil?[3] This absolute undecidability or, rather, incommensurability makes him a monstrous Thing, an Other *qua* Thing, not an intersubjective partner, but a thoroughly *inhuman* partner.[4] This Thing can also be a monstrous animal, from King Kong through Moby Dick to the gigantic white buffalo, obviously a new version of Moby Dick, the white whale, in J. Lee Thompson's *The White Buffalo* (1977); in this weird, highly idiosyncratic film, the old Bill Hickok returns to the Wild West, haunted in his dreams by the apparition of a White Buffalo (also a sacred native American animal); the whole movie points toward the staging and organizing of the *scene* of the final confrontation, when, on a narrow mountain pass, the buffalo will attack the hero and he will kill him. Significantly, Bronson wears dark sunglasses, the codified sign of the blinded gaze and of impotence, i.e. castration (Bronson's impotence is clearly ascertained in the film: when he meets his old love, Poker Jenny, he is unable to fulfill her expectations and to engage in sexual intercourse with her).[5] (It would be easy to propose here the elementary Freudian reading: the White Buffalo is the primordial father who is not yet dead and who, as such, blocks the hero's sexual potency—his desperate sound is homologous to that of shofar in Jewish religion; the scene the hero endeavours to stage is thus that of the parricide.) However, a further crucial feature, the Thing (White Buffalo) is linked not only to the motif of sexual impotence, but also to the destructive nature of American capitalism: when Hickok arrives at the final train station, he sees a mountain of white bones of the thousands of slaughtered buffalo (and, as we know from history, he was much responsible for their mass killing); the White Buffalo is thus clearly a kind of revenge ghost of all the dead buffalos.[6]

What is of special interest to our psychoanalytic perspective is, of course, the way this Thing —precisely insofar as it is in itself *asexual*—is inherently related to sexual difference: does not the gigantic volcanic rock north of Melbourne in Peter Weir's *Picnic at Hanging Rock* (1975) function as another version of such a Thing, more precisely, as a forbidden domain (Zone, precisely) in which ordinary mores are somehow suspended—once we enter this domain, the obscene secrets of sexual enjoyment become accessible? *Picnic* focuses on the strange events that took place at Appleyard College, an upper-class all-girls' school north of Melbourne, on St Valentine's Day, 14 February 1900, when the girls go for a picnic at Hanging Rock, a natural monument formed of ancient lava rock.[7] Before leaving, the angelic blond Miranda tells her orphan friend, Sarah, that she will not be at the school much longer. While having their picnic, four of the girls, Miranda, the rich heiress Irma, the rational Marion and the ugly Edith, decide to explore the rocks. Edith, fatigued and cranky, does not want to go on as the others do; she becomes frightened of something and runs screaming back to the picnic. The other three girls and Miss McCraw, one of their teachers, disappear in the Rock. Two boys who saw the girls while they were approaching the Rock go looking for them. While looking, one of the boys, the rich Michael, becomes delirious and injures himself on the rocks. He had found Irma, though: Irma is still alive, but she can't remember anything that happened to her. Mrs Appleyard, the headmistress with a drinking problem, decides that Sarah will not attend the college anymore because she is not receiving money from her guardian. After she tells Sarah of her fate to go back to the orphanage, she pushes Sarah off the roof of the building (or did Sarah herself commit suicide?). Some days later, Mrs Appleyard herself dies trying to climb Hanging Rock. What makes the enigma of Hanging Rock so interesting is the sheer multiplicity of interpretations the story suggests. First, at the level of "literal" solution to the mystery, there are five possibilities:

- the simple natural explanation: three girls and one of their mistresses fell into one of the deep crevices in the intricate stone structure of the rock, or were killed by the spiders and snakes which abound there;
- the criminal sexual explanation: they were abducted, raped and killed on the Rock, either by some sinister aborigines lurking there in wait for innocent visitors or by Michael and Albert, the two young male characters who obviously find the girls attractive and later save one of them;
- the sexual-pathological explanation: the girls' erotic repression led them to a violent self-destructive hysterical outburst;
- the primitive-religion supernatural explanation: the spirit of the mountain abducted these intruders, selecting only those who were attuned to its mode (and for that reason rejecting the fourth fat girl with no sense for sensual mysteries);
- the alien abduction explanation: the girls entered a different time-and-space Zone.[8]

On top of these, there are at least two "metaphoric" explanations: the story is based on the opposition between the stiff disciplinary Victorian atmosphere of the boarding school, located in an old neat house, and natural thriving unconstrained Life, located in the wild protuberance of the Rock. The stiff school atmosphere resonates with just-beneath-the-surface eroticism (semi-repressed lesbian longings of students for students, of students for teachers and teachers for students . . .). In contrast to this proverbial "Victorian" stiffness with its repressed longings, the Rock stands for the unbridled thriving of life in all its detailed, often disgusting shapes (close-ups of reptiles and snakes, associated with original sin, crawling around the sleeping girls, not to mention the wild, lush vegetation and flocks of birds).[9] So what could be more obvious than to read the story of the disappearance as a variation on the old topic of Victorian repression exploding into the open? The frigid Miss McCraw, the mathematics teacher, describes the birth of the Rock as the molten lava being "forced up from down below . . . extruded in a highly viscous state," more a description of hormones slowly awakening in the repressed pubescent girls than a natural phenomenon, a volcanic protuberance from the great depths of the earth. The Rock thus obviously stands for the unbridled life passion long controlled by social mores and finally erupting. It is also possible to give this an anti-colonialist twist: the Rock's evil act of abduction stands for resistance to English colonization (although, of course, such a sexualized notion of the Rock's revenge tells more about the phantasmatic content that colonialists have projected into the colonized Other than about this Other itself). In this reading, the Rock signals the elementary "passionate attachments" which take their revenge and undermine the disciplined routine of the School: at the end, even Mrs Appleyard, the authoritarian Headmistress, loses control of herself, goes to the mountain, and kills herself there by jumping from a high rock.

While the film does not resolve the enigma, it provides numerous hints which point to all these different directions (the strange red cloud seen when the girls disappeared points to the spirit of the mountain as the agent of abduction; all watches stopping at noon on the day of the picnic, the total amnesia of the survivors, and the same wound on their foreheads are standard signs of alien abduction and transposition into a different "time zone"). However, the pervasive atmosphere is that of predestined Doom (what happened was somehow ordained to happen, not a series of accidents, and it is as if Miranda, the angelic girl who leads the group to the mountain, had a presentiment of this Fate), identified with a non-phallic, non-heterosexual eroticism: although the eroticization of the Rock and its fatal attraction is obvious (Irma, the only surviving girl who is found later half-dead, is properly dressed when found, but, significantly, when they undress her to put her to bed, she is without corset, this symbol of Victorian constraint; Mrs McCraw, the frigid mathematics teacher who also disappears in the Rock, is last seen walking towards the Rock, blind to her surroundings, as if strangely possessed by it, and without her skirt, i.e. only in her underwear); the story emphasizes that the girls were not raped (the Doctor examining the surviving Irma reassures everyone that her hymen is "quite intact"). More than the standard phallic sexual experience, the Rock stands for the primordial experience of Libido, of Life in its unbridled thriving, perhaps for what Lacan had in mind with *jouissance féminine*.[10]

It is crucial that the only sex in the film is between the School's least refined and therefore least repressed inhabitants, the servants Tom and Minnie, who are totally indifferent to the spell of the Rock. The standard explanation would therefore be that the excessive, suffocating fatal sensuality of the Rock affects only those who are under the spell of the Victorian repression. But what if we turn this account around (repression prevents healthy sexual satisfaction and thus breeds misty decadently spiritualized perverted global sexualization) and posit that "straight" heterosexuality itself is based on the "repression" of some more primordial same-sex "passionate attachments," so that, paradoxically, the Victorian "repression" of heterosexuality itself is sustained by and enables the return of much more radically repressed attitudes? Freud emphasized that the repression of heterosexual urges can only be sustained if it draws its energy from the reactivation of much more primitive pre-phallic drives: paradoxically, repression on behalf of culture has to rely on libidinal regression. Here we have libidinal reflexivity at its purest: the very repression of (phallic) sexuality is sexualized, it mobilizes forms of pre-phallic perversity. One is reminded here of Elizabeth Cowie's reading of the famous concluding lines of Bette Davis to her lover in *Now, Voyager*, explaining why they should renounce further sexual contacts: "Why reach for the moon when we can have the stars?" Why straight heterosexual copulation, when, if we renounce it, I can have the much more intense pleasures of lesbian "primordial attachments"?

This is why poor Miss McCraw, the least sexualized of the teachers, this model of frigidity (measured by heterosexual standards), is the only one who joins the three girls and (in the eighteenth chapter) reappears as a mysterious obscenely sexualized "Clown-Woman." And, if we follow this line of reasoning to the end, do we not have to reinterpret the figure of the headmistress herself? What if, far from being the simple opposite of the Rock, Mrs Appleyard in a way *is* the Rock? What if her final suicide on the slopes of the Rock, rather than signalling her defeat in the face of the primordial passions of the Rock, points to their ultimate identity?

In Mimi Leder's cosmic catastrophic film *Deep Impact* (1998), the Thing is a rock still floating in space: a gigantic comet threatening to hit the Earth and to extinguish all life for two years. At the film's end, the Earth is saved due to the heroic suicidal action of a group of astronauts with atomic weapons; only a small fragment of the comet falls into the ocean east of New York and causes a colossal, hundreds-of-yards-high wave that flushes the entire north-east coast of the USA, inclusive of New York and Washington. This comet-Thing also creates a couple, but an unexpected one: the incestuous couple of the young, obviously neurotic, sexually inactive TV reporter (Tea Leoni) and her promiscuous father, who has divorced her mother and just married a young woman of the same age as his daughter (Maximilian Schell). It is clear that the film is effectively a drama about this unresolved proto-incestuous father/daughter relationship: the threatening comet obviously gives body to the self-destructive rage of the heroine, without a boyfriend, with an obvious traumatic fixation on her father, flabbergasted by her father's remarriage, unable to come to terms with the fact that he has abandoned her for her peer. The President (played by Morgan Freeman, in a politically correct vein) who, in a broadcast to the nation, announces the looming catastrophe, acts as the ideal counterpoint to the obscene real father, as a caring paternal figure (without a noticeable wife!) who, significantly, gives her a privileged role at the press conference, allowing her to ask the first questions. The link of the comet with the dark, obscene underside of paternal authority is made clear through the way the heroine gets in touch with the president: in her investigation, she discovers an impending financial scandal (large illegal government spending) connected with "ELLE"—her first idea, of course, is that the President himself is involved in a sex scandal, i.e. that "Elle" refers to his mistress; she then discovers the truth: "E.L.L.E" is a codename for the emergency measures to be taken when an accident that could lead to total extinction of life threatens Earth, and the government was secretly spending funds building a gigantic underground shelter in which one million Americans will be able to survive the catastrophe. The approaching comet is thus clearly a metaphoric substitute for paternal infidelity, for the libidinal catastrophe of a daughter facing the fact that her obscene father has chosen another young woman over her. The entire machinery of the global catastrophe is thus set in motion so that the father's young wife will abandon him, and the father will return (not to his wife, the heroine's mother, but) to her daughter: the culmination of the film is the scene in which the heroine rejoins her father who, alone in his luxurious seaside house, awaits the impending wave. She finds him walking along the shoreline; they make peace with each other and embrace, silently awaiting the wave; when the wave approaches and is already casting its large shadow over them, she draws herself closer to her father, gently crying "Daddy!," as if to search for protection in him, reconstituting the childhood scene of a small girl safeguarded by the father's loving embrace, and a second later they are both swept away by the gigantic wave. The heroine's helplessness and vulnerability in this scene should not deceive us: she is the evil spirit who, in the underlying libidinal machinery of the film's narrative, pulls the strings, and this scene of finding death in the protective father's embrace is the realization of her ultimate wish.[11] Here we are at the opposite extreme to *The Forbidden Planet* (Fred M. Wilcox, 1956): in both cases we are dealing with the incestuous father/daughter relationship, yet while in the *Planet*, the destructive monster materializes the father's incestuous death wish, in the *Impact* it materializes the daughter's. The scene on the waterfront with the gigantic wave sweeping away the embraced daughter and father is to be read against the background of the standard Hollywood motif (rendered famous in Fred Zinneman's *From Here to Eternity* (1953)) of the couple making love on the beach, brushed by waves (Burt Lancaster and Deborah Kerr): here, the couple is the truly deadly incestuous one, not the straight one, so the wave is the gigantic killing wave, not the modest shake of small beach waves.[12]

Furthermore, I want to focus on the specific version of this Thing: the Thing as the Space (the sacred/forbidden Zone) in which the gap between the Symbolic and the Real is closed, i.e. in which, to put it somewhat bluntly, our desires are directly materialized (or, to put it in the precise terms of Kant's transcendental idealism, the Zone in which our intuition becomes directly productive—the state of things which, according to Kant, characterizes only the infinite divine reason).

    This notion of the Thing as the id machine, a mechanism that directly materializes our unacknowledged fantasies, possesses a long if not always respectable pedigree. In cinema, it all began with Fred Wilcox's *The Forbidden Planet* (1956), which transposed onto a distant planet the story-skeleton of Shakespeare's *The Tempest*: a father living alone with his daughter (who had never met another man) on an island, their peace suddenly disturbed by the intrusion of an expedition. On *The Forbidden Planet*, the mad-genius scientist (Walter Pidgeon) lives alone with his daughter (Anne Francis), when their peace is disturbed by the arrival of a group of space-travellers. Strange attacks of an invisible monster soon start to occur, and, at the film's end, it becomes clear that this monster is nothing but the materialization of the father's destructive impulses against the intruders who disturbed his incestuous peace. (Retroactively, we can thus read the tempest itself from Shakespeare's play as the materialization of the raging of the paternal superego.) The id machine that, unbeknown to the father, generates the destructive monster is a gigantic mechanism beneath the surface of this distant planet, the mysterious remnants of some past civilization that had succeeded in developing such a machine for the direct materialization of one's thoughts and thus destroyed itself. Here, the id machine is firmly set in a Freudian libidinal context: the monsters it generates are the realizations of the primordial father's incestuous destructive impulses against other men threatening his symbiosis with the daughter.

    The ultimate variation of this motif of the id machine is arguably Andrei Tarkovsky's *Solaris* (1972), based on Stanislaw Lem's novel, in which this Thing is also related to the deadlocks of sexual relationship. *Solaris* is the story of a space agency psychologist, Kelvin, sent to a half-abandoned spaceship above a newly discovered planet, Solaris, where, recently, strange things have been taking place (scientists going mad, hallucinating, and killing themselves). Solaris is a planet with an oceanic fluid surface which moves incessantly and, from time to time, imitates recognizable forms, not only elaborate geometric structures, but also gigantic children's bodies or human buildings. Although all attempts to communicate with the planet fail, scientists entertain the hypothesis that Solaris is a gigantic brain which somehow reads our minds. Soon after his arrival, Kelvin finds at his side in his bed his dead wife, Hari, who, years ago on Earth, killed herself after he had abandoned her. He is unable to shake Hari off, all attempts to get rid of her failing miserably (after he sends her into space with a rocket, she rematerializes the next day). Analysis of her tissue demonstrates that she is not composed of atoms like normal human beings—beneath a certain micro-level, there is nothing, just void. Finally, Kelvin grasps that Hari is a materialization of his own innermost traumatic fantasies. This accounts for the enigma of strange gaps in Hari's memory—of course she doesn't know everything a real person is supposed to know, because she is not such a person, but a mere materialization of *his* phantasmatic image of her in all its inconsistency. The problem is that precisely because Hari has no substantial identity of her own, she acquires the status of the Real that forever insists and returns to its place: like fire in Lynch's films, she forever "walks with the hero," sticks to him, never lets him go. Hari, this fragile specter, pure semblance, *cannot ever be erased*—she is "undead," eternally recurring in the space between the two deaths. Are we thus not back at the standard Weiningerian anti-feminist notion of the woman as a symptom of man, a materialization of his guilt, his fall into sin, who can only deliver him (and herself) by her suicide? *Solaris* thus relies on science-fiction rules to enact in reality itself, to present as a material fact, the notion that woman merely materializes a male fantasy: the tragic position of Hari is that she becomes aware that she is deprived of all substantial identity, that she is Nothing in herself, since she only exists as the Other's dream, insofar as the Other's fantasies turn around her. It is this predicament that imposes suicide as her ultimate ethical act: becoming aware of how he suffers on account of her permanent presence, Hari finally destroys herself by swallowing a chemical stuff that will prevent her recomposition. (The ultimate horror scene of the movie takes place when the spectral Hari reawakens from her first failed suicide attempt on Solaris: after ingesting liquid oxygen, she lies on the floor, deeply frozen; then, all of a sudden, she starts to move, her body twitching in a mixture of erotic beauty and abject horror, sustaining unbearable pain. Is there anything more tragic than such a scene of the failed self-erasure, when we are reduced to the obscene slime which, against our will, persists in the picture?) At the novel's end, we see Kelvin alone on the spaceship, staring into the mysterious surface of the Solaris ocean.

In her reading of the Hegelian dialectics of lord and bondsman, Judith Butler focuses on the hidden contract between the two: "the imperative to the bondsman consists in the following formulation: you be my body for me, but do not let me know that the body that you are is my body."[13] The disavowal on the part of the lord is thus double: first, the lord disavows his own body, he postures as a disembodied desire, and compels the bondsman to act as his body; second, the bondsman has to disavow that he acts merely as the lord's body and act as an autonomous agent, as if the bondsman's bodily labouring for the lord is not imposed on him but is autonomous.[14] This structure of double (and thereby self-effacing) disavowal also renders the patriarchal matrix of the relationship between man and woman: in a first move, woman is posited as a mere projection/reflection of man, his insubstantial shadow, hysterically imitating but never able really to acquire the moral stature of a fully constituted self-identical subjectivity; however, this status of a mere reflection itself has to be disavowed and the woman provided with a false autonomy, as if she acts the ways she does within the logic of patriarchy on account on her own autonomous logic (women are "by nature" submissive, compassionate, self-sacrificing, etc.). The paradox not to be missed here is that the bondsman (servant) is all the more the servant, the more he (mis)perceives his position as that of an autonomous agent. The same goes for woman: the ultimate form of her servitude is to (mis)perceive herself, when she acts in a "feminine" submissive-compassionate way, as an autonomous agent. For that reason, the Weiningerian ontological denigration of woman as a mere "symptom" of man—as the embodiment of male fantasy, as the hysterical imitation of the true male subjectivity—is, when openly admitted and fully assumed, far more subversive than the false direct assertion of feminine autonomy. Perhaps the ultimate feminist statement is to proclaim openly "I do not exist in myself, I am merely the Other's fantasy embodied."[15]

What we have in *Solaris* are thus Hari's *two* suicides: the first in her earlier earthly "real" existence, as Kelvin's wife, and her second as the heroic act of the self-erasure of her very spectral undead existence. While the first suicidal act was a simple escape from the burden of life, the second is a proper ethical act. In other words, if the first Hari, before her suicide on Earth, was a "normal human being," the second one is a Subject in the most radical sense of the term, precisely insofar as she is deprived of the last vestiges of her substantial identity (as she says in the film: "No, it's not me . . . It's not me . . . I'm not Hari . . . Tell me . . . tell me . . . Do you find me disgusting because of what I am?"). The difference between Hari who appears to Kelvin and the "monstrous Aphrodite," who appears to Gibarian, one of Kelvin's colleagues on the spaceship (in the novel, not in the film: in the film, Tarkovsky replaced her by a small innocent blond girl), is that Gibarian's apparition does not come from "real life" memory, but from pure fantasy: "A giant Negress was coming silently towards me with a smooth, rolling gait. I caught a gleam from the whites of her eyes and heard the soft slapping of her bare feet. She was wearing nothing but a yellow skirt of plaited straw; her enormous breasts swung freely and her black arms were as thick as thighs."[16] Unable to sustain confrontation with his primordial maternal phantasmatic apparition, Gibarian dies of shame.

Is the planet around which the story turns, composed of the mysterious matter which seems to think, that is, which in a way is the direct materialization of Thought itself, not again an exemplary case of the Lacanian Thing as the "Obscene Jelly,"[17] the traumatic Real, the point at which symbolic distance collapses, the point at which there is no need for speech, for signs, since, in it thought directly intervenes in the Real? This gigantic Brain, this Other-Thing, involves a kind of psychotic short circuit: in short-circuiting the dialectic of question and answer, of demand and its satisfaction, it provides—or, rather, imposes on us—the answer before we even raise the question, directly materializing our innermost fantasies which support our desire. Solaris is a machine that generates and materializes in reality itself my ultimate phantasmatic objectal supplement or partner, which I would never be ready to accept in reality, although my entire psychic life turns around it.

Jacques-Alain Miller[18] draws the distinction between the woman who assumes her non-existence, her constitutive lack ("castration"), that is, the void of subjectivity in her very heart, and what he calls la femme à postiche, the fake, phony woman. This femme à postiche is not what common-sense conservative wisdom would tell us (a woman who distrusts her natural charm and abandons her vocation of rearing children, serving her husband, taking care of the household, etc., and indulges in the extravaganzas of fashionable dressing and make-up, of decadent promiscuity, of career, etc.), but almost its exact opposite: the woman who takes refuge from the void in the very heart of her subjectivity, from the "not-having-it" which marks her being, in the phony certitude of "having it" (of serving as the stable support of family life, of rearing children, her true possession, etc.)—this woman gives the impression (and has the false satisfaction) of a firmly anchored being, of a self-enclosed life, satisfied circuit of everyday life: her man has to run around wildly, while she leads a calm life and serves as the safe protective rock or safe haven to which her man can always return. (The most elementary form of "having it" for a woman is, of course, having a child, which is why, for Lacan, there is an ultimate antagonism between Woman and Mother: in contrast to woman who "n'existe pas," mother definitely does exist.) The interesting feature to be noted here is that, contrary to the commonsensical expectation, it is the woman who "has it," the self-satisfied femme à postiche disavowing her lack, who not only does not pose any threat to the patriarchal male identity, but even serves as its protective shield and support, while, in contrast to her, it is the woman who flaunts her lack ("castration"), who poses as a hysterical composite of semblances covering a void, who poses the serious threat to male identity. In other words, the paradox is that the more the woman is denigrated, reduced to an inconsistent and insubstantial composite of semblances around a void, the more she threatens the firm male substantial self-identity (Otto Weininger's entire work centers on this paradox); and, on the other hand, the more the woman is a firm, self-enclosed substance, the more she supports male identity.

This opposition, a key constituent of Tarkovsky's universe, finds its clearest expression in his *Nostalghia* (1983), whose hero, the Russian writer wandering around northern Italy in search of manuscripts of a nineteenth-century Russian composer who lived there, is split between Eugenia, the hysterical woman, a being-of-lack trying desperately to seduce him in order to get sexual satisfaction, and his memory of the maternal figure of the Russian wife he has left behind. Tarkovsky's universe is intensely male-centered, oriented on the opposition woman-mother: the sexually active, provocative woman (whose attraction is signaled by a series of coded signals, like the dispersed long hair of Eugenia in *Nostalghia*) is rejected as an inauthentic hysterical creature, and contrasted to the maternal figure with closely knit and kept hair. For Tarkovsky, the moment a woman accepts the role of being sexually desirable, she sacrifices what is most precious in her, the spiritual essence of her being, and thus devalues herself, turns into a sterile mode of existence. Tarkovsky's universe is permeated by a barely concealed disgust for a provocative woman; to this figure, prone to hysterical incertitudes, he prefers the mother's assuring and stable presence. This disgust is clearly discernible in the hero's (and director's) attitude towards Eugenia's long, hysterical outburst of accusations against him which precedes her abandonment of him.

It is against this background that one should account for Tarkovsky's recourse to static long shots (or shots which allow only a slow panning or tracking movement). These shots can work in two opposed ways, both of them exemplarily at work in *Nostalghia*: they either rely on a harmonious relationship with their content, signaling the longed-for spiritual reconciliation found not in elevation from the gravitational force of the earth but in a full surrender to its inertia (like the longest shot in his entire opus, the extremely slow passage of the Russian hero through the empty cracked pool with a lit candle, the meaningless test the dead Domenico ordains him to accomplish as the path to his salvation; significantly, at the end, when, after a failed attempt, the hero does reach the other border of the pool, he collapses in death fully satisfied and reconciled), or, even more interestingly, they rely on a contrast between form and content, like the long shot of Eugenia's hysterical outburst against the hero, a mixture of sexually provocative seductive gestures with contemptuous dismissing remarks. In this shot, it is as if Eugenia protests not only against the hero's tired indifference, but also, in a way, against the calm indifference of the long static shot itself which does not let itself be disturbed by her outburst. Tarkovsky is here at the very opposite extreme from John Cassavetes, in whose masterpieces the (feminine) hysterical outbursts are shot by a handheld camera in extreme close-up, as if the camera itself was drawn into the dynamic hysterical outburst, strangely deforming the enraged faces and thereby losing the stability of its own point of view.

Solaris nonetheless supplements this standard, although disavowed, male scenario with a key feature: this structure of woman as a symptom of man can be operative only insofar as the man is confronted with his Other Thing, a decentered opaque machine which "reads" his deepest dreams and returns them to him as his symptom, as his own message in its true form that the subject is not ready to acknowledge. It is here that one should reject the Jungian reading of *Solaris*: the point of Solaris is not simply projection, materialization of the (male) subject's disavowed inner impetuses; what is much more crucial is that, if this "projection" is to take place, the impenetrable Other Thing must already be here—the true enigma is the presence of this Thing. The problem with Tarkovsky is that he himself obviously opts for the Jungian reading, according to which the external journey is merely the externalization and/or projection of the inner initiating journey into the depth of one's psyche. Apropos of *Solaris*, he stated in an interview: "Maybe, effectively, the mission of Kelvin on Solaris has only one goal: to show that love of the other is indispensable to all life. A man without love is no longer a man. The aim of the entire 'solaristic' is to show humanity must be love."[19] In clear contrast to this, Lem's novel focuses on the inert external presence of the planet Solaris, of this "Thing which thinks" (to use Kant's expression, which fully fits here): the point of the novel is precisely that Solaris remains an impenetrable Other with no possible communication with us—true, it returns us our innermost disavowed fantasies, but the "Che vuoi?" beneath this act remains thoroughly impenetrable (Why does It do it? As a purely mechanical response? To play demonic games with us? To help us—or compel us—to confront our disavowed truth?). It would thus be interesting to put Tarkovsky in the series of Hollywood commercial rewritings of novels which have served as the base for a movie: Tarkovsky does exactly the same as the lowest Hollywood producer, reinscribing the enigmatic encounter with Otherness into the framework of the production of the couple.

Nowhere is this gap between the novel and the film more perceptible than in their different endings: at the novel's end we see Kelvin alone on the spaceship, staring into the mysterious surface of the Solaris ocean, while the film ends with the archetypal Tarkovskian fantasy of combining within the same shot the Otherness into which the hero is thrown (the chaotic surface of Solaris) and the object of his nostalgic longing, the home dacha (Russian wooden country house) to which he longs to return, the house whose contours are encircled by the malleable slime of Solaris' surface—within the radical Otherness, we discover the lost object of our innermost longing. More precisely, the sequence is shot in an ambiguous way: just prior to this vision, one of his surviving colleagues on the space station tells Kelvin (the hero) that it is perhaps time for him to return home. After a couple of Tarkovskian shots of green weeds in water, we then see Kelvin at his dacha reconciled with his father. However, the camera then pulls slowly back and upward, and gradually it becomes clear that what we have just witnessed was probably not the actual return home but still a vision manufactured by Solaris: the dacha and the grass surrounding it appear as a lone island in the midst of the chaotic Solaris surface, yet another materialized vision produced by it.

The same phantasmatic staging concludes Tarkovsky's *Nostalghia*: in the midst of the Italian countryside encircled by the fragments of a cathedral in ruins, that is, of the place in which the hero is adrift, cut from his roots, there stands an element totally out of place, the Russian dacha, the stuff of the hero's dreams. Here, also, the shot begins with a close-up of only the recumbent hero in front of his dacha, so that, for a moment, it may seem that he has effectively returned home. The camera then slowly pulls back to divulge the properly phantasmatic setting of the dacha in the midst of the Italian countryside. Since this scene follows the hero's successful accomplishment of the sacrificial-compulsive gesture of carrying the burning candle across the pool, after which he collapses and drops dead—or so we are led to believe—one is tempted to take the last shot of *Nostalghia* as a shot which is not simply the hero's dream, but as the uncanny scene which follows his decease and thus stands for his death: the moment of the impossible combination of Italian countryside in which the hero is adrift and of the object of his longing is the moment of death. (This deadly impossible synthesis is announced in a previous dream sequence in which Eugenia appears in a solid embrace with the hero's Russian maternal wife figure.) What we have here is a phenomenon, a scene, a dream experience, which can no longer be subjectivized—that is, a kind of non-subjectivizable phenomenon, a dream which is no longer a dream of anyone, a dream which can emerge only after its subject ceases to be. This concluding fantasy is thus an artificial condensation of opposed, incompatible perspectives, somehow like the standard optician's test in which we see through one eye a cage, through the other eye a parrot, and, if our two eyes are well coordinated in their axes, when we open both eyes, we should see the parrot in the cage (when I recently failed the test, I suggested to the nurse that, perhaps, I would be more successful if my motivation were stronger, if, say, instead of the parrot and the cage, the two images would be of an erect penis and a spread vagina, so that, when you open both eyes, the penis is in the vagina—the poor old lady threw me out. And, incidentally, my modest proposal was justified insofar as, according to Lacan, all phantasmatic harmonious coordinations in which one element finally fully fits the other are ultimately based on the model of the successful sexual relationship, where the male virile organ fits the feminine opening "like a key into the opening of a lock.")[20]

Tarkovsky added not only this final scene, but also a new beginning: while the novel starts with Kelvin's space travel to Solaris, the movie's first half hour takes place in the standard Tarkovskian Russian countryside with a dacha, in which Kelvin takes a stroll, gets soaked by rain and is immersed into humid earth. As we have already emphasized, in clear contrast to the film's phantasmatic resolution, the novel ends with the lone Kelvin contemplating the surface of Solaris, aware more than ever that he has encountered here an Otherness with which no contact is possible. The planet Solaris has thus to be conceived in strict Kantian terms, as the impossible apparition of the thought (the thinking substance) as a Thing-in-itself, a noumenal object. Crucial for the Solaris-Thing is thus the coincidence of utter Otherness with excessive, absolute proximity: the Solaris-Thing is even more "ourselves," our own inaccessible kernel, than the Unconscious, since it is an Otherness which directly "is" ourselves, staging the "objectively-subjective" phantasmatic core of our being. Communication with the Solaris-Thing thus fails not because Solaris is too alien, the harbinger of an intellect infinitely surpassing our limited abilities, playing some perverse games with us whose rationale remains forever outside our grasp, but because it brings us too close to what, in ourselves, must remain at a distance if we are to sustain the consistency of our symbolic universe. In its very Otherness, Solaris generates spectral phenomena that obey our innermost idiosyncratic whims, that is, if there is a stage master who pulls the strings of what goes on on the surface of Solaris, it is ourselves, "the Thing that thinks" in our heart. The fundamental lesson here is the opposition, antagonism even, between the big Other (the symbolic Order) and the Other *qua* Thing. The big Other is "barred," it is the virtual order of symbolic rules that provides the frame for communication, while in the Solaris-Thing, the big Other is no longer "barred," purely virtual; in it, the Symbolic collapses into the Real, language comes to exist as a Real Thing.

Tarkovsky's other science-fiction masterpiece, *Stalker* (1979), provides the counterpoint to this all-too-present Thing: the void of a forbidden Zone. In an anonymous bleak country, an area known as "the Zone" was visited twenty years ago by some mysterious foreign entity (a meteorite, aliens) which left behind debris. People are supposed to disappear in this deadly Zone, isolated and guarded by army personnel. Stalkers are adventurous individuals who, for a proper payment, lead people to the Zone and to the mysterious room at the heart of the Zone where their deepest wishes are allegedly granted. The film tells the story of a stalker, an ordinary man with a wife and a crippled daughter with the magic ability to move objects, who takes to the Zone two intellectuals, a writer and a scientist. When they finally reach the room, they fail to pronounce their wishes because of their lack of faith, while Stalker himself seems to get an answer to his wish that his daughter would get better.

As in the case of *Solaris*, Tarkovsky turned around the point of the novel: in the Strugatsky brothers' novel *The Roadside Picnic* (1971), on which the film is based, the zones—there are six of them—are the debris of a "roadside picnic," that is, of a short stay on our planet by some alien visitors who quickly left it, finding us uninteresting; stalkers themselves are also presented in a more adventurous way, not as dedicated individuals on a tormenting spiritual search, but as deft scavengers organizing robbing expeditions, somehow like the proverbial Arabs organizing raiding expeditions into the pyramids—another Zone—for wealthy Westerners. And, effectively, are the pyramids not, according to popular science literature, traces of an alien wisdom? The Zone is thus not a purely mental phantasmatic space in which one encounters (or onto which one projects) the truth about oneself, but (like Solaris in Lem's novel) the *material presence*, the Real of an absolute Otherness incompatible with the rules and laws of our universe. (Because of this, at the novel's end, the hero himself, when confronted with the "Golden Sphere"—as the film's room in which desires are realized is called in the novel—does undergo a kind of spiritual conversion, but this experience is much closer to what Lacan called "subjective destitution," a sudden awareness of the utter meaningless of our social links, the dissolution of our attachment to reality itself; all of a sudden, other people are derealized, reality itself is experienced as a confused whirlpool of shapes and sounds, so that we are no longer able to formulate our desire.) In *Stalker* as well as in *Solaris*, Tarkovsky's "idealist mystification" is that he shrinks from confronting this radical Otherness of the meaningless Thing, reducing and retranslating the encounter with the Thing to the "inner journey" towards one's Truth.

It is to this incompatibility between our own and the alien universe that the novel's title refers: the strange objects found in the Zone that fascinate humans are in all probability simply the debris, the garbage, left behind after aliens have briefly stayed on our planet, comparable to the rubbish a group of humans leaves behind after a picnic in a forest near a main road. So the typical Tarkovskian landscape (of decaying human debris half reclaimed by nature) is in the novel precisely *what characterizes the Zone itself from the (impossible) standpoint of the visiting aliens*: what is to us a miracle, an encounter with a wondrous universe beyond our grasp, is just everyday debris to the aliens. Is it then, perhaps, possible to draw the Brechtian conclusion that the typical Tarkovskian landscape (the human environment in decay reclaimed by nature) involves the view of our universe from an imagined alien standpoint? The picnic is thus here at the opposite extreme to that at Hanging Rock: it is not us who encroach upon the Zone while on a Sunday picnic, it is the Zone itself which results from the aliens' picnic.

For a citizen of the defunct Soviet Union, the notion of a forbidden zone gives rise to (at least) five associations: a zone is (1) Gulag, that is, a separated prison territory; (2) a territory poisoned or otherwise rendered uninhabitable by some technological (biochemical, nuclear) catastrophe, like Chernobyl; (3) the secluded domain in which the nomenklatura lives; (4) foreign territory to which access is prohibited (like the enclosed West Berlin in the midst of the GDR); or (5) a territory where a meteorite struck (like Tunguska in Siberia). The point, of course, is that the question "So which is the true meaning of the Zone?" is false and misleading: the very indeterminacy of what lies beyond the limit is primary, and different positive contents fill in this preceding gap.

Stalker perfectly exemplifies this paradoxical logic of the limit which separates our everyday reality from the phantasmatic space. In *Stalker*, this phantasmatic space is the mysterious Zone, the forbidden territory in which the impossible occurs, in which secret desires are realized, in which one can find technological gadgets not yet invented in our everyday reality, and so on. Only criminals and adventurers are ready to take the risk and enter this domain of the phantasmatic Otherness. What one should insist on in a materialist reading of Tarkovsky is the constitutive role of the limit itself: this mysterious Zone is effectively the same as our common reality; and what confers on it the aura of mystery is the limit itself, that is, the fact that the Zone is designated as inaccessible, prohibited. (No wonder that when the heroes finally enter the mysterious room, they become aware that there is nothing special or outstanding in it. The Stalker implores them not to impart this news to the people outside the Zone, so that they do not lose their gratifying illusions.) In short, the obscurantist mystification consists here in the act of inverting the true order of causality: the Zone is not prohibited because it has certain properties which are "too strong" for our everyday sense of reality; it displays these properties because it is posited as prohibited. What comes first is the formal gesture of excluding a part of the real from our everyday reality and of proclaiming it the prohibited Zone.[21] Or, to quote Tarkovsky himself: "I am often asked what does this Zone stand for. There is only one possible answer: the Zone doesn't exist. Stalker himself invented his Zone. He created it, so that he was able to bring there some very unhappy persons and impose on them the idea of hope. The room of desires is equally Stalker's creation, yet another provocation in the face of the material world. This provocation, formed in Stalker's mind, corresponds to an act of faith."[22] Hegel emphasized that, in the suprasensible realm beyond the veil of appearances, there is nothing, just what the subject itself puts there when he takes a look at it.

In what, then, does the opposition between the Zone (in *Stalker*) and the planet Solaris consist? In Lacanian terms, of course, their opposition is easy to specify: it is the opposition between the two excesses, the excess of stuff over symbolic network (the Thing for which there is no place in this network, which eludes its grasp), and the excess of an (empty) place over stuff, over the elements which fill it in (the Zone is a pure structural void constituted and defined by a symbolic barrier: beyond this barrier, in the Zone, there is nothing and/or exactly the same things as outside the Zone). This opposition stands for the opposition between drive and desire: Solaris is the Thing, the blind libido embodied, while the Zone is the void which sustains desire. This opposition also accounts for the different way the Zone and Solaris relate to the subject's libidinal economy: in the midst of the Zone is the "chamber of desires," the place in which, if the subject penetrates it, his desire or wish is fulfilled, while what the Thing-Solaris returns to subjects who approach it is not their desire but the traumatic kernel of their fantasy, the sinthome which encapsulates their relation to *jouissance* and which they resist in their daily lives.

The blockage in *Stalker* is thus opposed to the blockage in *Solaris*: in *Stalker*, the blockage concerns the impossibility (for us, corrupted, reflected, non-believing modern men) of achieving the state of pure belief, of desiring directly. The room in the midst of the Zone has to remain empty; when you enter it, you are not able to formulate your wish. In contrast to it, the problem of *Solaris* is over-satisfaction: your wishes are realized and materialized before you even think of them. In *Stalker*, you never arrive at the level of pure, innocent wish-belief, while in *Solaris*, your dreams and fantasies are realized in advance in the psychotic structure of the answer which precedes the question. For this reason, *Stalker* focuses on the problem of belief or faith: the chamber does fulfill desires, but only to those who believe with direct immediacy—which is why, when the three adventurers finally reach the threshold of the room, they are afraid to enter it, since they are not sure what their true desires and wishes are (as one of them says, the problem with the room is that it does not fulfill what you think you wish, but the effective wish of which you may be unaware). As such, *Stalker* points toward the basic problem of Tarkovsky's two last films, *Nostalghia* and *The Sacrifice* (1986): the problem of how, through what ordeal or sacrifice, it is possible today to attain the innocence of pure belief. The hero of *The Sacrifice*, Alexander, lives with his large family in a remote cottage in the Swedish countryside (another version of the very Russian dacha which obsesses Tarkovsky's heroes). The celebrations of his birthday are marred by the terrifying news that low-flying jet planes signaled the start of a nuclear war between the superpowers. In his despair, Alexander turns himself in prayer to God, offering him everything that is most precious to him to have the war not have happened at all. The war is "undone" and, at the film's end, Alexander, in a sacrificial gesture, burns his beloved cottage and is taken to a lunatic asylum.

This motif of a pure, senseless act that restores meaning to our terrestrial life is the focus of Tarkovsky's last two films, shot abroad; the act is both times accomplished by the same actor (Erland Josephson), who as the old fool Domenico burns himself publicly in *Nostalghia*, and as the hero of *Sacrifice* burns his house, his most precious belonging, what is "in him more than him-self."[23] To this gesture of senseless sacrifice, one should give all the weight of an obsessional-neurotic compulsive act: if I accomplish *this* (sacrificial gesture), the catastrophe (in *The Sacrifice*, literally the end of the world in an atomic war) will not occur or will be undone—the well-known compulsive gesture of "If I do not do this (jump two times over that stone, cross my hands in this way, etc., etc.) something bad will occur." (The childish nature of this compulsion to sacrifice is clear in *Nostalghia* where the hero, following the injunction of the dead Domenico, crosses the half-dry pool with the burning candle in order to save the world.) As we know from psychoanalysis, this catastrophic X whose outbreak we fear is none other than *jouissance* itself.

Tarkovsky is well aware that a sacrifice, in order to work and to be efficient, must be in a way "meaningless," a gesture of "irrational," useless expenditure or ritual (like traversing the empty pool with a lit candle or burning one's own house). The idea is that only such a gesture of just "doing it" spontaneously, a gesture not covered by any rational consideration, can restore the immediate faith that will deliver us and heal us from the modern spiritual malaise. The Tarkovskian subject here literally offers his own castration (renunciation of reason and domination, voluntary reduction to childish "idiocy," submission to a senseless ritual) as the instrument to deliver the big Other: it is as if only by accomplishing an act which is totally senseless and "irrational" that the subject can save the deeper global meaning of the universe as such.

One is even tempted here to formulate this Tarkovskian logic of the mean-ingless sacrifice in the terms of a Heideggerian inversion: the ultimate mean-ing of sacrifice is the sacrifice of the meaning itself. The crucial point here is that the object sacrificed (burned) at the end of *The Sacrifice* is the very ulti-mate object of the Tarkovskian phantasmatic space, the wooden dacha stand-ing for the safety and authentic rural roots of the home—for this reason alone, *The Sacrifice* is appropriately Tarkovsky's last film.[24] Does this mean that we nonetheless encounter here a kind of Tarkovskian "traversing of the fantasy," renunciation to the central element whose magic appearance in the midst of the strange countryside (planet's surface, Italy) at the end of *Solaris* and *Nostalghia* provided the very formula of the final phantasmatic unity? No, because this renunciation is functionalized in the service of the big Other, as the redemptive act destined to restore spiritual meaning to life.

What elevates Tarkovsky above cheap religious obscurantism is the fact that he deprives this sacrificial act of any pathetic and solemn "greatness," render-ing it as a bungled, ridiculous act (in *Nostalghia*, Domenico has difficulties in lighting the fire which will kill him, the passersby ignore his body in flames; *The Sacrifice* ends with a comic ballet of men from the infirmary running after the hero to take him to the asylum—the scene is shot as a children's game of catch). It would be all too simple to read this ridiculous and bungled aspect of the sacrifice as an indication of how it has to appear as such to everyday people immersed in their run of things and unable to appreciate the tragic greatness of the act. Rather, Tarkovsky follows here the long Russian tradition whose exemplary case is Dostoyevsky's idiot from the novel of the same name: it is typical that Tarkovsky, whose films are otherwise totally deprived of humour and jokes, reserves mockery and satire precisely for scenes depicting the most sacred gesture of supreme sacrifice (the famous scene of Crucifixion in *Andrei Roublev* (1966) is shot in such a way: transposed into the Russian winter countryside, with bad actors playing it with ridiculous pathos, with tears flowing).[25] So, again, does this indicate that, to use Althusserian terms, there is a dimension in which Tarkovsky's cinematic texture undermines his own explicit ideological project, or at least introduces a distance toward it, renders visible its inherent impossibility and failure?

There is a scene in *Nostalghia* that contains a Pascalian reference: in a church, Eugenia witnesses the procession of simple peasant women in honor of Madonna del Parto. They are addressing to the saint their plea to become mothers—that is, their prayer concerns the fertility of their marriage. When the perplexed Eugenia, who admits that she is unable to comprehend the attraction of motherhood, asks the priest who also observes the procession how one becomes a believer, he answers: "You should begin by kneeling down"—a clear reference to Pascal's famous "Kneel down and that act will render you feeble-minded" (i.e. it will deprive you of false intellectual pride). Interestingly, Eugenia tries, but stops halfway: she is unable even to perform the external gesture of kneeling. Here we encounter the deadlock of the Tarkovskian hero: is it possible for today's intellectual (whose exemplary case is Gortchakov, the hero of *Nostalghia*), this man separated from naive spiritual certainty by the gap of nostalgia, by asphyxiating existential despair—is it possible for him to return to immediate religious immersion, to recapture its certainty? In other words, does the need of unconditional faith, its redemptive power, not lead to a typically *modern* result, to the decisionist act of formal faith indifferent toward its particular content—that is, to a kind of religious counterpoint of Schmittean political decisionism in which the fact *that* we believe takes precedence over *what* we believe in? Or, even worse, doesn't this logic of unconditional faith ultimately lead to the paradox of love exploited by the notorious Reverend Moon? As is well known, Reverend Moon arbitrarily chooses the conjugal partners for the unmarried members of his sect: legitimizing his decision by means of his privileged insight into the working of the divine cosmic order, he claims to be able to identify the mate who was predestined for me in the eternal order of things, and simply informs a member of his sect by letter who the unknown person (as a rule from another part of the globe) is that to marry. Slovenes are thus marrying Koreans, Americans are marrying Indians, and so on. The true miracle, of course, is that this bluff *works*: if there is an unconditional trust and faith, the contingent decision of an external authority can produce a love couple connected by the most intimate passionate link. Why? Since love is "blind," contingent, grounded in no clearly observable properties, that unfathomable *je ne sais quoi* which decides when I am to fall in love can also be totally externalized in the decision of an unfathomable authority.

So what is false in the Tarkovskian sacrifice? One should always bear in mind that, for Lacan, the ultimate aim of psychoanalysis is not to enable the subject to assume the necessary sacrifice (to "accept symbolic castration," to renounce immature narcissistic attachments, etc.), but to *resist* the terrible attraction of sacrifice—attraction which, of course, is none other than that of superego. Sacrifice is ultimately the gesture by means of which we aim at compensating the guilt imposed by the impossible superego injunction (the "obscure gods" evoked by Lacan are another name for the superego). Against this background, one can see in what precise sense the problematic of Tarkovsky's last two films focused on sacrifice is false and misleading: although, no doubt, Tarkovsky himself would passionately reject such designation, the compulsion felt by the late Tarkovskian heroes to accomplish a meaningless sacrificial gesture is that of the superego at its purest. The ultimate proof of it resides in the very "irrational," meaningless character of this gesture—the superego is an injunction to enjoy, and, as Lacan puts it in the first lecture of his *Encore*, *jouissance* is ultimately that which serves nothing.[26]

NOTES

1. See Chapter XVIII of Jacques Lacan, *The Ethics of Psychoanalysis* (London: Routledge 1992).

2. Are the heroes of Wagner's first three great operas—*The Flying Dutchman, Tannhäuser, Lohengrin*—in a way also not split between their respective fatal Zone (the ghost-ship on which the Dutchman is condemned to wander eternally, the Venusberg of continual sexual orgies, the serene and for that reason infinitely boring kingdom of the Grail)? Is their problem not the same: how to ESCAPE suffocating existence in the Zone (the endless lonely years on a wandering ghost-ship; the excessive pleasure in Venusberg; and, probably, worse and most boring of all, the eternal spiritual bliss of the Grail) through the trustful love of a mortal woman?

3. "Is there anything that poses a question which is more present, more pressing, more absorbing, more disruptive, more nauseating, more calculated to thrust everything that takes place before us into the abyss or void than that face of Harpo Marx, that face with its smile which leaves us unclear as to whether it signifies the most extreme perversity or complete simplicity? This dumb man alone is sufficient to sustain the atmosphere of doubt and of radical annihilation which is the stuff of the Marx brothers' extraordinary farce and the uninterrupted play of jokes that makes their activity so valuable" (Lacan, *The Ethics of Psychoanalysis*, 55).

4. As has already been pointed out, the three brothers perfectly fit the Freudian triad of ego (Chico), superego (Groucho) and Id (Harpo); this is why the fourth, Zeppo, had to be excluded—there was no place for him in this triad.

5. The same goes for Max Ophüls' early German masterpiece *Liebelei*, in which we encounter the standard Oedipal constellation: the tragic hero's older mistress (the Baroness) is a mother-substitute whom he wants to abandon for the lower-class younger woman—the ensuing duel with the Baron, of course, is the duel with the paternal double-rival. However, the cliché to be avoided here is the notion that the paternal substitute's act is "castrating" (killing the hero in a duel): the exact opposite holds, i.e. it is the paternal figure who is "impotent", "castrated," and the duel with him stands for a ridiculous regression to the imaginary rivalry with the father (whose impotence is signaled by his strange gaze and monocles)—often, the figure who prevents the realization of sexual intercourse is a ridiculous castrato, his outrage a mask, an index of his impotence. *Liebelei* thus tells the story of the hero's failure to break out from the incestuous closure into "normal" exchange, i.e. to accomplish the shift from the incestuous object to a foreign woman. We are thus opposed here to the standard reading of the severe, military, or parental figure in Ophüls' films as that of "castrating father" (see, for example, for the Baron in *Liebelei*, Susan White, *The Cinema of Max Ophüls* (New York: Columbia University Press, 1995), 95): this spectacled/stiff paternal figure who obstructs the love relationship is the exact opposite, i.e. not castratING, but castratED, i.e. his stiffness masks a ridiculous lifelessness and impotence (the reason the Baroness needs a younger lover!). The general point to be made here is how, effectively, deconstructionist film theory often resorts to terms like "phallic" or "castration" with a rather crude insensitivity . . .

6. Hickcok is also presented as the Indian killer; his acts in the film—befriending an Indian warrior who is also tracking down the Buffalo—are acts of coming to terms with his murderous past in the service of the American colonization of the West.

7. This already introduces the first element of mystery: although a persistent rumor asserts that the movie is based on a real-life mysterious disappearance, there is no basis whatsoever for this claim. Why has this conviction persisted for decades without any foundation in fact?

8. Incidentally, Joan Lindsay, the author of the novel on which the film is based, seemed to prefer a combination of these last two explanations in the eighteenth chapter of the novel, entitled "The Secret of Hanging Rock" and published only in 1987, after her death.

9. It is interesting to note how today, the notion of Evil seems again to exceed in both directions the boundaries of "mid-level" human affairs as its proper locus: not only is the notion of some trans-human, global Evil again operative (say, in the guise of the sense of the looming global ecological catastrophe for which humanity as such is responsible, although it cannot be attributed to the intention of any concrete individual), but we also increasingly experience Evil as a threat looming at the level of the invisible small, of micro-organisms (such as the new viruses resistant to all antibiotics). The impact of films like *Picnic at Hanging Rock* relies on this new sensibility for the dimensions of Evil which are simultaneously more global, impersonal, and looming at the micro-level, such as the bursting forms of minuscule life on the Rock.

10. Therein resides the difference between this story and E. M. Forster's novel *Passage to India* (1924), in which an unresolved sexual enigma also occurs in the cave of a gigantic rock: although *Passage to India* is much more complex in its description of colonialist deadlocks, we are dealing unambiguously with a sexually frustrated heroine longing for the standard heterosexual experience.

11. Interestingly enough, the other big 1998 blockbuster-variation on the theme of a gigantic comet threatening Earth, *Armageddon*, also focuses on the incestuous father/daughter relation. Here, however, it is the father (Bruce Willis) who is excessively attached to his daughter: the comet's destructive force gives body to *his* fury at his daughter's love affairs with other men of her age. Significantly, the denouement is also more "positive," not

self-destructive: the father sacrifices himself in order to save Earth, i.e. effectively—at the level of the underlying libidinal economy—erasing himself out of the picture in order to bless the marriage of his daughter with her young lover.

12. However, apropos of this Hollywood ideological inscription of the global catastrophe into the framework of the motif of the "production of a couple," we should not forget that not every link of this kind is *eo ipso* ideological. When we are dealing with what Alain Badiou would have called the declaration of Love as a Truth-Event, as the flash of the dimension of Immortal Truth within the process of generation and corruption, the only way to render visible, to represent, this dimension of an unconditional insistence is through the "nonsensical," "miraculous" notion of the *stasis* of time: it is as if, in the flash of the Truth-Event, the very course of time is temporarily halted. There is something of this miracle even in such a common melodrama as Claude Lelouch's *Viva la lie* (*Long Live Life*, 1984), in which the rotation of Earth around its axis suddenly stops: in the middle of Paris, morning never arrives, there is constant night; fascinated people gather in public places and just stare at the dark sky . . . At the film's end, this miracle/catastrophe is nicely accounted for as the dream of the hero who wanted to "stop the flow of time" in order not to miss the encounter with his beloved.

13. Judith Butler, *The Psychic Life of Power* (Stanford: Stanford University Press 1997), 47.

14. Do we not encounter here the same double disavowal as in Marxian commodity fetishism? First, commodity is deprived of its bodily autonomy and reduced to a medium which embodies social relations; then, this network of social relations is projected into a commodity as its direct material property, as if a commodity has by itself a certain value or as if money is by itself an universal equivalent.

15. And, perhaps, this paradoxical double disavowal enables us to discern the subversive potential of the masochist contract: in it, the second-level disavowal is cancelled, i.e. the servant *openly assumes the position of the servant*, and—since he is all the more the servant, the more he (mis)perceives his position as that of an autonomous agent—he thereby (at the level of the "subject of enunciation") *effectively* asserts himself as an autonomous agent. In short, what we obtain in masochism, instead of the servitude masked as autonomous agency, is autonomous agency masked as servitude.

16. Stanislaw Lem, *Solaris* (New York: Harcourt, Brace & Co., 1978), 30.

17. The formula of Tonya Howe (University of Michigan, Ann Arbor) on whose excellent seminar paper "*Solaris* and the Obscenity of Presence" I rely here.

18. See Jacques-Alain Miller, "Des semblants dans la relation entre les sexes," in *La Cause freudienne 36* (Paris, 1997), 7–15.

19. Quoted from Antoine de Vaecque, "Andrei Tarkovski," *Cahiers du Cinema* (1989), 108.

20. Is not the exemplary case of such a fantasmatic formation combining heterogeneous and inconsistent elements the mythical Kingdom/or Dukedom/of Ruritania, situated in an imaginary Eastern European space combining Catholic central Europe and the Balkans, the Central European noble feudal conservative tradition with the Balkan wilderness, modernity (train) with primitive peasantry, the "primitive" wilderness of Montenegro with the "civilized" Czech space (examples abound, from the notorious *Prisoner of Zenda* onwards)?

21. Is the logic here not the same as that of the false imitation of business class in economy class in British Airways: some years ago, I was served simple paper napkins as if they were humid towels, arrayed on a tray and delivered with tweezers? Also, on smaller planes, the separation between business and economy class is often purely symbolic, i.e. a barrier holding a curtain is shifted back- or forward, depending on how many business-class tickets are sold.

22. de Vaecque, "Andrei Tarkovski," 110.

23. This opens up a possible connection with Lars von Trier's *Breaking the Waves*, which also culminates in an act of sacrifice of the heroine: if she goes to the boat with the violent sailor and lets herself be beaten up, probably to death, this sacrifice will revive her crippled husband.

24. Interestingly, although it is difficult to imagine two more different universes than Tarkovsky's and David Lynch's, it is possible and productive to establish links between them at the level of particular visual, etc. *sinthoms*—a wooden house burns at the end of *The Sacrifice* as well as at the end of *Lost Highway*! The meaning of this act, of course, is the opposite: for Tarkovsky, the house stands for the authentic safety of the Home, while the Lynchean House is the ultimate site of obscene crime and *jouissance*.

25. See de Vaecque, "Andrei Tarkovski," 98.

26. To avoid a crucial misunderstanding, the point of our rejection of the sacrificial gesture as false is not to reduce it to some hidden "pathological" motivation. Psychoanalysis proper involves the very opposite of "spoiling" an act's ethical grandeur by unearthing its common causes (explanations like "the hero's suicidal sacrifice was merely the result of his unresolved Oedipal guilt-feeling . . ."): for Lacan, an act proper is precisely a gesture that cannot be explained, accounted for, through the reference to its "historical (or social or psychological) context," since it stands for an intervention which, "out of nothing," retroactively redefines the very contours of what counts as a "context." So, when we encounter a gesture like that of Mary Kay le Tourneau (the thirty-six year-old schoolteacher imprisoned for a passionate love affair with her fourteen year-old pupil, one of the great recent love stories in which sex is still linked to authentic social transgression), the business of psychoanalysis is not to "explain" this act as the outcome of some underlying unconscious mechanism for which the subject is ultimately not responsible, but, on the contrary, to SAVE THE DIGNITY OF THE ACT.

CHAPTER 10

Wounds of the Past: Andrei Tarkovsky and the Melancholic Imagination

Linda Belau and Ed Cameron

I bring unhappiness to everybody.

Andrei Tarkovsky

By means of a leap into the orphic world of artifice (of sublimation), the saturnine poet, out of the traumatic experience and object of mourning, remembers only a gloomy or personal tone. He thus comes close, through the very components of language, to the lost Thing. His discourse identifies with it, absorbs it, modifies it, transforms it.

Julia Kristeva

TARKOVSKY AND THE SIGNIFICATION OF NON-MEANING

One of the most critically engaging dimensions of Andrei Tarkovsky's films is their pre-modern quality. This pre-modern quality, according to Thomas Redwood, is embodied in the "obscure, difficult, baffling, [and] esoteric"[1] nature of the films, qualities that make the films resistant to viewer comprehension and critical interpretation. While this is not the only significant dimension of his cinematic work, it is, nonetheless, the one that is most striking to both viewers and critics, particularly since this so-called pre-modern value lies in his films' affinity with the primal and the pre-rational, especially as Tarkovsky himself has promoted the disconnection of the image from meaning.[2] In this sense, then, there is also something unspeakable about his work that is equally striking. It is important to note here, though, that the primal should be distinguished from the pre-modern as a specifically temporal or historical determinative: rather than designating the primal as primitive, surmountable, or dispensable, the primal in Tarkovsky's artistic vision is correlative to a spiritual ideal, to that which can only be revealed and not signified. For Tarkovsky, the cinematic image "stretches out to infinity, and leads to the absolute."[3] It is not defined by temporality or its historicity. Thus, it can be argued that Tarkovsky partakes of the mystic endeavor of revealing the "irreducible mystery of the uncanny, effectively preserv[ing] the Holy in a space that is independent of and impervious to anthropological and scientific appropriation."[4]

Tarkovsky's wish to promote the primal operates as an artistic reaction to what he considered the "contemporary spiritual blight"[5] he found in both his own Soviet socialist society and his adopted-in-exile consumer Western culture. His obsession with the ineffable has, thus, been understood, by at least one critic, as an artistic attempt to fill this "spiritual void left by a materialist age."[6] Spanish filmmaker Victor Erice has argued that Tarkovsky's cinematic vision revolves around "the hope of finding spiritual plenitude,"[7] that "his filmmaking became a cause with religious echoes," and that for Tarkovsky art was "a form of prayer."[8] Several critics have argued, for this reason, that for Tarkovsky cinema is a form of revelation, a microcosm of divine creativity. In this paper, we argue that what makes Tarkovsky's films unique and stylistically separate from those of his most prominent filmmaker influences (Mizoguchi, Antonioni, Fellini, Bresson, Bergman, and Buñuel) is his utilization of an aesthetic medium in service to a strictly religious mode of melancholic sublimation. Through a psychoanalytically inflected argument, we further consider how Tarkovsky's auteur perspective is conditioned in and through what Jacques Lacan calls the Thing, that which is lost through the advent of signification.

Tarkovsky's specifically melancholic style of religious sublimation is strongly tied to a mode and mood that runs throughout all his films. As his films are mourning the loss of spirituality in contemporary materialist society, they stylistically tie themselves to what has been lost, especially since melancholia attaches to and sublimation aims toward the Thing that suffers from the signifier.[9] The generally recognized obscurity of Tarkovsky's films circulates around their thematic, structural, narrative, and stylistic attachment to the lost object (Thing), which distorts and destabilizes coherence while remaining structurally exiled from signification. In her detailed study of melancholia as an artistic endeavor, Julia Kristeva maintains that "the Thing falls away from me along the outposts of significance where the Word is not yet my Being [. . .] before being an Other, the Thing is the receipt that contains my dejecta [. . .] it is a waste with which, in my sadness, I merge."[10] By attending to these "outposts of significance" (the planet Solaris, the mirror reflection, the Zone), as he does within his cinematic universe, Tarkovsky artistically attempts to reveal that spiritual essence that has been lost to and voided from the contemporary world. As Kristeva continues, "aesthetic and particularly literary creation, and also religious discourse in its imaginary, fictional essence, set forth a device whose prosodic economy, interaction of characters, and implicit symbolism constitute a very faithful semiological representation of the subject's battle with symbolic collapse."[11] Tarkovsky's use of disembodied slow-tracking long takes, his creation of temporal discontinuity, his penchant for narrative incoherence, and his signature "trance" style, all formally exhibit a turning away from signification and a subsequent attachment to the lost object and an impossible past that is the indicative feature of melancholia.

Tarkovsky has himself indicated that he has striven to create a cinema that simultaneously enchants and repels. Examining Leonardo's portrait of *A Young Lady with a Juniper*, Tarkovsky argues that his cinematic style approaches Leonardo's ability to affect spectators simultaneously in two opposing ways: "She is at once attractive and repellent. There is something inexpressively beautiful about her and at the same time repulsive, fiendish [. . .] beyond good and evil."[12] He also concedes that he used Leonardo's portrait of the young woman in his film *Mirror* (1974) "in order to introduce a timeless element" and to "emphasise in her and in the actress, Margarita Terekhova, the same capacity at once to enchant and to repel."[13] The simultaneous enchanting and repelling descriptor given to Tarkovsky's actress, who incidentally plays both the narrator's mother and wife in *Mirror*, echoes the psychoanalytic characterization of the Thing as the lost primordial maternal object, that always-only lost symbiotic relationship with the mother before the advent of signification.[14] This lost object, that which is endlessly mourned by melancholia, is enchanting because it harkens to a utopian plentitude, but repellent because it threatens the socio-symbolic network with collapse. Turning toward the Thing means turning away from the symbolic order and codifiable meaning. Simultaneously enchanting and repelling also echoes Tarkovsky's view of his own signature long takes. According to critic Sean Martin, "Tarkovsky proposed that if a take is lengthened, boredom naturally sets in for the audience. But if a take is extended even further, something else arises: curiosity."[15] The tedious nature of Tarkovsky's long takes epitomizes his film's repellent style, one aspect of his films that turns off the vast majority of film viewers. However, when his long takes persist to the point of developing a life of their own, something else emerges: a glimpse of the Thing at the threshold of meaning.[16] In this manner, Tarkovsky's films formally intimate melancholia and thereby make non-meaning significant. Eschewing received meaning and significance, much like the melancholic, Tarkovsky's three final Soviet films (*Solaris* (1972), *Mirror*, and *Stalker* (1979)), we argue, indirectly reveal the primordial essence of reality that has been voided from the contemporary socio-symbolic network, as well as his own feeling of exile within the given reality principle caused by this voiding.

Arguably, *Nostalghia* (1983) is Tarkovsky's most melancholic film, the film where Tarkovsky expresses melancholia to the utmost degree. Tarkovsky also considered his penultimate film superior to all his other features because it completely eschews any narrative in favor of pure mood.[17] He also claimed that it was the only film where he was able to wholly express himself: "My previous pictures were a creative act for me; I made them as a professional filmmaker and I separated my films from myself. *Nostalghia* on the other hand is an exact reprint of my state of mind; it was my deed."[18] Tarkovsky's claim, here, can be read in two ways. With *Nostalghia*, the director is finally able to delve uninterrupted into and fully indulge in the true depths of his melancholic emotional state. The film even concludes with a dedication to his lost mother, who died in 1979. On the obverse side, however, *Nostalghia* could be understood as having taken up the reins of mourning, functioning as a sort of working-through of melancholia. Unlike melancholia, which resists signification, nostalgia functions as a signifier of the lost object of melancholia. In nostalgia, the Thing that emerges in melancholia becomes signified as a temporal and locatable object from the past, like a childhood home. Because of Tarkovsky's self-imposed exile in the West and his decision to film *Nostalghia* in Italy, the alienation felt by his protagonist/avatar Andrei Gorchakov represents a certain homesickness for a specific past that can be located in his lost mother country. The free-floating melancholic techniques of his earlier Soviet films become in *Nostalghia* methods to signify a specific loss in reality. Tarkovsky's characteristic long takes, in *Nostalghia*, no longer offer a glimpse of the Thing at the threshold of meaning as they start to symbolize the definite feeling of exilic longing; the final image of the family dacha within the cathedral dramatically symbolizes the home, a terrestrial object, as sacred; Eugenia's fusion with the mother clearly signifies Andrei's desire for the lost primordial love back in Russia; etc. This symbolization of the object results in an idealization and misses the sublimatory aim toward the Thing expressed in his Soviet films.[19] Nostalgia houses a comforting place for the object, a place that prolongs desire; whereas sublimation indicates that the object is out of place, that the object remains meaningless within the given coordinates of reality, of the Other. Because of his expressionistic signifying of the Thing of melancholia into an object that is now lost, *Nostalghia* does not pursue the melancholic sublimatory aim of Tarkovsky's final Soviet films. However, it does propose a form for the melancholia of his previous three films. It makes the melancholic nature of *Solaris*, *Mirror*, and *Stalker*—the three films focused on here—stand in relief.

SOLARIS AND THE TREK TO OTHERNESS

Critic Simonetta Salvestroni has argued that, by the end of his time on the space station orbiting the planet Solaris, the protagonist Kris Kelvin is able to break his prosaic ways and accept Otherness, albeit one less fantastic than the materialized hallucination of his dead wife Hari.[20] However, it must be added that Kelvin's acceptance of absolute Otherness, as developed in Tarkovsky's film, only comes at the expense of breaking with the Other, the socio-symbolic pact that governs reality. In fact, like most science-fiction fare, *Solaris* lends itself quite readily to an allegorical understanding. Kelvin's space odyssey is really one man's attempt to reach the absolute Otherness that circulates around the edges of his melancholic condition, especially as melancholia's fixation on the lost object, its fixation on what was lost upon the advent of signification, requires the withdrawal from the realm of the Other. Life on the space station provides Kelvin the unique experience of lacking the lack, of lacking the very lack that is introduced by the advent of the signifier. Through interstellar isolation, Tarkovsky is able to hyperbolically demonstrate the melancholic's estranged relation to the Other and the concomitant connection to absolute Otherness on his way to making film a substitute for prayer, where non-meaning itself becomes significant.[21]

Countering Stanislaw Lem's novel from which the film is adapted, Tarkovsky's decision to begin the film's narrative on earth at the isolated family dacha indicates that Solaris' effects on Kelvin's mental state derive more from his prior mental state than from the alienating effects of space travel. Solaris' existence is, therefore, more of a culmination of a deteriorating mental condition than a cause of the condition. The opening-credit sequence of the film is assisted by mesmerizing organ music, a bizarre blending of futuristic science fiction and antiquated instrumental accompaniment. The film's promise of moving forward to the future of space exploration is thereby subtly undercut by a musical movement from a lost, archaic past. The first visual image reinforces Kelvin's psychological condition with its arresting extreme slow-motion, slow-tracking close-up shot of reeds swaying in water.[22] This is one of those Tarkovsky shots that persists long enough to transform the spectator's boredom into a poetic intimacy with otherness. The attending tilt to Kelvin solidifies his association with this poetic withdrawal among the pre-symbolic imagery in the same way that Tarkovsky's patented lyrical interludes of this type estrange his film's ostensible narrative from itself. Kelvin is also first shown frozen within Tarkovsky's trance style, meandering through the grounds of the family dacha as if completely alienated from reality. The caged birds and various pictures of framed balloons in arrested flight placed on the walls inside the family domicile further foreshadow the possibility that Kelvin's "flight" into space never really leaves the terrestrial realm. The isolation of the family dacha and Kelvin's apparent isolation there manage to demonstrate the manner in which Kelvin's loneliness, his separation from the socio-symbolic system, predates his expedition to the desolation of outer space. The manner in which Kelvin's trip to Solaris is portrayed—exclusively through an extreme close-up of Kelvin's eyes—designates the trip more as a journey into the inner recesses of Kelvin's mind than it does as an attempt to reach the furthest reaches of the universe.[23] Both Kelvin's isolation at the family dacha and his isolation in outer space spatially demonstrate how he has put himself out of service to the Other, how, in his failure to mourn, he has alienated himself from earthly desires.

Through this allegorical reading, the planet Solaris figures as Kelvin's black sun, the "mass of jelly" consuming everything into its orbit while ridiculing the very coordinates of space and time—the aprioristic foundations of the reality principle. Here, the otherworldly existence within the claustrophobic confines of the space station figure Kelvin's already established deprivation from reality caused by his inability to mourn the death of his wife, a loss that is apparently already a replication of the loss of his mother. Kelvin's trip to the heavens mimics the melancholic's attempt to dwell in the impossible and to make the always already unobtainable object appear as lost. By providing Kelvin with a simulation of his dead wife Hari, the massive planet Solaris solidifies Kelvin's attachment to the impossible lost object and his alienation in the past. The planet's oceanic surface, shown numerous times throughout the film, also approximates the gelatinous amniotic goo of the pre-symbolic period, a period before the advent of the father's signifier and any demarcation of reality. When Snaut informs Kelvin that the planet reads dreams in order to prey on guilt, he essentially confirms the self-abuse and lowering of self-regard that is so indicative of melancholia. The melancholic abuses himself for the loss suffered because the melancholic incorporates the lost object into the ego and preys on it for leaving, for becoming lost. All three of the station's inhabitants—Kelvin, Snaut, and Sartorius—are preyed on by some lost object of their past. While Sartorius experiments on his object as a way of placating his guilt, Snaut just refuses to sleep in an attempt to keep his guilt at bay. Kelvin, on the other hand, fully indulges in his proximity to the lost object. Gibaran, the fourth inhabitant of the station, succumbed to the truly devastating effects of melancholia, having committed suicide and dying of "hopelessness" prior to Kelvin's arrival. Ultimately, the guilt of the melancholic stems from the initial existential guilt associated with the fact that the lost object only exists as lost. It is what is given up in the first place upon entry into the socio-symbolic order of language. Solaris, therefore, promises a reencounter with this paradoxical object, but, like melancholia, it also demands a break from reality and a possible flight into madness.

If Solaris functions as the black sun of melancholia, then Hari functions as the Thing, the embodiment of the lost object that is impossible to mourn.[24] What was lost to signification with the advent of the signifier, according to Lacan, can only be embodied in a misrecognized leftover because it suffers from the signifier.[25] Any representation of the Thing can only proceed indirectly because it remains elusive to symbolic representation. This is why the so-called guests that Solaris provides to the astronaut hosts operate as approximations. That the human inhabitants of the station function as "hosts" for the planet's "guests" specifies the inner nature of the film's space exploration. During Snaut's birthday celebration in the station's library, Hari complains that the humans treat the guests as external hindrances while ignoring the fact that these guests are really just part of "your conscience."[26] In this manner, Hari indicates the extimate nature of the uncanny guests. These guests, like herself, are simultaneously external agents and representations of the most intimate kernel of the station crew members' psychological state, the lost object embodied in the Thing having been incorporated into the ego.[27] Hari's continuous resurrections signal Kelvin's desired attachment to the lost object in favor of a stable connection with reality. When Hari revives from the dead, after having ingested liquid oxygen, Snaut accuses Kelvin of turning a scientific problem into a "common love story," exactly what Tarkovsky has done to Lem's science-fiction novel. Only Tarkovsky's love story is not as "common" as Snaut would indicate. When Kelvin later explains, "You love that which you can lose. Yourself, a woman, a homeland," he, in essence, weds himself, by implication, to the lost object itself. In a 2011 interview, Natalya Bondarchuk, the actress who played Hari, points out that the first time we see Hari in the film, whether or not it occurs during Kelvin's dream or immediately upon his waking, the manner in which Tarkovsky films her indicates that when she is looking at Kelvin and at the spectator it is Solaris or God looking through her eyes.[28] At this point in the film, with the early introduction of Hari before she becomes too humanized, we, as spectators, are witnessing the Thing, a Thing that is gazing out from a melancholic space that predates the advent of signification. Her placement at the edge of a signifiable universe demonstrates the Thing's disruption of the socio-symbolic universe that is necessary for an encounter with Otherness. Her abrupt introduction is Tarkovsky's representation of Otherness; it doesn't appear as otherworldly as it should, situated as it is in a science-fiction film, because the encounter does not really require a trip to the outer reaches of the universe. It only requires a withdrawal from the given coordinates of reality. Rather than using the science-fiction genre to explore the possible future of scientific innovation, Tarkovsky uses the genre to critique the limitations of science's quotidian bias, its pedestrian reduction of the unknown to mere things yet unknown. This critique of science, incidentally, emerges again in Tarkovsky's final Soviet film, *Stalker*.

Hari's connection to the lost maternal object is made through several juxtapositions between Kelvin's wife and his mother. During a screening of home movies, the simulated Hari is introduced to Kelvin's past. The home videos show Kelvin as a child with his parents on a snow-covered hilltop. These scenes are then juxtaposed with scenes obviously from later as Hari appears in one shot at the family dacha. The home movies are oddly shot in Tarkovsky's signature slow-pan style, thus eliminating their realist effect. The order of the clips also creates a poetic association, conceiving Hari as a mother substitute. During Kelvin's fever dream, as the planet is bombarded with his encephalogram rays, he lies in bed and hallucinates a vision of his mother in his quarters. His mother then transmogrifies into Hari and then into what appears to be multiple women shown from behind that could be either Kelvin's mother or Hari. When Kelvin eventually emerges from his bed, he has been transported to a sepia-infused version of his family dacha, only many walls and much of the furniture are covered in the plastic sheeting familiar from the environment on the space station, thereby situating Kelvin in a liminal space between various temporal moments. In the dacha, Kelvin has a conversation with his mother, telling her how he is very lonesome now. His mother notices how he has become rather "unkempt" these days, signaling his melancholic withdrawal from material concerns. Skakov argues that the "blue monochrome colour scheme underlines the uninhabited nature of the place and its otherworldliness."[29] The blue-filtered color scheme also references the "blues," and, thereby, highlights the melancholic nature of this attachment to the lost mother. At the end of the film, it is difficult to tell whether Kelvin has left Solaris' orbit as he is shown occupying the family dacha, or whether the family dacha now exists as a hallucination on one of Solaris' newly formed islands, or whether Kelvin has simply brought his melancholia back with him to Earth. Either way, the family dacha itself ultimately becomes the embodiment of sorrow and loss, personified in the house's emotional tears.[30] This connection between the lost maternal object and a general melancholic mood will have a stronger gravitational pull in Tarkovsky's next feature, *Mirror*.

MIRROR AND THE REFLECTION OF THE LOST OBJECT

By the time Tarkovsky made his fourth feature, *Mirror*, in 1974 he understood that his native Soviet society was not very receptive to his "long boring films," as he called them.[31] His loss of home was becoming evident as he increasingly came to realize that only the West could appreciate his films.[32] This mourning over the emerging loss of his homeland is represented in *Mirror* as the reflective combination of his own subjective memories and the recent objective history of Russia. Although seen as contrived or clumsy by several critics, the narrator's deathbed scene that occurs at the end of the film positions the entire narration between two deaths, in a liminal state on the edge of the socio-symbolic order. From this place, the confusing and ambiguous narrative mixing of highly subjective memory sequences, screen memory sequences, and dream sequences with relatively objective sequences, ranging from second-hand memories to newsreel footage, makes more sense. Also, the constant temporal shifts to different historical and personal periods helps reinforce the understanding of the film's mode of narration as approximating a highly idiosyncratic stream of consciousness, an interior imaginary monologue with questionable veracity and reliability.[33] In this sense, the entire trajectory of the narrative (for lack of a better term) could be appreciated as a dying man's scattered reminiscences as he approaches that object which has always been lost. Christy Burns' perceptive categorizing of Tarkovsky's art as a refusing of modernity, thereby, could itself be reenvisioned to understand Tarkovsky's cinema as organized around a pre-modern drive, a drive to articulate that which has been left behind by modernity, that which is structurally lacking, and that which has never been sufficiently mourned, as opposed to a mourning of actual lost place or lost childhood.[34]

Most of the reflections strewn through the narrative of *Mirror*, under this perspective, demand to be seen as contributing to a dramatizing of the impossible return to a pre-symbolic time of childhood, to a time before the unspoken schism between Aleksei and his mother, a foundational schism that creates the very lost object that the circular, atemporal narrative of the film attempts to locate. The titular mirror and the countless mirrors placed throughout the *mise-en-scène* testify to the looking-back, *nachträglich* nature of the film's narrative, as narrative usually tends to progress forward rather than to regress backward.[35] The pre-credit opening documentary television program viewed by young Ignat, depicting a stuttering young man cured by hypnosis, ontogenetically reproduces the initial emergence of the signifier by allegorically illustrating that full faith in the symbolic order requires a sort of manipulation by hypnosis.[36] One must be cured of linguistic skepticism in any of its symptoms in order to become a fully functioning member of the socio-symbolic pact. The babbling of the pre-linguistic, pre-symbolic child—figured here as the stuttering student—must be redirected and brought under the domination of the paternal signifier that orders the symbolic system. The stuttering of the young student represents, for Tarkovsky, what is lost, what is given up upon entry into the law of the father's economy. The poetic babblings that make up the entirety of the film's narrative not only indirectly highlight what has been given up but attempt to sublimate that pre-symbolic textual material into an effort to draw attention to the lost object. The opening black-and-white simulated television program presents a glimpse of that lost object, and the rest of the film is articulated around the melancholic drive to draw near that impossible object.

So much of the childhood reminiscences of Aleksei on his deathbed circulate around the family dacha, an abode throughout Tarkovsky's film career that embodies that nurturing remnant of the past that has been lost to the adult individual and to the increasingly modernized Soviet society. The natural imagery of the slow-motion swaying of the grasses that appear ubiquitous in the environs of the dacha in Tarkovsky films embodies, according to Michael Dempsey, "a vision of lost harmony" and "a primal peace, which we can regain."[37] The loss of the family dacha, envisioned at the end of *Mirror* when the dacha is shown in ruins, signals the spiritual blight of Tarkovsky's contemporary society. In the opening post-credit scene, Aleksei's memory presents a screen memory of his mother's fling with a doctor on his way to the train station in Tomshino.[38] It is clear that Aleksei's father is already missing from the family structure, having left in 1935. This initial reminiscence signals the loss of the father and the opening up to the melancholic ruminations and mood that take up the entirety of the film's narrative. Without the paternal quilting point organizing the narrative of the dying Aleksei's memories, he is free to fixate on what was lost between him and his mother. Aleksei's first narrative voice-over intrusion reinforces the missing father: "We usually recognized our folks when they raised from behind the bush in the middle of the field. If he turns towards the house, it's Father. If not, it is not Father, which means he will never come again." Subtitle translation aside, the ambiguity of the personal pronouns of this initial narrator voice-over indicates that the final "he" might actually refer to Aleksei's father, as if the erotic activity between the strange doctor and his mother discloses that his father is never coming back.

During this initial flashback sequence at the ancestral homestead, the first of the four poems written by Tarkovsky's own father Arseny is recited in a supplemental voice-over. In this highly autobiographical film, Tarkovsky's father—who had abandoned his own family—figures as the missing father of Aleksei, a father whose presence is only demonstrated as an absent voice. In the poem, the melancholic mood of the film is established with the words, "When the night fell, I was blessed." These words refer to the dying Aleksei's desire to reunite with the lost object. The final sequence of the film makes this desire an actuality by morphing the prenatal into a post-mortem sequence. The dying Aleksei imagines (experiences?) a primal-scene sequence at the ancestral farmstead where his parents discuss whether they want a boy or a girl, only to morph into his prenatal mother's reverse shot of his current elderly mother walking hand in hand with the five-year-old Aleksei and his little sister at the same location. The camera slowly tracks them through the fields and by the light of the sinking sun until it reverse tracks into the woods and into the darkness where Arseny's poem promises blessedness. This impossible sequence reaches poetic heights as it dramatizes the impossible success of the melancholic drive's attempted reconnection with the lost maternal Thing.[39] The first newsreel footage juxtaposing the evacuation of the Communist children-victims of the Spanish Civil War with footage from Valeri Chkálov's balloon flight over the North Pole itself juxtaposes the sorrowful descent into darkness with the rising to the heavens that Tarkovsky makes as the ultimate figure of a melancholic demeanor. This newsreel footage is appropriately accompanied by

Pergolesi's *Stabat Mater* with its famous melancholic choral libretto, "Stood the mournful Mother weeping," further orienting the film's melancholic mood into a sublimation of the lost maternal object.

STALKER AND MELANCHOLIC EMPTINESS

Following suit with the two previous films, Tarkovsky's final Soviet film, *Stalker*, made perhaps when he was feeling the most exiled within his Motherland, goes the furthest in creating a film that dramatizes "the hope of finding spiritual plenitude." Revelation as an artistic practice, revealed by *Stalker*, can be better understood through Lacan's three types of sublimation outlined in *Seminar VII*.[40] Lacan articulates the three human discourses' sublimatory signifying of the unknown (*das Ding*)—the emptiness of our knowledge. Science forecloses this emptiness by articulating the unknown as not only immanent but as accessible. With more time, effort, and technology, science believes it can uncover the unknown and make it known, transforming the Thing into mere things yet unknown. In contrast, art organizes itself around this emptiness by articulating the unknown as paradoxically immanent yet inaccessible. In this manner, art is able to expose the Thing negatively as the limit of its own vision and nothing more. Religion, however, avoids this emptiness by articulating the unknown as transcendental and therefore inaccessible. For religion, the unknown can only be encountered through an indirect revelation of the eternal realm, making the Thing divine. The story of *Stalker* circulates around this unknown and presents these three discursive approaches to the limits of human comprehension. What unknown knowledge lies at the heart of the melancholic Zone? The Zone's relatively vibrant color and near impenetrable location reflect its pre-symbolic otherworldliness and its location in a realm alien from the given socio-symbolic system at "the edge of despair's abyss."[41] The tedious trek of the three explorers and the tediousness of Tarkovsky's long-take tracking shots capture the monotony of the drive as it circumnavigates the missing object.[42] According to Stalker, the magical room at the heart of the Zone cannot be approached in a direct line; just like the movement of desire itself and the Thing that desire avoids, it can only be approached in a round-about manner. Also, all who risk the trip into the Zone, it seems, are prompted by a deep sadness and by a melancholic drive to reconnect to the lost object that emanates from the mysterious impenetrable empty room of the Zone.[43] At the end of their monotonous and circumlocutory expedition through military armed barricades and an uncharted post-industrial environ that has been reclaimed by nature, none of the three explorers actually enters the room, as its emptiness, not its fullness, is its essence.

The three explorers' professions (a physics professor, a literary writer, and an amateur seer) themselves reflect Jacques Lacan's three human discourses' (science, art, and religion) relation to the unknown—the emptiness of our knowledge. Their approach to the unknown enigma of the Zone illustrates their differing modes of sublimation; they are basically caricatured by the film's narrative as the "intellectual aristocracy," each one representing one of the three human discourses. Since Professor is a man of science, he is naturally skeptical of anything that cannot be probed by scientific instruments. His primary desire seems to be the discovery of something new for the scientific world, a discovery that he hopes will make him the envy of scientists everywhere. He claims that the inherent value of the Zone is revealed by its being treated like a national treasure. For him the Zone is only a mystery, is only an unknown because it has not been investigated properly. His desire to destroy the room with the bomb components he has smuggled in his rucksack metaphorically illustrates his scientific drive to rid the world of anything beyond the reach of scientific measurement and comprehension.

Before the illegal trek to the Zone commences, Writer is heard explaining to his female companion that the world is boring because it is "run by cast-iron laws." The implicit Nietzschean critique of the laws of physics is confirmed when he concludes, "There is no Bermuda Triangle. There's the triangle A-B-C. It is all so tedious. [. . .] In the Middle Ages life was interesting." In the Middle Ages, in other words, there was still a sense of mystery, still aspects of existence beyond understanding's grasp. Writer's reason for his trip to the Zone seems to revolve around the Zone's presence as an enigma, the only mystery left in the modern world. Early in the film, and confirming his aesthetic credentials, he recalls a fable of an ancient vase in a museum that leaves the museum patrons in awe, until it is revealed as a fake, a joke pulled on the art world. However, this joke nonetheless highlights the mode of sublimation proper to art: the vase, when it was seen as authentic and because of its situation in a museum, was not only elevated to the pedestal of art but through its presence created the very empty place that art occupies. Like all objets d'art, the vase creates the very immanent but unknowable emptiness inherent in the symbolic order. As Lacan argues, the Thing can only be represented by emptiness,[44] and art brings this Thing indirectly to our attention by creating the empty space it itself occupies. Writer has lost his inspiration and sees the Zone as the promise that this emptiness still exists in the modern scientific age ruled by concrete materialism.[45]

Stalker, clearly the spiritual hero of the film, stands as the character most alienated by the modern materialist world. He lives in a severely run-down apartment, economically squeaking by on the fringes of the black market through his illegal guided trips into the forbidden region of the Zone. Against his wife's pleas to give up his fringe existence and his risk of imprisonment, he tells her that he is "imprisoned everywhere." The spiritual blight of the contemporary materialist world, where churches have been replaced by nuclear power plants, has made him more aware of the root cause of his melancholia than any of his self-absorbed customers. He, more than his clients, feels most at home when he is outside the socio-symbolic space within the reclaimed, post-industrial wasteland of the Zone.[46] That the Zone is filmed in vibrant color when his everyday reality is filmed in grimy, two-dimensional sepia tones indicates the fullness that the Zone promises. Stalker himself is prohibited from entering the room because for him its emptiness directly correlates to the fullness that only exists in the transcendental realm of the heavenly afterlife.[47] This transcendental realm is intimated near the end of the film in the only color scenes outside the Zone: the elevated high-angle crane shot of Monkey, Stalker's daughter, provides a transcendental viewpoint, and the mysterious image of the telepathic moving of the glasses by Monkey, a child of the Zone, at the very end of the film. These images are accompanied by *The Ode to Joy*, indicating a spiritual power beyond the comprehension of scientific understanding. In this dramatization, Stalker, like his maker, exemplifies the religious mode of sublimation where the emptiness of melancholia on Earth can be elevated into the promise of a return of the lost object of the transcendental realm that has been forsaken by his contemporary spiritually atrophied culture.

CONCLUSION

A targeted focus on the melancholic affect that pervades Tarkovsky's late Soviet cinema illustrates his fundamentally poetic critique of the reality principle, the contemporary notion of reality that eschews the space of the primordially spiritual. By relying on a realist aesthetic that outstrips itself, Tarkovsky is able to intimate a more spiritual realm, a realm of spirituality that exists beyond the realm of the Other and persists as the cure for modern melancholia. By creating a depressing yet intriguing cinema, Tarkovsky uses all three of his final Soviet films—*Solaris*, *Mirror*, and *Stalker*—to provide an implicit critique of limiting modern notions of reality by imagining a reality where the attractive yet repellent Thing has not been forsaken.

NOTES

1. Thomas Redwood, *Andrei Tarkovsky's Poetics of Cinema* (Newcastle: Cambridge Scholars Press, 2010), 2.
2. Andrey Tarkovsky, *Sculpting in Time: Reflections on the Cinema*, trans. by Kitty Hunter-Blair (Austin: University of Texas Press, 1989), 110.
3. Ibid., 104.
4. Simon D. Podmore, *Kierkegaard and the Self Before God: Anatomy of the Abyss* (Bloomington: Indiana University Press, 2011), 76. For Tarkovsky's interest in mysticism, especially nineteenth- and early twentieth-century Russian Orthodox mysticism, see Tony Partridge and Maria Diaz-Coneja, "Art as Revelation: Andrei Tarkovsky's Films and the Insights of Victor

Erice," *Journal of European Studies* 42.1 (2011): 23–43; and Redwood, *Andrei Tarkovsky's Poetics of Cinema*, 28–36.

5. P. Adams Sitney, "Andrei Tarkovsky, Russian Experience, and the Poetics of Cinema," *New England Review* 34.3–4 (2014): 234.

6. Redwood, *Andrei Tarkovsky's Poetics of Cinema*, 29.

7. Victor Erice, "The Ruins of History," trans. by Maria Diaz-Coneja and Tony Partridge, *Journal of European Studies* 42.1 (2011): 72.

8. Ibid., 69.

9. Jacques Lacan, *The Seminar of Jacques Lacan, Book VII: The Ethics of Psychoanalysis, 1959–1960*, trans. by Dennis Porter (New York: Norton, 1992), 118.

10. Julia Kristeva, *Black Sun: Depression and Melancholia*, trans. by Leon S. Roudiez (New York: Columbia University Press, 1989), 15.

11. Ibid., 24.

12. Tarkovsky, *Sculpting in Time*, 108.

13. Ibid.

14. Sigmund Freud, of course, relied on a different, more famous Leonardo portrait when drawing the psychoanalytic association between mourning, the lost maternal object, and sublimation. "Leonardo Da Vinci and a Memory of His Childhood," *The Standard Edition of the Complete Psychological Works of Sigmund Freud, Vol. XI*, ed. and trans. by James Strachey (London: Hogarth Press, 1957), 59–137.

15. Sean Martin, *Andrei Tarkovsky* (Harpenden: Kamera Books, 2011), 46. There is obviously some correlation that can be made between Tarkovsky's understanding of boredom and the pre-modern notion of melancholia known as *acedia*. There is also a strong affinity in Tarkovsky's work between boredom, the absence of meaning, and the failure of interpretation. For more on the relationship between religious insight and boredom, see Michael L. Raposa, *Boredom and the Religious Imagination* (Charlottesville: University of Virginia Press, 1999). Tarkovsky was also an adamant critic of the limits of interpretation. See Tarkovsky, *Sculpting in Time*, 176–200; and Martin, *Andrei Tarkovsky*, 25.

16. The passing discomfort of boredom that eventually clears the way to an encounter with otherness incidentally echoes Martin Heidegger's conception of profound boredom. See, for example, *The Fundamental Concepts of Metaphysics: World, Finitude, Solitude*, trans. by William McNeill and Nicholas Walker (Bloomington: Indiana University Press, 2001).

17. John Gianvito (ed.), *Andrei Tarkovsky: Interviews* (Oxford, MS: University of Mississippi Press, 2006), 183.

18. Ibid., 159.

19. For the distinction between the object and the Thing, see Lacan, *The Seminar of Jacques Lacan, Book VII*, 101–14.

20. Simonetta Salvestroni, "The Science-Fiction Films of Andrei Tarkovsky," trans. by RMP, *Science-Fiction Studies* 14.3 (1987): 300.

21. Kristeva, *Black Sun*, 138. Kristeva claims that in a similar manner painting functions for the sixteenth-century Dutch painter Hans Holbein as a substitute for prayer.

22. Nariman Skakov claims that in *Solaris*' opening nature shots, Tarkovsky "appears to follow the semi-pagan Russian cult of Mother Damp Earth." *The Cinema of Tarkovsky: Labyrinths of Space and Time* (London: I. B.Tauris, 2012), 81. The association of Tarkovsky's imagery with the worship of the lost mother illustrates his affinity with melancholia, as the melancholic attaches to the lost maternal object.

23. Toward the end of the film, in the final scene in the space station's library, Tarkovsky has the camera slowly track into an extreme close-up of Kelvin's ear while he is ruminating on various spiritual concerns, thereby reinforcing the importance of the inner journey over mere space exploration. Slavoj Žižek argues that Kelvin's journey to space as only a

materialization of his inner psychological journey betrays Tarkovsky's Jungian proclivities. "The Thing from Inner Space," *Sexuation*, ed. Renata Salacl (Durham, NC: Duke University Press, 2000), 234.

24. In his interpretation of Tarkovsky's sci-fi films, Žižek deploys the notion of the Thing as a kind of fantasy-projection machine, "a mechanism that directly materializes our unacknowledged fantasies," and that thereby broaches the divide between the symbolic and the real. He ultimately differentiates the planet Solaris from *Solaris*, which functions as the Thing that materializes the traumatic kernel of fantasy and the Zone from *Stalker*, which produces the empty place that sustains desire. See "The Thing from Inner Space," 216–59. In another examination, Žižek claims that the planet Solaris is itself the ultimate embodiment of the damp, heavy nature that indicates Tarkovsky's "spiritual corporeality." He claims that "this gigantic material Thing which thinks literally gives body to the direct coincidence of matter and spirit." See *The Fright of Real Tears: Krzysztof Kieślowski Between Theory and Post-Theory* (London: BFI, 2001), 102–3. In both cases, Žižek posits the planet itself as the massive Thing that invades reality. We, on the other hand, are positing Hari herself as the particular maternal uncanny Thing that haunts the melancholic, preventing him from sustaining the desire of the Other.

25. Lacan, *The Seminar of Jacques Lacan, Book VII*, 118.

26. During this sequence, Sartorius accuses Kelvin of losing touch with reality because he is too deeply obsessed with "noble thoughts," even referring to him as a "second-rate Dostoevsky." Dostoevsky was, of course, a melancholic and subject of Kristeva's study of melancholia. See Kristeva, *Black Sun*, 173–217. Dostoevsky was also a major influence on Tarkovsky. See Sitney, "Andrei Tarkovsky, Russian Experience, and the Poetics of Cinema," 235.

27. Jacques Lacan created the concept of "extimacy" out of a portmanteau of "external" and "intimacy," as a conceptual translation of "uncanny," and as demarcating an external strangeness that is actually intimate. The Thing, in this instance, appears as an external stranger but is actually quite intimate (part of the station crew's most hidden secrets). See Jacques-Alain Miller, "Extimatè," trans. by François Massardier-Keney, *Lacanian Theory of Discourse: Subject, Structure, and Society*, ed. Mark Bracher et al. (New York: New York University Press, 1994), 74–87 for a further elaboration of Lacan's concept.

28. "Natalya Bondarchuk on *Solaris*," *Solaris*, directed by Andrei Tarkovsky (1972; Criterion Collection, 2011), DVD.

29. Skakov, *The Cinema of Tarkovsky*, 93.

30. Toward the end of the film, when Snaut informs Kelvin that the planet has transformed with tiny "islands" sprouting up across the surface of its vast ocean, he echoes his earlier metaphor that the planet extracts "islands" of memory from the crew members of the Solaris space station. When the metaphorical islands of memory become literal islands, the past is taking over the present, and time is surely out of joint. Tarkovsky himself makes this *Hamlet* reference in relation to the temporally disturbed appearance of the tea-drinking woman and her servant from *Mirror*. See Skakov, *The Cinema of Tarkovsky*, 121.

31. In the above-referenced 2011 interview with Natalya Bondarchuk (Hari), she confesses that Tarkovsky often used to claim, "If I can't make a long boring film, then I'll shoot myself." At least jokingly, Tarkovsky professed his aesthetic drive to sublimate his melancholia.

32. *Solaris* had won the Grand Prix at Cannes and the Catholic Church award from the Vatican. The latter award, for obvious reasons, was hidden from the public in the Soviet Union.

33. Johnson and Petrie describe the narrative, likewise, as "a mosaic of what the narrator knew firsthand, what he was told, what he dreamed or imagined, and what happened

around him as part of the historical process that he shared with millions of other people."
Vida T. Johnson and Graham Petrie, *The Films of Andrei Tarkovsky: A Visual Fugue*
(Bloomington: University of Indiana Press, 1994), 116.

34. Christy L. Burns,"Tarkovsky's *Nostalghia*: Refusing Modernity, Re-Envisioning Beauty,"
Cinema Journal 50.2 (2001): 104–22. Peter King similarly argues that *Mirror* represents an
impressionistic vision of "loss and the attempt through memory to regain what is lost."
"Memory and Exile: Time and Place in Tarkovsky's *Mirror*," *Housing, Theory and Society*
25.1 (2008): 67. Likewise, Skakov claims that Tarkovsky cinematically represents the
impossible return to childhood through his narrative violation of the "finite categories"
of space and time, thus transcending the mundane: Skakov, *The Cinema of Tarkovsky*, 132.
Neither, however, focuses on the peculiar and particular structure of melancholia as the
reason for the unraveling of the narrative thread.

35. A mirror is essentially Tarkovsky's metaphor for the Freudian repetition compulsion:
"*Mirror* is not a casual title. The storyteller perceives his wife as the continuation of
his mother, because wives resemble mothers and errors repeat themselves—as strange
reflection. Repetition is a law, experience does not get transmitted, everyone has to live it."
Gianvito, *Andrei Tarkovsky: Interviews*, 44.

36. Most critics read this scene as the poet getting his voice back, allowing the epic lyric to
begin. However, it might be advantageous to understand this opening cure of a stutterer
as a critique of the successful endeavor to limit the poetic voice, especially since the young
man is a student at a tech school.

37. Michael Dempsey, "Lost Harmony: Tarkovsky's *The Mirror* and *The Stalker*," *Film
Quarterly* 35.1 (1981): 13.

38. Jeremy Mark Robinson claims that the collapsing fence that occurs when the doctor
shares a seat with Aleksei's mother functions as the five-year-old Aleksei's repressed
displacement of a sexual encounter, especially reflected in the doctor's words, "It is nice
to fall down with a pretty woman." *The Sacred Cinema of Andrei Tarkovsky* (Maidstone:
Crescent Moon Publishers, 2006), 412.

39. The melancholic's drive to dwell with the lost object by withdrawing from reality can,
tragically, often lead to suicide. Aleksei's cause of death seems to baffle those around him.
The doctor concludes that some can die of guilt, perhaps the cause of his suicide. Natalya
Bondarchuk also concludes that Tarkovsky's own death was ultimately caused by his
sorrow. "Natalya Bondarchuk on *Solaris*."

40. Lacan, *The Seminar of Jacques Lacan, Book VII*, 128–32. For a theological study of the
relationship between religious revelation and sublimation, see Karl Barth, *The Revelation
of God as the Sublimation of Religion*, trans. by Garrett Green (New York: Bloomsbury,
2007).

41. Dempsey, "Lost Harmony: Tarkovsky's *The Mirror* and *The Stalker*," 17.

42. Lacan claims that sublimation is the proper itinerary of the drive. Lacan, *The Seminar of
Jacques Lacan, Book VII*, 210–13.

43. The Zone's association with melancholia is reinforced by a poetic voice-over from the
"Book of Revelation" that occurs about midway through the three travelers' expedition:
"There was a great earthquake; And the sun became black as a sackcloth of hair and the
moon became of blood. And the stars of heaven fell unto the earth." Gerard Nerval,
of course, described his melancholia as a "black sun" (*soleil noir*) in his poem "The
Disinherited," a metaphor he derived from William Blake and Heinrich Heine.

44. Lacan, *The Seminar of Jacques Lacan, Book VII*, 130.

45. Writer is often portrayed through his animosity toward scientific inquiry, and Professor
criticizing him for his ignorance and inability to think in abstract terms and insisting that
"mankind exists in order to create works of art."

46. The reclamation of the industrial wasteland by the Zone indicates that there is something beyond the material.
47. Dempsey characterizes Stalker as both a "certifiable fool" and yet "a genuine seer." Dempsey, "Lost Harmony: Tarkovsky's *The Mirror* and *The Stalker*," 17. This favorite traditional Russian and Tarkovskian association between the prophet and the fool echoes the traditional melancholic relationship between the pathological psyche and creativity.

CHAPTER 11

The Flesh of Time: *Solaris* and the Chiasmic Image

Robert Efird

Despite his professed disappointment over its realization, *Solaris* (1972) is perhaps Andrei Tarkovsky's most well-known and well-studied film. The reasons are not surprising; not only does the work engage in a thoughtful dialog with its literary hypotext, it raises new and difficult questions as to the deeper nature of being, perception, and memory. As both the film and novel unfold, an apparently living, thinking ocean covering a distant planet penetrates the minds of the scientists who hover above, and somehow generates neutrino-based, physical realizations of their memories, fantasies, or twisted psychoses. In fact, the full genesis of the "guests," as the scientists on the space station call them, is never entirely clear, but the premise itself seems to question our understanding of the links between the incorporeal reality of memory or thought and the physical reality of the world before us. In Tarkovsky's hands this becomes a penetrating inquiry into time, consciousness, and the forces that make up the fabric of reality. *Solaris*, for whatever its flaws relative to the rest of the director's career, is perhaps the most explicit example of Tarkovsky using cinema as an ontological practice.

Perhaps the best starting point for delving into these questions is provided by Slavoj Žižek and his discussion of the filmmaker's seemingly contradictory "cinematic materialism," where "the heavy, damp matter (earth) which, far from functioning as the opposite of spirituality, serves as its very medium."[1] And indeed, Tarkovsky's expressions of spirituality are consistently and intensely physical. As with Dostoevsky, whose influence on the filmmaker is unmistakably profound, "the spiritual life is immanent in man and not transcendent."[2] However, as Berdyaev's description of the novelist continues, this seeming materialism "does not imply that he denied all transcendental reality."[3] In fact, it is precisely through the visible that the filmmaker attempts to express the immanence of the spirit: "Through the image is sustained an awareness of the infinite: the eternal within the finite, the spiritual within matter, the limitless given form."[4] Tellingly, Žižek relates the materialism he finds in the films to Schelling's notion of *geistige Körperlichkeit*, "spiritual corporeality."[5] But in using Stanislaw Lem's novel as a kind of catalyst and forcing this concentration on the physical, Tarkovsky also seems to be attempting to open a window onto what, remaining with Schelling's terminology, we could call an "abyss of the past" or *erste Natur*. As Maurice Merleau-Ponty refines it, this is "the fundamental stuff of all life and of every existing being, something terrifying, a barbaric principle that one can overcome but never put aside."[6]

The usual diversions and perversions aside, Žižek's commentaries on *Solaris* remain some of the most penetrating and enlightening insights into the film. Even conclusions that lead along a much different path than I will take here do much to prepare the ground for a deeper consideration. For instance, in describing the planet Solaris as an "id-machine," "a mechanism that directly materializes our unacknowledged fantasies," we are led to the somewhat obvious (and, unfortunately, accurate) take that "*Solaris* relies on science fiction rules to enact in reality itself, to present as a material fact, the notion that woman merely materializes a male fantasy."[7] Though Tarkovsky's Kris Kelvin is hardly the most positive of protagonists, this latent misogyny is not inconsistent with the usual positioning of women in Tarkovsky's films. But the description of the "id-machine" also leads to the notion that the planet forces "the direct materialization of thought itself" and comprises "an otherness which directly 'is' ourselves, staging the 'objectively subjective' fantasmatic core of our being."[8] In fact, Tarkovsky uses the genre of science fiction, which, as commentators on the film have long been pointing out, was considered a relatively inoffensive genre in the face of Soviet censorship, as a means of figuration for something more expansive and transcendent than even Lem's remarkable novel would allow. The seeming paradox Žižek mentions, the spiritual within the physical and the "objectively subjective," is actually the major characteristic of *Solaris* as a work of art, and one that extends beyond simply this subjective/objective binary and into the ambivalent structure of the film itself, emerging as a subtle, though occasionally conspicuous, concentration on the horizon between matter and spirit.

As this structure is built according to a kind of transverse aesthetic pivoting on the edge of the actual and the virtual, the various iterations of Hari would seem to mark a zenith of this apparent tension and, at the very least, provide a possible means for uncovering the film's deeper ontological underpinnings. On the more basic level, perhaps the immediate significance of this character, who appears as two simulacra based on the memories Kelvin has of his dead wife, is in her presentation as a seemingly magic materialization of the virtual. As Mark Riley points out in another exceptional study of the film, "proximity to the planet and its ocean [. . .] links the specificity of individual memory to the realization of an influential pre-individual condition manifest in the planet itself."[9] Complicating things for Kelvin and the other scientists, however, is the fact that the guest, as both Riley and Žižek are quick to point out, lacks the substantial human identity of the original. In fact, the question as to whether Hari or any of the other guests are actual people in the strictest sense would seem to be settled in the negative—if nothing else, they are composed of a different substance. And yet, though it is quite troubling to the characters, this is not the only question at the heart of the film. Riley also describes Hari quite accurately as "a point of immanence specified by the proximity of the corporeal Kelvin and, most importantly his memory of his wife [. . .] to the pre-individuation manifest in Solaris as a kind of transcendental ground."[10] And with this, the question of Hari's identity here takes a back seat to something more profound. The character is the focal point of Tarkovsky's exploration of the indiscernible zone between the material and the spiritual, while the ocean of Solaris may be understood here as something beyond expression in traditional filmic or linguistic terms, the analog of a process at the heart of reality, rendered perhaps more intelligible (though, admittedly, not always clearly) through this novel approach to cinema.

It is in this respect, I think, that Merleau-Ponty's somewhat ambiguous notion of Flesh becomes particularly relevant when considering *Solaris*. It should go without saying that the filmmaker does not demonstrate the concept through his practice (there is nothing to indicate he ever read Merleau-Ponty), but rather that—in an exploration of time and consciousness very much his own—he arrives at what appears to be a surprisingly comparable ontological stance. Though the correspondences between the philosopher and the filmmaker are rarely noted, particularly in light of the more obvious parallels between Tarkovsky and thinkers like Gilles Deleuze and Henri Bergson, Merleau-Ponty's concept may offer considerably more insight into the enigmas posed by this film. For both the philosopher and the filmmaker it is the exploration of time, time as duration or even *aion*, in the sense Deleuze describes as "the locus of incorporeal events, and of attributes which are distinct from qualities," that emerges as central to their ontology.[11] And in this non-physical unfolding there is a compelling expression of the invisible nature of reality itself as time becomes, according to Merleau-Ponty's description in *Phenomenology of Perception* (1945), "not an object of our knowledge, but rather a dimension of our being."[12] Both look deeply beyond the apparent solidity of the surface visibility to explore the actual medium of the material and the spiritual, and it is here that the concept of the flesh, which Deleuze and Guattari describe as "both a pious and a sensual notion, a mixture of sensuality and religion," becomes particularly salient.[13] Tarkovsky's abundant concern for the physical, so accurately noted by Žižek, works to reveal "a quality pregnant with texture, the surface of a depth, a cross section upon a massive being," and thus, in the words of the filmmaker, an examination of "life beneath the surface."[14] Unfortunately there is no concise explanation of the concept of flesh, and Merleau-Ponty's sudden death in 1961, when he was in the midst of completing *The Visible and the Invisible*, makes it difficult to determine whether the philosopher himself had yet arrived at a definitive outline. By its very nature, however, the flesh remains something mysterious, the non-physical substrate of both the visible world and the virtual, intimately connected with the differential process of time and the constitution of consciousness:

> As the formative medium of the object and the subject, it is not the atom of being [. . .] We must not think of the flesh starting from substances, from body and spirit—for then it would be the union of contradictories—but we must think it, as we said, as an element, as the concrete emblem of a general manner of being.[15]

Rather than masking ambiguity, the flesh is, in a sense, the ambiguity itself; the point of differentiation or, as Merleau-Ponty explains, "the dehiscence of the seeing into the visible and of the visible into the seeing."[16] As such, this is not a condition of stasis but rather a continuous and unfixed bursting forth along an ante-predicative horizon.

Perhaps most importantly for the present study, this horizon is described by the philosopher as a mirror-like chiasm, the dynamic point of intertwining of sensible and sentient, visible and invisible, as well as the non-physical locus of differentiation. This "double belongingness to the order of the 'object' and the order of the 'subject'" is perhaps best expressed in the coincidence between what sees and what is seen or, in Merleau-Ponty's most explicit example, what is touching and what is touched.[17] And though we certainly find numerous analogs of this in Tarkovsky's work, the best place to begin with *Solaris* may be in the chiasmic relation of dream and reality.

THE DREAM CHIASM

Few moments in Tarkovsky's oeuvre express the intertwining of the material and the spiritual with the intensity of the oneiric or quasi-fantastic sequences. The tendency to mingle diegetic reality with dream or memory already forms the dénouement of Tarkovsky's student work, *Steamroller and Violin* (1961), and is precociously refined by the time of his first feature, *Ivan's Childhood* (1962). In all of his films, dream sequences figure as pivotal structural and thematic events, caesuras in the course of the quotidian where time, space, and subjectivity fall from expected patterns and open onto expressions of raw being or sensation. In this respect, *Solaris* is both typical and unique. Here, as we so often see, the border between actual and virtual is left unmarked and fluid, with dream and reality each drifting into the space of the other. But *Solaris*, unlike its predecessor *Ivan's Childhood*, does not enter the oneiric space of its protagonist until late in the film. And even here it is somewhat unclear (given what occurs in the film's final moments) if what we witness—Kelvin's return to his home on Earth and the encounter with his dead mother—is in fact a fevered reverie or yet another level of physical reality generated by proximity to the planet's thinking ocean. The ambiguity here is reinforced by a striking departure in Tarkovsky's usual pattern, where the threshold between the real and the phantasmatic is crossed in a manner seemingly unlike that of any other work. With the movement of the dream into physical reality, what we see, by the end of the film, is the seemingly total interpenetration of both worlds.

Given the context of Tarkovsky's career, it would seem a safe assumption, whatever may have been said in interviews or diaries, that the centrality of dreams (such as the conversation Kelvin has with the dead Gibarian) in Lem's novel was a major factor in the choice to make an adaptation of *Solaris*. And again, following the novel, and in a marked difference with the other films, the dream image gains a physical reality that continues to manifest itself over the course of the story. The simulacra emerge, as Kelvin is told by Snaut, when the ocean invades the scientists' thoughts as they sleep and dream. And thus the awkward conversation at Snaut's birthday celebration midway through the film becomes perhaps central to how we initially understand the deeper ontological concerns of the film. At Snaut's insistence, Kelvin reads Sancho Panza's exhausted discourse from *Don Quixote*, where sleep is:

> the general coin that purchases all things, the balance and weight that equals the shepherd with the king, and the simple with the wise. One only evil, as I have heard, sleep has in it, namely, that it resembles death; for between a man asleep and a man dead, there is but little difference.[18]

It is especially important that it is from this liminal, interstitial space that the memories or fantasies of the scientists assume physical reality, that the line between life and death becomes a chiasm, a reversibility that, while never moving into absolute coincidence, reverberates on both sides of the divide. In the dream, the empirical body of waking reality is subdued, yet the sentience of embodiment remains, albeit tilting on the very edge of emptiness or the interior. Merleau-Ponty explains in working notes from November 1960 that the unique chiasmic structure of the dream "as being in the world without a body" is "the true *Stiftung* [institution] of Being," in so far as "the dream is *inside* in the sense that the internal double of the external sensible is *inside*."[19] As Marc Richir elaborates, the *Stiftung* of Being in the dream takes place as the "'pure' condensation of the perceptible 'there is' in the essence by the *épochè* of the dream."[20] In *Solaris*, as in so much of Tarkovsky's work, the dream floats "on the edge of being, neither in the for Itself, nor in the in Itself, at the joints, where the multiple *entries* of the world cross."[21]

Despite the fact that we do not initially see the dreams, the filmic realization of these events, the interpenetration of the interior sentience and the exterior of the sensible is perhaps most striking in the moments just before the initial appearances of the Hari simulacra—and resonates quite effectively with the passage from Cervantes and the nearly indiscernible line between life and death. In both sequences, just prior to the moment she appears, the camera hovers at the foot of the bed as Kelvin sleeps, slowly tracking up from his feet to his head in an inverted homage to the conclusion of Pasolini's *Mama Roma*, where the camera tracks down the body of the bound Ettore as his life drains away. But this earlier film is itself charged, as one must assume Tarkovsky was well aware, with the distorted, otherworldly perspective of Andrea Mantegna's 1480 painting, *Lamentation over the Dead Christ*. Subtle as these references may be, they reverberate along other facets of the film's crystalline surface: the adherence of the past to the present, the various "resurrections" of the dead Hari, and the unnatural or schizophrenic perspectives we see in a number of the scenes peripheral to these events. It bears mentioning as well that these shots of Kelvin sleeping are also closely matched to the shot of the dead Gibarian lying in the station's freezer and awaiting his burial back on Earth.

But most important is the evocation of a transitional state, effected here by delving deep into cultural memory with the passing of Ettore into death and the quickening of the dead Christ, and expanded with the similarity between the sleeping Kelvin and the dead Gibarian. In *Solaris*, as in all of Tarkovsky's films, sleep and dreams mark the interstice between this physical world and that of the mind and spirit. The appearances of the first and second Hari on the station, in this regard, are thus not unlike the waking dream of *Ivan's Childhood* or the eerie dreams of Gorchakov in *Nostalghia* (1983). What is most distinctive, however, is precisely this physical realization, something to which the director hints in these other films (such as with the sudden appearance of the dog in the actual physical space of the hotel room in Gorchakov's first dream), but which can only be convincingly pursued within the genre of science fiction. Moreover, and critical to the more profound points of this film, the physical realizations of Kelvin's dreams (or memories) are to all appearances self-aware, capable of their own inner development and emotional crises.

HARI

While the question of Hari's actual humanity may be easily answered in the negative—she is composed of a different substance—she offers perhaps the most productive area to explore Tarkovsky's "spiritual materialism." And her lack of identity, emphasized by both Žižek and Riley, is a feature the filmmaker is at pains to foreground. But rather than this negating her as a person (and we must keep in mind that she may also be understood as an analog encouraging a deeper understanding of the human condition), Hari's incarnation in fact brings with it a description of being not as a static state but one of constant change and becoming.

Her actions and statements leave little doubt that she is very much a sentient creature (Lem's novel seems to make clear that the guests are, subjectively, human) and one quite different from both the planet and Kelvin, the physical product of an internal scission of these two different consciousnesses that reverses back and now sees the parent subjectivities as objects. The lack of what we commonly understand as identity is something that both simulacra of Hari sense, as is evident by their professed lack of memories and inability to immediately recognize themselves. In fact, their sudden incarnation here makes it clear they have not had time to construct such a thing, other than what they may have borrowed from Kelvin's thoughts. As the second simulacrum grows, however, she does seem to be developing her own identity or personality, different (but not totally divorced) from both Kelvin and the original. Thus the principle of identity here is very much a secondary consideration, second to the differentiation and dehiscence that created these individuals and continues to manifest throughout their existence. As Riley notes, "The visitor determines a differentiation that refuses to sustain any clear duality. Its manifestation is the interaction of a multiplicity and therefore can no longer be interpreted as the action of the subjective upon the objective."[22]

The initial moments following the appearance of the first Hari are especially critical in this regard. After waking the sleeping Kelvin with a kiss and a caress, she finds an old photograph of the real Hari he has brought with him to the station: "Who is this?" It is only when she rises and faces the mirror on the wall

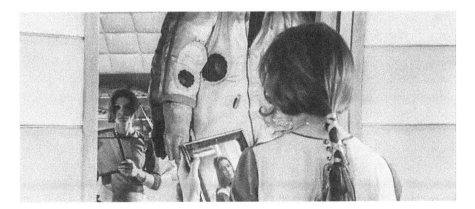

Figure 11.1 Hari with the photograph of her prototype in *Solaris*.

she realizes, in a statement delivered with just the flicker of a question: "This is me" (Figure 11.1). If we consider a photograph, following Vivian Sobchack, as "a figure of transcendental time made available against the ground of lived and finite temporality [. . .] never engaged in the activity of becoming," the void of Hari's memory and the lack of any formed identity through her differentiation from the consciousness of Kelvin is drawn here in especially sharp relief.[23] And not surprisingly, it is the mirror which elicits the simulacrum's self-awareness, in what one may see as a particularly twisted exemplar of Lacan's mirror stage. Hari, in this moment, becomes aware of herself as a seeing subject in the world. But the implications Tarkovsky draws forth run slightly deeper. The concentration on physicality, particularly what is visible and touchable, is strong in the first moments of Hari's appearance; her first act is to kiss and caress Kelvin. And it is, again paradoxically, this focus on the visible that draws a contrast between the invisible event of seeing and the subjectivity created in the seeing being. As Sobchack, very much under the influence of Merleau-Ponty's ideas, describes the child at the mirror, "it is this primordial knowledge of the body that contextualizes the visible Other seen in the mirror and informs the visible Other with subjective as well as objective status."[24] The difference between the fluidity of the mirror and the stasis of the photograph is explicitly the difference of becoming, the actual figuration of the chiasmic nature of the flesh. It is in such a manner that the mirroring of the seeing and the seen here finds its closest analog to the dehiscence of the seer into the physical world of the visible as the body of the incarnated being, particularly in the case of Hari and the other simulacra, who becomes "a presentation of a certain absence."[25]

This is rendered even more distinctly with the second simulacrum. Again, her interaction with Kelvin, after he summons her to the bed, begins with kissing and caresses. Her appearance before the mirror, however, takes place some time later, and reveals her to be far more advanced in her self-consciousness than her predecessor. Following the screening of Kelvin's home movie, where the original Hari is visible, the simulacrum moves into the bathroom and approaches the mirror. It is here, as they stare at their reflections, that she announces to Kris that she does not know herself, that she has no memory, though in fact she does remember things he attempts to deny. It would appear that what she remembers is only what Kelvin knows and, at a glance, we could see this as the ultimate denial of her full humanity. But could it not be in this questioning, this acknowledgment of the inner void, that she reaches a point of sentience at least comparable with Kelvin and, in this confrontation with herself and him before the mirror, perhaps even moves to a higher awareness? It is no accident that this existential shock to Hari comes as she sees her reflection—and perhaps even more importantly, if only metaphorically, that Kris is shown in (and soon disappears from) the same space. As Riley observes, "the visitor could be interpreted as the surface meaning of incorporeal on the corporeal. Kelvin's visitor/wife is the realization of an incorporeal event from his past."[26] Again, Hari is not a person in the sense that Kelvin is, but neither is she merely an unstable assemblage of neutrinos. What we see in Hari's questioning of herself (and Kelvin) before the mirror is perhaps a stark example of

> the coiling over of the visible upon the seeing body, of the tangible upon the touching body, which is attested in particular when the body sees itself, touches itself seeing and touching the things, such that, simultaneously, *as* tangible it descends among them, *as* touching it dominates them all and draws this relationship and even this double relationship from itself, by dehiscence or fission of its own mass.[27]

Whatever we may think of simulacrum, Hari's status as an actual person, all indications are this is an incarnate subject and thus, despite the difference in substance, herself of the same time/space fabric as the world around her, unfolding and changing with the movement of time and differentiation. And it is from here that in the next few sequences (apparently with the help of the cynical Sartorious) she becomes entirely aware that she is not the original but, as she herself puts it, someone completely different.

It is worth returning to Riley's observation here that the simulacrum "could be conceived as a point of immanence specified by the proximity of the corporeal Kelvin and, most importantly, his memory of his wife [. . .] at the time of her death to the pre-individuation manifest in Solaris as a kind of transcendental ground."[28] But it should be emphasized that the movement from virtual to actual, or from multiplicity to singularity, is never something completed, nor are the two ever in absolute coincidence with Hari. What the film brings forth is rather the dynamic, chiasmic intertwining, which is, in reality, not limited to a determinate time and place but manifested everywhere; the transcendental ground described by Riley certainly finds its visible point of contact in Hari and the ocean, but in fact (and quite subtly) permeates the entirety of the film. To again draw the comparison to Merleau-Ponty, we could say the emergence of Hari is from "a possibility, a latency, and a *flesh* of things."[29] Here this is the means through which the invisible possibilities become visible, physical—the flesh is the incarnation in a lived body, whose chiasmic nature encompasses both subject and object. As such, this chiasm is both sentient and sensible, and the intertwining of these two natures encompasses "overlapping and fission, identity and difference."[30]

INTERSUBJECTIVITY AND THE FLESH OF TIME

And the film is constantly drawn to these chiasmic expressions, what Merleau-Ponty would call the interlacing of the visible and the invisible, which frequently burst into view through particularly complex variants of the Deleuzian time-image. In fact, if we consider the relationship between the closely matching shots from the opening moments and the conclusion (as well as the dozens of other mirrored images that appear throughout), we can see how fully integrated the concept of this chiasm is in the very structure of the film itself. Here we should pause, however, and return to the use of the reflections in the scene described above. As Merleau-Ponty makes abundantly clear, the mirror is a particularly effective means of revealing the chiasm of the flesh: "The flesh is a mirror phenomenon and the mirror is an extension of my relation with my body."[31] As a site of differentiation, the temporary presence of Kelvin in this shot is especially suggestive of both the scission that moves at the site of the chiasm and the internal threshold of the physical and the spiritual both within him and the simulacrum, as well as the intersubjective space between the consciousnesses that create her. And while it is impossible here to give an exhaustive account of the way the filmmaker uses mirrors in this film—the instances are far too numerous—one may see, even given this single example, the extent to which Tarkovsky's expressions of materiality and time parallel (perhaps even exceed) the range of similar concepts in the work of Deleuze and Merleau-Ponty. For the former, the image of the mirror is equally chiasmic and emblematic of the movement of time, and thus serves an equally practical role in describing the unfolding distinction between the virtual and the actual, or the spiritual and the physical through the infinite contraction of the present and the perpetual dilation of the past. As an exemplar of the time-image the mirror provides (particularly in this instance) a multiplicity of perspectives and, correlative to this, the coexistence of moments—the point of distinction between the present and the past: "[t]he past does not follow the present that it is no longer, it coexists with the present it was. The present is the actual image, and *its* contemporaneous past is the virtual image, the image in the mirror."[32] As so often in these films, Tarkovsky enhances the expression of time with the rhythmic appearance of water, first as drops partially obscuring Hari's face in the mirror and finally, at the end of the shot, as a flow from the ceiling, a visual rhyme to the film's opening shot of water flowing over seaweed (itself mirrored at the conclusion) as well as the bizarre, reversed image of rain falling inside the house in the final moments. Thus the impression created is that this scission, the point of indiscernibility between the actual and the virtual, while appearing to be localized within certain scenes or shots, is in fact distributed throughout the entirety of the film and reveals the underlying ground upon which reality (diegetic or otherwise) is produced.

But equally compelling are the individual instances where the expression of time as a differential force displaces the presentation of space, the moments when this underlying ground unexpectedly bursts into view. Here it is not just that we find an analog to the chiasm of actual and virtual, but a dispersal of the empirical alignment of time and space, and with this the traditional subjective/objective distinction itself lapses into indiscernibility and opens onto intersubjectivity. While Hari manifests as an acute instance of this phenomenon, there are numerous other instances which suggest the process is in effect even without any of the visitors on the screen. This is exemplified most spectacularly in a sequence shortly before the appearance of the first simulacrum: Kelvin's second conversation with Snaut.

The shot begins with the seated Snaut facing the camera as he tends to his wounded hand and then spinning his chair and rising to meet the now exhausted Kelvin. The camera initially follows him to the right of the screen, but soon begins to trace a circular pattern to the left, alternating (in a single shot) between the two characters and mingling with the perspectives of each. The circularity of the movement is immediately reminiscent of the rotating camera in the "Skomorokh" episode of *Andrei Rublev*, which itself seems to move into and out of the central character's field of vision. But added to this are especially jarring disjunctive movements—not unlike those of Rublev's conversation with the dead Theophanes in the ransacked Vladimir cathedral and Gorchakov's visit to Domenico in *Nostalghia*. Here, both Kelvin and Snaut disappear from view as the camera moves about the room and reappear in impossible positions seconds later. Watching closely, we see that even their gazes indicate the uncanny refraction of time and space. However, there is no ready or clear diegetic explanation for the breakdown of the sensory-motor schema; this is no visit from an otherworldly apparition (at least not yet), nor can the movements of the characters be explained by some kind of mental abnormality (Snaut in fact insists that the frightened Kelvin is perfectly sane). Rather, this interruption of the empirical sequentiality of time and movement, complete with the perceptual indiscernibility characteristic of the time-image (as well as the mirrored imagery and graphic matching mentioned above), functions as a kind of synecdoche of the psychic encounter with the planet and the opening of the indeterminate chiasmic zone between the individual entities themselves. The similar placements of Kelvin and Snaut at different times within this single shot (the camera pans across their faces as they stand, successively, at the same point in the room), coupled with the distortion of movement and perspective, reinforces this and suggests that with the opening of a "zone of indiscernibility," in which time is revealed as not simply the succession of spatial moments but as change or differentiation, we are reaching deeply into a more distinctive expression of flesh as "the formative medium of the object and the subject," an intersubjective space not unrelated to Žižek's "objectively subjective" heart of being.[33]

Time, as the fabric common to all things, appears as the force that divides the subject from itself, the locus of difference. As expressed in the film, time becomes apprehensible through the image and interpreted, to borrow Miguel de Beistegui's formulation, "as the transcendental a priori, or the nonworldly event in which the world happens."[34] As he continues, time "is the preindividual flux whence all individuals emerge, this not primarily as the differentiation of a pregiven and always presupposed identity [. . .] but as the realization of an onto-logical potential."[35] This differentiation or realization, as expressed throughout Tarkovsky's work (the scenes at the mirror offer perhaps the most immediate examples) and with particular strength in *Solaris*, is paradoxically the force that unites seemingly separate entities. If we consider this against the flesh, the dehiscence of the seeing subject into the visible world—related perhaps to this movement through the preindividual flux—we may in fact be able to relate the intercorporeal features of Merleau-Ponty's concept to Tarkovsky's expressions of time. Returning for a moment to the sequence of Hari and Kelvin before the mirror there is, I think, undeniably a similar chiasmic density to the flesh, the "coiling over of the visible upon the seeing body." And yet, as the philosopher insists, this chiasmic unity, the "adherence of the sentient to the sensed and of the sensed to the sentient" is not a limited, individual event:

> Why would not the synergy exist among different organisms, if it is pos-sible within each? Their landscapes interweave, their actions and their passions fit together exactly [. . .] For, as overlapping and fission, iden-tity and difference, it brings to birth a ray of natural light that illumi-nates all flesh and not only my own.[36]

Thus, Tarkovsky's image of time is not simply, as Riley puts it, "the reappraisal of the subordination of temporality to movement and the spatial," but quite specifically an opening onto the intersubjective space emerging from this inter-corporeality, a point of intertwining existence extending, as Merleau-Ponty says of the flesh, "everywhere and forever, being an individual, [. . .] being also a dimension and a universal."[37]

Returning to Riley's description of Hari cited earlier, "a point of immanence specified by the proximity of the corporeal Kelvin [. . .] to the pre-individuation manifest in Solaris," it seems that this "point" is in fact the visible, aesthetic manifestation of the universal dynamic process. The "chiastic structure", to borrow Véronique Fóti's expression, "that unifies the synergic sentient body also interlinks sentient beings with one another."[38] And it is perhaps just such an interlink which joins the ocean, the simulacra, and the scientists. The "tran-scendental ground" provided by the ocean of Solaris is here the joint through which the larger, all-encompassing process of time finds its acute artistic figura-tion. What is perhaps most unique about *Solaris* among Tarkovsky's films (and indeed those of any other filmmaker) is precisely this expression of temporal flesh and density emerging along the horizon between which the spiritual and the physical intertwine, the bursting forth of time and difference as at once the force that divides the subject from itself and fractures open the zone between subject and object, myself and the other. There is, of course, always an inherent danger of using these philosophical descriptions in this context—*Solaris* is in no way a philosophical tract—but at the same time, given the larger apprehension of reality the film provokes, this may provide the most effective means for discerning what the film is doing at its deepest level. Again, it is not only the manipulation of time to express the sensation of the infinite, non-physical world lurking behind the visible; Tarkovsky effectively reveals the inherence of the spiritual within the material by presenting a striking temporalization of virtualities at, simultaneously, the level of diegetic reality (with the materialization of Hari) and within the structure of the film itself through these expressions of temporal duration. But this expression depends almost completely on its physicality; Tarkovsky presents us with images designed to make us look beyond their frame and focuses on the material as a means of revealing the spiritual. In this respect, perhaps more than any other, the parallels with the work of Merleau-Ponty are at their strongest. As the philosopher describes the appearance of phenomena,

> each appearance of the thing that falls before our perception is still nothing but an invitation to perceive more and a momentary pause in the perceptual process. If the thing itself were attained, it would from then on be stretched out before us without any mystery. It would cease to exist as a thing at the very moment that we believed we possessed it.[39]

In *Solaris*, it is precisely through art that such a concept is properly articulated, as the physical, visible image necessarily leads beyond itself and, as the filmmaker himself put it, "stretches out into infinity, and leads to the absolute."[40]

NOTES

1. Slavoj Žižek, *The Fright of Real Tears: Krzystof Kieslowski: Between Theory and Post-Theory* (London: British Film Institute, 2001), 103.
2. Nicholas Berdyaev, *Dostoievsky*, trans. by Donald Attwater (London: Sheed & Ward, 1934), 50.
3. Ibid.
4. Andrei Tarkovsky, *Sculpting in Time*, trans. by Kitty Hunter-Blair (Austin: University of Texas Press, 1987), 37.
5. Žižek, *The Fright of Real Tears*, 102.
6. Maurice Merleau-Ponty, *Nature: Course Notes from the Collège de France*, trans. by Robert Vallier (Evanston, IL: Northwestern University Press, 2003), 38.
7. Žižek, "The Thing from Inner Space," September 1999, http://www.lacan.com/zizekthing.htm.
8. Ibid.
9. Mark Riley, "Disorientation, Duration and Tarkovsky," in Ian Buchanan and Patricia MacCormack (eds), *Deleuze and the Schizoanalysis of Cinema* (London: Continuum, 2008), 54.
10. Riley, "Disorientation, Duration and Tarkovsky," 57.

11. Gilles Deleuze, *The Logic of Sense*, trans. by Mark Lester (New York: Columbia University Press, 1990), 165.
12. Maurice Merleau-Ponty, *Phenomenology of Perception*, trans. by Donald A. Landes (London: Routledge, 1965), 438.
13. Gilles Deleuze and Felix Guattari, *What is Philosophy?* trans. by Hugh Tomlinson and Graham Burchell (New York: Columbia University Press, 1994), 178.
14. Maurice Merleau-Ponty, *The Visible and the Invisible*, trans. by Alphonso Lingis (Evanston, IL: Northwestern University Press, 1968), 136; Tarkovsky, *Sculpting in Time*, 21.
15. Merleau-Ponty, *The Visible and the Invisible*, 147.
16. Ibid., 153.
17. Ibid., 137.
18. Miguel de Cervantes, *Don Quixote de la Mancha*, trans. by Charles Jarvis (Oxford: Oxford University Press, 1999), 1076.
19. Merleau-Ponty, *The Visible and the Invisible*, 262.
20. Marc Richir, "Le sensible dans le rêve," in R. Barbaras (ed.), *Notes de cours sur L'origine de la géométrie de Husserl: Suivi de, Recherches sur la phénoménologie de Merleau-Ponty* (Paris: PUF, 1998), 253 ("c'est-à-dire la 'condensation' en quelque sorte 'pure', par l'*épochè* du rêve, de l' 'il y a' sensible dans le *Wesen*").
21. Merleau-Ponty, *The Visible and the Invisible*, 260.
22. Riley, "Disorientation, Duration and Tarkovsky," 56.
23. Vivian Sobchack, *The Address of the Eye: A Phenomenology of Film Experience* (Princeton: Princeton University Press, 1992), 59.
24. Sobchack, *The Address of the Eye*, 119–20.
25. Merleau-Ponty, *The Visible and the Invisible*, 136.
26. Riley, "Disorientation, Duration and Tarkovsky," 55.
27. Merleau-Ponty, *The Visible and the Invisible*, 146.
28. Riley, "Disorientation, Duration and Tarkovsky," 57.
29. Merleau-Ponty, *The Visible and the Invisible*, 133.
30. Ibid., 142.
31. Ibid., 255.
32. Gilles Deleuze, *Cinema 2: The Time-Image*, trans. by H. Tomlinson and R. Galeta (Minneapolis: University of Minnesota Press, 1989), 79.
33. Merleau-Ponty, *The Visible and the Invisible*, 147.
34. Miguel de Beistegui, "Toward a Phenomenology of Difference?" *Research in Phenomenology* 30.1 (2000): 63.
35. Ibid.
36. Merleau-Ponty, *The Visible and the Invisible*, 142.
37. Riley, "Disorientation, Duration and Tarkovsky," 52; Merleau-Ponty, *The Visible and the Invisible*, 142.
38. Véronique M. Fóti, "Chiasm, Flesh, Figuration: Toward a Non-Positive Ontology," in *Merleau-Ponty and the Possibilities of Philosophy* (Albany: SUNY Press, 2009), 188.
39. Merleau-Ponty, *Phenomenology of Perception*, 242.
40. Tarkovsky, *Sculpting in Time*, 104.

CHAPTER 12

Cinema as Spiritual Exercise: Tarkovsky and Hadot

Anne Eakin Moss

The French philosopher Pierre Hadot strove to reconcile the strategies and aims of philosophy and religion by calling for "spiritual exercise" to enable the practice of "philosophy as a way of life."[1] Born in 1922 and sequestered in a seminary for most of World War II, Hadot left the Catholic Church in 1952 to marry and pursue a scholarly career. Responsible for introducing Ludwig Wittgenstein to French philosophy, Hadot was elected to the Collège de France as chair of the History of Hellenistic and Roman Thought in 1983 on the recommendation of Michel Foucault.[2] Though Andrei Tarkovsky was born ten years later than Hadot, and died prematurely in 1986, the mature work of both men was infused by the introspective post-war atmosphere of disillusionment and Existentialism, Socialist hopes and disappointment, Cold War anxiety and Soviet stagnation.[3] Tarkovsky's poetic and explicitly "spiritual" films resonate with Hadot's philosophy in their pursuit of "cosmic consciousness"—a term that is Hadot's but could just as well refer to the sea on the planet Solaris.[4]

Hadot examines ancient Greek philosophy with philological and historiographical tools, considering philosophy as a way of life, rather than a system of ethics, politics, or formal logic. For Hadot, philosophy is an embodied, ongoing practice that orients the self within a larger whole, one that can be likened to meditation, art, and science.[5] "[I]n each philosophical school," he writes, "we find the same conception of the cosmic flight and the view from above as the philosophical way par excellence of looking at things."[6] Tarkovsky's films, in dialog with the great philosophical novels of the nineteenth century and dissident poetry of the twentieth century, as well as medieval and Renaissance painting, Russian Orthodox theology and Existentialist philosophy, strive to teach a practice of attention that seems quite similar to what Hadot describes as "the fundamental Stoic spiritual attitude"—"a continuous vigilance and presence of mind, self-consciousness which never sleeps, and a constant tension of the spirit."[7] Hadot's call for the artist that "must paint in a state in which he feels his unity with the earth and the universe" could just as well be Tarkovsky's Andrei Rublev as it is Hadot's Paul Klee or Cézanne.[8] It could just as well be Tarkovsky himself.

How are we to take this similarity? What does it mean to think of cinema *as* spiritual exercise and as philosophy more generally? What are the stakes and pay-off of such a comparison? Here I offer two primary avenues of inquiry. The first is to ask how Hadot's analysis of ancient philosophy and his concept of spiritual exercise might illuminate Tarkovsky's films and film practice in some new way. What can looking at Tarkovsky's films and filmmaking as kinds of spiritual exercise tell us about the films themselves, and then perhaps, about the possibilities of cinema as a medium and Tarkovsky's role in expanding those possibilities? I touch on each of the major films, noting how their themes of spiritual seeking follow a progression through Tarkovsky's oeuvre that leads all the more to a notion of spiritual exercise without the promise of recompense, epitomized in Tarkovsky's last film, *The Sacrifice* (*Offret*, Sweden, 1986), as the faithful daily watering of a dead stick. Then I examine specific visual techniques in the films and the ways in which they encourage a mode of viewing that is non-linear and might be considered spiritual exercise in itself. The second avenue of inquiry is to ask how Tarkovsky's films might illuminate Hadot's notion of spiritual exercise, and further, how they might suggest a way of understanding cinema itself as a form of spiritual exercise for the modern age. And in so doing, they may offer a way to understand how the media of communication negotiate the practice of religion, philosophy, and spiritual exercise in modernity.[9]

FILMMAKING AS SPIRITUAL EXERCISE

On the most basic level, Tarkovsky's films can be seen as vivid narrative illustration of spiritual exercises in Hadot's terms. Each of the protagonists of his seven major films demands of himself extreme forms of mental concentration, focused on goals that depart from the everyday and can only be seen as spiritual or metaphysical. The child spy, icon painter, cosmonaut, autobiographical subject, stalker, writer, and father are all quixotic seekers of some transcendent aim, their quests characterized by deep attention to the world around them. Hadot, in his inaugural lecture to his chair at the Collège de France, describes the writings of Platonism, Aristotelianism, Stoicism, and Epicureanism as linked in so far as they seek "not so much to inform the reader of a doctrinal content but to form him, to make him traverse a certain itinerary in the course of which he will make spiritual progress." That itinerary is not clear-cut, but one "in which all the detours, starts and stops, and digressions of the work are formative elements."[10] The same could be said of the path laid out for the heroes of each of Tarkovsky's films, and even for his actors across the seven feature films, as they are seemingly reborn in new roles. Events and actions bear less narrative significance for the heroes than they do spiritual signifi-cance. The transcendent aim which they seek, though arguably achieved in the first two films—Soviet victory and the enduring art of the icon—recedes in the later films, never to be explicitly consummated, nor revealed. Alexander may have reversed the apocalypse in *The Sacrifice*, but Little Man will still water the dead tree. Hadot concludes his inaugural lecture with the assertion that ancient philosophy's enduring legacy is its pursuit of "the feeling for the seriousness and grandeur of existence."[11] In his oeuvre, Tarkovsky demonstrates cinema's ability to take on that legacy. As he declared in his essays on filmmaking, art "makes infinity tangible."[12] Both men aspire to make the spiritual sensible in the everyday.

The hero of Tarkovsky's lyrical Thaw-era debut feature, *Ivan's Childhood* (1962), is a twelve-year-old boy orphaned in the course of the Great Patriotic War and now a reconnaissance spy for the Soviet army. Jean-Paul Sartre defended the film in *l'Unita* (the Italian communist party journal) from accusations of petit-bourgeois expressionism, praising its beauty and calling it "absolutely Soviet." He observed that "the film's lyricism—its churning skies, its tranquil waters, its countless forests—are life itself for Ivan."[13] Sartre's observation is borne out by the film's portrayal of Ivan's point of view and his dreams, which mirror but intensify the fractured experience of wartime existence. Ivan experiences the world with all of his senses, as if a string ready to pick up the slightest vibra-tion around him. His intensity of attention and "concentration on the present moment" resembles that of the Stoic philosopher.[14] His past is gone and he looks forward to no future, only the present of his mission. If Sartre is right that the film's "lyricism" is Ivan's "life," then it is because Ivan is ideally oriented within the fractured world of the war, registering its signs with the dismay and horror of a child, but answering to them with the responsibility and seriousness of a war hero. When Galtsev discovers that Ivan has been executed in German captivity, he assigns himself and the viewer the task of his last line: "I must think about this." Having been martyred, Ivan has achieved a form of perfection, of being one with the Soviet world, that is inaccessible to the scarred Galtsev, and to the spectator of Soviet Russia in 1962.

Tarkovsky turned to the Slavic past in search of a source of spiritual iden-tity in his next film. In an interview with the Soviet film journal *Ekran* in 1965, Tarkovsky described the hero of his new film, which after several years of struggle with conservative post-Thaw Soviet censorship would become a three-hour saga based on the life of the medieval Russian Orthodox icon painter Andrei Rublev (*Andrei Rublev*, 1966). He said that Rublev is "a person seeing the world with a painful keenness, reacting with utmost sensitivity to everything he encounters . . ." and that "he strove to express an all-embracing harmony of the world, the serenity of the soul."[15] Compare Pierre Hadot's interpretation of Plato's *Phaedo* and the *Republic*: "the whole of the philosopher's speculative and contemplative effort becomes a spiritual exercise, insofar as he raises his thought up to the perspective of the Whole, and liberates it from the illusions of individuality (in the words of Friedmann: 'Step out of duration . . . become eternal by transcending yourself')."[16] The young bell maker, played by a slightly older Nikolai Burlyayev (Ivan in *Ivan's Childhood*), searches for the right kind of clay to cast the bell by reaching out to the world with all his senses, seeking to create an object that will mediate daily between the human and the divine. The color shots of Rublev's icons that burst forth at the end of *Andrei Rublev* suggest transcendence after Rublev's long struggle with human individuality—his vow of silence and refusal to paint after witnessing human violence, all of which the spectator experiences as duration via long takes to be discussed further below.

Kris Kelvin, the hero of *Solaris* (1972), is sent to the space station orbiting the planet Solaris to find out what happened to the mission, and gets drawn into contemplating the mystery of the planet that sends him fleshy apparitions of his dead wife. Kris asks, at the end of the film, "Why are we being tortured like this?" and the lone remaining scientist answers, as if in Hadot's words, "In my opinion, we have lost our sense of the cosmic. The ancients understood it perfectly." Kris ponders what to do at the end of the film, after the last of the repeated incarnations of his simulacrum wives has "annihilated" herself—to return to Earth or stay on the station. Ultimately, his decision echoes Hadot's admonition to the "*Spectator Novus*" of modernity, that "we must separate ourselves from the 'everyday' world in order to rediscover the world qua world":[17]

> Do I have the right to turn down even an imagined possibility of contact with this Ocean which my race has been trying to understand for decades? Should I remain here? . . . What for? In the hope that she'll return? But I don't harbor this hope. The only thing left for me is to wait. I don't know what for. New miracles?

The next sequence allows us at first to think that Kelvin has returned to his father's house on Earth. Kris looks into the window of his father's house and ponders all the objects in it, which we've seen at some length earlier in the film. Like one of those "spot the differences" pages, everything is made strange. Hadot, coincidentally seeming to echo Viktor Shklovsky, writes: "Philosophy . . . deepens and transforms habitual perception, forcing us to become aware of the very fact that we *are perceiving the world*, and that the world *is* that which we perceive."[18] However, the final shot zooms out to reveal that the return of the prodigal son is taking place not on an altered Earth, but on an island-simulacrum on the surface of Solaris. Interpreting this much-debated ending through the prism of Hadot's philosophy, Kelvin has not indulged in escapism by remaining on Solaris, but has demonstrated his commitment to spiritual exercise in the form of examining the obstacles in the self that prevent the perception of the world qua world. Kris has to be in the cosmic in order to see the everyday.[19]

Hadot concludes his inaugural lecture with a quotation from Communist fellow traveler Georges Friedmann, who in 1942 demanded of his reader, "every day, a 'spiritual exercise,'" on the grounds that "very rare, are those who, in order to prepare for the revolution, wish to become worthy of it."[20] The revision-ist culture of the Thaw, in literature and cinema, similarly, revealed the extent to which the Soviet revolution never allowed for care of the self. More hereti-cally, it questioned whether or not the real revolution had come. Tarkovsky's monumental focus on the individual quest of self-understanding, set against the backdrop of the signature international competition of the Cold War, the space program, insisted that Russian culture still had a spiritual program to offer as well.

Tarkovsky's next film, the autobiographical *Mirror* (1974), takes the film-maker's own spiritual exercise as its subject. It begins with the young mother in stillness, waiting for the father's return, and ends with the old mother (played by Maria Vishnyakova, Tarkovsky's real mother) in movement, as if the film freed her, or the hero's memory of her, to reconcile past and present. Further, the process of making the film might be seen as a demonstration of the abil-ity of filmmaking itself to be spiritual exercise. *Mirror* was conceived first as a dialog (as an interview with his mother filmed with hidden cameras) and latterly as a confession.[21] Filmmaking is of necessity a dialogic process of nego-tiation toward a shared vision among director, cameraman, cinematographer, actors, studio, and state censorship apparatus, yet *Mirror* gives the impression of an intensely first-person meditation. Tarkovsky's work on the film lasted ten years from its conception in 1964 to its production in 1973–4. In *Sculpting in Time*, Tarkovsky professed, "The aim of art is to prepare a person for death, to plough and harrow his soul, rendering it capable of turning to good."[22] The film's engagement with the religious was the product of a long negotiation with the censorship state that demanded the filmmaker cut elements of the screenplay that had a "biblical tone" and that he "relieve the entire film of mysticism."[23] Yet if spiritual exercise serves as an attempt to "find the truth that lives within each of us that can be found and used," this film can be seen as its epigone. The making of the film also demanded the vigilance and attention to the world depicted in all of his films. Tarkovsky was told he would be given enough film for three takes per shot, but received only about enough for one.[24] He carefully selected every object that made its way into the *mise-en-scène*—to the extent of rebuilding his mother's dacha from photographs and having the fields around it planted with exactly the kind of grass (buckwheat) that he saw in his memory, taking literally his call for art "to plough and harrow his soul."[25] The artistic transformation of Tarkovsky's personal history took the form of spiritual exercise in its very production, and demanded the same of the viewer in the durational and puzzle-like experience of the final product of the film.

SPECTATORSHIP AS SPIRITUAL EXERCISE

From the turning point of *Mirror*, the second half of Tarkovsky's filmic production, *Stalker* (1979), *Nostalghia* (1983), and *The Sacrifice*, shifts the emphasis from filmmaking as a process of spiritual exercise, to teaching the viewer to exercise a spiritual kind of seeing in a modern, secular, and technological age. The Stalker guides his companions through the mysteriously transformed world of the Zone, teaching them to see the natural environment as alien and to place every footfall with intention. Refusing to follow his translator and guide, Eugenia, from the very start, the traveling writer of *Nostalghia* casts his eye over Italy, recalling Russia all along, and finds himself attracted more to the madman Domenico than the earthly beauty of Eugenia. And finally, the father of *The Sacrifice* guides his family and friends in how to see the world at the end of time, though the postman Otto reminds him that there is no such thing as truth. Each of these films poses a complex cinematographic puzzle to the viewer, and thematizes the relationship between seeing and knowing. Beyond narrative illustration of characters engaged in spiritual exercise, Tarkovsky's cinematography—his extremely careful and controlled *mise-en-scène*, long takes, painterly shot composition, deliberate use of color and contrast, aural composition, and non-linear montage—guides and instructs the spectator to look at and listen to his vision of the world with the same kind of deep attention as well as estrangement.

In frustrating the rules of classical Hollywood narrative continuity, Tarkovsky can be seen as training the spectator in something like the Stoic art of living—to teach us to "switch from our 'human' vision of reality, in which our values depend on our passions, to a 'natural' vision of things, which replaces each event within the perspective of universal nature."[26] This "'human' vision of reality, in which our values depend on our passions," might be associated with classical Hollywood continuity, with its logic of the shot/reaction shot that sutures the viewer to a specific, and usually human, viewing position, one conditioned by voyeuristic desires. Tarkovsky's aesthetics instead prevent the viewer from engaging in "habitual perception," imposing a "'natural' vision of things, which replaces each event within the perspective of universal nature." Rather than a subjective point of view that focuses the viewer's attention on human agency, Tarkovsky's cinematography asks us to contemplate the contingent relationship of the subject, character, and viewer to the material and moral world around them both.

Fredric Jameson somewhat astonishingly accuses Tarkovsky's films of lacking in self-reflexivity, criticizing them for the hypocrisy of the "valorization of nature without human technology achieved by the highest technology of the photographic apparatus itself. No reflexivity acknowledges this second hidden presence, thus threatening to transform Tarkovskian nature-mysticism into the sheerest ideology." Robert Bird retorts that "Tarkovsky's entire cinematic project was aimed precisely at exploring the cinematic apparatus and investigating its impact upon human experience—as much sensory as intellectual and spiritual."[27] Considering the narrative repurposing of documentary footage through *Mirror*, Bird writes that "Though it is not specifically a critique of the Soviet imaginary, *Mirror* seeks to redefine the viewer's very attitude towards images, not as the storehouse of the known, but as a possibility for envisioning the new."[28] Indeed, the hallmark of auteur cinema, and Tarkovsky's in particular, is the self-conscious cinematographic transformation of the filmed world, and the personal signature of that transformation is generally recognizable to the art cinema goer. The "revelation of the device" demanded by Jameson may be seen explicitly in the shadow of the microphone at the beginning of *Mirror*. But even when the technological apparatus remains hidden, the auteur's mark can also be seen in the films' essayistic form and mode of representation. Tarkovsky's long takes and compound images, which he called "imprinted time," and Giles Deleuze took as prime examples of the "time-image," often come from an impossible point of view, and force the viewer to contemplate the passage of time, the logic of the gazes within the shot, and the relationship of the universal to the particular.[29] These contemplative, long-duration shots generate moments of "essayism" that Timothy Corrigan defines as "a figurative disruption or digression that questions, at its heart, the experiential mode of film narrative itself."[30] In his essayistic narrative films, Tarkovsky demands that the viewer reflect on the experience of cinema, of memory, and of the progress of the spirit through the course of the film, and through the course of engaging with his oeuvre, in the dialog generated by all seven of his major films together.

Thus the return of Anatoly Solonitsyn, who played the title character in *Andrey Rublev*, as the passing doctor at the beginning of *Mirror*, and the mysterious breeze that blows through the grass at the beginning of *Mirror*, seeming to push the doctor back to the dacha, and that same breeze that seemingly returns to warn the same actor, playing the Writer in *Stalker*, to turn back from the direct path to the room, all reminds the viewer to view each individual scene in light of the whole artistic project. The viewer engages in similar work when comparing the repeated images of levitating women, wandering dogs and horses, and rain that falls inside houses and in sheets that do not wet the character and do not extinguish fire across the films. The films demand that the spectator never finalize his or her understanding of an individual image. Actors grow old from film to film, like the central figures of Richard Linklater's *Boyhood* (2014). Recognizing these connections serves to estrange the viewer from "nature-mysticism" and remind them of the aesthetic mediation of the images on-screen. Tarkovsky's filmic poetics intend to make the viewer a participant in the sense-making of the film. Via associations such as these, the viewer is invited to become "co-creator."[31] Hadot writes, "The experience of modern art thus allows us to glimpse—in a way that is, in the last analysis, philosophical—the miracle of perception itself, which opens up the world to us. Yet we can only perceive this miracle by *reflecting* on perception, and *converting our attention*."[32] Tarkovsky insists on redefining the viewer's mode of engagement with images and transforms this engagement from a ritual of distraction, as Walter Benjamin might have it, into spiritual exercise.

What Hadot, illustrated here by Tarkovsky, demonstrates is the possibility of philosophy to reconnect us to the world. That connection is not something to be achieved, but to be practiced over time, throughout a life. Seeing Tarkovsky's cinematography as spiritual exercise does not demand, then, a purely affective, associative mode of spectatorship, but on the contrary, requires cognition, memory, and analysis. What Nora Alter has written about the essay film genre holds true for Tarkovsky's narrative films as well: "Like 'heresy' in the Adornean literary essay, the essay film disrespects traditional boundaries, is transgressive both structurally and conceptually, it is self-reflective and self-reflexive."[33] Tarkovsky's films engage in a kind of reflexivity that is intensely cognitive and intellectual, and rewarded by dialog between spectator and image. "Spiritual exercise" differentiates itself as well from the ritual and aura of worship, aspiring to an everyday form of life. Ultimately both Hadot and Tarkovsky want to rejuvenate the practice of living.

SPIRITUAL SPECIAL EFFECTS

The contemporary philosopher of religion Hent de Vries, for whom Hadot is an important influence, draws a connection between the cinematic special effect and the religious notion of the miracle, arguing that the special effect cannot be "thought or experienced—without some reference to (or conjuring up of) the miracle and everything for which it stands." At the same time, he argues, "[c]onversely, . . . thinking the miracle was never possible without introducing a certain *technicity* and, quite literally, a *manipulation* of sorts."[34] In the chapel at the beginning of *Nostalghia*, the birds do not burst forth from the statue of the Madonna miraculously, but are released with an audible snap from her dress by the hands of the kneeling supplicant. Tarkovsky asks us (and Eugenia) to see this both as miracle and a deliberate effect, part of a ritual constructed to inspire faith, in other words, synecdochic to the miracle itself. Tarkovsky was extremely wary of the special effect, fearing any introduction of fakery or falseness into his films, and asserting that "outward effects simply distance and blur the goal which I am pursuing."[35] He nonetheless used cinema trickery in a number of signature techniques that depart from a mimetic reproduction of reality and can leave no doubt in the viewer of the fact of technical manipulation.

In the remainder of this essay, I look at three of these signature techniques in Tarkovsky's filmic language to show how they ask the viewer to engage in a mode of spectatorship that can be likened to spiritual exercise, and might be considered "spiritual special effects." The first is the compound image, which serves as something like a temporal covering shot, combining images in impossible time and space. Just as Tarkovsky claims to be "sculpting in time," Hadot cites Plotinus' metaphor of the sculptor, which says that seeing the soul in its "immortality and immateriality" requires that you "'remove from it everything that is not itself."[36] Rather than transcendence, I argue, these shots point to the ongoing work of spiritual exercise, invoking the miraculous, yet redefining it for the secular, modern era. I discuss here the final shots of *Solaris* and *Nostalghia*. The second is an approximately 360 degree pan, which, while not exactly a special effect, violates the 180 degree rule that conventionally governs continuity cinema, and seems to situate the viewer at the center of the film's world. I examine two examples, one from *Andrei Rublev*, and the second from *Nostalghia* (though this shot is not strictly speaking a full 360 degrees, it suggests that illusion). Like the long-duration shots that Tarkovsky allegedly said generate "a new intensity of attention" over the time of viewing, these shots force the spectator to think about what does not match up, then to pass through boredom and confusion to decide on some linkage on the spiritual level.[37] Finally, I touch on the repeated scenes of levitation through Tarkovsky's oeuvre, from Ivan's dream at the beginning of *Ivan's Childhood*, to the scene of weightlessness in the library in *Solaris*, to the floating women and couple in *Mirror* and *The Sacrifice*. These moments of transcendence, whether framed as dream, science, allegory, or witchery, are all connected to mother figures and stand for the fecund possibility of the miraculous.

The zooming-out sequence at the end of *Solaris*, which reveals the scene of the prodigal son to be taking place on the surface of the planet Solaris, not Earth, allows the spectator the view from above. Yet it also incorporates a special effect-shot, combining dacha and planet, presumably by means of a matte, designed to reconcile the film's worlds and offer its last word on the planet's effects on Kris. Though Burton "filmed only clouds" and neither the scientists nor we get to see his view of the "giant baby," the ending gives us a non-subjective and impossible view of Kris' epiphanic reunion with his father. Hadot considers the science of physics to be a form of spiritual exercise in its pursuit of the "imaginative 'overflight' which causes human affairs to be regarded as of little importance." Kris might be on the surface of the planet, but we are with Seneca, ". . . casting a contemptuous glance at the narrow globe of the earth from above . . ."[38] However, as Hadot would also assert, the spectator does not achieve transcendence by possessing this view. Instead, as much debate over the meaning of the ending of *Solaris* attests, spectators are put in dialog with the deliberately composed image, forced to ask what that view entails, costs, or demands. What responsibility do we as viewers have to, and for, transcendent vision? In psychoanalytic film theory the establishing or initial shot is the "site of *jouissance*," of the overweening sense of control over the image, which offers the spectator a vision of "imaginary plenitude, unbounded by any gaze, and unmarked by difference." Conventional rules of continuity, as Kaja Silverman further explains, usually require the initial shot to be followed with a reaction shot that assigns the transcendent view to a character in the narrative. Continuity cinema thus aims to make "the viewing subject . . . aware of the limitations on what it sees."[39] Although it may seem to reverse this conventional sequence, I would argue that Tarkovsky does not allow the covering shot or "overflight" at the end of *Solaris* to give us unbounded plenitude, but instead demands reflection and reflexivity in dialog with Tarkovsky's oeuvre. The documentary shots of aviators hanging from Soviet stratospheric balloons —agents of the overhead view—in *Mirror* serve as a metafilmic comment on the truth claims of documentary. And the crash of the medieval hot-air balloon in the prolog to *Andrei Rublev* insists on the failure of the attempt to transcend. The only reaction to the peasant's flight is the mute rolling of the horse.

Tarkovsky's shots of landscapes, earth, tree trunks, and water exceed the subjectivity of the characters to which they are sutured, if they are sutured at all. These complex, absorptive shots demand attention to texture, detail, movement—both the surface and depth of the cinematic image. When the doctor at the beginning of *Mirror* falls off the fence, he gets a new view of the earth that prefigures the Stalker's awestruck contemplation of the Zone: "Look at these things, these roots, bushes . . . Plants feel, are aware, maybe even perceive. [. . .] They don't hurry, while we speak banalities." The natural environment seems to look back at the characters and the viewer, challenging any attempt to encompass or control the view. Hadot's citation from Plutarch captures the attitude toward the world demanded by Tarkovsky: "For the world is the most sacred and divine of temples, and the one most fitting for the gods. Man is introduced into it by birth to be a spectator: not of artificial, immobile statues, but of the perceptible images of intelligible essences . . ."[40]

At the end of *Nostalghia*, a zooming-out shot similar to the end of *Solaris* compounds all the problematics of the film—the particular (the house) and the universal (the ruined cathedral), Andrei and dog as intellect and nature. These endings insist on the viewer's investment in the image as such, not as the narrative perspective of a character, and demand analysis and engagement rather than insisting on an illusion of transcendence. Just as Kris goes to the surface of Solaris to contend with his experience of human existence, the final sequence of *Solaris* frames the world as a perceptible image contingent on the cosmic. As the final sequence of *Nostalghia* zooms out to reveal the enclosing cathedral, Russian peasant song fills the space, combining the Western and Eastern, sacred and folk. Finally snow falls over the image, as if to mediate between image and viewer on a tactile level.[41] Though Tarkovsky rejected Eisenstein's intellectual montage, this layered shot requires dialectical thinking. Rather than a finalized synthesis, it suggests the spiritual seeking of the exile's lot.

Toward the beginning of *Andrei Rublev*, Rublev and his companions take refuge from the rain in a stable where they interrupt the blasphemous performance of an itinerant jester. In a moment of stillness and waiting, one of the monks leaves to inform on the jester. He pronounces "God sends monks, the devil sends jesters" at the beginning of a 360 degree pan around the stable which ends with a view through the window of his cassocked figure reporting to the mounted noble in the window at the end of the shot.[42] Tarkovsky brilliantly evokes an ethics of spectatorship by inscribing the viewer in the center of this pan, which takes in each of the individuals in the barn as a communal whole, bounded by four walls textured to give their reality a sensuous certainty. There is a tension between the little girl who almost catches our eye and the boy who scratches at the wall, the intense gaze of Rublev, and the shifting eyes of the jester, all of which alerts us, without words, to the ethical responsibilities inherent in looking closely at our neighbor. By placing the spectator in the center of the humble hut that might as well be a manger, Tarkovsky prevents passive viewing or the assumption of superiority.

At the center of *Nostalghia* (at approximately 1 hour, 19 minutes in the Kino Lorber release) is another circular black-and-white panning shot that, unlike the shot in *Andrei Rublev*, disavows the reality of physical space rather than asserting it. As Eugenia reads the letter from Sosnovsky ("I could try not to return to Russia, but the thought kills me, because I would die if I never again saw my homeland"), Andrei lies back to relieve a nosebleed, and seems to have a vision of home. His wife wakes upon hearing her name, and leaves the house to join a young boy, a girl, and an old woman, who all look out expectantly from the hilltop. This sequence returns the viewer to the scene of the opening credits, in which these four figures, dog, and horse are all visible in a long shot from the house looking out over a lake. In the dream sequence, the almost two-minute-long shot pans from a close-up of each of the three women standing in mute expectation, seemingly looking for Andrei, and then pans without an evident cut to reveal, impossibly, the same group of women, plus the boy, dog, and horse, in a long shot suddenly reversed and yet searching still (Figures 12.1, 12.2). Andrei's absence unites the shot conceptually, yet its spatial impossibility requires of the

Figure 12.1 Gorchakov's wife in the dream sequence in *Nostalghia*.

Figure 12.2 Gorchakov's family in the dream sequence in *Nostalghia*.

viewer the work of understanding what his absence means to him and us. As the sacristan says to Eugenia (in a close-up looking out directly at the spectator, and thus an utterance meant to address both character and audience) at the beginning of the film in the chapel, about the procession in honor of the Madonna del Parto about to occur: "If there are any casual onlookers who are not suppliants, then nothing happens." Do the women in Andrei's dream wait in vain because of Andrei's lack of belief? Because of ours? "But you should at least kneel down," continues the sacristan. Cinema as spiritual exercise asks of the viewer that we at least kneel down—grant to the filmmaker the possibility of a miracle, wait for it, and take up dialog with it.

In Tarkovsky's last film, the levitation of Alexander while he lies with the witch Maria represents Otto's promise for the last chance to save the world from apocalyptic destruction. This abrupt departure from indexical reality does not demand that the viewer reevaluate the genre of the film in each case, shifting expectations to the fantastic. After all, the scene of floating in *Solaris* has a perfectly scientific explanation. Similarly, the plastic sheet heavy with water, hung over Domenico's bed in *Nostalghia*, seen retrospectively in light of these other images, stands in for his wife, driven away by the family's seven-year imprisonment to his paranoia. If these symbols have a degree of equivalence across Tarkovsky's oeuvre, then the special effect of levitation does not ask us to reevaluate our understanding of the genre or mimetic quality of the film, and reclassify it as fantasy rather than realistic drama, but instead it tells us that we might find this special effect in our experience of reality. In other words, Tarkovsky asks the spectator to believe in the special effect in so far as it reproduces mimetically the *experience* of the miraculous, the transcendent, and the spiritual.

I have argued for an affinity between Tarkovsky and Hadot in their attitude toward the divine and the world, and I have attempted to demonstrate that affinity through a very brief overview of Tarkovsky's seven major films, examined in Hadot's terms. Hadot's emphasis on practice and duration rather than transcendence or revelation draws attention to the themes of seeking and observation as well as the techniques of long take and complex vertical montage, and offers a way to think about Tarkovsky's production over the course of his oeuvre. Through Hadot's lens, the fruitless searches of Tarkovsky's ruined men in the second half of his oeuvre are as philosophically productive as the transcendent aims of the heroes of the first half. In fact, the outcome is irrelevant to the practice of living a philosophical life, which need not take the form of what is generally considered philosophy at all. Running hands through clay, wading through a swamp, and crossing a pool with a lighted candle—these can all be seen as embodied forms of philosophical practice in so far as they exercise the spirit by bringing the self into dialog with the "cosmic" whole. Hadot emphasizes the work of philosophy in its etymology: "philo-sophia: the love of, or progress toward, wisdom." He writes, "To the same extent that the philosophical life is equivalent to the practice of spiritual exercises, it is also a tearing away from everyday life. It is a conversion, a total transformation of one's vision, life-style, and behavior."[43] This idea allows us to see Tarkovsky's heroes' behavior as a form of philosophy, and offers a new way of thinking about the work asked of the spectator of one of his films.

In turn, Tarkovsky's films illuminate the modern relevance and transformation of ancient philosophical practice as described by Hadot, and offer a self-reflexive vision of the role of cinema in modern spiritual life. They offer a way of seeing cinematic practice, both as filmmaker and spectator, as spiritual exercise. The relationship between Tarkovsky and Terrence Malick, Lars von Trier, Chantal Akerman, Chris Marker, Spike Jonze, or any number of filmmakers of a contemplative or reflexive bent, might be thus considered through the lens of spiritual exercise. De Vries proposes:

> To speak of special effects *in terms of miracles* . . . implies that one *generalize* the applicability of the world of religion—its concept and imaginary, its semantic and figural archive—to include almost everything that, at one time or another, had set itself apart from religion (or from which religion had sought to distance itself, in turn). The magical and the technological thus come to occupy the same space, obey the same regime and the same logic.[44]

In the making and in the viewing, in its themes and its presentation, Tarkovsky's cinema demands the work of reconciling the world of religion with the world of technology. Robert Bird comes to a similar conclusion with respect to the cinematic shot in Tarkovsky: "it conveys . . . a sober recognition of the role visual media have come to play in determining the very constitution of human reality."[45] Tarkovsky's films also reveal the role that media and especially cinema play in human aspirations toward the divine, and the everyday practice of those aspirations. The view from above, the cosmic consciousness, or the miraculous is not something given or answered by Tarkovsky, but an idea that is posed and withdrawn, a position to be desired, but never obtained.[46]

NOTES

1. See particularly Pierre Hadot, *Philosophy as a Way of Life: Spiritual Exercises from Socrates to Foucault*, ed. Arnold Davidson and trans. by Michael Chase (Oxford: Blackwell, 1995); hereafter *Spiritual Exercises*.
2. Pierre Hadot, *The Present Alone Is Our Happiness: Conversations with Jeannie Carlier and Arnold I. Davidson*, trans. by Marc Djaballah (Stanford: Stanford University Press, 2009), 22, 40–1.
3. Sartre's interest in Tarkovsky is well documented. See Jean-Paul Sartre, "Letter on the Critique of *Ivan's Childhood*," in Nathan Dunne (ed.), *Tarkovsky* (London: Black Dog, 2008), 35–45. In an interview, Hadot asserts, "Not until Nietzsche, Bergson, and existentialism does philosophy consciously return to being a concrete attitude, a way of life and of seeing the world." Hadot, *Present Alone*, 108.
4. Hadot, *Spiritual Exercises*, 85.
5. See Pierre Hadot, "Forms of Life and Forms of Discourse in Ancient Philosophy," trans. by Arnold Davidson and Paula Wissing, *Critical Inquiry* 16 (Spring 1990): 483–505, 499; also Hadot, *Spiritual Exercises*, 97.

6. Hadot, *Spiritual Exercises*, 242.

7. Ibid., 84.

8. Ibid., 255.

9. Hent de Vries lays out the stakes of this problematic in his introduction to the volume *Religion and Media*, eds Hent de Vries and Samuel Weber (Stanford: Stanford University Press, 2001), 3–42.

10. Hadot, "Forms of Life," 499.

11. Ibid., 505.

12. Andrey Tarkovsky, *Sculpting in Time: The Great Russian Filmmaker Discusses His Art*, trans. by Kitty Hunter-Blair (Austin: University of Texas Press, 2008), 39.

13. Sartre, "Letter," 42.

14. Hadot, *Spiritual Exercises*, 84.

15. John Gianvito (ed.), *Andrei Tarkovsky: Interviews* (Jackson: University Press of Mississippi, 2006), 12–15.

16. Hadot, *Spiritual Exercises*, 97.

17. Ibid., 258.

18. Ibid., 253. Italics in original.

19. Robert Bird's interpretation of the end of *Solaris* resonates with Hadot here: "between our intuitions of a transcendent source (i.e., the Ocean) and the insecurity of corporeal life we erect systems of representation—threads of understanding—which never form themselves into a clear design, yet comprise the very fabric that weds consciousness to corporeality." *Andrei Tarkovsky: Elements of Cinema* (London: Reaktion Books, 2008), 162.

20. Cited in Hadot, "Forms of Life," 505. The same quotation also begins his book *Exercices Spirituels et Philosophie Antique*, 3rd edn (Paris: Institut d'Études Augustiniennes, 1993), 13.

21. See Natasha Synessios, *Mirror*, KINOfiles Film Companion 6 (London: I. B.Tauris, 2001), 10–40.

22. Tarkovsky, *Sculpting in Time*, 43.

23. Synessios, *Mirror*, 38.

24. Ibid., 27.

25. Synessios, *Mirror*, 44.

26. Hadot, *Spiritual Exercises*, 83.

27. Jameson cited in Bird, *Andrei Tarkovsky*, 12.

28. Bird, *Andrei Tarkovsky*, 145.

29. Gilles Deleuze, *Cinema 2: The Time-Image*, trans. by Hugh Tomlinson and Robert Galeta (Minneapolis: University of Minnesota Press, 2007). Nariman Skakov insightfully distinguishes between "Deleuze's theory and Tarkovsky's praxis," noting that while Deleuze "presents the image of time devoid of any moral or theological 'burden,' the latter's temporal 'sculptures' are overwhelmingly anthropocentric, and they strive towards a certain divine ideal." *The Cinema of Tarkovsky: Labyrinths of Space and Time* (London: I. B.Tauris, 2012), 5.

30. Timothy Corrigan, "Essayism and Contemporary Film Narrative," in Caroline Eades and Elizabeth Papazian (eds), *The Essay Film: Dialogue, Politics, Utopia* (New York: Wallflower, 2016), 15–27, 15.

31. Synessios, *Mirror*, 11.

32. Hadot, *Spiritual Exercises*, 256. Italics in original.

33. Nora Alter, "The Political Im/perceptible in the Essay Film: Farocki's *Images of the World and the Inscription of War*," *New German Critique* 68 (Spring/Summer 1996): 165–92, 171.

34. Hent de Vries, "Of Miracles and Special Effects," *International Journal for Philosophy of Religion* 50 (2001): 41–56, 48. De Vries' study of Hadot, *Spiritual Exercises: Concepts and Practices*, is under contract with Harvard University Press.

35. Tarkovsky, *Sculpting in Time*, 204; see also 30, 71–2, III. See also Naum Abramov, "Dialogue with Andrei Tarkovsky about Science-Fiction on the Screen," in Gianvito (ed.), *Andrei Tarkovsky: Interviews*, 32–7.

36. *Spiritual Exercises*, 100.

37. Cited in Bird, *Andrei Tarkovsky*, 197.

38. Hadot, *Spiritual Exercises*, 98.

39. Kaja Silverman, *The Subject of Semiotics* (New York: Oxford University Press, 1983), 203.

40. Hadot, *Spiritual Exercises*, 98.

41. On the way in which cinema atmospheres mediate between screen and viewer, see Antonio Somaini, "Walter Benjamin's Media Theory: The *Medium* and the *Apparat*," *Grey Room* 62 (Winter 2016): 6–41.

42. Robert Bird performs a careful reading of this shot in *Andrei Tarkovsky*, 194–8.

43. Hadot, *Spiritual Exercises*, 103.

44. de Vries, "Of Miracles and Special Effects," 51–2.

45. Bird, *Andrei Tarkovsky*, 205.

46. An earlier draft of this essay was originally presented at the workshop, "A 'Spiritual Exercise' Every Day," convened by Sabrina Bouarour and Sara ElAmin at The Humanities Center, Johns Hopkins University, 4 December 2014. I am grateful to the conveners and participants for their feedback and encouragement.

CHAPTER 13

Memory and Trace

Mikhail Iampolski

FROM SUBJECTIVE TO DE-SUBJECTIVIZED MEMORY

Soviet culture was oriented toward the future. It was teleological, unfolding time in anticipation of an imminent communism, even after communism no longer seemed achievable. Historical novels were written and historical-revolutionary films were made, of course, but the historical past in these works was usually a distortion of the present. They did not look to history in the interest of understanding and reconstructing the past. In this sense, a long period in Soviet culture all the way through the 1970s and 1980s was fundamentally ahistorical, or more precisely, represented a radical break from the historicism inherited from the nineteenth century.

One of Tarkovsky's unique qualities is that he was among the first in Russian culture to discover the forgotten theme of historicism and recognize that the future, even more so than the present, has deep roots in the past. The emergence of Tarkovsky, in my view, marks the end of historical teleology. Through his work he identified the boundary beyond which the future began to fade and disappear from public consciousness and the past once again came into its own. I would even go so far as to claim that Tarkovsky is responsible for the atrophy of the future and the viability of the past.

The challenge of reconstructing the past struck Tarkovsky with full force during the filming of *Andrei Rublev* (1966). Tarkovsky described the origin of his interest in history thusly: "The film is set in the fifteenth century, and it turned out to be excruciatingly difficult to picture 'how everything was.' We had to use any sources we could: architecture, the written word, iconography."[1] Tarkovsky ruled out the use of painting, as he considers painting the opposite of cinema in that it is based on direct observation of the world. Hence his conclusion:

> We cannot reconstruct the fifteenth century exactly, however thoroughly we study all the things that remain from it. Our awareness of that time is totally different from that of the people who lived then. But nor do we think of Rublev's 'Trinity' in the same way as his contemporaries, and yet the 'Trinity' has gone on living through the centuries: it was alive then, and is so now, and it is a link between the people of that century and this.[2]

Rublev's painting was to him entirely outside of history. Tarkovsky determined that a historical reconstruction must be based not on documentation of the era, but on materials that transcend time, that fall out of time. In this sense, he unquestionably continued the Soviet cultural tradition by associating *Rublev* with "the truth of direct observation" and "physiological truth." Yet neither of these truths is historical; both are explicitly anti-historical.

This changed as he worked on *Mirror* (1974). In *Mirror* the integration of the past into the present, which was explored in *Rublev*, remains absolutely paramount. It appears here even at the level of plot. By this time the conflation of present and past has even acquired a name: "memory." The film came together with difficulty, and Tarkovsky described it as a chaotic, disorganized aggregate of episodes that only found unity when all the pieces of the mosaic fell onto the unifying, subjective experience of time. Tarkovsky acknowledged that until the very last moment he did not see any way to bind this mixture together into a single temporal perspective.

Tarkovsky's decision to root the film in memory—his own and those of his family—encountered resistance from even his closest friends and associates. Cameraman Vadim Yusov refused to work on the film, as he found "the frankly autobiographical nature of the work distasteful from an ethical point of view; he was embarrassed and irritated by the unduly personal, lyrical tone of the whole narrative, and by the author's desire to talk exclusively about himself."[3] Two episodes were critical for conceptualizing *Mirror*. The first concerned the reconstruction of the house in which the director spent his childhood:

> *Mirror* is also the story of the old house where the narrator spent his childhood, the farmstead where he was born and where his father and mother lived. This building, which over the years had fallen into ruins, was reconstructed, "resurrected" from the photographs just as it had been, and on the foundations which had survived. And so it stood exactly as it had forty years earlier. When we subsequently took my mother there, whose youth had been spent in that place and that house,

her reaction to seeing it surpassed my boldest expectations. What she experienced was a return to her past; and then I knew we were moving in the right direction. The house awoke in her the feelings which the film was intended to express . . . [4]

The second episode involved a buckwheat field that was once in front of the house and that had been sown with clover and oats for many years. Tarkovsky rented this field:

[W]e rented the field and sowed it with buckwheat at our own risk. The people in the *kolkhoz* couldn't conceal their amazement when they saw it come up. And we took that success as a good omen. It seemed to tell us something about the special quality of our memory—about its capacity for penetrating beyond the veils drawn by time, and this was exactly what the film had to be about: it was its seminal idea. I do not know what would have happened to the picture if the buckwheat had not grown . . . I shall never forget the moment it started to flower.[5]

What is at stake here is memory's capacity to make contact with reality. That which I remember is rooted in reality to such a degree that it can sprout shoots in a real field. This rootedness, this materiality, the corporeality of memory, is vital for Tarkovsky, who strove to overcome a purely mental visualization of the past. Bergson wrote that memory and affect are always interwoven with our perceptions. Perception, accordingly, is rooted in corporeality, which is essential for the experience of time as duration. Tarkovsky was convinced that a similar affective experience allows the viewer and the artist to literally penetrate into another's memory and relive the time of others. As he recalled,

When the set had been built up on the foundations of the ruined house, we all, as members of the team, used to go there in the early morning, to wait for the dawn, to experience for ourselves what was special about the place, to study it in different weather conditions, to see it at different times of the day; we wanted to immerse ourselves in the sensations of the people who had once lived in that house, and had watched the same sunrises and sunsets, the same rains and mists, some forty years previously. We all infected each other with our mood of recollection, and our feeling that the communion between us was sacred. And the completion of work came as a painful wrench, as if that was the moment at which we should have been starting on it: by that time we had almost become part of one another.[6]

In this case, immersion in the memory of another, the ability to "permeate each other," is connected with place, but the director attached much more importance to living the time of another. For this reason the significance of the long takes, the documentation of time, and his critical attitude toward montage is continually emphasized. For *Mirror*, a key revelation was the discovery of footage of the Soviet Army crossing Lake Sivash that "stunned" Tarkovsky. By his own admission, "I had never come across anything like it. As a rule one was faced with poor quality films, or short snippets recording day to day life in the army."[7] Here a scene extended in time stretched before him. "I could hardly believe that such an enormous footage of film should have been spent on recording one single event continuously observed. It had clearly been filmed by an outstandingly gifted camera-man."[8] The duration of the episode had a power that was nothing short of magical, and facilitated the viewer's entry into the visual and emotional experience of the cameraman who, as Tarkovsky learned, died on the day of this extraordinary shoot: "There came onto the screen an image of overwhelming dramatic force—and it was mine, specifically my own, as if the burden and the pain had been borne by me."[9]

An experience of the bygone past that has been prolonged in time renders what is observed as simultaneously "mine" and "not mine." It is like a memory that has lost its connection to the experiencing subject and become transformed into the viewer's pseudo-memory. Yet such a transformation can only take place if what has been captured has been seemingly removed from consciousness and become almost objective. Of course, this de-subjectification of experience is nothing new. Modern science entirely proceeds from the objectification of experience, in which knowledge gained through empirical observations and controlled experiments is of equal value to any researcher or observer. But with Tarkovsky we are dealing with a strange objectification that maintains a direct link with the subjective consciousness. It is the intimate lived experience of an individual permeating me that we have become accustomed to associating with memory. It is precisely here that the inconsistency in Tarkovsky's efforts to "sculpt time" manifests itself.

FILM AS DURATION AND MEMORY

Since Kant, time has been considered a form of consciousness. But this form of experience is not to be understood as phenomenological. We feel and think in time, but time in and of itself is not an external reality, or as philosophers would say, "a phenomenon." This critical stance, however, is continually subject to question within the framework of artistic production, where the ancient metaphor of time as a stream or a river plays a fundamental role in attributing phenomenological qualities to time. This metaphor is used to great effect by Tarkovsky, who loved to "synchronize" the movement of the camera and water, and align his vision with the world. In these shots the subjectivity of experiencing time as a stream merges with the flow of the stream outside of consciousness. This duality was well expressed by Borges in his classic essay "A New Refutation of Time": "Time is the substance of which I am made. Time is a river that sweeps me along, but I am the river."[10]

The French phenomenologist Claude Romano, who was critical of the analogy between time and consciousness and streams, rightly remarked that the consciousness responsible for constituting time as a flow must itself be placed in the flow of time in order to carry out this operation:

> So that one may ask where time originates (and answer: in the soul, the ego, the mind, the conscience), we must have from the beginning implicitly conceived of time as a kind of process—an *arche*-movement, a stream, a flow, an elongation, a distension—and, consequently, understood it from the beginning according to the specifications which in principle are valid only for those changes or objects that are found *in* time. In short, to conceive of time as originally subjective, it is necessary to conceive of time as a temporal, or better, intra-temporal phenomenon, which is obviously a contradiction in terms.[11]

This contradiction is only strengthened by the fact that time is not, in the strict sense of the word, a phenomenon that can be described. It is precisely in this distinction between the time of consciousness and the time of the world that Tarkovsky encountered many difficulties. According to his understanding of the era of *Mirror*, time that flows outside of us seems to flow into the diegetic time of the film, which is experienced subjectively.

Maurice Merleau-Ponty, who discussed the metaphor of time as a stream in *The Phenomenology of Perception*, unequivocally came to the conclusion that this metaphor does not have any heuristic meaning:

> We say that time passes or flows by. We speak of the course of time. The water that I see rolling by was made ready a few days ago in the mountains, with the melting of the glacier; it is now in front of me and makes its way toward the sea into which it will finally discharge itself. If time is similar to a river, it flows from the past towards the present and the future. The present is the consequence of the past, and the future of the present. But this often repeated metaphor is in reality extremely confused. For, *looking at the things themselves*, the melting of the snows and what results from this are not successive events, or rather the very notion of event has no place in the objective world. When I say that the day before yesterday the glacier produced the water which is passing at this moment, I am tacitly assuming the existence of a witness tied to a certain spot in the world, and I am comparing his successive views: he

was there when the snow melted and followed the water down, or else, from the edge of the river and having waited two days, he sees the pieces of wood that he threw into the water at its source. [. . .] Change presupposes a certain position which I take up and from which I see things in process before me: there are no events without someone to whim they happen and whose finite perspective is the basis of their individuality. Time presupposes a view of time. It is, therefore, not like a river, not a flowing substance. The fact that the metaphor based on this comparison has persisted from the time of Heraclitus to our own day is explained by our surreptitiously putting into the river a witness of its course. [. . .] If the observer sits in a boat and is carried by the current, we may say that he is moving downstream toward his future, but the future lies in the new landscapes which await him at the estuary, and the course of time is no longer the stream itself: it is the landscape as it rolls by for the moving observer. Time is, therefore, not a real process, not an actual succession that I am content to record. It arises from *my* relation to things.[12]

At some point Tarkovsky begins to understand that the flow of time in the world is a construct of the observer. He also realizes that in cinema we are dealing with the director's construct, which ultimately and inevitably begins to look like a violent imposition on the viewer:

Let us say that I want to have time flowing through the frame with dignity, independently, so that no-one in the audience will feel that his perception is being coerced, so that he may, as it were, allow himself to be taken prisoner voluntarily by the artist, as he starts to recognize the material of the film as his own, assimilating it, drawing it in to himself as new, intimate experience. But there is still an apparent dichotomy: for the director's sense of time always amounts to a kind of coercion of the audience, as does his imposition of his inner world. The person watching either falls into your rhythm (your world), and becomes your ally, or else he does not, in which case no contact is made. And so some people become your "own," and others remain strangers; and I think this is not only perfectly natural, but, alas, inevitable.

I see it as my professional task then, to create my own, distinctive flow of time, and convey in the shot a sense of its movement—from lazy and soporific to stormy and swift—and to one person it will seem one way, to another, another.[13]

It turns out that time is just a manifestation of the director's vision. And the film director resembles Merleau-Ponty's observer in a boat. And yet, there is something important to be gained from this observation. Tarkovsky likens the

experience of time to falling into a rhythm, with rhythm arising from the interaction of immutable elements. Merleau-Ponty identifies the motionless banks
that "float" past the observer as creating a rhythm that is differentiated from
the continuous flow of water that has no distinguishing characteristics. This
is important for understanding cinema, which creates the illusion of movement, flow, and action through montage—the assemblage of still images and
individual components. Tarkovsky is known for his aversion to montage, but
this antipathy clearly evinces his underestimation of the role of discrete parts
in creating rhythm. Deleuze insightfully acknowledged this contradiction in
Tarkovsky's aesthetics:

> . . . Tarkovsky says that what is essential is the way time flows in the
> shot, its tension or rarefaction, "the pressure of time in the shot." He
> appears to subscribe to the classical alternative, shot or montage, and
> to opt strongly for the shot ("the cinematographic figure only exists
> inside the shot"). But this is only a superficial appearance, because
> the force or pressure of time goes outside the limits of the shot and
> montage itself works and lives in time. What Tarkovsky denies is that
> cinema is like a language working with units, even if these are relative
> and of different orders: montage is not a unit of a higher order which
> exercises power over unit-shots and which would thereby endow
> movement-images with time as a new quality. The movement-image
> can be perfect, but it remains amorphous, indifferent and static if it is
> not already deeply affected by injections of time which put montage
> into it and alter movement.[14]

Only injections of minute particles of time can create rhythm, which, according to the director himself, is a vehicle for the viewer to enter the temporality
of a film.

Since, according to Tarkovsky, memory and observation are the central
components of film, cinema cannot be oriented toward the future and is rel-
egated to a purely nostalgic outlook. This idea is more complex than it seems.
Freud argued that perception and "becoming conscious and leaving behind
a memory-trace are processes incompatible with each other in the same system."[15] If traces of what has been perceived were to take hold in the system
of perception, that is, if they were to become firmly implanted within the
memory of this system, the potential to create new perceptions would soon be
obstructed by mnemonic traces. According to Tarkovsky, cinema resolves the
incompatibility between perception and memory. The viewer of a film assimi-
lates what is recorded in the memory of another. But this distribution of roles
(one recollects, the other sees) did not satisfy Tarkovsky, who idealized the
combination, the amalgamation, of two systems within a single experience—I

do not merely see, I am simultaneously immersed in the memory of another, who becomes me.

Fredric Jameson proposed that vehicles for the transmission of information are adaptive mechanisms that prevent the traumatic experiences registered in our memory from entering into our consciousness. Jameson writes: "a whole series of mechanical substitutes intervenes between consciousness and its objects, shielding us perhaps, yet at the same time depriving us of any way of assimilating what happens to us or of transforming our sensations into any genuinely personal experience."[16] Tarkovsky believed in the ability of film to facilitate this kind of assimilation. Jameson's position, however, seems to me to be well founded. Film is not a neutral, artificial, prosthetic memory, but carries out a role that Tarkovsky had not anticipated.

The fact is that film not only exhibits duration, which, according to Bergson or Deleuze, creates an external model of consciousness. It functions like memory, if we can hypothesize a type of memory that records only once. Film captures a trace of light that lands on celluloid and irreversibly passes from the faculty of perception to memory. The trace left on the film, consistent with Freud's reasoning, makes further perception impossible. Moreover, according to Deleuze, the image remains apart, distinct from the body; unlike perception and memory, it is not embodied. Despite the fact that the image was shot from a particular point of view, again according to Deleuze, it is not fixed enough to be subjective and relate to subjective experience. Deleuze speaks in this regard about the film image not as an analog of subjectivity, but as a thing that he, in the spirit of Whitehead, considers an image: "The thing is the image as it is in itself, as it is related to all the other images to whose action it completely submits and on which it reacts immediately. But the perception of the thing is the same image related to another special image which frames it, and which only retains a partial action from it, and only reacts to it mediately.[17] In perception thus defined, there is never anything else or anything more than there is in the thing: on the contrary, there is 'less.'"[18] Film, while not quite a thing, is closer to things than to perception, although the latter itself is merely a special variant of thing. Film can thus help to mitigate trauma, as trauma is transformed from subjective to objective experience. Per Whitehead and Bergson, Deleuze defines the thing: "The thing is an image and, in this respect, is perceived itself and perceives all the other things inasmuch as it is subject to their action and reacts to them on all its facets and in all its parts."[19] Film is also a thing that reacts to the world. Deleuze writes: "In short, things and perceptions of things are *prehensions*, but things are total objective prehensions, and perceptions of things are incomplete and prejudiced, partial, subjective prehensions."[20] Deleuze emphasizes that cinema does not at all focus on a subjective mode of perception, which for him is characteristic of "vast acentered and deframed zones" that separate it from subjectivity.[21] The memory of cinema, in this instance, is first of all not personal memory, but the memory of a thing that reacts to the world around it and retains traces of its impact.

THE SHIFT FROM MEMORY TO TRACE

In *Sculpting in Time*, which was written from 1977 to 1984, the period after the completion of *Mirror* and during much of the work on *Stalker* (1979), Tarkovsky mentions and systematically uses the Japanese term *sabi*, which was explicated by Vsevolod Ovchinnikov in *A Branch of Cherry Blossom*. Tarkovsky cites Ovchinnikov:

> It is considered that time, *per se*, helps to make known the essence of things. The Japanese therefore see a particular charm in the evidence of old age. They are attracted to the darkened tone of an old tree, the ruggedness of a stone, or even the scruffy look of a picture whose edges have been handled by a great many people. To all these signs of age they give the name, *sabi*, which literally means "rust." *Sabi*, then, is a natural rustiness, the charm of olden days, the stamp of time [—or patina—A.T.].
>
> *Sabi*, as an element of beauty, embodies the link between art and nature.[22]

Tarkovsky notes: "In all respects the Japanese ideal of *sabi* is the cinematographer."[23]

Traces of time are cinematographic in the sense that it is not only things, but film that imprints these traces of time on itself. These traces are often called deictic, and their imprinting relates precisely to what Deleuze called the "thing" as a type of image, that is, an "acentered" image without any subjectivity. Neither mossiness nor a lived-in quality has any relation to subjective memory. As Ovchinnikov points out, *sabi* realizes the link between art and nature. The mossiness of a stone transforms that stone, whatever its aesthetic appearance, into a natural phenomenon. A gradual decomposition of matter and immersion into nothingness takes place. Leonard Koren writes that when we speak about *sabi* (or *wabi-sabi*), we have in mind "these delicate traces, this faint evidence, at the borders of nothingness."[24]

These impersonal traces of time enchant Tarkovsky, who does not, however, completely abandon the hope of translating them into traces of subjective memory. If we ignore the activity of the subject, traces cease to exist. A subject is needed in order to turn the fragments of the world around us into a *trace*, that is, into a sign existing in the present that corresponds to a past action or an absent being. We need a Sherlock Holmes to turn a pile of ashes on the ground into the traces of a crime.[25] Traces become apparent only in the process of their interpretation through the consciousness of another. Andreas Buller defines the concept of trace this way: "Traces are 'immanent things.' And the immanent is born and constituted exclusively in the human mind. Discrete 'traces' exist in the minds of individuals."[26] Buller considers the trace to be a product of the imaginary alienation of the other. "The historical trace," he writes, "is in essence the 'alienation' or 'expression' of the OTHER. It must be noted that while it is the 'expression' or 'manifestation' of the OTHER, the trace emerges exclusively from the point of view of the one who perceives it. The 'alienated' takes on the character of the 'expressed' or 'manifested' in an act of human understanding."[27]

Traces conceal things and are imprinted on film in equal measure, without any intentionality or subjectivity, outside of the memory system. But for Tarkovsky they are initially still directly connected with consciousness, albeit a strange consciousness that is outside the subject. The shift from memory to the trace occurred with the transition from *Solaris* to *Stalker*. In *Solaris* the Ocean is able to recreate memories in three-dimensional simulations. Everything is still rooted in memory but is shifting toward a natural, objective indexicality, a trace alienated from memory. The trace here is unquestionably the "alienation of the OTHER." Tarkovsky himself said of the film: "As concerns a certain alienation [of perspective], it was in a way important for us to put a sort of transparent glass between the image and the viewer so that it kind of appeared as if one were seeing not with one's own eyes, as if one were trying to take an objective position, which tends to be somewhat colder. This isn't so much an effect of the cameraman's style as our desire to see not what is dear to me personally as the filmmaker, but what has become (or may become), a symbol of beauty for mankind, so to speak, from nature's perspective."[28] This alienation of perspective indicates a gradual departure from identification with memory, as was the case in *Mirror*. The director no longer seeks to immerse the viewer or the film crew in the place and time of his past and remove the distinction between his own experience and the experience of another. The orientation has shifted, and the need to see the world "not with one's own eyes, as if one were trying to take an objective position" has become foregrounded. Regarding the film's conflict, the director noted that Kelvin understands that the Hari revealed to him by the Ocean is a purely external object, yet he "cannot separate himself from it." The trace, while external, is still considered even by Tarkovsky himself to be internal and immanent. *Solaris* is entirely built upon this enmeshing of trace and memory.

In *Stalker*, however, the world of memory gradually recedes, and Japanese *sabi* comes into its own, almost without limit. During the filming of *Stalker*, Olga Surkova wrote: "I watched the rushes in black and white with Tarkovsky and Liusia Feiginova in the editing room. They were extremely interesting in texture and atmosphere. It was thoroughly worthwhile for Rashid[29] to spend all day yesterday stripped to the waist, in thigh-high rubber boots, building the columns. Even Tarkovsky was pleased (everything was produced according to his sketches) as he applied paint and affixed moss, creating a sense of dilapidation and abandonment. A dam, splash marks, slippery walkways, stagnant water, all in greyish-brown, green tones."[30] The Zone in *Stalker* appears to possess certain mysterious psychic powers, but these are no longer oriented toward memory, only toward alienated traces of time. Tarkovsky's focus now is to reproduce these traces of time. In her diary, Surkova wrote: "Today I was in a pavilion. Two pipes were elevated on a platform and a water tank was between them. The pipes were decrepit, covered with bitumen . . . Three weeks ago I was in two other pavilions that Andrei had designed. One with vessels, test tubes, and other odds and ends submerged in stagnant water. The other was a strange, desolate landscape . . . With dunes made of some kind of white substance . . . And everywhere there was ruin, erosion, decay, the state of disrepair after the death of civilization."[31]

In theory, the details that make up the temporary texture of things cannot be remembered. Memory is selective; it recalls gestalt that has names and forms, but it cannot record the vast quantity of textured traces that now occupied Tarkovsky's attention. Surkova transcribed the revealing conversation that the director had with his cameraman Vladimir Kniazhinskii on this subject:

> Tarkovsky: The texture in the pavilion should look like stone and stucco, and the stucco was once painted but now it's flaking . . . In short, I'm for having a lot of minute details in this room . . .
> Kniazhinskii: I'm against that, Andrei. To fill this set with "minutiae" we'd have to bring in ten elephants!
> Tarkovsky: But if there isn't any minutiae everything will look phony.

In *Nostalghia* (1983), as in *Stalker*, the theme of ruin acquires substantive meaning. In ruins, the artificial gradually grows into the organic, the natural state in which indexicality almost completely breaks with the themes of memory, duration, and corporeality. The famous final scene from *Nostalghia*—in which a home in the Russian countryside, drawn from the memories of the film's protagonist, is revealed within the ruins of a Gothic cathedral—fully attests to the trace's absorption of memory. *Nostalghia* is permeated with the contradiction between others' traces of time, history, and the waning influence of memory.

In 1927 Siegfried Kracauer published a remarkable essay on photography in which he compared photography with memory. According to Kracauer, memory retains only that which has meaning and personal significance and can be understood as a repository for truth. From the perspective of memory, "photography appears as a jumble that consists partly of garbage."[32] Memory, which bears within it the meaning of the world and its truth, is threatened by photography. Photography's chaos of preserved traces, its unlimited expansion of an archive of minutiae, leads to the disappearance of images associated with memory. In the end, as Kracauer writes, "all memory-images are bound to be reduced to this type of image [repositories for truth], which may rightly be called the last image . . ."[33] It is as if an infinite, chaotic accumulation of traces of truth led to a kind of apocalypse, the survival of the last image in which meaning and memory are retained. Kracauer believed that the accumulation of traces and the expansion of the photographic archive that led to a decline in memory were also an attempt to banish "the recollection of death, which is part and parcel of every memory-image."[34] Traces accumulate in the mode of the infinite present, which becomes an apocalyptic reality.

The world of traces from which subjectivity disappears is paradise, the only state of man that preceded the knowledge and universal symbolization of the world. But paradise is also a place without memory. Memory arises as a consequence of expulsion from paradise and the eternal nostalgia associated with this loss. In defending the right of reality to be imprinted on film without symbolic organization on the part of the subject, we are trying to preserve a world that is fated to disappear. This is why the world of traces is so closely related to the aesthetics of ruins. As Chantal de Gournay observed, "there is no art or creative work worthy of this designation that does not include within it the virtuality of death."[35]

It seems that Tarkovsky's later films are altogether consistent with Kracauer's description. In April 1981 Tarkovsky gave an interview in which he shared his ideas about the changing nature of time and his understanding of these changes. He spoke of the disappearance of temporal perspective and the collapse of the future into a present that is widely expanding beyond the given moment: "Before the past was somewhere far away, far beyond the horizon. Today it has merged with the present. Can we say that society is prepared for this? Our time differs from the past in that now the future is immediately in front of us. It is in our hands."[36] This suspension of the movement of time, its depletion, lends it an extra-historical, apocalyptic quality that becomes the central motif of *The Sacrifice* (1986). Furthermore, in Tarkovsky's view, the end of time is not at all associated with death: "Death does not preoccupy or interest me because I do not believe in death. Today the main concern is that man does not trust nature."[37] Nature is the symbol of the disappearance of the historical into the eternal, the non-historical, the infinite space of traces. *Sabi* conclusively destroys memory and creates a particular tension in Tarkovsky's outlook in the last years of his life. Memory ultimately is de-subjectivized, the subject disappears and undergoes a profound crisis, and the zone of acentric indexicality extends to the entire world into which the subject disappears and is replaced by a thing in the Deleuzian sense of the word.

Translated by Lisa Ryoko Wakamiya

NOTES

1. Andrei Tarkovsky, *Sculpting in Time*, trans. by Kitty Hunter-Blair (Austin: University of Texas Press, 1989), 78.
2. Ibid., 79.
3. Ibid., 135.
4. Ibid., 132.
5. Ibid., 132, 133.
6. Ibid., 136.
7. Ibid., 130.
8. Ibid., 130.
9. Ibid., 130.
10. Jorge Luis Borges, *Selected Non-fictions* (Harmondsworth: Viking Penguin, 1999), 332.
11. Claude Romano, *L'aventure temporelle* (Paris: Presses Universitaires de France, 2010), 60; Claude Romano, *Avantiura vremeni. Tri esse po fenomenologii sobytiia* (Moscow, 2017), 117.
12. Maurice Merleau-Ponty, *Phenomenology of Perception* (London: Routledge, 2013), 477–8.
13. Tarkovsky, *Sculpting in Time*, 120–1.
14. Gilles Deleuze, *The Time-Image (Cinema)* (Minneapolis: University of Minnesota Press, 1989), 42.
15. Sigmund Freud, *Beyond the Pleasure Principle* (Mineola, NY: 2015), 19.
16. Fredric Jameson, *Marxism and Form. Twentieth-Century Dialectical Theories of Literature* (Princeton: Princeton University Press, 1971), 63.
17. "La perception de la chose, c'est la même image rapportée à une autre image spéciale qui la cadre, et qui n'en retient qu'une action partielle et n'y réagit que médiatement." Gilles Deleuze, *Cinéma I. L'Image-mouvement* (Paris: Minuit, 1983), 93; Gilles Deleuze. *The Movement-Image* (Minneapolis: University of Minnesota Press, 1986), 63.
18. Deleuze, *The Movement-Image*, 63.
19. Ibid., 63.
20. Ibid., 64.
21. Ibid., 64. Mark Hansen criticized this idea of Deleuze's as well as the suggestion of cinema's "embodiment" as a system in Mark Hansen, *New Philosophy for New Media* (Cambridge, MA: The MIT Press, 2004).
22. Cf. Tarkovsky, *Sculpting in Time*, 59.
23. Andrei Tarkovsky, *Arkhivy. Dokumenty. Vospominaniia* (Moscow, 2002), 159. [This sentence from the Russian text is omitted from the English translation of *Sculpting in Time*.]
24. Leonard Koren, *Wabi-Sabi for Artists, Designers, Poets & Philosophers* (Berkeley: Stone Bridge Press, 1994), 42.
25. On the detective's responsibility to turn the world into a collection of traces, see Pierre Bayard, *L'affaire du chien des Baskerville* (Paris: Minuit, 2008).
26. Andreas Buller, *Tri lektsii o poniatii 'sled'* (St Petersburg: Aleteiia, 2016), 28.
27. Ibid., 33.
28. Andrei Tarkovsky, "Poiasneniia k fil'mu *Soliaris*," *Kinovedcheskie zapiski* 14 (1992): 50.
29. Surkova does not recall the last name of the artist named Rashid. In the credits the artist is identified as Tarkovsky himself.
30. Ol'ga Surkova, "Khroniki Tarkovskogo. *Stalker*," *Iskusstvo kino* 9 (2002). Reprinted at: http://www.tarkovsky.su/library/syrkova-stalker-journal-1/ (accessed 8 September 2019).
31. Ol'ga Surkova, "Khroniki Tarkovskogo. *Stalker*," *Iskusstvo kino* 10 (2002). Reprinted at: http://www.tarkovsky.su/library/syrkova-stalker-journal-2/ (accessed 8 September 2019).
32. Siegfried Kracauer, "Photography," *Critical Inquiry* 19.3 (Spring 1993): 426.

33. Ibid., 426.
34. Ibid., 433.
35. Chantal de Gournay, "Le deuil de l'image. De la photographie à l'image virtuelle," *Réseaux* 11.61 (1993): 130.
36. Andrei Tarkovsky, "Reshaiushchie vremena," *Iskusstvo kino* 12 (2012). Reprinted at: http://tarkovskiy.su/texty/Tarkovskiy/Sweden.html (accessed 8 September 2019).
37. Ibid.

Legacy

Introduction to Part IV

O ur volume logically concludes with the discussion of Tarkovsky's influence on both domestic and international cinema, exemplified by Andrei
Zvyagintsev and Lars von Trier respectively. Both are often hailed as the heirs
of the Russian master, yet they have not received sufficient critical attention in
this regard. The two chapters in this section aim to rectify this shortcoming.
Lisa Ryoko Wakamiya's chapter traces the presence of Tarkovskian thematic
and stylistic motifs in a series of Zvyagintsev's films, such as the father/son
relationship in *The Return* (2003), elegiac visual techniques in *The Banishment* (2007), and the Brueghelian landscape in *Loveless* (2017). The author also
discusses how it is important for Zvyagintsev to maintain his own authorial
autonomy from the depersonalizing influence of the inherited tradition.

In the concluding chapter, Sergey Toymentsev and Anton Dolin focus on
von Trier's lifelong engagement with the Russian master, which was openly
admitted in his 2009 *Antichrist*'s shocking dedication. To unravel the complex
relationship between the two directors, the authors place them in the context of
Harold Bloom's rhetorical matrix of revisionary ratios and trace several stages
of Tarkovsky's influence on the Danish director: the early stage of antithetical
completion, when the latter continuously attempted to push the former's messianic project to new limits, and that of counter-sublime, characterized by von
Trier's impossible yet compulsive desire to forget Tarkovsky. The chapter also
examines how von Trier simultaneously attacks and reinvents Tarkovsky's spiritualist ideology of redemption from the position of European cynicism most
vividly exemplified by Peter Sloterdijk's *Critique of Cynical Reason* (1983).

CHAPTER 14

Zvyagintsev and Tarkovsky: Influence, Depersonalization, and Autonomy

Lisa Ryoko Wakamiya

When confronted with the question of influence, the director Andrei Zvyagintsev most frequently invokes the films of Andrei Tarkovsky. "People often ask me if Tarkovsky was an influence on my filmmaking," he stated while promoting his second film, *The Banishment* (2007). "If his films did have any influence on me, it was not in a conscious way." He immediately, however, follows this disavowal with acquiescence. "I think it's impossible for any Russian filmmaker not to feel a certain influence coming from the work of Tarkovsky," he concedes. "The question is how the influence manifests itself; whether it's just pure repetition and imitation or something deeper."[1]

Influence has long been associated with the anxious acknowledgment of an existing canon, or alternatively, with a free-flowing process in which "a variety of writings, none of them original, blend and clash."[2] By denying the Bloomian anxiety of influence and its model of strong artists and the acolytes who overpower them, Zvyagintsev rejects the idea that the history of cinema consists of selected canonical texts and their imaginative echoes. At the same time, doing away with auteurs altogether and immersing himself in a "tissue of quotations" is a condition he cannot abide. Rather, viewing Zvyagintsev's films against Tarkovsky's reveals influence in the form of a cinematic pedagogy in which the subordination of the self makes it possible for a film to emerge and immediately to become embedded in a network of inherited discourses. In contrast to Tarkovsky, for whom the commitment to the creative act is foregrounded, Zvyagintsev's work thematizes and performs the loss of enjoyment by which the subject becomes inscribed into the symbolic. The question of how Tarkovsky's influence might manifest itself in ways that produce "something deeper," namely, whether such a model of influence can advance innovative claims about the relationship between cinematic representation and the world of human experience, is the subject of this essay.

INFLUENCE AND THE SYMBOLIC FATHER

When asked to explicate artistic truth, Zvyagintsev related the following anecdote: "Let's say two men, Petrov and Ivanov, are sitting and having a conversation. If we consider this in terms of artistic truth, on a vertical axis that extends deep down to the classical tradition or to antiquity, Petrov and Ivanov become different figures . . . one becomes a father and the other a son. They become situated within the entire corpus of world culture."[3] The story that Zvyagintsev relates here is simple on its surface, yet it illustrates the extent to which he sees the epistemological journeys toward self-knowledge in his films—and the films themselves—as embedded within deep structural relations. The father/son relationship, like the teacher/student binary, assumes the subordinate may yield to or challenge his mentor but will not challenge the broader regime that structures their relations. For Zvyagintsev, the individual is inevitably bound up in traditionally depicted intersubjective relations and their inherited discourses.

Zvyagintsev describes watching Tarkovsky's films as a formative pedagogical experience. He was an eighteen-year-old student of theater in Novosibirsk when he first encountered them during a retrospective screening. "I didn't understand anything then, I knew nothing, heard nothing, about who Tarkovsky was. I only knew that I had to go, because at the Pedagogical Theater School they told the students to go and watch. Of course there were things I didn't understand, but it made a strong impression on me." In the same conversation, he describes later watching Michelangelo Antonioni's *The Adventure/L'avventura* (1960), which "revolutionized my conception of cinema." Ingmar Bergman's *Autumn Sonata/Höstsonaten* (1978) moved him to the point of tears. He then saw the films of Robert Bresson. "All of this," he says, "enters into you, and if I may say so, becomes yours—something kindred in which you discover yourself."[4] It was Tarkovsky's films that inspired Zvyagintsev to become a filmmaker.[5]

For Zvyagintsev, watching films, filmmaking, and commenting on his own and others' films are processes of learning and acquiring knowledge. Even telling someone to do something, as when Zvyagintsev was told to watch Tarkovsky's films, is a kind of pedagogy. As a method of instruction it rests on the presumption that the pedagogue knows what is best for the learner; learning cannot be left to chance or undirected experience. This is the model of instruction and learning at the heart of Zvyagintsev's debut film *The Return/Vozvrashchenie* (2003). An unnamed Father returns to his wife and sons after a twelve-year absence. His interactions with his two sons during a week-long road trip consist primarily in lessons that take the form of injunctions:

—Call me Dad, like a son should! Got it?
—Yes, Dad!
—Well done, son.

The trip is a "week-long 'crash course' in the crafts of manhood," during which the boys are taught how to drink, objectify women, create traction to extract the tires of a car stuck in mud, repair the hull of a boat, and more generally, apply their newly acquired skills when confronted with unexpected difficulties.[6] The question "Who is he?" which dominates the early part of the film following the Father's arrival, is soon replaced by the questions "Why did he come back?" and "What does he want?" as the boys struggle to fulfill the Father's constant, often cruel, demands. While the older son readily accepts the Father's stated identity and seeks his approval, the younger son questions his identity and avows, "if he touches me again, I'll kill him." The Father's inscrutable aims become a screen against which the sons project their respective wish-fulfillment fantasies. Both sons see their wishes fulfilled, and at the same time develop a relationship to the symbolic paternal function. In his analysis of *The Return*, Barnaby B. Barratt notes, "the experiential odyssey undertaken by every father-son pairing concerns how we can love (or at least direct and contain our brutality) not only in a world steeped in violence, but also in context of aggressive, rageful and hateful feelings that are an ingredient of every relationship." The film depicts the formation of masculinity and what it means to become the symbolic father, while illustrating the grief concerning "our pseudo-omnipotent, narcissistic and thoroughly delusional notion that we could ever speak from the location of the phallus, mean exactly what we say, be master of our psychic life and own our 'own' desires."[7]

In an uncharacteristically candid description of the film, Zvyagintsev stated that it is "about the metaphysical incarnation of the soul's movement from the Mother to the Father," foregrounding the boys' movement from the maternal home and the formative, if brief, period of pedagogical experience with their father that integrates them into a preconstituted symbolic order.[8] The process of learning depicted here is not so much one of self-discovery as of integrating the self in relation to others, language, and the law. This trajectory may be productively contrasted with the father-son relations Tarkovsky presents in *Mirror* (1974), arguably his most autobiographical film. In a 1975 public appearance, Tarkovsky stated that "the purpose of *Mirror*, its inspiration, is that of a homily: look, learn, use the life shown here as an example." How striking, then, that the example presented in *Mirror* concerns the attenuated presence of the father and the son's struggle with the Law of the Father. But in place of rivalry with the father over the mother and the coming-into-being of the symbolic father following the Father's death, Tarkovsky's film focuses on the son's desire to unite with his father in their sameness.[9]

Helena Goscilo argues that Tarkovsky's decision to cast the same actress to play both the autobiographical protagonist's mother and wife, the same actor to play Tarkovsky in the 1940s and Tarkovsky's son in the 1960s, and his real-life father—the poet Arseny Tarkovsky, who abandoned his family when Tarkovsky was four years old—to read his poetry in voice-over, renders "analysis of [*Mirror*'s] father-son relations virtually superfluous," in that the film "confirms, yet again, Tarkovsky's unresolved psychological problems with this father, his Oedipal 'confusion' of mother and wife [. . .] and his wishful identification with his father [. . .] the adolescent transfer of cathexis to the father as the norm of male identity formation."[10] To the degree that a pedagogical example is presented in *Mirror*, it acknowledges preexisting order—such as the move from the realm of the imaginary to the symbolic—in conflict with individual autonomy. Goscilo describes Tarkovsky's struggle as an attempt to "reconcile his psychological trauma with his philosophical convictions," resulting in films "that creatively revised not history, but his story."[11]

Mirror unveils an individual and idealized drama that unites the once-distant father and desiring son in the creative realm, and Tarkovsky's insistence upon the artist's autonomy aligns with his willingness to explore and rewrite profoundly personal traumas in his films. In contrast, Zvyagintsev's *The Return* yields to preexisting order. With Father dead and the sons' wish fulfillment actualized, the Oedipal drama unfolds to suggest that the paternal function is bound to somehow influence the future development of the adolescent boys. *The Return* mourns the inevitable loss of the imaginary and reconciliation of the self to the symbolic, a structure that is likewise evident in Zvyagintsev's account of his own education. He identifies his canon—Tarkovsky, Antonioni, Bergman, Bresson—then situates himself in relation to it, experiencing self-loss in the process of becoming a filmmaker himself. In his films there is no subversion of canonical discourses or practices, but adaptation to them and attribution of authorship in the form of thematic and visual citation.

INFLUENCE AND DEPERSONALIZATION

If *The Return* established Zvyagintsev among critics as Tarkovsky's foremost heir, his second film, *The Banishment/Izgnanie* (2007), with its long takes of the Russian countryside and tracking shots over debris-laden pools of water, can be read as a visual panegyric. Tarkovsky's influence is typically identified with a set of visual and thematic trademarks. As Nick James notes, "Whenever an elegiac film incorporates long single-camera takes, is happy not to distinguish between real time, action, dream and memory, and wants to drink in the landscape, that word ['Tarkovskian'] is in the wind [. . .] If there are grasslands swirling, white mist veiling a house in a dark green valley, cleansing torrential rains, a burning barn or house, or tracking shots across objects submerged in water, a Tarkovsky name-drop is never far away." According to James, *The Banishment* is "the most straightforward, even blatant, case of Tarkovsky's influence in action. Many of [Zvyagintsev's] shots of lustrous or weather-obscured landscapes are so redolent of the master as to approach parody."[12] Birgit Beumers likewise observes that the "frequent shots of the wind ruffling the fields and the swaying rye [. . .], the use of mirrors [. . .], the reference to water, both as a purifying source and as a surface for reflection," reveal a "reliance on citation." The allusions to Tarkovsky, Bergman, Bresson, and Antonioni in *The Banishment*, in her view, "are obtrusive and too obvious."[13]

In interviews surrounding the release of *The Banishment*, Zvyagintsev aligned the phenomenon of influence—his juxtaposition of pure repetition and something deeper—with the process of depersonalization. It may be argued that the film's overriding concern, as in *The Return*, is the self's relation to others. More specifically, as the reviews that saw undisguised imitation rather than influence in the film attest, the film's visual citations of canonical directors and adaptation of William Saroyan's novel *The Laughing Matter* (1953) enact the struggle to constitute the self within inherited discourse. Diegetically this is most apparent in a bedtime scene in which a neighbor's daughter reads St Paul's First Letter to the Corinthians aloud and the viewer must consider how the characters situate themselves in relation to the words of Scripture. The child's reading of I Corinthians and its "Hymn to Love," undertaken at the request of a pregnant wife trapped in a loveless marriage, is intended as an edificatory experience for the gathered children and explicative of the mother's condition ("If I . . . do not have love, I am nothing"). The mother has already once attempted suicide, and is deeply alienated from her husband, who is convinced that the unborn child is not his and has arranged for an abortion against her will. The distant and non-communicative father of the child, who more than anyone would be enlightened through the reading, whether for edification or explication, is absent from the scene.

Zvyagintsev's incorporation of I Corinthians in *The Banishment* is constructed as a series of citations. He immediately prefaces the scene with a visual reference to Leonardo da Vinci's *The Annunciation* (1472), signaling both the mother's pregnancy and alluding to Tarkovsky's own visual citations of Leonardo in *Mirror* and *The Sacrifice* (1986). The same verse from I Corinthians, including the "Hymn to Love," is quoted in full by Tarkovsky in his book, *Sculpting in Time* (1986), and is read by the protagonist of Tarkovsky's *Andrei Rublev* (1966). In *Rublev* the recitation of I Corinthians urges uniformity of belief and strict patterns of behavior in response to dissension in the community of believers. Yet it is the "Hymn to Love" within it that allows Rublev to overcome the literalism of the doctrine and accept others.[14] The exhortation to love allows Rublev to accept with compassion a holy fool who has desecrated the sacred space of a cathedral, thus challenging her marginalization on the part of the community's believers. The "Hymn to Love" empowers Rublev to overcome the contradiction between judgment and acceptance. In contrast with the epiphanic moment of interpretation and revelation in Tarkovsky, the absence of any such revelation or insight in Zvyagintsev's film expresses the prohibition of interpretive freedom on his protagonists. They are bound to accepting doctrine and constituting themselves in relation to it, or are otherwise distanced from any potential for interpretive engagement.

At the time he was filming *The Banishment*, Zvyagintsev described filmmaking as a process of depersonalization. "When you make a film, you acquire the ability to see yourself from outside. You see yourself as in a mirror [. . .] In the mirror you see not only yourself, but yourself among other things."[15] "Yourself among other things," or "things including yourself," is a curious locution here. It acknowledges a multiplicity of other things that one sees and does not enumerate, things that may be like or similar to the self and might have been mentioned in its place. The absence of individual autonomy implied in this statement is consistent with the film's thematization of the struggle to constitute the self amid prevailing discourses. Unsurprisingly then, Zvyagintsev extended processes of depersonalization in *The Banishment* to other potential sources of authorial or interpretive autonomy. The language of Saroyan's novel *The Laughing Matter*, on which *The Banishment* is based, became subordinated to other, more culturally embedded texts, such as 1 Corinthians (and by extension, Tarkovsky's *Rublev*), Leonardo's *The Annunciation*, and Masaccio's *Expulsion of Adam and Eve from Paradise* (1425). "Eve is the only name from Saroyan's story that remains in the film," Zvyagintsev admits.

Similarly, Zvyagintsev was initially drawn to Artem Melkumian's "literary screenplay" for *The Banishment* based on Saroyan's novel, but a few months later he and his co-author Oleg Negin radically rewrote it, removing much of the dialogue altogether. Melkumian's screenplay, according to Zvyagintsev, "was very heavyweight and beautiful, full of long monologues and repetitions" but "impossible to film in a satisfying way [. . .] I had to cut it remorselessly."[16] Zvyagintsev noted that Melkumian had a deeply personal relationship to Saroyan's novel, which Melkumian credited with changing his life during a period of deep depression.[17] This personal connection, which likely extended into the screenplay, was removed to underscore the film's archetypal narratives and emphasize essential likenesses within human experience. Of actors, Zvyagintsev has claimed that they often "like to steal the show and overestimate the value of their ideas,"[18] and *The Banishment* offers its actors little, if any, opportunity for individual expression or creative interpretation. Explaining his method for directing the actors in this film, he observed that, "If you have a tree trunk and you need it to be smooth and you see, 'oh there is a twig or a branch,' you come and cut it. Similarly, if something is not necessary in the actor's personality for a particular part, you just remove it."[19]

For Zvyagintsev the inherited tradition is part of an order that plays a restrictive role in the constitution of the creative self. Unable to challenge the regime into which his films come into being, Zvyagintsev cannot reenact the

Tarkovskian epiphany that liberates the interpreter from authoritative readings. He instead cites canonical narratives while removing the potential for interpretive autonomy. Ironically, this process may in itself be an act of depersonalization and citation. Zvyagintsev has identified Robert Bresson's *L'argent* as one of his ideals, in part because "in this film [. . .] he brought his method to perfection. There's nothing there at all! Absolutely nothing!"[20] By communicating through discourse inherited from others and negating the autonomy of the self, *The Banishment* alternates between citation and refusing sovereignty to the self who cites. As such, the film itself remains open to interpretive contestation. Zvyagintsev's acts of citation and depersonalization point to one way to articulate one's relationship to inherited discourse, although it leaves the film open to the question of what happens when depersonalization is not recognized as such by viewers, but as imitation.

INFLUENCE AND AUTONOMY

Tarkovsky's visual citations of works of art, according to Vida Johnson and Graham Petrie, function on multiple levels, with the works of Leonardo and Pieter Brueghel the Elder shaping "the very foundations of his aesthetic thinking."[21] Brueghel's *Hunters in the Snow* (1565) figures prominently in *Solaris* (1972) and *Mirror*, and in both films accompanies episodes that explore the workings of memory. Zvyagintsev's *Loveless/Nelyubov* (2017), not coincidentally, visually reconstructs *Hunters in the Snow* at its conclusion, and a comparison of how Brueghel's painting figures in Tarkovsky's and Zvyagintsev's films throws into sharp relief how Zvyagintsev's more recent films have explicitly articulated an approach to visual citation that highlights the differences between how the two directors conceptualize the relationship between individual creativity, interpretation, and the world of human experience.

The first encounter with *Hunters in the Snow* in *Solaris* takes place in the space station's library, where Kris Kelvin observes the replica of his dead wife Hari studying a reproduction of the painting. The camera's gaze merges with Hari's; tracking shots focus on details from the painting, and these meditations on sections of the canvas are interspersed with brief fragments from a home video made by Kelvin's father that captures scenes from Kelvin's childhood. It is as if we are witnessing the process by which the replicated Hari builds an inventory of memories and an understanding of human experience. The space station then enters a thirty-second interval of zero gravity, and as the objects in the library begin to float, so do Hari and Kelvin. He reaches for her, and as the two hold each other, rotating gracefully in the air, the camera returns twice to *Hunters in the Snow*. Events in quick succession—recalling memories, understanding another's past, and sharing experiences—all take place against the measured contemplation of Brueghel's canvas. It appears that Hari has understood what it means to be human.

And yet, immediately following this experience, Hari kills herself. Why? Earlier in the film, when Kelvin first shows her the home movie shot by his father, the sequence of images distresses her. When Father looks up with an expectant smile to return his wife's gaze, a young Kelvin interrupts their interaction and chases his father through the snow. When Mother anxiously looks around a corner, it is to observe the young Kelvin returning from collecting firewood. When Mother, resplendent in a white fur coat, moves to get a better view of something, it is to observe the small fire that Kelvin has made. A shot of the adolescent Kelvin turning to face the camera and smile is immediately followed by an image of his mother looking back at him. These interactions between mother and son contrast with the final shots of the home movie, in which Hari is standing in front of Kelvin's mother's house. In the first shot, presumably taken before she enters the house, she waves happily. In the second, she gazes at the viewer solemnly. "That woman in the white coat hated me," Hari says after watching the film and recalling the original Hari's memories. "We drank tea and she kicked me out." Kelvin tries to change the details, claiming that his mother had died before he and Hari met, but he eventually admits that following the meeting between her and his mother, he and Hari parted and never saw each other again. She soon learns that the original Hari, unable to navigate the overbearing relationship between Kelvin and his mother, killed herself.

Given the structure of the home movie Kelvin shows to the replicated Hari, her knowledge of human experience is necessarily limited. She does not know a husband extricated from maternal desire. When we next see *Hunters in the Snow* in *Solaris*, Kelvin is dreaming of his mother's home on Earth, where a reproduction of it hangs on the wall. A disoriented Kelvin and his mother briefly face the image, when Kelvin suddenly admits that he had forgotten his mother's face. She expresses regret that he is unhappy and berates him for not calling, then observes that his arm is dirty and brings a basin with water to wash it. Here, the apparition of the anxious, overbearing mother returns, and when Kelvin wakes from a fevered dream, he learns that the resurrected Hari has killed herself again. The original Hari kills herself after the encounter with his mother; the replicated Hari kills herself twice, both times immediately after we see *Hunters in the Snow*. Hari is entirely a product of Kelvin's memories, in which *Hunters in the Snow* is linked with the maternal home. Hari's fragmented examination of the painting in the library may give her insight into human experience, but this insight is broken up by her recollections of the home movie, and possibly her memory of seeing the painting in Kelvin's mother's home. These memories render impossible any relationship with Kelvin. It can be argued that the film within the film is a *mise-en-abyme*, a synchronic treatment of the diachronic process of the entire film, in which Brueghel's painting and its attendant associations with Kelvin's past and Hari's inability to acquire her own subjectivity remain unresolved until the very last moments of the film, when Kelvin reconciles with his father and Hari is indisputably dead.

In his analysis of *Solaris*, Nariman Skakov cites from Tarkovsky's diary entry for 12 March 1971, made during the film's shooting: "It occurred to me that the film made by Kelvin the elder, which Chris takes with him, should be made like a poem. (Base it on one of father's poems)."[22] The poems of Tarkovsky's father, Arseny Tarkovsky, figure prominently in *Mirror*, where the voice of the elder Tarkovsky can be heard reciting them, but in *Solaris* the selected poem appears in visual, rather than textual, form. Skakov notes that poem, "supposedly 'As a child I once fell ill . . . ' which later appears in *Nostalghia*," is rendered as "a spectral sequence of several images in the home video." These images, which were originally conceived as a separate short film based on the poem, are briefly described by Tarkovsky in *Sculpting in Time*.[23] Skakov's revelation helps to demonstrate that the father's gaze is both diegetic (Kelvin says his father shot the home video, although he added a little) and extra-diegetic, in that the elder Tarkovsky's verse structures the images in the home video. Tarkovsky argued that "in cinema [. . .] you have to impart your own experience with the greatest possible sincerity," so that the viewer has "the opportunity to live through what is happening on the screen as if it were his own life, to take over, as deeply personal and his own, the experience imprinted in time upon the screen."[24] In *Solaris*, Brueghel's canvas and Kelvin's father's visual poem communicate Kelvin's profound connection with his family, nature, and human experience, and simultaneously Hari's inability to assimilate herself into these narratives to acquire a subjectivity of her own.

In Zvyagintsev's *Loveless*, *Hunters in the Snow* is reproduced toward the end of the film. By this point in the narrative, it is evident that the parents whose son has gone missing have given up hope of ever seeing him again. They have sold the apartment they shared with their son, and given his long absence, their impending divorce, and respective relationships with other people, they have no intention of keeping the apartment in the hope that their son might return. As the apartment is being dismantled in preparation for new tenants, the camera slowly pans past the workmen and frames the action taking place outside the window. The ambient sound of the workmen's labor accompanies a stationary shot of trees on a snowy hill in the foreground, people engaged in activities that draw the viewer's eye toward the center of the composition, and a landscape receding beyond the hill. This view, a reconstruction of *Hunters in the Snow*, is one that the missing boy would have seen from his desk in his bedroom.

Figure 14.1 Brueghelian landscape in *Mirror*.

Figure 14.2 Brueghelian landscape in *Loveless*.

The next shot is at ground level, and the engaging sounds of children at play as they sled across the snowy landscape remind the viewer again of the boy's absence and his inability to perceive or partake of the action. This shot visually echoes a sequence from Tarkovsky's *Mirror*, itself a visual paraphrase of *Hunters in the Snow*. In Tarkovsky's film, a young boy resolutely walks uphill toward the camera with a small briefcase in his left hand, as children are sledding in the background. As he approaches, documentary footage of the fall of Berlin is interspersed with close-up shots of the boy's face and the Brueghelian scene behind him. The function of the scene is to question whether it is an accurate reenactment of the narrator's wartime childhood experience or his son's imagined version of the narrator's story. The blurred lines between memory, fiction, and history illustrate the film's autobiographical premise. In *Loveless* we see, as in *Mirror*, a boy walking uphill toward the camera, only he is carrying a snowboard in his left hand. Less determined than Tarkovsky's young protagonist, the boy turns around to make sure that a younger boy is following him. The stationary shot ends before the boy gets any closer, ending any possibility for further signification. Zvyagintsev's paraphrases of Brueghel and Tarkovsky reveal that both visual sources represent fields of human experience—shared activity, family, memory, history—from which the missing boy is absent. The viewer, like the missing child, is removed from any possibility for further interpretive engagement with Zvyagintsev's visual sources. If Brueghel's painting stands for the potentially structured social field for both Tarkovsky and Zvyagintsev, its radical inaccessibility in the latter's film may be coordinated with the contemporary "death of the Master" and the concomitant decline of meaningful symbolic action on the part of the subject.

Zvyagintsev's acts of depersonalization in response to influence may be described as visual continuity accompanied by interpretive obstruction. This method of integrating past tradition into the present is consistent with Zvyagintsev's claim that following *The Banishment* and with the subsequent release of *Elena* (2011), *Leviathan* (2014), and *Loveless*, he has turned from drama to tragedy. A drama is "showing us all the time the *reasons* why something is taking place," according to Zvyagintsev, but tragedy keeps us "torturing ourselves by trying to crack the riddle: *why* did what happened happen? We are not given *reasons*."[25] Zvyagintsev's acts of depersonalization, his turn to tragedy, and withdrawal of interpretive possibility should be contrasted with Tarkovsky's own attitudes toward influence, in which the individual is of paramount importance.

During a public address in Rome, Tarkovsky openly discussed the question of influence:

> What is influence? It is, for example, the artist's selection of the environment in which he wants to work. The people, the collaborators, with whom he wants to work and with whom he will feel comfortable. It is only this. And then if you ask me what influence I have received from names like, for example, Bresson, Antonioni, Bergman, Kurosawa, Mizoguchi, I must say none. I have no desire to imitate them. Because it would be impossible to do so, to begin with. And moreover, if my goal was the imitation of great directors, I would be distancing myself from the true goal of cinema, since the main goal of any kind of art is to find a personal means of expression, a language with which to express what is inside of you. Therefore, the influence that these directors, whom I adore, have on me lies in the fact that I find myself in the pleasant company of filmmakers.[26]

Both imitation and influence situate the filmmaker in relation to the work of others. For Tarkovsky, imitation, like "attempts to construct *mise en scène* from a painting," is tantamount to "killing cinema." "No *mise en scène* has the right to be repeated, just as no two personalities are ever the same."[27] Because filmmakers do not "work in a vacuum," the matter of influence is more complex. Influence includes the "fatal influence of other people," as Tarkovsky writes in *Sculpting in Time*, but more frequently, as here, he describes a sphere of influence that aligns the artist's subjectivity with his collaborators, authentic expression ("the true goal of cinema"), and filmmakers whom he holds in particular esteem.[28]

In April 1972 Tarkovsky composed a list of his "top ten" favorite films at the request of his friend Leonid Kozlov. Tarkovsky "took [Kozlov's] proposition very seriously," and after writing a list of directors' names, then a list of films, he carefully numbered the films and typed and signed the document:

1. *Le Journal d'un curé de campagne*
2. *Winter Light*
3. *Nazarin*
4. *Wild Strawberries*
5. *City Lights*
6. *Ugetsu Monogatari*
7. *Seven Samurai*
8. *Persona*
9. *Mouchette*
10. *Woman of the Dunes* (Teshigahara)

The earlier written draft that listed directors' names included Dreyer, and Antonioni and Vigo (whose names are crossed out), in addition to those whose films are included on the typed final draft: Bergman, Bresson, Buñuel, Chaplin, Kurosawa, Mizoguchi, and Teshigahara. The list constitutes his canon, and as such, names directors *of* influence. They destroy genre: "What is Bresson's genre? He doesn't have one. Bresson is Bresson. He is a genre in himself." Likewise, Antonioni, Fellini, Bergman, Kurosawa, Dovzhenko, Vigo, Mizoguchi, Buñuel, "each is identified with himself." Chaplin "is Chaplin." Each has an individual approach to editing: "You will always recognize the editing of Bergman, Bresson, Kurosawa or Antonioni [. . .] because each one's perception of time, as expressed in the rhythm of his films, is always the same."[29] Tarkovsky's list of directors of influence formalizes his view that the artist must be responsible only for himself.[30] He cannot allow himself to be *under* another's influence.

Hailed as the "heir to the Russian master Andrei Tarkovsky" and pronounced one of Tarkovsky's "most assiduous imitators," Zvyagintsev most recently has been described as "a seer of the social and spiritual divides in

Vladimir V. Putin's Russia." The suggestion that Zvyagintsev is now a film-maker of "social issues [. . .] fills [him] with horror."[31] Rather, his move to the genre of tragedy affiliates his depersonalized work with continuity and tradition. In the protracted courtroom scenes in *Leviathan*, in which the desperate protagonist's appeals are overruled by the judge's uninterrupted, monotonous reading of her verdict, the inevitable ruling signals that "nothing's going to change."[32] Similarly, *Loveless* begins in October 2012, when opposition movements in Russia were driven by optimism and momentum for political change; it ends in 2015, when it is evident that no change will come. Entrenched bureaucracies are ideal settings for Zvyagintsev's contemporary tragedies and their interpretive obstructions. In antiquity, he notes, "the spectators knew the story just as well as the author," and yet one was still compelled to watch a performance: "it is only what is open widest of all that remains more concealed and mysterious than anything else."[33]

The importance of genre for confronting the unknowable in the present is not lost on Zvyagintsev. Emphasis on the "molar" aspect of contemporary existence, to use Deleuze's term, dominates Zvyagintsev's tragedies. Whether a governing apparatus or deep-rooted family dynamic, these forces are associated with unyielding inevitability. The protagonists' efforts to challenge this state of affairs only deepen their entanglement, resulting in a sacrifice of the self to inertia. If this sounds very much like the organizing structure of his previous films, the components are the same: it is the shift in genre that accounts for difference. *The Banishment* cited constantly, situating the citing self among others' discourses with ambivalent results. The later tragedies likewise cite—*Leviathan* can be read as a retelling of the Book of Job, with references to Hobbes' political philosophy—and no attempt at interpretive liberation is sought or even possible.

Tarkovsky emphasized the director's need to reject genre and formulate a distinct relationship to time in order to assert his autonomy. Zvyagintsev's work in the genre of tragedy links his work to tradition, yet the question at the center of tragedy—"how could this have happened?"—commits his work to the historical present. The attendant questions raised by Zvyagintsev's films reflect concerns of our time: Does the difference in how Tarkovsky and Zvyagintsev respectively interact with past tradition reflect a contemporary crisis in the status of autonomy? Can autonomy repressed by depersonalization ever lead to any meaningful outcomes for interpretation? Zvyagintsev's films ask these questions again and again. This understandably leads to readings of his films as political or religious allegories, but these are also questions about influence. T. S. Eliot defined depersonalization as "a continual surrender of [the artist] as he is at the moment to something which is more valuable."[34] In the case of Zvyagintsev, the value of tradition is to remember the possibilities of interpretation and to underscore the absence of such possibilities now.

NOTES

1. James Norton, "The Sins of the Father: Andrei Zvyagintsev in Conversation," *Vertigo* 3.8 (Winter 2008). https://www.closeupfilmcentre.com/vertigo_magazine/volume-3-issue-8-winter-2008/the-sins-of-the-father-andrei-zvyagintsev-in-conversation/
2. Roland Barthes, "The Death of the Author," in *Image, Music, Text*, trans. by Stephen Heath (New York: Hill & Wang, 1977), 146.
3. Andrei Zvyaginsev, Interview with Vladimir Pozner (aired on 29 May 2011). https://www.youtube.com/watch?v=gS7oTyY__zs
4. Marina Timasheva, "Master-Klass Andreia Zviagintseva," *Radio Svoboda*, 5 June 2009. https://www.svoboda.org/a/1748340.html
5. "It was Tarkovsky's films that first inspired me to start making films myself. But Michelangelo Antonioni and Ingmar Bergman have been big influences too." Rebecca Davies, "Andrei Zvyagintsev Interview," *The Telegraph*, 12 August 2008. http://www.telegraph.co.uk/culture/film/3558368/Andrei-Zvyagintsev-interview.html
6. Barnaby B. Barratt, "Fathering and the Consolidation of Masculinity: Notes on the Paternal Function in Andrey Zvyagintsev's *The Return*," *The Psychoanalytic Review* 102:3 (2016): 351.
7. Ibid., 360.
8. David Gritten, "The director who came in from the cold," *The Daily Telegraph*, 6 November 2004, 22.
9. Helena Goscilo, "Fraught Filiation: Andrei Tarkovsky's Transformations of Personal Trauma," in Helena Goscilo and Yana Hashamova (eds), *Cinepaternity* (Bloomington: Indiana University Press, 2010), 264–5.
10. Ibid., 262–3.
11. Ibid., 268.
12. Nick James, "The Tarkovsky Legacy," *Sight and Sound* 25.11. http://www.bfi.org.uk/news-opinion/sight-sound-magazine/features/deep-focus/tarkovsky-legacy
13. Birgit Beumers, "Andrei Zvyagintsev: The Banishment," *Kinokultura* 18 (October 2007). http://www.kinokultura.com/2007/18r-izgnanie.shtml
14. Nariman Skakov, *The Cinema of Tarkovsky: Labyrinths of Space and Time* (London and New York: I. B.Tauris, 2012), 60–1. In his film *Blue*, Krzysztof Kieslowski likewise cites from 1 Corinthians to acknowledge the need to find a place for the self among others through a love that comes at the cost of the very self.
15. "Ты видишь в зеркале не только себя, а и себя в том числе." Artur Solomonov, "Nastoiashchee proizvedenie iskusstva sozdaet treshchinu v gladi nashikh predstavlenii o mire, o nashikh sviaziakh s liud'mi," *The New Times* 10 (16 April 2007). https://newtimes.ru/articles/detail/13036
16. Davies, "Andrei Zvyagintsev Interview." http://www.telegraph.co.uk/culture/film/3558368/Andrei-Zvyagintsev-interview.html. Zvyagintsev also cut 40 seconds from the film "in three places" between its screening at the Cannes Film Festival and its commercial release (in Andrei Zvyagintsev, *Master Klass* (Moscow: ARTKino/Mir Iskusstva, 2010), 27.
17. Iulia Anokhina and Vladimir Gasparov (eds), "Master-klass Andreia Zviagintseva. Fragment No. 3," in *Dykhanie kamnia. Mir fil'mov Andreia Zviagintseva* (Moscow: Novoe literaturnoe obozrenie, 2014), 141.
18. "Why are European countries lining up for the new Zvyagintsev film?" *Russian Beyond*, 14 March 2017. https://www.rbth.com/arts/movies/2017/03/14/why-are-european-countries-lining-up-for-the-new-zvyagintsev-film_719531
19. Davies, "Andrei Zvyagintsev Interview."

20. Zvyagintsev, *Master Klass*, 9.

21. Vida T. Johnson and Graham Petrie, *The Films of Andrei Tarkovsky: A Visual Fugue* (Bloomington: Indiana University Press, 1994), 254.

22. Skakov, *The Cinema of Andrei Tarkovsky*, 85.

23. Ibid., 85.

24. Andrey Tarkovsky, *Sculpting in Time: Reflections on the Cinema* (Austin: University of Texas Press, 1987), 183.

25. Andrey Zvyagintsev, Oleg Negin, and Mikhail Krichman, *The Making of Andrey Zvyagintsev's film* Elena, trans. by Katherine Judelson (London: Cygnet, 2014), 204–5.

26. Dmitry Trakovsky, *Meeting Andrey Tarkovsky*, 2008.

27. Tarkovsky, *Sculpting in Time*, 78, 25; Trakovsky, *Meeting Andrey Tarkovsky*.

28. Tarkovsky, *Sculpting in Time*, 235.

29. Ibid., 121.

30. Ibid., 150, 233. In an interview to promote *Loveless*, Zvyagintsev noted Tarkovsky's handwritten draft list of influential directors. Zvyagintsev is often described as being under Tarkovsky's influence, yet here he identifies an influence on Tarkovsky: "there was this huge cross on Michelangelo Antonioni. It is my understanding that's because he realized that Antonioni was where he came from" (Ksenija Pavlovic, "Interview With Andrey Zvyagintsev: "Oh Russia, Where Do You Go?" *The Pavlovic Today*, 25 November 2017. https://thepavlovictoday.com/exclusive/interview-andrey-zvyagintsev-oh-russia-go/)

31. Zvyagintsev et al., *The Making of Andrey Zvyagintsev's film* Elena, 198.

32. Ibid., 197.

33. Ibid., 205.

34. T. S. Eliot, *Selected Essays* (London: Faber & Faber, 1948), 13.

CHAPTER 15

Von Trier and Tarkovsky: From Antithesis to Counter-sublime

Sergey Toymentsev and Anton Dolin

"DEDICATED TO ANDREI TARKOVSKY"

Throughout his career Lars von Trier was often compared to Andrei Tarkovsky in terms of visual style, religious thematics, and symbols. Yet when he openly dedicated his infamous *Antichrist* (2009) to the Russian director in the closing credits, virtually no one from film critics and cinephiles alike could take this dedication seriously. Indeed, how could a horror film representing sex, violence, and cruelty in an obscene and pornographic fashion (e.g. infanticide, genital mutilation, knee-drilling, etc.) resemble any of Tarkovsky's films? As early reviewers recall, "one of the loudest laughs during the first screening was at von Trier's dedication of the film to Andrei Tarkovsky,"[1] a dedication which was invariably dismissed as "tongue-in-cheek,"[2] "presumptuous,"[3] "brazenly incongruous,"[4] "a liberty too far,"[5] "a final flip of the bird to the Cannes audience,"[6] "a move that felt like rubbing salt in the wounds of those who hated *Antichrist*."[7] Many viewers would agree that to "dedicate a film of such anarchy to the patron saint of cinema seems . . . a little blasphemous"[8] and that "Trier is to Tarkovsky . . . what a street thug with a switchblade is to . . . a saint on a pillar."[9] Von Trier himself, however, insisted he was not playing a joke on the audience by this dedication. In his defense, he explained in the Cannes press conference: "Tarkovsky . . . he's a real God . . . I've seen his films many, many times . . . He's the generation before me. I feel related to him . . . If you dedicate a film to a director, then nobody will say that you're stealing from him, so this was the easy way out."[10]

Antichrist is not the only film where von Trier formally pays homage to Tarkovsky. His name is listed first in von Trier's thanks in the end credits of both volumes of *Nymphomaniac* (2014), another bold exploration of the feminine *jouissance* in which "countless quotes from Andrei Tarkovsky"[11] are loosely interspersed among equally countless sex scenes and lengthy genital close-ups. As could be expected, many reviewers deemed such reverential visuals as "ironic,"[12] "excessive" and "puzzling," by claiming that "von Trier, the secular cynic, has no heart for Tarkovsky's immanence,"[13] that he "lacks Tarkovsky's spirituality and Christian commitment to salvation or grace," and that in *Nymphomaniac* he "is, in a sense, shitting (or pissing or ejaculating) all over Tarkovsky, in an attempt to sully everything he stands for."[14]

Despite unsympathetic reviews of von Trier's tributes to Tarkovsky, the question of their connection has not been completely bypassed in the incredibly rich literature on the former. Scholars regularly mention Tarkovsky among chief cinematic influences on von Trier, along with Carl Theodor Dreyer, Ingmar Bergman, and David Lynch,[15] yet in most cases the discussion does not go any further than underlying their key differences or pointing to examples of visual citation. Amy Simmons, for example, has only few comments on the subject in her book-length study of *Antichrist*: by admitting the trace of the Russian director in the "film's attention to landscapes," she points out that "whereas the contemplative Andrei Tarkovsky generally emphasised divine omnipotence, von Trier grapples with theological contradictions by . . . revealing the darker, and more misogynistic aspects of the Christian tradition."[16] Simmons' perceptive observation certainly sheds some light on where both auteurs stand in relation to religion, yet it hardly clarifies the reason for *Antichrist*'s scandalous dedication. B. M. S. Thomsen, on the contrary, takes *Antichrist*'s dedication at its word and argues that von Trier draws his inspiration mainly from Tarkovsky's *The Sacrifice* (1986) by reenacting such symbolic components as madness, apocalypse, witch, and wooden house, among others[17] (even though von Trier explicitly stated in an interview that *The Sacrifice* "was a big mistake" and he didn't like it[18]). For Sinnerbrink, it is von Trier's *Melancholia* (2011) that appears to be thematically indebted to Tarkovsky's last film (as well as aesthetically to *Solaris*): whereas Tarkovsky's protagonist sacrifices himself for the world, von Trier's film goes a step further by staging an aesthetic spectacle of world-sacrifice that gestures toward the emergence of a new post-humanist world.[19]

The list of sketchy juxtapositions between the two directors, where Tarkovsky usually stands for modernist cinema and von Trier for a postmodernist one, can certainly be extended, yet their systematic comparison is yet to come. Given that Tarkovsky's shadow keeps following von Trier from one film to another—from his early student shorts to *Nymphomaniac*—it would be worthwhile to examine their affinities and divergences in greater detail as well as attempt to explain von Trier's motives for such a long-standing influence. In what follows, we will discuss Tarkovsky's presence in von Trier's films in both stylistic and thematic aspects by borrowing Harold Bloom's notions of antithetical completion and *daemonization* from his rhetorical matrix of revisionary ratios. We hope that Bloom's theory of poetic influence will help us not only to highlight von Trier's most evident examples of visual citation as well as clarify his differing treatment of essentially Tarkovskian motifs, such as Christ figure, sacrifice, and apocalypse, but also to trace the evolution of his engagement with the Russian director throughout his long and prolific career, which we divide into two main stages or phases: those of antithesis and counter-sublime. We will also focus on how von Trier simultaneously attacks and rein-vents Tarkovsky's spiritualist ideology of redemption from the position of European cynicism most vividly exemplified by Peter Sloterdijk's *Critique of Cynical Reason*. Refracted through the rampant cynicism and nihilism of von Trier's provocations, we argue, Tarkovsky's legacy is by no means devalued or destroyed but, paradoxically enough, acquires a new lease on life in more complicated post-secular conditions.

ANTITHETICALLY COMPLETING TARKOVSKY

Von Trier's passion for Tarkovsky's films has never been a secret, thanks to his generous statements of appreciation of the latter's influence. "I was very inspired by Tarkovsky," he says, "I won't make any bones about that."[20] Refer-ring to him as "god" and "one of the biggest idols"[21] in numerous interviews, von Trier especially worships *Mirror* (1974), which was the first Tarkovsky film he was exposed to at film school. As he recalled in a 1990 interview, "There they showed a long clip from *The Mirror* by Andrei Tarkovsky. What I saw was a long take without cuts, a camera tracking a road. It was simply unbeliev-able—like a revelation to me! At the time I had of course seen a lot of films with different aesthetics and I was always interested in the divergent—in unusual things—but the images from this Tarkovsky film seemed to me to have come from another planet."[22] Much later, in a 2009 interview, von Trier's mem-ory of the first encounter with Tarkovsky still remained fresh: "When I saw *The Mirror* for the first time on a small TV set, I was in ecstasy. If we talk about religion, this is a religious relationship."[23] "I was hypnotised! I've seen it 20 times . . . to me he is God."[24] Furthermore, von Trier was one of the main contending bidders for the Tarkovsky archive placed up for auction at Sotheby's in 2012, thanks to whom it was sold for $2.4 million.[25]

At the same time, von Trier is quite adamant to defend his artistic autonomy by claiming that his "stolen material has been processed into something new" and that he "[doesn't] strive to reproduce [his] sources of inspiration mechanically."[26] As he insisted in one of his early interviews, "I create some images that are parallel to Tarkovsky's . . . But I don't think it's a loan from [him] so much as it's inevita-ble occurrence of parallels because of everyone agreeing on the basic elements."[27] His admitted use of elements "parallel to Tarkovsky's" and processing them "into something new" resonates with Bloom's revisionary mode of antithetical comple-tion or *tessera* according to which a "poet antithetically 'completes' his precursor, by so reading the parent-poem as to retain its terms, but to mean them in another sense, as if the precursor has failed to go far enough."[28] As a reaction-formation or "the antithetical defense of reversal-into-the-opposite,"[29] this ratio "represents any later poet's attempt to persuade himself (and us) that the precursor's Word would be worn out if not redeemed as a newly fulfilled and enlarged Word of the ephebe."[30] Furthermore, in the process of antithetical completion "the precursor is regarded as an over-idealizer" and the poet's quest for originality requires "'correcting' the excessive metaphysical idealism of his poetic father." By completing their precursors' legacy via its reversal, later poets, Bloom argues, "deceive themselves into believing they are tougher-minded than their precursors."[31] By adopting Bloom's theory in the cinematic context, we may say that von Trier largely retains Tarkovsky's stylistic terms, yet thematically he remains antithetical to the latter's spiritualist project. Given that idealism is the primary target for mockery and criticism in all of his films, von Trier indeed seems to be tougher-minded than his idealist Russian precursor. In what follows, we will discuss both aspects of his antithetical "anxiety of influence" in chronological order.

Tarkovsky's influence is undoubtedly most traceable in von Trier's early career, when he designed his films in a deliberately radical fashion as if they were truly made on another planet. As he explains, at that time his main desire was "to make a clean break from polished Danish filmmaking,"[32] in which Tarkovsky's cinema seemed like a proper example to follow. Von Trier's student seven-minute short *Nocturne* (1980), focusing on a light-sensitive woman tormented by insomnia, and, to a greater extent, graduation film *Images of a Relief* (1982), sympathetically portraying a group of desperate German soldiers after the liberation of Copenhagen in 1945, diligently reproduce the key components of Tarkovskian technique. As he comments on the sepia color of the latter, "this business of tinting black-and-white film is an unashamed imitation of Tarkovsky, a bit like his *Mirror*." Furthermore, the somber choral music dramatically accompanying the visuals "was also inspired by Tarkovsky."[33] Besides the features mentioned by the director, *Images of a Relief* actively employs excruciatingly long takes, the insertion of documentary footage, dreamlike imagery, dilapidated factory, forest, rain, the combination of water and fire, and levitation. Von Trier's turn to the topic of World War II could also be influenced by early Tarkovsky, yet with a twist: whereas *Ivan's Childhood* (1962) is focused on Russian soldiers fighting Germans, in *Images* it is the defeated Germans who become the heroes. Despite its being accused for romanticizing Nazism, the film's idiosyncratic style toned down its controversy among the critics and instantly earned von Tier a reputation as a virtuoso filmmaker daring to address provocative subjects.

Von Trier's debut feature, *The Element of Crime* (1984), a hyperstylized post-apocalyptic neo-noir thriller, stands out as the most Tarkovskian film. Whereas his previous film was striving to assimilate *Mirror*'s stylistic components, this one fully absorbed *Stalker*'s dystopian aesthetic of decay. The film is structured as a hypnosis session, during which an amnesiac hard-boiled detective named

Fisher is transported from Cairo to Europe in order to retrieve from his memory the circumstances of his last case about the serial killer he was investigating there. The film's title alludes to the criminological treatise written by Fisher's mentor, who puts forth the idea that to track down a criminal one must assume the criminal's point of view and thus trace the genesis of a crime back to its very motive or "element." This "element," von Trier explains, is "a locality that provides a sort of 'centre of infection' for crime, where, like a bacteria it can grow and spread at a certain temperature and in a certain element—moisture, for instance;" it is "the force of nature that intrudes upon and somehow invades people's morals."[34] By implementing this method, Fisher delves deeper into the case until he can no longer distinguish his own actions from the murderer's. Settiing out to extract the element of crime by merging with the murderer's mind, Fisher the mind-hunter, therefore, gets swallowed up by that element itself. For many critics, the film's loopy and cryptic narrative seemed only a pretext for von Trier's exuberant and overly ambitious stylization of visual form, for which he won the award for Best Technique in Cannes. On closer inspection, however, both *Element*'s plot and its stylistic manifestation are strategically parallel to each other: just as the protagonist's agency is usurped by the perpetrator's evil nature, the narrative's intelligibility is literally overshadowed by the material excess of the film medium. As von Trier comments, "In *The Element of Crime* nature encroaches on the human . . . The inquiring humanist who leaves his home terrain and journeys out into nature ends up going to rack and ruin."[35] In terms of the production design, *Element*'s triumph of nature over culture is represented by Europe as a flooded wasteland akin to *Stalker*'s Zone mashed up with other decadent milieus from Francis Ford Coppola's *Apocalypse Now* (1979), Ridley Scott's *Blade Runner* (1982), Luc Besson's *Le Dernier Combat* (1983), and the like. As Torben Grodal observes, "Lyrical Tarkovsky-elements are welded together with elements from American war films, detective flicks, science fictions, and pornography."[36]

It would be safe to suggest that for von Trier, at least in his early career, Tarkovsky is primarily associated with the pantheist celebration of nature in its elemental beauty. *Element* cites the Russian director right from the start by opening with an image of a donkey trying to stand on its feet, which is inspired by *Andrei Rublev*'s poetic scene of a horse rolling over on the river shore (while the donkey's sequence followed by the stills of Muslim mosques should probably be viewed as a reference to Egypt as the film's geographical setting). Fisher's hypnotic return to Europe opens with underwater shots of human debris and decomposing corpses of horses floating in the murky depths, which resonates with *Stalker*'s lengthy dream sequence with an overhead shot of the riverbed. The voice-overs accompanying both sequences share the same apocalyptic theme: Fisher cites Coleridge's *Rime of the Ancient Mariner* ("water, water everywhere . . ."), while Stalker's wife cites Revelation 6: 12–17. By echoing *Andrei Rublev*'s infamous scene of a horse falling off the stairs, *Element* also includes a similar one with a horse slipping off the dock into the water. Furthermore, von Trier intensifies *Stalker*'s sepia color and pervasive dampness by shooting his entire film with high-pressure sodium-vapor lamps at night in the rain, which lends it a sharp yellow tone. And yet, despite these multiple borrowings, von Trier never wanted to be a slavish imitator of others' findings. Even though their visualization of post-apocalyptic landscape is somewhat parallel, both Tarkovsky and von Trier diverge starkly in terms of its symbolization: whereas for the former nature (even in its decay) points toward spiritual redemption, for the latter it adds nothing beyond the death of civilization, except chaos and moral degradation. In *Element*, therefore, von Trier turns Tarkovsky's style inside out: by leaving its poetic beauty intact, he purges it of any religious connotations and adds to it a sinister dimension, a tendency which is fully realized in his *Antichrist*. In fact, Tarkovsky did have a chance to see *Element* and, if we believe von Trier's words, "he hated it . . . He thought it was a load of crap."[37]

In his subsequent features, von Trier steadily continued winking visual nods to Tarkovsky, although with a less systematic intensity. In *Epidemic* (1987) a naïve doctor, Mesmer, hanging from a helicopter over marshland, is transported to a plague-stricken countryside to help the people, which is a direct quote from *Andrei Rublev*'s prologue about Yefim's attempted flight in a hot-air balloon, a scene that symbolizes the artist's suicidal idealism. The natural scenery in *Medea* (1988) is heavily inspired by the uncanny ambience of Tarkovskian landscapes. *Element*'s dark and watery post-apocalyptic landscape partly reappears in *Europa* (1991) as the allegory of post-war Germany haunted by the atrocities of the past. In *Breaking the Waves* (1996), the final sequence with the ringing bells miraculously suspended in the sky references *Andrei Rublev*'s equally miraculous ending in which the young Boriska manages to cast a perfect bell through his faith alone. In *Dogville* (2003) the scene in which Grace attempts to escape in a freight truck stuffed with apples in boxes parallels a dream sequence from *Ivan's Childhood* where Ivan and his sister have a ride on a truck loaded with apples. *Manderlay* (2005) includes scenes with a burning horse rushing through the night as well as a donkey slaughtered for dramatic purposes, which is, again, a reference to *Andrei Rublev*'s raid sequence with a burning cow and a butchered horse. Even though von Trier decided to cut all the scenes showing the dead donkey out of the film under pressure from animal rights organizations and the burning horse shot was computer-generated, he, just like Tarkovsky, would never feel embarrassed for mutilating animals for art's sake. As he responds to the animal welfare activists regarding half-dead horses in *Element*, "these were horses that were going to be put down anyway and thrown to the lions at the zoo, so why couldn't we use them in our film instead?"[38]

While retaining much of Tarkovsky's style, von Trier nevertheless emphatically rejects the former's quasi-religious utopianism. By fully admitting his own cynicism, he even likens himself to Tom in *Dogville*, one of his most cynical characters, who organizes the enslavement and ritual rape of Grace, while presenting himself as the moral leader of the town: "he's thoroughly cynical. But then so am I."[39] Furthermore, it is from the position of his incurable cynicism that he antithetically completes Tarkovsky's project. Whereas Tarkovsky's films celebrate the quixotic idealism of his overly committed heroes or Christ figures (e.g. Ivan, Andrei Rublev, Stalker, Gorchakov, Domenico, Alexander),[40] von Trier incessantly undermines all possible grounds for such actions, yet simultaneously looks for better alternatives. As he formulated the principal theme of his films in a 2000 interview: "The films that I have made have all had to do with a clash between an ideal and reality. Whenever there's been a man in the lead role, at a certain point this man finds out that the ideal doesn't hold. And whenever it was a woman, they take the ideal all the way."[41] A similar statement we read in his 2005 interview: "All my life I've been interested in the discrepancy between philosophy and reality, between conviction and its implementation."[42] And yet, while emphasizing the irreconcilable gap between his characters' naïve romanticism and brutal reality via irony, sarcasm, and provocation, von Trier, who himself used to be a communist and a Catholic in the past, has never abandoned his belief in the necessity of idealism and still thinks idealists must be given a chance. As he said in a 2005 interview with Stig Bjorkman, "We live in total chaos so we need to create ideals in order to survive. Otherwise life would be unbearable."[43]

VON TRIER'S CYNICISM IN SPIRAL EVOLUTION

Von Trier's compulsive yet ambivalent critique of idealistic convictions, which strives to discredit any manifestation of the utopian impulse without dismissing it altogether, is similar to Peter Sloterdijk's concept of modern cynicism elaborated in his *Critique of Cynical Reason* (1983) and denoting an "enlightened false consciousness" as the final stage of the Enlightenment, in which the Enlightenment critique is turned against itself due to the disillusionment with it. Such consciousness, he argues, "no longer feels affected by any critique of ideology; its falseness is already reflexively buffered."[44] Hopelessly addicted to the critique's "relentless drive against illusions," modern cynics are unable to form a belief in any ideal or stable values except their own self-preservation, which paradoxically aligns with "moral self-denial."[45] "Because everything has become problematic," he sums up, "everything is also somehow a matter of indifference."[46] Just like von Trier is drawn toward unmasking "the discrepancy between philosophy and reality," Sloterdijk similarly insists on the "schizoid logic"[47] of modern cynicism afflicted by the "deep schism that runs through modern consciousnesses and that seems to separate the rational and the real."[48] Besides their failure to engage in any committed political action, Sloterdijk emphasizes the psychological and existentialist predicament of present-day cynics by defining them as "borderline melancholics, who can keep their symptoms of depression under control and can remain more or less able to work." The "new, integrated cynicism," he says, "covers up a mass of offensive unhappiness and the need to cry."[49]

Sloterdijk's historical diagnosis of European cynicism as modernized unhappy consciousness in the post-1968 era, parallel with Foucault's lectures on the subject at the Collège de France in 1983–4, sheds light on the intellectual and ideological environment in which von Trier launched his career. His cynicism blew wide open already in his very first short film *The Orchid Gardener* (1977) dedicated to a girl "who had died of leukemia immediately after the shooting of this film" with the dates of birth and death in the opening credits. As he recalled later, "That was entirely fabricated. A complete lie. And manipulative and cynical, because I realized that if you started a film like that, then the audience would take it a lot more seriously."[50] Yet it is not that von Trier is shamelessly proud of his cynicism. On the contrary, just as the modern cynic's drive for self-preservation, according to Sloterdijk, runs parallel with that for self-destruction manifested in such "broken modes of consciousness . . . [as] irony, cynicism, stoicism, melancholy, sarcasm, nostalgia, voluntarism, resignation to the lesser evil, depression and anesthesia,"[51] von Trier is well known as a long sufferer of depression and multiple anxieties which often stand in the way of his filmmaking. Furthermore, just as Sloterdijk hopes to find a cure for his "cynical reason" in the "cheeky" Greek *kynicism* of Diogenes (outside modernity) and Buddhist meditation (outside Europe), von Trier's attraction to Tarkovsky's cinema can also be understood as the former's need for therapy which the latter's unabashed messianism and mysticism could certainly provide. As von Trier confesses, "But when I want to allow myself a moment of ultimate enjoyment, it would suffice for me to watch Tarkovsky's *Solaris* for half an hour and it warms my heart—he fascinates me."[52]

It is important to emphasize that von Trier is by no means a proponent of cynicism, no matter how cynical his films may seem. Being a hard-core cynic himself, he is nevertheless a consistent critic of cynicism if we look at his trilogies as a continuous endeavor to overcome this "discrepancy" between an ideal and reality rather than as a straightforward critique of idealism. All thematically coherent, each of them foregrounds an idealistic protagonist who either perishes or succeeds in his or her pursuit of a certain ideal. The *Europa* trilogy focuses on a male rational idealist, the *Golden Heart* trilogy triumphantly champions female emotional idealism, the incomplete *America: Land of Opportunities* trilogy deals with female rational idealists, and the *Depression* trilogy pushes female emotional idealism to the limit by exceeding it to mania. In the light of von Trier's spiral evolution, in which different versions of idealism are cyclically reshuffled and rematched, all these trilogies may easily be viewed as his persistent recontextualization of Tarkovsky's messianic humanism in the setting of Western cynicism: in its original form it will fail miserably, of course, as the male idealists of the *Europa* trilogy effectively demonstrate, yet it might stand a chance of being successfully adopted after its gender and mental health boundaries are revised. Whereas the naïve protagonists from the *Europa* trilogy are semi-satirical characters treated by von Trier with irony and ridicule despite their lofty aspirations (in *Element* Fisher chases a serial killer who leads him to himself, in *Epidemic* the young doctor Mesmer spreads contamination by trying to save people, in *Europa* the American Leo comes to post-war Germany to help its reconstruction yet ends up becoming a Nazi collaborator), the heroines of the *Golden Heart* trilogy excel as truly Tarkovskian Christ figures capable of self-sacrifice, martyrdom, and devotion to the cause. In *Breaking the Waves* Bess believes she could cure her paralyzed husband by prostituting herself; as a result of such conviction, she loses her life yet her husband is healed. Many scholars pointed out thematic similarity between Bess' sacrifice and Alexander's in Tarkovsky's *The Sacrifice*: both protagonists perform the "same act of meaningless sacrifice as the ultimate guarantee of sense"[53] by ecstatically turning in prayer to God and offering everything they have in exchange for saving other people. The same sacrificial logic is enacted in two other installments of the trilogy: in *Idiots* (1998) Karen seems to be the only one who goes truly insane in the group of radicals searching for their "inner idiot" by "spassing" (i.e. acting mentally disabled in public); in *Dancer in the Dark* (2000) Selma chooses the death penalty instead of spending the money saved for her son's operation on a trial lawyer. These semi-hagiographic melodramas celebrating women in their sublime act of sacrifice, however kitschy, ironic, and grotesque they are, came the closest to reproducing, or antithetically completing, Tarkovsky's Christological narrative on Western soil, despite the critics accusing von Trier of implicit misogyny.

Von Trier's unfinished *America* trilogy, however, reverses his gradual ascent toward humanist ideals and reveals him as a bitter and uncompromising cynic over again. Not only does his *Dogville* unleash a devastating critique of the hideous underside of democratic ideals allegorically represented in the Dogville hypocritical residents exposed as a community of cynical liars and rapists, the film equally questions the credibility of the actions of its Christ-like protagonist Grace guided by the ethic of self-sacrifice. In contrast to the theological rhetoric of his previous trilogy, in *Dogville* von Trier replaces the hermeneutic of sacrifice with that of justice and thus converts his heroine into a rational idealist who eventually prefers a violent retribution over sufferings and redemption. Even though Grace's conversion into a rational justice seeker was welcomed by some critics,[54] in *Manderlay*, *Dogville*'s sequel, her naïve enterprise to teach freedom and equal rights to former slaves in a colony is portrayed with the same satirical attack as the male idealists in von Trier's first trilogy. As he points out, "It's true that Grace's idealism resembles Leo's. The difference is that Leo was only trying to do good, while Grace implements her idealism with a gun in her hands."[55] It is no wonder, then, that the *America* trilogy still remains unfinished since in its two films von Trier has already made it is quite clear that female rational idealism is as much futile to cure his cynicism as its male counterpart and to find a better remedy for it he had to conjure up a belief based on passion rather than intellectual conviction. His clinical depression of 2006–7 helped him find such a way out in the form of manic idealism that becomes the subject of his next trilogy and, as in a spiral, thematically overlaps with the female emotional idealism of the *Golden Heart* trilogy.

VON TRIER'S COUNTER-SUBLIME

Von Trier's *Depression* trilogy marks a new phase in his engagement with Tarkovsky, that of *daemonization* or personalized counter-sublime according to Bloom's classification of revisionary ratios. In this ratio the later poet turns against the precursor's sublime and, to repress it, establishes an alternative version of it by undergoing the so-called *daemonization* in which "the ephebe is daemonized [and] his precursor necessarily is humanized."[56] Bloom outlines three domains in the precursor's work against which the later poet reacts in his or her subliminal appropriation of them: the landscape, the inner self, and the precursor's glance. As he writes,

> To appropriate the precursor's landscape for himself, the ephebe must estrange it further from himself. To attain a self yet more inward than the precursor's, the ephebe becomes necessarily more solipsistic. To evade the precursor's imagined glance, the ephebe seeks to confine it in scope, which perversely enlarges the glance, so that it rarely can be evaded.[57]

By losing "reciprocity with the world" and becoming more introspective instead, the later poet, therefore, develops his or her counter-sublime as a further intensification of the precursor's sublime, in which the depersonalized landscape reappears as uncanny and the poet's dehumanized self as demonic. In Freudian terms, the formula of *daemonization* is as follows: "Where my poetic father's *I* was, there *it* shall be," or even better, "there my *I* is, more closely mixed with *it*."[58] That is to say, the precursor's influence can be transcended and absorbed into tradition only through the later poet's plunging into the unconscious, which is viewed as a "self-crippling act" where the latter's "Oedipal phase *develops backwards* to enrich and make yet more inchoate the id"[59] in order to clear imaginative space for a new creative identity. The influence of the precursor's sublime, however, cannot be forgotten altogether, it can only be repressed and later recognized as "the return of the repressed"[60] in the poet's counter-sublime, which "reduces the precursor's human glory by handing back all his hard-won victories to the daemonic world."[61] In terms of tropes, the poet's subliminal overcoming of the precursor via repression manifests itself as "an exaggerated representation, the overthrow called hyperbole, with characteristic imagery of great heights and abysmal depths."[62] As we will see below, hyperbole as the "trope of excess, of the violent overthrow,"[63] and grotesque as the sublime's "dialectical brother"[64] are the main stylistic characteristics of von Trier's counter-sublime.

It wouldn't be an exaggeration to state that von Trier expresses his admiration for Tarkovsky's cinema in terms of the sublime. For example, while trying to describe *Mirror*'s opening scene—the long tracking shot showing the mother sitting on a fence—he uses such words as "captivating," "mesmerizing," "shocking" and sincerely admits he still can't understand its beauty after seeing it multiple times. As he says, "It's hard to say what's special about it. It was magical if something was from Mars, and not from Earth. It's almost like David Bowie, he was kind of from Mars."[65]

Whereas in his early student works von Trier strived to imitate Tarkovsky's subliminal aesthetic (for example, in the scene of Leo's levitation over the forest in *Images of a Relief*), in the *Depression* trilogy, particularly rife with references to the Russian director, he aims to suppress it by overshadowing it with grotesque, hyperbole, and irony. In this regard, it is no wonder *Antichrist*'s dedication to Tarkovsky strikes many viewers as "blasphemous" and "brazenly incongruous": instead of paying homage to his legacy, von Trier's objective here is rather to reach closure with the influence of his precursor by repressing it through hyperbolic distortions of his counter-sublime. In the DVD commentary to *Antichrist*, von Trier, unfortunately, doesn't point to any Tarkovsky citation and claims he was primarily inspired by the "mood" of *Mirror*. Yet we may still decode this "mood" in terms of visual references present in the film. The most obvious one is Eden, an isolated log cabin in the forest, reminiscent of *Mirror*'s wooden country house of Alexei's childhood in Zavrazhye enfolded by trees (as well as Gorchakov's Russian house in the fog from *Nostalghia*'s dream sequences). Both dwellings are uncanny representations of Eden-before-the-Fall located in mythological time and space and intimately associated with the feminine and the maternal. Early in the film the forest surrounding the cabin is visualized by familiar tropes of the Tarkovskian natural scenery: oneiric landscape covered by thick greenery and blooming flora, rustling leaves, gusts of wind across a high-grass field, clouds of fog, birch forest, the bare trunk of a dead tree, etc. As many commentators pointed out, in *Antichrist* nature plays a character of its own which evolves from an idyllic rehabilitation retreat to a shocking "Satan's church" that hyperbolically distorts the Tarkovskian landscape through the prism of the horror aesthetic characterized by "the stylized gothic/supernaturalist images of a sublime but malevolent nature."[66] Both manifestations of nature acquire gender markers in the film: whereas He perceives it as the source of life and healing, She fears it as the demonic force of destruction. For example, on their train ride to

Eden, to demonstrate the therapeutic effect of nature, He asks her to imagine herself lying on the grass and melting with it: "Don't fight it . . . just. . . . Turn green." By following his instructions, She visualizes her body lying on the grass and literally turning green (Figure 15.1), which references Stalker's ecstatic sinking into the grass with his eyes closed on arrival in the Zone (Figure 15.2).

Figure 15.1 She lying in the grass in *Antichrist*.

Figure 15.2 Stalker lying in the grass in *Stalker*.

According to the feminist reading of the scene, her hypnotically induced becoming the grass "re-inscribes the feminine subject of the film through a relation of submission or capitulation to nature,"[67] which should be viewed as "the stereotype of women's intimate relationship with nature" imposed by "Dafoe's discourse projected on the screen."[68] In the light of *Antichrist*'s dedication, however, this scene could also be interpreted as von Trier's ironic mockery of Tarkovsky's Taoist celebration of nature as spiritual "comfort zone,"[69] which is proved to be no more than a male fantasy. As *Antichrist* powerfully demonstrates, nature that extends far beyond plants and animals effectively traverses such fantasy through the violent eruption of the Real of which She has always been aware. In Bloomian terms, we may say that in *Antichrist* von Trier's counter-sublime estranges and demonizes the Tarkovskian landscape by turning it into the representation of the unconscious or what Sinnerbrink calls "supernaturalism" that "covers both the horror of excessive life in nature (the rotting plant roots, insect sounds, dead trees) and a 'beyond' of nature (occult forces that defy rational explanation)."[70]

As many viewers were quick to notice,[71] *Melancholia*'s references to Tarkovsky's imagery are hard to miss: the burning canvas of Breughel's *The Hunters in the Snow* (1565) that stands for a miniature of Earth in *Solaris* (1972), Justine as Millais' Ophelia floating down a water stream familiar from many of Tarkovsky's films, a falling horse, an apple orchard, Justine's sarcastic suggestion to meet apocalypse with Beethoven's Ninth reminiscent of Domenico's self-immolation accompanied by Beethoven's "Ode to Joy". The entire plot of *Melancholia* could be viewed as an inversion of *Solaris*: whereas Tarkovsky's characters perish on a planet away from Earth, von Trier's meet their end on Earth smashed by a rogue planet. And yet, *Melancholia* may seem closer to *Nostalghia*, given that both films are equally preoccupied with apocalypse, redemption, and the incurable state of despondency of their protagonists. In fact, melancholia and nostalgia are medically synonymous terms. Furthermore, in *Melancholia* von Trier extensively employs Tarkovsky's favorite method of visual rhymes and thematic parallels. In *Nostalghia*, for example, we see Italy's landscape overlap or resonate with Russia's, Gorchakov's nostalgia with Domenico's madness (as well as Sosnovsky's nostalgia), his Russian wife Maria with the beautiful Italian interpreter Eugenia, his messianic passage with a candle in the pool with Domenico's self-immolation in Rome's Piazza del Campidoglio, among others. Similarly, *Melancholia* juxtaposes Justine's personality with Claire's, draws parallels between the melancholic Justine and the planet Melancholia, and has Wagner's prelude to *Tristan und Isolde* as a suspenseful soundtrack to the film's agonizing waiting for the end of the world. Unlike Tarkovsky, however, von Trier never intends to magically revert the planet's collapse in a way that *The Sacrifice* does. Instead of "*The Sacrifice*'s valorisation of self-sacrifice," as Sinnerbrink points out, *Melancholia* "presents an aesthetic staging of the sublime spectacle of world-destruction as an ironic gesture of cinematic self-sacrifice."[72] It is against Tarkovsky's moral and theological sublime that von Trier juxtaposes his emphatically aesthetic counter-sublime from start to finish: namely, the prelude's series of *tableaux vivants* shot in slow motion and the literal representation of the apocalypse in the end.

As "an orgy of the sublime and the ridiculous,"[73] *Nymphomaniac* takes Tarkovsky's legacy a step further by placing it into a pornographic context. Following the repressive injunction of its subtitle "Forget about Love," the film grotesquely violates all normative standards of love, family, and marriage by foregrounding the Sadean manic heroine stricken by loveless apathy and inexhaustible lust. As Linda Badley observes, what distinguishes *Nymphomaniac* from most of von Trier's previous films is its "cinematic adaptation of a Sadean discourse or rhetoric of excess"[74] manifested in the film's compulsion to say and show everything. As von Trier himself admitted, the works of the Marquis de Sade intersecting sex and intellectual thought were the main source of inspiration for *Nymphomaniac*.[75] And yet, why is Tarkovsky listed first in von Trier's thanks at the end of the film? In the light of the revisionary ratio of *daemonization*, *Nymphomaniac* should be viewed as an aggressive reaction against the precursor's sublime whose "all hard-won victories [are handed back] to the demonic world."[76] In other words, what *Nymphomaniac*'s counter-sublime methodically attacks is Tarkovsky's subliminal celebration of love and family values. The entire narrative of the film seems to be modeled after *Mirror*'s non-linear biography permeated by intertextual allusions. In fact, one of *Nymphomaniac*'s chapters is indeed titled "The Mirror." As for *Nymphomaniac*'s citations, most of them refer to the most intimate representations of love in Tarkovsky's films. For example, toward the end of Volume I Joe uses the concept of three-voice polyphony, introduced by one of Seligman's intellectual digressions, to describe her sexual experience with three complementary partners. The contrapuntal polyphony of Bach's organ prelude "Ich ruf zu dir, Herr Jesu Christ" is then illustrated by Joe's copulating lovers standing for each musical voice, with the screen split into thirds. In this sexual-musical analogy, Joe's love to one of them serves as "the secret ingredient" in her harmonious polyamory and is compared to Bach's cantus firmus. As is known, the same Bach prelude is used as the central musical theme in *Solaris*: it accompanies the levitation scene with Kris and Hari floating in the spaceship's library as well as Kris' imaginary return to home in the end. Both sequences are quite moving and are regarded as subliminal since they symbolize the transcending power of love in the cosmic context. Von Trier's Sadean polyamorous visualization of Bach's prelude functions, therefore, as his counter-sublime to Tarkovsky's matrimonial and familial sublime. Tarkovsky's levitation motif is also referenced by Joe's orgasmic levitation during which she has a vision of the whore of Babylon and another woman whom she mistakes for the Virgin Mary from the reproduction of Andrei Rublev's icon on Seligman's wall. This story prompts Seligman to proceed with another digression on the differences between the Eastern Church ("the church of happiness") and the Western Church ("the church of suffering"), according to which she structures the next chapter of her sexual biography. In the final chapter Joe compares herself with a broken and barren oak she discovers on the mountain and names it as her "soul" tree, a tree which is borrowed from *The Sacrifice*'s first and last scenes and which symbolizes generational continuity between Alexander and his son.

All three installments of the *Depression* trilogy employ the same structure of the counter-sublime by methodically dehumanizing and hyperbolically distorting various forms of Tarkovsky's sublimity: *Antichrist* overshadows Tarkovskian landscapes with gothic "supernaturalism," *Melancholia* presents the viewer with the aesthetic spectacle of the apocalypse in contrast to *The Sacrifice*'s moral redemption, *Nymphomaniac* demonstratively forgets about Tarkovsky's ethics of love and family values via adapting a Sadean rhetoric of excess. In this regard, "Forget about Tarkovsky" could well be a suitable subtitle for the entire *Depression* trilogy, where each of its films equally dramatizes the authorial struggle for artistic autonomy from the precursor's influence.

CONCLUSION

To sum up, von Trier's long-term engagement with the Russian director has undergone several stages of influence throughout his career: from his utter fascination with *Mirror* in his student years and desire to imitate its visual technique in his first films to continuous attempts to overcome the haunting influence of Tarkovsky's legacy by either antithetically completing or aggressively dehumanizing it. Whereas *The Element of Crime* massively adopts Tarkovsky's style yet strips it off from its spiritual dogmatism, the *Golden Heart* trilogy pushes his messianic idealism much further by converting his male protagonists into Christ-like women as the agents of redemption. The *Depression* trilogy openly admits the Danish auteur's indebtedness to Tarkovsky ("if you are stealing, then dedicate"[77]) but only to cynically denounce everything that the latter stands for, such as the spirituality of nature, belief in humanity and this world, and love. Von Trier's latest film, *The House That Jack Built* (2018), where male manic idealism supersedes its female counterpart, could be viewed as an ascetic extension of the same tendency which, this time, condemns or demonizes the Tarkovskian cult of the house, although this speculation is yet to be substantiated by further analysis.

NOTES

1. Mark Brown, "Cannes film festival: Can Lars von Trier be having a laugh at us?" *The Guardian*, 18 May 2009. https://www.theguardian.com/film/filmblog/2009/may/18/cannes-film-festival-lars-von-trier-antichrist

2. Peter Bradshaw, "Who's afraid of the talking fox? I am," *The Guardian*, 19 May 2009. https://www.theguardian.com/film/2009/may/19/cannes-antichrist-father-children-von-trier

3. Xan Brooks, "Mangy Foxes and Fake Firs: the Reel Chaos of the Cannes Film Festival," *The Guardian*, 18 May 2009. https://www.theguardian.com/film/2009/may/18/cannes-film-festival-antichrist-lars-von-trier

4. Dennis Lim, "*Antichrist* is controversial, but therapeutic for director Lars von Trier," *Los Angeles Times*, 23 May 2009. https://www.latimes.com/archives/la-xpm-2009-may-23-et-antichrist23-story.html

5. Elizabeth Renzetti, "Bedevilled by von Trier's *Antichrist*," *The Globe and Mail*, 24 July 2009. https://www.theglobeandmail.com/arts/bedevilled-by-von-triers-antichrist/article4281308/

6. Peter Sciretta, "Early Buzz: Lars Von Trier's *Antichrist*," */Film*, 17 May 2009. https://www.slashfilm.com/early-buzz-lars-von-triers-antichrist/

7. Allan Hunter, "*Antichrist*—Lars Von Trier Interview," *The List*, 23 July 2009. https://film.list.co.uk/article/19091-antichrist-lars-von-trier-interview/

8. Zachary Wigon, "Lars von Trier is 'The Best Director in the World,'" *TribecaFilm.com*, 19 October 2009: https://www.tribecafilm.com/stories/512c11891c7d76d9a90007ba-lars-von-trier-is-the-bes

9. Nigel Andrews, "Beauty and the Unspeakable," *The Financial Times*, 23 July 2009, 11.

10. Hunter, "*Antichrist*—Lars Von Trier Interview."

11. Tarja Laine, "Mea maxima vulva: Appreciation and Aesthetics of Chance in *Nymphomaniac*," in Rex Butler and David Denny (eds), *Lars Von Trier's Women* (New York: Bloomsbury Publishing USA, 2016), 233–46, 234.

12. Max Carpenter, "Lars von Trier Digs Deep in *Nymphomaniac*," *The Grail*, 10 April 2014. http://www.reedthegrail.com/film-reviews/2014/4/10/lars-von-trier-digs-deep-in-nymphomaniac

13. Carson Lund, "*Nymphomaniac*: Vol. II," *Letterboxd.com*, 6 April 2014. https://letterboxd.com/lund_carson/film/nymphomaniac-vol-ii/

14. Caveh Zahedi, "Lars von Trier's *Nymphomaniac*: Volume I & Volume II," *Talkhouse.com*, 2 May 2014. https://www.talkhouse.com/caveh-zahedi-i-am-a-sex-addict-talks-lars-von-triers-nymphomaniac-volume-i-volume-ii/

15. See Caroline Bainbridge, *The Cinema of Lars Von Trier: Authenticity and Artifice* (London: Wallflower Press, 2007), 13; Linda Badley, *Lars von Trier* (Urbana: University of Illinois Press, 2010), 3.

16. Amy Simmons, *Antichrist* (New York: Columbia University Press, 2015), 58.

17. Bodil Marie Stavning Thomosen, "*Antichrist*—Chaos Reigns: the Event of Violence and the Haptic Image in Lars von Trier's Film," *Journal of Aesthetics & Culture* 1.1 (2009).

18. Jan Lumholdt and Lars von Trier, *Lars von Trier: Interviews* (Jackson: University Press of Mississippi, 2003), 55.

19. Robert Sinnerbrink, "Anatomy of *Melancholia*," *Angelaki* 19.4 (2014): 111–26.

20. Mette Hjort and Ib Bondebjerg, *The Danish Directors: Dialogues on a Contemporary Danish Cinema* (Intellect Ltd, 2003), 215.

21. Aske Alexander Foss, "B&O What Moves You? Lars von Trier," *Vimeo*, 2012. http://vimeo.com/51020281

22. Lumholdt and von Trier, *Lars von Trier: Interviews*, 72.

23. Hunter, "*Antichrist*—Lars Von Trier Interview."

24. David Jenkins, "Lars Von Trier discusses *Antichrist*," *Time Out* (no date). https://www.timeout.com/london/film/lars-von-trier-discusses-antichrist-1

25. Tatiana Yershova, "The Battle for Tarkovsky's Archive," Russkiy Mir Foundation, 30 November 2012. https://www.russkiymir.ru/en/publications/139752/

26. Lumholdt and von Trier, *Lars von Trier: Interviews*, 74.

27. Ibid., 7.
28. Harold Bloom, *The Anxiety of Influence* (New York: Oxford University Press, 1997), 14.
29. Harold Bloom, *A Map of Misreading* (New York: Oxford University Press USA, 2003), 98.
30. Bloom, *The Anxiety of Influence*, 67.
31. Ibid., 69.
32. Lumholdt and von Trier, *Lars von Trier: Interviews*, 74.
33. Stig Bjorkman, *Trier on von Trier* (London: Faber & Faber, 2005), 47.
34. Ibid., 70.
35. Hjort and Bondebjerg, *The Danish Directors*, 215.
36. Torben Grodal, "Frozen Flows in von Trier's Oeuvre," in Torben Kragh Grodal, Bente Larsen, and Iben Thorving Laursen (eds), *Visual authorship: creativity and intentionality in media* (Copenhagen: Museum Tusculanum Press, 2005), 129–68, 143.
37. Paul Thomas Anderson, "Flashback Friday: PT Anderson Talks With Lars Von Trier," *Cigarettes & Red Wines*, 22 April 2011: http://cigsandredvines.blogspot.com/2011/04/flashback-friday-pt-anderson-talks-with.html
38. Lumholdt and von Trier, *Lars von Trier: Interviews*, 67.
39. Ibid., 252.
40. For example, in an interview Tarkovsky calls Stalker "one of the last idealists." Quoted from Vida T. Johnson and Graham Petrie, *The Films of Andrei Tarkovsky: A Visual Fugue* (Bloomington: Indiana University Press, 1994), 149.
41. Lumholdt and von Trier, *Lars von Trier: Interviews*, 148–9.
42. Quoted from Simmons, *Antichrist*, 83.
43. Stig Bjorkman, *Lars von Trier: Interview* (Sankt-Peterburg: Azbuka-klassika, 2008), 319.
44. Peter Sloterdijk, *Critique of Cynical Reason* (Minneapolis: University of Minnesota Press, 1988), 5.
45. Ibid., 22.
46. Ibid., xxxii.
47. Ibid., 96.
48. Ibid., 217.
49. Ibid., 5.
50. Lumholdt and von Trier, *Lars von Trier: Interviews*, 252.
51. Sloterdijk, *Critique of Cynical Reason*, 122.
52. Bjorkman, *Lars von Trier: Interview*, 318.
53. Slavoj Žižek, *The Parallax View* (Cambridge, MA: The MIT Press, 2009), 85.
54. See, for example, Carleen Mandolfo, "Women, Suffering and Redemption in Three Films of Lars von Trier," *Literature and Theology* 24.3 (2010): 285–300.
55. Bjorkman, *Lars von Trier: Interview*, 320.
56. Bloom, *The Anxiety of Influence*, 100.
57. Ibid., 105.
58. Ibid., 110.
59. Ibid., 109–10.
60. Ibid., 106.
61. Ibid., 109.
62. Harold Bloom, *Poetry and Repression: Revisionism from Blake to Stevens* (New Haven: Yale University Press, 1976), 18.
63. Ibid., 131.
64. Ibid., 132.
65. Foss, "B&O What Moves You? Lars von Trier," Vimeo, 2012: http://vimeo.com/51020281
66. Robert Sinnerbrink, *New philosophies of film: Thinking images* (London: A. & C. Black, 2011), 170.

67. Magdalena Zolkos, "Violent Affects: Nature and the Feminine in Lars von Trier's *Antichrist*," *Parrhesia* 13 (2011): 178–89, 183.
68. Patrícia de Almeida Kruger, "Mutilated Emancipation: Lars von Trier's *Antichrist* as a Critical Approach to the Representations of Women in History," in *Transgressive Womanhood: Investigating Vamps, Witches, Whores, Serial Killers and Monsters* (Leiden: Brill, 2019), 231–40, 237.
69. Donato Totaro, "Nature as 'Comfort Zone' in the Films of Andrei Tarkovsky," *Offscreen* 14.12 (2010). https://offscreen.com/view/nature_as_comfort_zone
70. Sinnerbrink, *New philosophies of film*, 206.
71. See, for example, Vladislava Vardits, "Andrei Tarkovskiy i Lars von Trier: stsenarii kontsa sveta," in Norbert Franz, *Andrej Tarkovskij: Klassiker—Классик—Classic—Classico* (Universitätsverlag Potsdam, 2016), 573–86.
72. Sinnerbrink, "Anatomy of *Melancholia*," 121.
73. Dave Calhoun, "*Nymphomaniac*, Vol 1 & Vol 2," *Time Out*, 21 March 2014. https://www.timeout.com/london/film/nymphomaniac-vol-1-vol-2
74. Linda Badley, "'Fill All My Holes': Nymph () maniac's Sadean Discourse," *Ekphrasis. Images, Cinema, Theory, Media* 14.2 (2015): 21–39, 26.
75. Howard Feinstein, "Lars von Trier: 'I will never do a press conference again'," *Indie Wire*, 20 May 2011. https://www.indiewire.com/2011/05/lars-von-trier-i-will-never-do-a-press-conference-again-54069/
76. Bloom, *The Anxiety of Influence*, 109.
77. Jenkins, "Lars Von Trier discusses *Antichrist*," *Time Out*. https://www.timeout.com/london/film/lars-von-trier-discusses-antichrist-1.

Index